S0-ACR-540

ADVANCED BASS FISHING

John Weiss

Drawings by Sylvia Schwartz

OUTDOOR LIFE BOOKS

Published by

Outdoor Life Books
Times Mirror Magazines, Inc.
380 Madison Avenue
New York, NY 10017

Distributed to the trade by

Stackpole Books
Cameron & Kelker Sts.
Harrisburg, PA 17105

Originally published by E. P. Dutton, Inc., 1976

Library of Congress Cataloging in Publication Data

Weiss, John, 1944-
Advanced bass fishing.

Includes index.
1. Bass fishing. I. Title.
SH681.W4 1985 799.1'758 85-7119
ISNB 0-943822-43-2

Manufactured in the United States of America

This book is dedicated to Inky Davis, a long-time friend and one of the country's most accomplished bass experts, with whom I've spent thousands of hours on the water.

Contents

Introduction

The rapid rate at which our knowledge of bass behavior has increased in recent years makes compiling a comprehensive book on bass fishing a formidable challenge. Very frankly, I feel like David just moments before he faced down Goliath.

You see, bass have inhabited North American waters for tens of thousands of years and yet 95 percent of what we know about the species—their habits in various types of water, methods of catching them consistently under a variety of conditions, and even effective management techniques—has been learned during only the last ten years. Moreover, our knowledge is increasing so rapidly it's incredibly difficult for any fishing writer to keep abreast of the almost weekly press releases containing new findings by the nation's biologists, fishery scientists, leading tackle companies and angling experts.

So where does a fishing writer begin? Indeed, is it even possible for anyone to correlate the enormous and continually growing amount of angling know-how with the relevant, but oftentimes obscure, biological facts to produce a book that is not only readable but complete? Probably not. It's unlikely that any single person has learned, or ever will learn, everything there is to know about bass behavior and successful bass fishing. To add to a writer's confusion, not to mention his reader's bewilderment, even the most highly respected biologists often heatedly disagree on various facets of bass behavior.

Despite these difficulties, I feel the attempt to assemble bass-fishing information from diverse sources into a single book is worthwhile. Such wide-ranging works can substantially help anglers across the country to enlarge their perspective, sharpen their insight and skills, and improve their levels of fishing success.

The first edition of *Advanced Bass Fishing,* came off the press about eight years ago. Although that book contained the latest scientific data gleaned from the country's most revered bass-fishing luminaries, I look back upon it as merely a germinating seed. The book you're now holding is based upon its predecessor but contains far greater detail and a wealth of updated information. It's the seed of my earlier book sprouted and matured into a full-grown plant.

You might well ask, aren't there already a number of other bass-fishing books on the market? Absolutely! In fact, the selection is almost mind-boggling. The trouble is, virtually all other bass books assume their readers are novices. These elementary books serve a valid purpose because newcomers are getting into bass fishing every day of the year. Yet vastly outnumbering the beginners are experienced anglers who have long since graduated from grade school and are now seeking a college education.

They've already, many times over, paid their dues to the angling world in the form of billions of hours upon America's lakes, reservoirs, rivers, streams and ponds. They've bought sleek fiberglass bassboats for zipping around the most expansive reservoirs and in many cases have second, smaller boats for working natural lakes and rivers. They make regular use of electric motors, live wells, sonar equipment, boron rods, precision reels, superior lines, and lures that look so lifelike you almost expect them to swim off on their own. Today's modern bass angler even has his own unique vocabulary that may sound like a foreign language to someone who's not a member of the fraternity.

Advanced Bass Fishing is for the estimated 20 million accomplished fishermen who annually devote substantial portions of their fishing time to searching out the most popular of all gamefish species. Unfortunately, a good many of these veteran bass anglers aren't satisfied with their catches and all too often return at day's end with not much more to show for their efforts than a medium-rare neck and an exercised casting arm. They may catch a few keeper-size fish, and occasionally they even luck into a three- or four-pounder. But the real lunkers, weighing from four to ten pounds or even more, which a few select fishermen seem to bring in with exasperating regularity, remain for many forever elusive.

One reason for this state of affairs is that bass fishing is not as easy as it used to be. New lakes are not popping up like spring mushrooms as they did during the reservoir-construction boom of the 1940s, '50s and '60s. Consequently, each lake is now subjected to more intense fishing pressure than ever before. In most waters, bass populations are simply not as abundant today as they were 30 years ago. And even in waters where bass numbers are high, the fish have become wary and likely to avoid anything that even remotely makes them suspicious their welfare is in jeopardy. As a result, for today's bass fisherman, simply being good is not enough: to be consistently successful, you have to be better than good.

Advanced Bass Fishing will help the experienced, but frequently dissatisfied, angler become just that—better than good—by carefully examining the three elements that are essential to success. Throughout the book I'll frequently be discussing bass from a biological standpoint, better to explain how they function in an underwater environment. I'll also be going into considerable detail about locating bass in different bodies of water. This is important because in the final analysis locating the fish is the key to success. If you can't find 'em, you surely can't catch 'em! The third component concerns use of the various techniques and related tackle items that are most likely to produce under a wide variety of weather and water conditions.

This practical, advanced know-how is almost certain to revolutionize your approach to bass fishing because it takes you step by step through many of the techniques the experts use to find and boat large numbers of big fish on a regular basis.

However, it's also necessary to temper your bass-fishing expectations with a realistic attitude, because there's not an angler in the world who can hope to crank in a record breaker on every outing. To frame an analogy, ten-point whitetail bucks are not nearly as plentiful as forkhorns; similarly, ten-pound bass are not as abundant as two-pounders. But there are indeed big fish out there and you should be boating your fair share.

Consider, for a moment, my friend Doug Hannon of Odessa, Florida. This 35-year-old fishing whiz has, to date, caught over 300 bass topping ten pounds apiece (the largest, incidentally, being close to 16 pounds). Then there's veteran tournament pro Roland Martin, who recalls the memorable outing in which he boated five bass over ten pounds in a single day. This incredible event took place at Santee–Cooper in South Carolina. There's also the awe-inspiring state record catch made by Jim Phelps when fishing California's San Vicente Reservoir: That one-day, five-fish limit weighed over 43 pounds. Or, to really cause your heart to thump, consider the unbelievable one-day catch made by tackle manufacturer Tom Mann and his pal Dave Lockhart on Alabama's Lake Eufaula. The two partners caught 25 bass that weighed an astounding 155 pounds: The heaviest ten bass on that string averaged nine pounds apiece and the largest tipped the scales at better than 13 pounds!

These tales are not meant to discourage you. Indeed, you should begin not by setting your sights on unrealistic trophies but by asking yourself, "How well did I do last year, particularly in catching bass over three pounds?"

The experts—Doug Hannon and Roland Martin and Tom Mann and

Doug Hannon, one of the country's foremost bass-angling authorities, has released hundreds of bass over ten pounds.

all those who consistently land the big ones—obviously know something that most bass anglers do not. Furthermore, they've honed their skills so sharply that they can put that learning into practical use whenever they fish their favorite waters. What their success doesn't depend on is "luck." In fact, my friend Billy Westmoreland, a renowned bass-fishing expert from Celina, Tennessee, is fond of saying luck is a four-letter word spelled W–O–R–K.

The premise that underpins this book, therefore, is that acquiring an intimate knowledge of bass behavior is the key ingredient in heavying-up any stringer. Sophisticated lures, tackle, electronic equipment, and boats and motors are only tools enabling an angler to carry out his task more efficiently and effectively. Liken the entire thing, if you will, to a master mechanic with thousands of dollars worth of wrenches and diagnostic equipment. Those tools are invaluable to him, yet without his knowledge, training and understanding of how car engines work, the tools are worthless.

So right at the start, let's make it perfectly clear that no amount of any brandname fishing or boating equipment, by itself, will make you a successful bass angler, even though many advertisements try to make you believe so.

For example, I know many consistently *un*successful anglers who in recent years have traded in their low-powered johnboats and aluminum V-bottoms for sleek bassboats with high-performance hulls and outboards of such size that they throw up roostertails at only half-throttle. Although fully convinced that these symbols of success would bring it, they're still not catching any more bass than before.

Thousands of other anglers, in search of a quick remedy for their unsuccessful fishing outings, annually succumb to the new-lure syndrome. They are so naive as to believe that big bass will turn themselves inside-out trying to get at some revolutionary lure design—an incredible but widespread fantasy.

Even more frequently, the winner of a national bass tournament may reveal at the televised weigh-in that he made his winning catch on a black plastic worm with a red firetail, whereupon the tackle company that manufactures the bait, to its sheer delight, is overnight swamped with orders. Seldom does the tournament champ have a chance to tell the rest of the story: That the black worm with the red tail was simply the lure he happened to be throwing when he finally located the bass; that the real key to his catch was not the particular lure itself but how he evaluated the existing weather and water conditions, established a pattern, and eventually began making contact with bass 18 feet deep on secondary breaklines; and that had he switched lures during the heat of the action to a chrome jigging spoon or chartreuse leadhead tailspinner, they would probably have proven equally effective.

There are no revolutionary lure designs, magic lure colors, expensive marine equipment or sophisticated electronic gadgetry that, *in themselves,* will pay off consistently for anyone. But in all fairness to the marine and tackle manufacturers, I can say unequivocally that high-quality gear, compared to inferior discount-house stuff, is a definite aid, provided the angler couples the use of these tools with a thorough understanding of how bass live and move and feed.

Nurturing the proper attitude—one of confidence—is yet another essential ingredient to success because, in truth, bass are not very intelligent. Nor are they clever, wily or capable of outwitting anglers, as many of my fellow writers often suggest. It is true that bass possess highly refined survival instincts and when subjected to intense angling pressure may exhibit a wide variety of avoidance reactions. But generally they are very stupid creatures completely at the mercy of their environment.

Once an angler has realized that bass aren't overly intelligent, he'll see that successful bass fishing entails little more than learning about bass behavior and applying that knowledge to varying situations on the water. As his confidence builds, it will feed upon itself, allowing the angler to each day draw upon his previous experiences to enjoy even greater success. When Doug Hannon sets out for a day's fishing, for example, *he absolutely knows* he'll catch at least one ten-pound bass. Yet without that mental outlook and self-generated confidence, he wouldn't even come close to achieving that daily goal.

Throughout this book it is important to remember that all bass have the same needs, regardless of where they may be found. The bass you catch in Minnesota, California or New Jersey have the same biological requirements as the bass I catch in Ohio, Canada, Texas or Florida. They need food; they need cover or some form of bottom contour or structure they can relate to; they need the proper amount of dissolved oxygen in the water; and if there is to be continued propagation of their kind, they require suitable water temperatures and spawning habitat. Further, their day-to-day activities are influenced by a host of other variables: weather, pH, amount of light penetration, the age and related fertility of the water they're inhabiting, the balance among themselves and other fish species sharing the same water, and so on. Once an angler has acquired detailed knowledge of how bass react under varied circumstances, he should be able to visit any body of water anywhere in the country and, taking existing conditions into account, soon be catching bass.

Although the biological needs of bass, with only slight exceptions, do not change from locale to locale, what often does change is the nature of the waters they inhabit. Naturally, a shallow swampland reservoir in South Carolina is going to differ markedly from a canyonland reservoir in Arizona, but in either case the bass still must eat, spawn, and find places for hiding and resting. Even though the day-to-day activities of bass will be influenced by a myriad of things over which they have no control, they are highly adaptable creatures that have an uncanny way of "making do" with whatever resources are available.

Before beginning the first chapter, I'd like to introduce a number of very special people who appear throughout this book. Although modern American bass angling has benefited by the contributions of countless experts, these people stand head and shoulders above all others. There's Doug Hannon, whom we've already met, but also another Florida resident, Glen Lau, who specializes in the underwater filming of fish behavior. Next comes Paul Johnson, a longtime friend who is vice-president for the Berkley Company in Spirit Lake, Iowa. Unlike many tackle company representatives whose minds are geared solely to selling their company's products, Paul is not only committed to research but also to investing prodigious efforts in the teaching of new knowledge to anglers nationwide.

Of course, no mention of bass fishing is complete without heralding the accomplishments of Mr. BASS. Everyone should already know this is Ray

Ray Scott, known as Mr. BASS, founded the prestigious Bass Anglers Sportsman Society in 1968. At a tournament weigh-in ceremony, he interviews professional angler Ricky Clunn.

Scott who, 16 years ago, founded the Bass Anglers Sportsman Society. Along with his topnotch magazine editor Bob Cobb and tournament director Harold Sharp, Scott has united bass anglers nationwide into a cohesive assemblage of the most skilled anglers ever brought together under a single umbrella. Readers of this book who are not already members of B.A.S.S. can take a giant stride forward in their bass education by joining the organization, located at Number One Bell Road, Montgomery, AL 36141.

Still further back in America's bass-fishing limelight stands Buck Perry. A former physics professor, originally from North Carolina, Perry has a knowledge of the earth's composition that borders on the phenomenal. He frequently serves as a consultant to state departments of natural resources in their fish management programs, and even to state highway departments needing advice about the stratification of terrain. Since a good many of today's best bass waters are manmade impoundments created over previously dry land, Perry's knowledge of the earth's crust has contributed immensely to his fishing insight. This knowledge is important because, as we shall see later, bass spend the majority of their time right on the bottom and in association with some type of contour, structure or unique composition of bottom materials.

It is Buck Perry who is responsible for most of what we know about the deep-water lives of bass and their movements. It was he who first coined the terms *structure, sanctuary,* and *migration route,* among others —terms that now, many years later, are a part of the casual vocabulary of bass anglers and play an important role in their varied approaches to finding and catching bass.

Finally, there are the brothers Al and Ron Lindner of Brainerd, Minnesota, young scientists and former students of Buck Perry who have taken many of Perry's early findings and greatly expanded upon them. Their organization and namesake magazine, *The In-Fisherman,* bring together the elite of freshwater anglers. There simply is no other regularly published journal of scientific lore and recent research findings that brings so much useful information together to help bass anglers, as well as those who regularly pursue other species. For more information, write to In-Fisherman, P.O. Box 999, Brainerd, MN 56401.

Of the Lindners' numerous achievements, two that are the most significant to bass anglers have to do with the classification of lakes and reservoirs and with predator-prey relationships in various bodies of water. These two subjects are particularly relevant in determining where fish are located and selecting the tactics that usually are most successful in catching them.

This book, then, aims to make you a better-than-good bass angler. You won't find much flowery prose, humorous anecdotes, or nostalgic recollections and pipe smoking in its pages. What you will find instead is a wide range of factual, little written about information gleaned from the country's most proficient guides, tournament professionals, tackle manufacturers, underwater photographers and fishing scientists. These people (and I include myself) are not romantics and armchair anglers by any stretch of the imagination; nor are they self-ordained know-it-alls. They're still students themselves who never spend a day on the water without learning something new, and they're teachers who are dedicated to helping average people with average intelligence become expert fishermen.

With all of this in mind, look upon this book not as something to be quickly skimmed through and then placed on a closet shelf but as a reference to be studied and consulted often. When you run headlong into a problem during a frustratingly tough day on the water and you feel defeated, look on the positive side. You've indeed learned something—what *doesn't* work. Then, take a few minutes to thumb through an appropriate section of this book, and you'll undoubtedly learn what *will* work next time you're confronted with similar conditions.

John Weiss
Chesterhill, Ohio

CHAPTER

1

The Bass Species

Looking at the bass species, we could easily get entangled in a lengthy discussion of their historical backgrounds, native ranges, expanded ranges through transplanting, and on and on. But few, other perhaps than ichthyologists, get excited by such discussions. Most anglers, I suspect, simply want to know how to catch more bass than they've been getting, especially those elusive rascals that are half as long as a tall man's leg. Nevertheless, I will briefly review the various bass species in order to set the stage for the rest of the book and introduce the cast of characters.

Although there are eleven strains and/or species of bass, the great majority of anglers in North America pursue only four species. These are all, upon occasion, referred to as *black bass*, but this term is gradually falling out of usage, in part because the four species are definitely not always black in color. The four most sought-after species are the largemouth bass (*Micropterus salmoides*); the smallmouth bass (*Micropterus dolomieui*); the spotted bass (*Micropterus punctulatus*), which is sometimes also known as the Kentucky bass, although the species is not restricted to the state of Kentucky alone; and the Florida bass (*Micropterus salmoides floridanus*), which is a subspecies of the largemouth.

Biologists also recognize other species such as the redeye bass, Suwanee bass and Guadalupe bass; digging still deeper into various textbooks would reveal the identity of other strains. All of these minor species are very limited in distribution across the continent, and you may even have to count scales, refer to anatomical charts showing dorsal fin spines and uncase your set of calipers to make a positive identification and distinction between them.

This book is concerned only with the northern largemouth, smallmouth, spotted and Florida bass, since any of the other species are likely to constitute only incidental bonus catches made upon rare occasion while fishing for one of the other four.

Distribution and Habitat

At the present time, Alaska is the only state that does not have at least one strain of bass. The various bass species were not always this widely dispersed, though. Their dispersal beyond their native ranges has occurred during the last several decades through the efforts of adventuresome, experimentally minded, often rebel biologists associated with state and federal fishery agencies or independent fishery societies. A recent example is the transplanting of Florida bass into southern California waters where they customarily live at depths of 60 feet, gorge themselves upon foot-long rainbow trout and consequently grow to outlandish sizes. In fact, these unique fish constitute the majority of the largest bass caught by anglers in the last five years.

The northern largemouth, however, has the most widespread range, mainly because it is the most adaptable of all the bass species. Originally restricted to the region of the Great Lakes and their drainage tributaries, the largemouth is now found from the southern portions of the eastern Canadian provinces to the arid desert lands of Mexico; its range extends into Hondurus and the waters of Cuba. East to west, the largemouth's range stretches from the brackish tidal marshes of the Atlantic seaboard across the country to the deep lakes of the Pacific northwest. All in all, the largemouth is not only the most widely distributed but also the most prolific of all the bass species.

The largemouth is primarily an inhabitant of natural lakes, manmade reservoirs, sluggish rivers, tide zones, farmponds and stripmine pits, but it is an occasional resident of swift rivers and streams, too. The fish doesn't seem to thrive in cooler, rushing waters and in most rivers and streams seldom reaches its maximum growth potential. Additionally, in such environments it almost exclusively resides in quiet, deep pools out of the main current or along shorelines where heavy cover or unique bank configurations retard the velocity of the current.

Providing the water is not too cold or moving too swiftly, the largemouth may set up housekeeping under a wide variety of conditions, with only two exceptions. The species is not as adaptable as many other fish species to high levels of pollution, and given the choice, it will avoid bottom areas of lakes and other waters that are overly muddy. But if muddy water is unavoidable from time to time, the largemouth will tolerate it and simply make do. In general, then, the water may be clear, stained, murky, warm, cool, shallow, deep, free of cover or infested with swamp cover and chances are excellent that *Micropterus salmoides* and its offspring will get along just fine.

In later chapters, I'll spend a good deal of time discussing how to catch lunker smallmouth, spotted and Florida bass, but the primary emphasis throughout this book will be on the largemouth—the "basic" bass. If you learn how this species lives and moves and feeds, and how to catch it, you can easily adapt this knowledge to catching the other basses as well. They are individuals in their own right—make no mistake about that—but their habits are not significantly different from those of the largemouth.

This isn't to say that it's always possible to be specific when categorizing different fish or the habitats in which they live. The vast array of local conditions that exists across North America makes it impossible to deal in anything but generalizations. Therefore, you need to remain flexible in thinking about and applying the basic principles, trends and tendencies discussed in this book to the particular local conditions you may be fishing under.

Take, for example, the short, stocky body shape of the largemouth. Right off, this body shape indicates that this bass is equipped to maneuver in tight cover situations and ambush prey at close range with short bursts of speed. It is not a body shape for swimming at sustained speeds in open-water pursuit of prey, like the more elongated northern pike, muskie, trout and salmon.

Based simply on their body shape, we can conclude that largemouths are most at home when they are in and around various types of cover or bottom structures, the actual depth having to do primarily with the season. But the particular environment in which largemouths live may have an overriding influence on their specific location within a body of water. When I fish New York's St. Lawrence River, for example, I know most largemouths will be hugging inside weedlines close to the banks. This is purely a survival measure designed to avoid encounters with the pike and muskies regularly patrolling the outside, deep-water edges of the same weeds. Conversely, in a crystal clear, deep, infertile lake such as Tennessee's Dale Hollow, which has a marked absence of shoreline weeds and also a marked absence of species that might prey upon bass, largemouths (and smallmouths and spotted bass, too) may congregate in open water to pursue schools of threadfin shad.

It's important to note these things in the beginning because from time to time we'll be looking at live baits, lures and presentation methods. But we must never lose sight of the fact that a bass's location and behavior always depend on the particular environment in which it lives.

Identifying Bass Species

Besides the largemouth's blocky, truncated body shape, its chief distinguishing physical characteristic is an enormous mouth, which enables it to feed on large and varied prey. Although the largemouth spends only a very small portion of each day actively feeding, I've often boated a fine bass only to discover a smaller fish still blocking its gullet, the tail of the hapless victim still protruding from the bass's mouth. And other times I've slipped a nice bass into a live well and watched it almost immediately regurgitate more minnows and crayfish than anyone would believe possible. Despite its superior equipment for predation, the largemouth goes through often lengthy periods of relative dormancy during which it appears to feed little, if at all. These spells of reduced feeding, which are discussed in detail in later chapters, may be brought on by changes in water or weather conditions (e.g., during cold-front or cold-water periods)

The most distinguishing feature of the largemouth bass is its gaping maw. Although feeding may be sporadic at times, largemouths frequently go on incredible binges.

or by changes in the fish's biological condition (e.g., during spawning).

Even if we restrict our attention only to the four main bass species, distinguishing among them can be difficult because in certain waters they may look remarkably similar. Since correct identification of the species may be critically important to fishing success, let's see how to tell them apart:

Largemouth Bass. When the mouth of a largemouth bass is closed, the rear of the upper jaw extends past a vertical line drawn from the rear edge of the eye. The forward portion of the spiny dorsal fin and the rear soft portion are very nearly separated from one another, whereas in the other basses the dorsal fin is either continuous or more nearly so.

The largemouth's coloration may vary from region to region and even within the same body of water. The species generally is a vibrant grass-green along the sides, and progressively darker toward the dorsal area. The underbelly is nearly always dirty white. In certain waters, however, largemouths may be almost totally black; in others they may be silvery. A dark lateral line is usually visible on smaller fish, running from the gill flaps to the tail, but in larger bass this line may not be so pronounced. Also, there may be dark, splotchy markings along the sides of the fish.

All of the bass species seem to adapt their coloration to their habitat, which adds to the confusion among anglers as to which bass they've caught. A bass caught in thick weeds, for example, may be dark green. Yet if that same bass were caught an hour later as it was cruising over a sandbar it would undoubtedly appear tan. On the other hand, bass caught in very deep water, in very muddy water, or when suspended and chasing baitfish in open midlake regions, often appear very pale and milky green. This changing camouflage is of course a distinct advantage to the bass in its predatory activities.

Florida Bass. Like the largemouth, the Florida bass also engages in frenzied feeding upon occasion. But since it lives in a more stable environment, it exhibits a more regular lifestyle.

Being a subspecies of the largemouth bass, the Florida bass is almost identical in appearance to its more wide-ranging relative, although it sometimes takes on slightly darker hues. Other than the huge sizes Florida bass commonly attain, and their occasional darker color, they differ physiologically from northern largemouths only in the number of rows of scales above and below the lateral line (see discussion later in this chapter).

Smallmouth Bass. A more selective feeder than the largemouth, the smallmouth bass also has a noticeably smaller mouth. This trait, however, probably does not explain the relative infrequency of cannibalistic gorgings exhibited by smallmouths; rather, their feeding behavior can be attributed to the rather sparse and infertile environments which they inhabit.

In contrast to a largemouth bass, when the mouth of a smallmouth is closed, the rear of the upper jaw does *not* extend beyond the eye. The forward and rear (spiny and rayed) portions of the dorsal fin are joined.

As with largemouths, coloration of smallmouths may vary between and even within bodies of water. Generally, they take on a greenish bronze hue on the upper two-thirds of the body, with a sort of yellowish brown underbelly. There is no distinct, dark lateral line but there are an average of three dark stripes fanning out from the snout to the rear of the gill covers, yielding to darker, irregular splotches along the sides of the fish.

Spotted (Kentucky) Bass. The feeding characteristics of spotted bass are often a combination of those exhibited by largemouths and smallmouths. Often spotted bass will go on a binge; at other times they seem to feed hardly at all.

Identification of spotted bass is the most difficult of all because the species has the same general coloration as the largemouth and smallmouth. To add to any angler's dismay, the spotted bass has the dark lateral line of the largemouth, yet its mouth is like that of a smallmouth in that the rear corner of the upper jaw extends to, but not beyond, the eye. Unique to this species, however, are several rows of dark dots between the lateral line and the ventral region, extending full length from the gill flaps to the base of the tail. There are also spots (really splotches) of dark gray along the dorsal region. But since all bass species may vary somewhat in appearance, according to the makeup of the water they inhabit, identification based on markings and color alone may not be possible.

When fishery biologists are unsure of the species of a particular bass, they often count the rows of scales between the lateral line and the front of the dorsal fin. The spotted bass has nine rows of scales, the smallmouth eleven, the largemouth seven, and the Florida bass from seven to nine.

Of course, this method of identification is not practical when you are on the water. Then, I recommend distinguishing between the largemouth and smallmouth by comparing their jaws and keeping in mind the three dark stripes the smallmouth sports on its gill covers. If you are still in doubt, open the fish's mouth and run your finger over the tongue. If it's a spotted bass, you'll feel a small oval patch of very soft teeth; the tongues of largemouths, smallmouths and Florida bass are smooth to the touch. (Smallmouths, spotted bass, and the Florida subspecies are discussed more thoroughly in Chapters 18–20, respectively.)

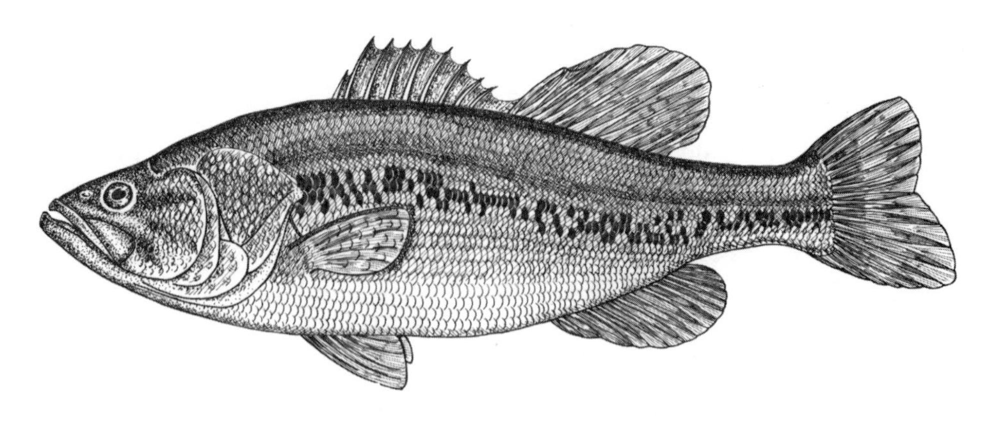

LARGEMOUTH BASS

SMALLMOUTH BASS

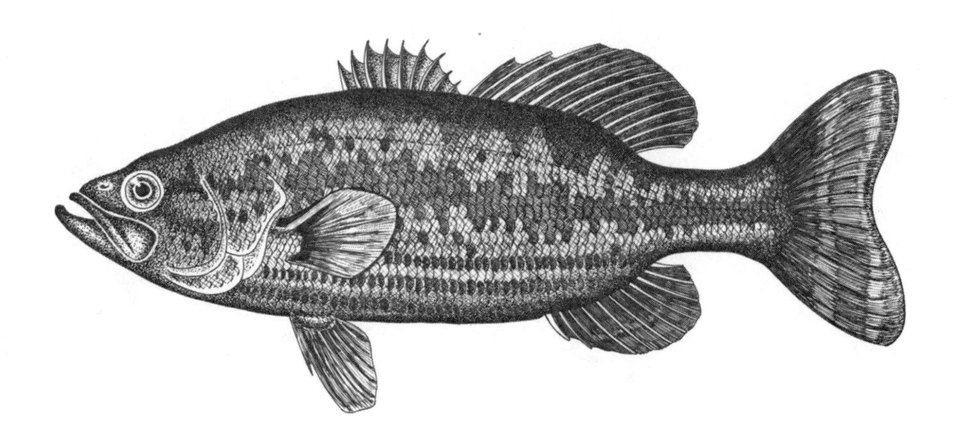

SPOTTED BASS

Size and Movements

A "lunker" largemouth caught north of the Mason–Dixon line is any fish that weighs four pounds or more. But in the deep South, where anglers may encounter the Florida strain of bass, you'll have to net one of better than ten pounds to raise admiring eyebrows among locals. A smallmouth of better than four or five pounds, anywhere, is an impressive trophy, and

Johnny Morris, honcho of Bass Pro Shops, unhooks a chunky spotted bass. Note the rows of dots along the ventral region; an even surer sign of its identity is the small oval patch of soft teeth on the tongue of a spotted bass.

a spotted bass weighing more than three or four pounds should have you ego-tripping for at least a month.

In any body of water, however, it's always the females of each bass species that attain the greatest weights. Males rarely grow larger than three or four pounds. Affectionate labels such as "sows," "hawgs," "bucketmouths," "mules" and "horses" always refer to female bass.

Finally, to set the stage for coming chapters, I should mention that except in unique environmental circumstances no bass, regardless of species, lives the year-round in one place in any body of water. This is not to say they are migratory like walleyes or salmon. But within their home ranges they do periodically shift from one place to another. There are both seasonal movements in which the fish may travel substantial distances (generally less than a quarter-mile on the average) and shorter temporary sojourns (sometimes only 20 yards) on a daily and even hourly basis. Moreover, as individuals of any bass species grow older and larger, they seem to become more and more restricted in their movements. Compared to young bass that often engage in chase-and-catch feeding behavior, sometimes roaming in schools, larger bass are more sedentary, preferring to wait in ambush for their prey.

CHAPTER

2

Spring Spawning

In the Introduction I noted that all bass have the same biological needs, regardless of where they are found, and that their habits, although generally similar, are also influenced by the particular environments in which they live. This is why any discussion of the various species must always bear qualifications such as "generally," "usually," and "most often." A good example of such environmental influences is the spawning and reproduction of largemouth bass. Prolonged spells of cold weather may delay normal spawning, whereas unseasonable heat waves may trigger early egg laying. Also, radical fluctuations in water level due to heavy rains, drought, or the deliberate manipulation of flood-control structures often determine when and how deep bass will build their nests and whether the spawning attempt will be successful or disastrous.

The spawning activities of bass take place in three stages. There is the *prespawn* stage in which bass move to their spawning grounds in large numbers and are quite responsive to lures and live baits. Next comes the *spawning* stage in which the fish are actually on their nests, engaged in laying and fertilizing their eggs. During this period the fish do not actively feed, but strike responses can be elicited. Finally comes the *postspawn* stage in which the bass begin drifting away from the spawning grounds. The females, in particular, go into an almost comatose recuperative period; however, males may recover from spawning and resume feeding almost immediately.

Time of Spawning

Water temperature is the single most influential element in determining when bass spawn. Largemouths get the show rolling the minute the temperature passes 60° F. The most active, purposeful spawning, however, occurs when the water reaches 65° in conjunction with a new moon or full moon. And everything from that point on proceeds according to nature's plan if nothing interferes to interrupt, slow down or speed up spawning activities.

I have seen bass move onto their beds in Ohio during late May when the water temperature approached 62°. Then, when a last touch of winter reduced the water temperature to 57°, the fish moved off their beds and into deeper waters, where they held at *waiting stations* until the water was once again suitable for spawning. Many times these *false spawns* or delays ruin the reproduction cycle because the roe-laden females eventually refuse to move onto the beds; after a period of time their bodies will absorb or assimilate the eggs, so no young are born that year.

Such a disruption of the breeding cycle may explain the occasional marked absence of a certain age-group of bass in particular waters. Fish

Water temperature is the most important factor influencing the spawning behavior of all bass species.

of one, two, five and six pounds may be caught regularly, with few or no three- or four-pounders ever showing up on anglers' stringers. It is likely the majority of one or two generations of offspring never made it into being because the spawning habits of the adult bass were drastically altered during those respective years.

Under normal conditions of water and weather, latitude is the governing factor as to when, exactly, bass will begin spawning activities in any

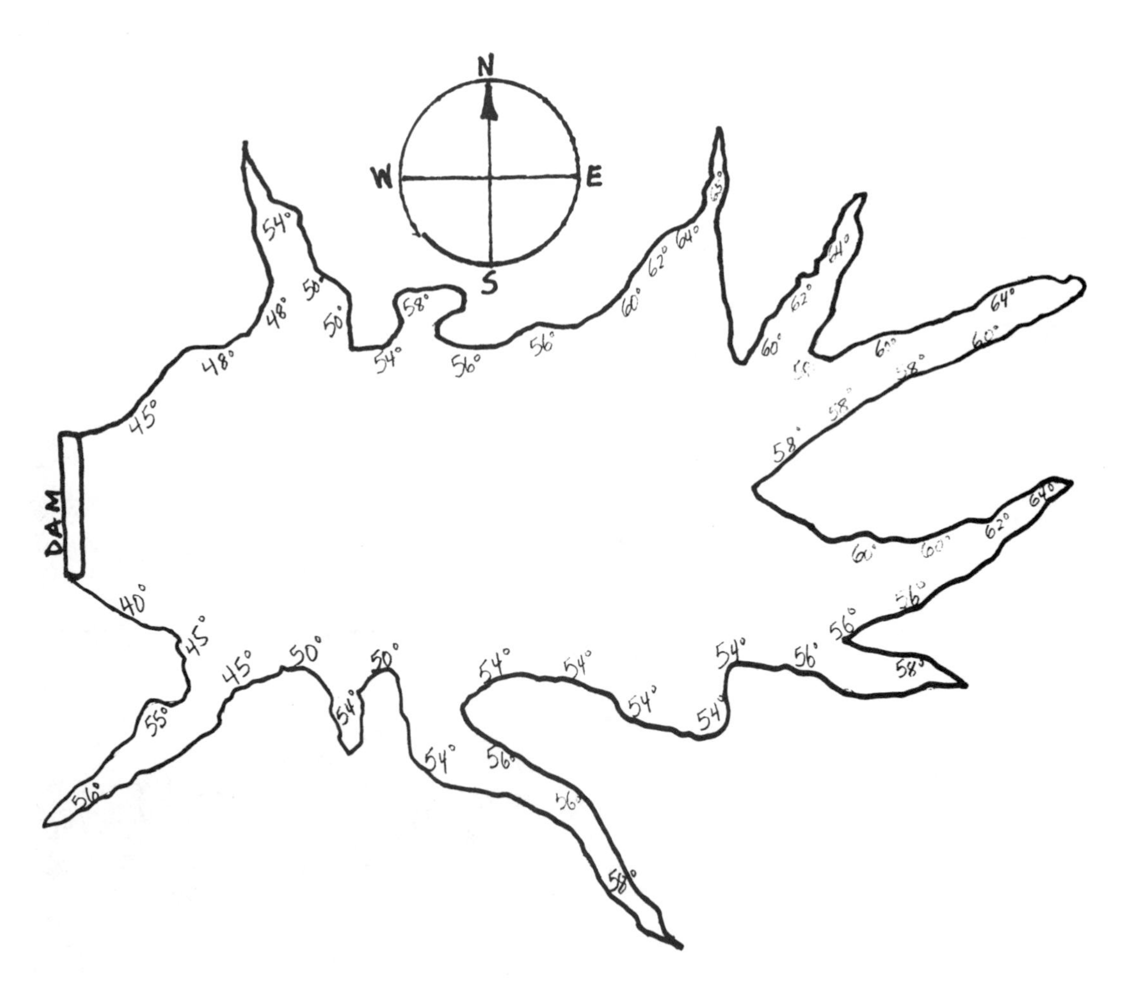

Bass may be in various stages of spawning depending on where they live in a given lake. The warmest waters in this typical lake occur in the eastern, shallow headwaters and also along the north and northwestern shorelines, which are protected from prevailing west-to-east weather. Along exposed southern shorelines and in the deeper western area of the lake near the dam, the water is significantly cooler.

In this aerial photograph of a sprawling Midwest reservoir, it's easy to make educated guesses as to where bass-spawning activity would take place.

given region. In Florida and other deep South states, desirable water temperatures may occur as early as February or March. In fact, a certain percentage of bass may be engaged in spawning activities every month of the year in the deep South because of the consistently warmer temperatures and frequent heat spells found there. Farther north in the Kentucky region, the spawn doesn't begin until late April or May. And in the northern border states and southern regions of the Canadian provinces, the reproduction process may not begin until June.

Even within a particular body of water, spawning activities may span many weeks. Naturally, since the shallow headwater region of a lake will be the first to warm, spawning behavior gets underway there first. Slightly deeper regions farther down the shoreline may not reach spawning temperature for another ten days, and the deepest part of a lake, near a dam, may not warm to suitable temperatures for still another two weeks. Moreover, in any large body of water, the northern and northwestern coves and shoreline banks always receive more of the slanting rays of the warming springtime sun than do other places. Such locations also are generally protected from the last cold winds of winter and therefore will usually be the first places where bass engage in homemaking activities.

These observations suggest some helpful tactics. For example, an enterprising angler faced with tough postspawn fishing in a northwestern cove near the headwaters of his favorite lake can simply zip to the other side of the lake and likely find bass in a spawning mode. Or, he can motor downlake toward the dam and find bass there in an aggressively feeding prespawn stage. Likewise, if a bit later he finds tough postspawn fishing in the deeper part of the lake near the dam, he should know automatically what to do: Move to the shallow headwater region of the lake where the bass have long since finished spawning, have recuperated, and are now beginning to follow their normal summertime patterns.

Depth and Location of Bass Beds

The spawning process itself begins when the male bass move into the shallows. The term *shallow* as used here and throughout this book is only a relative term. Male largemouths may select bedding sites and begin constructing nests in water only six inches deep. I have seen them in shallow southern bayous, bulldogging about with their dorsal fins and the humps of their backs completely out of the water as they bloodied their tails fanning away debris from a bedding site. On the other hand, I've also located largemouth beds as deep as eight or ten feet in certain crystal-clear northern lakes.

The *depth* at which bass choose to spawn is determined by the degree of water clarity and the amount of underwater cover. These two factors influence the amount of sunlight that can penetrate the water. If the water is gin clear and little cover is present, more light can penetrate. Then bass may make their beds somewhat deeper than usual. Conversely, if the water is murky and substantial amounts of brush are present, the beds will invariably be somewhat shallower. In most cases an angler can expect to find largemouths spawning at depths averaging between three and five feet, though as already noted there may be exceptions to the rule.

The *locations* of spawning sites are determined by bottom composition and wind and wave action. Ideally, the bottom should be of hard-packed sand, shell, pea-gravel, clay, or marl (loosely packed clay and limestone),

Although bass will spawn on main-lake shorelines, they much prefer quiet backwaters. Males are the first to move inshore to select bedding sites.

with a very thin layer of mud covering the hard material. Largemouths seem to like to sweep out their nests, and the combination of hard bottom materials covered with marginal amounts of soft mire is the best of all conditions they search for.

At the same time, however, the prospective spawning site should be as free as possible from siltation, which is the deposition of finely granulated sediment on the bottom. Small amounts of sediment can be kept in suspension by the continual fanning action of the bass's tails, but sudden or massive amounts of sediment settling upon the eggs will suffocate them.

Because of potential siltation, and also because shallow water warms much faster, bass beds in lakes and reservoirs are found predominantly in quiet coves, bays and creek arms adjacent to the main body of water. But if few such shallows occur in a body of water, bass will spawn right along the banks of the main lake, usually where some type of protection is afforded the beds. Small cuts in the banks, downwind sides of points jutting out from the shore, or places where felled trees are lying in the water are examples of locations where wind and wave action will not disturb the beds by roiling the water unduly and covering the eggs with greater amounts of debris than the parent bass are able to keep in suspension. Keep in mind, though, that you'll probably find ten beds back in protected embayments and shallow creek arms for every one located along the banks of the main body of water.

Bass also like to have some type of object they can back up against, or some type of natural *cul de sac* they can lie within, from which they can defend the bedding site against other fish that try to eat the eggs. So when you're scouting for bedding locations, be alert for logs, tree trunks, stumps, rocks and similar cover.

It should also be mentioned that while bass are typically schoolfish for the greater part of the year, they disperse or scatter when the mating season approaches, searching out their own bedding locations away from others of the same species. In short, they become very territorial. Nevertheless, bass-spawning beds may be rather concentrated in certain regions in any given body of water, simply because the most ideal sites are always at a premium.

Generally, a largemouth's spawning bed is circular, measuring from 12 to 25 inches in diameter by about six inches deep. The contrast in appearance between spawning beds and surrounding bottom materials makes them easy to spot in clear water when you look through polarizing sunglasses to eliminate reflective glare from the surface. The beds appear, against a rather dark background, as pale, saucer-shaped depressions, the result of the males using their tails and pectoral and anal fins to clean away muck, leaves, decayed vegetation and other bottom debris, leaving clean sand, gravel or clay.

The Female's Role

While the male bass are building inshore spawning nests, females heavy with eggs begin moving from their deep-water winter homes to areas near the annual spawning grounds. At certain select locations (*holding stations*), they wait for their suitors to escort them for the remainder of their journeys. In larger and deeper lakes and reservoirs, frequent sites for female holding stations are sharply sloping points that extend from shorelines and guard the entrances to bays, ponds, marshes and creek arms. If no bays or coves are nearby and the bass are forced to spawn along the main banks of a lake or reservoir, the female holding stations may be nearby drop-offs or other bottom contour situated directly adjacent to much deeper water. In shallower lakes and reservoirs, the holding stations may be along the edges of inundated stream channels or perhaps an old riverbed.

Of course, a drop-off or winding stream channel may extend for hundreds of yards; attempting to figure out where, exactly, the various holding stations are situated can be a brain-racking task. Glen Lau of Ocala, Florida, who specializes in underwater filming of gamefish behavior, has shed a good deal of light on the subject. He has discovered that the holding stations female bass elect to use usually contain one or more *rubbing logs.*

Rubbing logs may consist of stumps, standing timber or almost any type of felled tree lying on the bottom in the types of locations described already. It's believed that female bass select holding stations with rubbing

Before being escorted to spawning sites by males, females heavy with eggs select offshore holding stations near deeper water. Here, anglers fish rubbing logs, in the form of standing timber, which often indicate the location of female holding stations.

logs because they bump and rub against these objects in an instinctive attempt to loosen the eggs from their skeins. This loosening action subsequently allows the females to more easily deposit eggs on the spawning beds.

In the reproductive cycle of basses, the male largemouth plays, by far, the more active role in the spawning behavior of the species. We've already seen how the buck selects a suitable bedding site and then fans out the nest. Next, the male searches out a nearby "ripe" female and herds her from the vicinity of the holding station to the bedding location, often nipping pestiferously at her. Once she is on the bed, he may swim continual circles around her to discourage her from leaving, and he may repeatedly bump her ventral region with his nose to trigger her into dropping her eggs.

In most cases, a female bass will drop only a portion of her eggs at any one time. Days later, with another male, she may drop more eggs on some other bed not far away. These females usually constitute the *cruisers* seen working back and forth in shallow bays and coves or along various main-lake shorelines. Most likely, they have already spawned once and are biding their time, waiting to be escorted to still another bedding site. These multiple attempts at egg laying are undoubtedly nature's insurance policy, since a certain percentage of beds or eggs each year are sure to be accidentally destroyed. This frequently happens when land slippage occurs, when there are radical fluctuations in water level that suddenly leave beds high and dry, or when there are abrupt changes in water temperature.

The total number of eggs dropped by any female largemouth, of course, depends upon the size of the fish. A three-pound bass may intermittently drop 8,000 eggs or more during the course of her inshore reproduction efforts. Studies conducted by numerous biologists, however, have shown that bass are averse to overcrowding. When bass populations build up, especially in smaller bodies of water, the males excrete into the water a chemical substance that prevents females from dropping their eggs. Conversely, where bass populations are very low, females manufacture and deposit more eggs than usual, and the males manufacture more milt to fertilize them.

Tips for Spring Fishing

While both male and female bass may engage in normal feeding behavior during very early spring as the water begins to warm, their later preoccupation with spawning most often causes all feeding to cease. Yet when bass are on their beds, they may still be caught rather readily. It is important for the angler to know, however, that strikes at this time do not reflect feeding behavior, per se, but other types of behavior, and he should gear his tactics accordingly.

For example, consider the nonfeeding strikes of the female bass, which may occur for one of two reasons. First, the female eventually may be angered into striking by repeated presentations of the lure; this occurs quite often with largemouths and Florida bass but, unexplainably, seldom with female smallmouths and spotted bass. Second, the female may see debris such as a twig or leaf (or perhaps an angler's worm) drift into the bedding area, whereupon she inhales it, swims a short distance from the bed and then exhales or blows it out of her mouth. In this case, the strike is not really a strike at all but the female bass merely engaging in her usual housekeeping.

The male largemouth, on the other hand, can be coaxed quite easily into striking when he is on the bedding site. As with the female, it is not a predatory feeding urge that causes him to take the angler's lure. By instinct he is very protective of the bedding site and will attack any intruders that approach the nest with the apparent intention of dining upon the eggs or newly hatched fry.

Just recently, for example, I was casting along a shoreline when I saw a big "ball" of half-inch bass minnows hovering near the surface. I threw my plug near the school, knowing in advance what would happen. Sure enough, a two-pound male bass instantly darted out of nowhere and violently slapped the lure with the *side* of his head. He wasn't interested in "eating" my plug, just killing it or chasing it away from his offspring.

Therefore, if a fisherman is able to spot bass-spawning beds visually, or if he has found the cover and bottom conditions typically associated with beds, he is almost certain to experience several distinct types of action. The first cast or two is sure to bring a vicious strike and a rather smallish bass may be hooked. This is the male and many anglers then make the mistake of continuing to work farther down the shoreline. If they would continue to fish the immediate area where the first fish was caught, using a much slower retrieve with long pauses between each movement of the lure, succeeding casts might eventually hook the much larger female bass. Her strike, or take, however, will probably be much lighter. Look for a gentle "mouthing" of the bait and be ready to set the hook immediately. If this tactic proves unsuccessful, and the angler is convinced there is a much larger fish on or near the bed, repeated casting to the area may eventually be rewarded with an arm-jolting strike.

On numerous occasions I've located a huge female on a bed and had consecutive casts to her result only in massive boils of water beneath my lure. That, in itself, is enough to make the hairs on any angler's neck bristle! But then, as many as 30 casts later, she may eventually become infuriated and really knock hell out of the lure. My guess is that the initial boiling-water episodes beneath the lure are her attempts to rid the nest area of the intruder, but failure in that finally prompts her as a last resort to try and kill it—in so doing she often hooks herself.

A few additional spring spawn-fishing tips might also be in order. First, when the water is cloudy and spawning beds cannot be seen easily, it's always wise to work the sunny sides of stumps, brush piles, felled trees or other locations that appear suitable for spawning. Although bass normally are quite averse to bright light and will retreat for the shaded sides of cover when in shallow water, the spawning weeks are an exception to the rule. As already noted, bass usually construct their nests so they are exposed as much as possible to the warming effects of the sun.

Also, if your shallow-water spawn-fishing efforts result only in small bass, the reason probably is that the fish are still in their earliest prespawn stages when the majority of fish in the shallows are males. To begin picking up the larger female bass, shift your efforts to the the mouths of embayments, the drop-offs, the edges of stream channels on the bottom, and similar holding stations adjacent to deep water where there is some type of timber.

Fishing for bass in the spring when they are on or near spawning sites can produce exciting action, large fish, and a nearly full stringer during a single day on the water. This is because bass are much easier to locate in spring than later on when the spawn is ended and the fish have evaporated (or so it seems, to many anglers) back into the depths. But there has long been controversy—indeed, even cursing and butting of heads—about whether catching spawning bass does harm to future bass populations.

Does it really make any difference whether a big female bass (or a male, for that matter) is caught a month or two before the spawning season, or a month or two afterward? That particular bass is still being removed, isn't it? On the other hand, a fish taken before spawning, obviously, can't produce offspring. Although more research is needed in this area, one thing is certain: If you release bass taken during the spawning season, they will return to their bedding sites and very shortly resume their reproduction efforts. As for fish kept for the table, sportsmen worthy of the title never keep more fish than they can put to good use. In the final chapter of this book, I'll examine the topic of catch-and-release ethics and procedures in much greater detail, but for the moment let's consider the remainder of the spawning process.

The Fate of Fry

After depositing her eggs, the female largemouth plays no further role in the egg- or fry-rearing process, and she gradually begins to drift away from the bedding site. The eggs hatch from two to five days after they have been fertilized by the buck. Although the male largemouth remains near the bed to protect the young fry from predators for a short while, he eventually succumbs to his increasingly ravenous hunger and becomes a leading predator himself, gobbling up as many of the fry as possible. This response —a well-planned scheme on the part of Mother Nature—causes the offspring to scatter and for the very first time begin fending for themselves. Self-preservation becomes the name of the game, and the young remain in or around heavy shoreline cover, hiding from those who would make a meal of them in short order.

The growth rate of fry, once they are completely free of the yolk sacs

The nemesis of bass lakes, bass anglers, and bass themselves are hoards of stunted panfish that invade spawning sites and decimate eggs and newly hatched fry.

which have nourished them until this time, is determined by many factors. Initially they feed upon plankton and other minute aquatic organisms, later switching to the smallest crustaceans and terrestrials, including various insect forms that commonly flit about most shallow-water areas during the late spring and summer. When the fry are about five inches long, they may also feed heavily upon small minnow species.

Growth rates of any of the bass species, then, are in direct proportion to the fertility of the waters they inhabit, the length of the growing season each year, and the numbers of other fish competing for the food supply in a body of water. Under favorable conditions, when there is plenty of food and not too many competitors, young bass can grow, in weight and length, quite rapidly.

The situation is not always so favorable, however. In many smaller lakes and reservoirs across the country, and especially in farmponds and ranch tanks, bluegill and crappies also inhabit the water. If these species are not controlled and their numbers soar, they can have a devastating effect upon bass in two ways. First, swarms of small panfish invade the bass nests to devour the eggs and newly hatched fry, preventing the bass population from replenishing itself as it would if the massive numbers of panfish were not present. Also, the panfish seriously deplete the food supply that small bass require during their early growth stages. As a result, such small bodies of water may harbor a certain number of large bass, but contain few of the smaller ones that in theory would eventually take their places. As the large bass are caught or die of old age, the lake or pond is left with nothing other than panfish; these continue to reproduce, outrun their available food supply and in time become even more stunted. Sometimes stocking more bass will remedy the problem, especially if adults, capable of curbing the panfish numbers, are used. But often the imbalance in fish populations is so great that the only solution is to apply rotenone to kill all fish life (or completely drain the body of water) and start all over with renewed stockings of both bass and panfish.

So there can be no doubt that the lives of young bass are laced with precarious uncertainties and threats to their well-being. Panfish and crayfish, among many predators, will try to make a meal of them while they are still dependent and struggling under the burden of their yolk sacs. Larger panfish and smaller gamefish will swoop down upon them in the fry stage and decimate both their numbers and available food supply. Even their own parents cannot be trusted. Mother abandons them, and several days later Father tries to swallow them! Only three to five percent of any spawning will survive these initial ravages, and they are likely to become meals for still larger predator gamefish as they near yearling size. For the great majority, there will be no escape and no tomorrow. But young bass adept at hiding and adaptable to nature's code of "eat or be eaten" eventually grow large enough that they need no longer fear the other fishes and creatures inhabiting the same weedbeds and rocky drop-offs.

Life is not smooth sailing, or swimming, from here on, however. Even as increasing size and approaching maturity begin to protect a young bass, its greatest competitor—man—appears on the scene. Sporting gentlemen will attempt to fool it into biting upon metal, plastic and wooden imitations of its food. They will tempt the bass with real food in which they have concealed hooks! Or they will try to capitalize upon its famed pugnacity and provoke it into striking, whether hungry or not. The bass may survive many of these encounters by release during its early years, and may survive still again in later years by using brute strength to smash anglers' gear. But the one encounter with man that the bass cannot survive is the thoughtless destruction of its habitat by channelization or the pollutive effects of raw sewage, chemical spills and acid rain falling from the sky.

Despite all of these threats to their well-being, largemouth bass, and to a slightly lesser extent the other basses, continue to thrive in many North American waters. They grow fat, they increase in numbers, and they yield the unpredictable excitement of an often spectacular battle with those who brave the elements to search them out on their home grounds. It's not at all surprising that the various bass species are the most sought-after gamefish. That they are able to overcome seemingly insurmountable odds and still survive—even flourish—is testimony to the tenacity of these species.

Postspawning Behavior of Adult Bass

When the spawning process is completed and the bass fry have been left to make it on their own, the parent bass go through a brief recuperative period of lethargic inactivity, after which their appetites steadily begin to increase. As mentioned in Chapter 1, bass do not feed continually but usually restrict their active foraging to certain indeterminate times of day. As the water continues to warm after spawning, however, bass's metabolic rates increase; as a result, the periods of active feeding become appreciably longer than during the earlier cold-water months. The faster their systems burn food stores to create energy, the more food bass must acquire during each feeding session. In addition, the long winter months and subsequent spawning activity significantly reduce their body weight. The need to replenish lost body weight and the increased metabolic rate, brought on by warmer water, make for periods of sometimes stupendous fishing.

Since bass are averse to bright light, and shallow water makes them feel ill at ease, when they leave the spawning grounds they usually hide in and around some type of cover that affords shade and seclusion. An angler, leisurely drifting down shorelines studded with remnants of felled trees, stumps, boulders, mats of floating vegetation and other cover, if he is careful in his approach, can expect consistent action, either by eliciting feeding responses or by forcing the fish to strike. Now is a time of year when explosive action can be enjoyed with a variety of surface plugs and other shallow-water runners. The flyrodder is sure to be there, too, his line uncurling like a ballerina's arm as it ever so gently and methodically lays poppers or deerhair bugs near suspected bass lairs.

The places where the bass are found soon after spawning are only temporary stations as they day by day gradually drift toward their summer homes. With each passing day of the postspawn period, any shoreline plugger's chances of coming home with a heavy stringer progressively diminish. In lakes and reservoirs most of the larger fish are beginning to congregate along the edges of the depths. In the weeks to follow, they will be spending most of their time *in* the depths. Left behind will be the younger bass (many of them from the previous year's spawning) in various stages of growth and ranging from two to 12 inches in length, to find whatever food and hiding the shallow shoreline cover may provide. The young bass will remain in these places until they have grown to a respectable size and, like their parents, discover they can no longer tolerate the bright sunlight and unsafe conditions that prevail in the shallow haunts.

At this time of year, many less-accomplished anglers begin to offer explanations as to why they are no longer catching bass larger than the minimum keeper size. They may sincerely believe the large bass have stopped biting. "The dog days are approaching," they claim, "and the bass are becoming inactive."

The truth of the matter is that the large bass are now more active than ever! They are feeding heavily during those times of day when their biological clocks tell them to replenish fuel supplies, and when they are not actively foraging, they often can be easily provoked into striking. Moreover, because they now are beginning to congregate in schools, they can be caught in larger numbers than during any other time of year.

The problem is that most anglers are still plugging the shallow bays where they found bass during the brief prespawn, spawn and postspawn periods. But the largest bass have long since moved away from those places and won't return again until the following spring.

CHAPTER

3

Structure Is Their Home

At the conclusion of their spawning activities, bass begin to congregate along the deep-water edges of cover. The inquisitive angler might ask why they gradually move toward deeper water and where they plan to go next.

The answer is that bass have an instinct to school. In numbers there is safety, particularly if the members composing a school are of like size. Consequently, in one school there will be bass averaging 1½ pounds; in another, fish averaging 2½ pounds; and so on. One time I was fishing with tournament pro Ricky Green on Montgomery Lake in Alabama when we discovered a bonanza of bass on a deep bar. We began yanking them in, one after another, and during the course of an hour caught 37 fish. Amazingly, not one of the bass was an inch longer or shorter than the others, and all of them weighed within an ounce of two pounds.

There is an inverse relationship between the size and number of individual fish in a school: The larger they are, the fewer there are—and the more tightly they group together. The very largest bass in any given body of water may sometimes group together in twos and threes, but just as often they are loners. In the case of largemouths and Florida bass, such fish may be more than eight or nine pounds. But in the case of smallmouths and spotted bass, which typically do not grow as large, individual school members usually average only two to three pounds.

In addition to having a schooling instinct, bass beyond the yearling size (that is, nine to 13 inches in length and averaging a pound in weight) are basically deep-water fish. Fortunately for anglers, schools of bass (of all species) occasionally travel or *migrate* from their deep-water haunts to shallower areas, making them easier to catch. But the larger the individual fish in a school, the less willing they are to leave deep water; and when they do migrate, the less likely they are to move as far into the shallows as do schools comprised of smaller fish.

Bass head for deep water for several reasons. First, as bass grow, their behavior becomes more shy and retiring. This is largely a survival instinct, which in bass is highly refined. Anything that even hints that their survival may be in jeopardy causes them to retreat hastily.

For a moment, let's look at the world from the bass's viewpoint. From the very day they are hatched from their eggs, the precautionary instincts off all bass urge them to flee from activity—human or otherwise—or risk being eaten. In the fry, fingerling and yearling stages of growth, they learn they can escape from larger predators by vanishing into the dark recesses of shoreline weeds and rocks. As they grow still older and larger, with their innate tendency to school getting stronger, they soon are faced with little choice but to retreat to deeper waters, the only place large enough for a group to hide from disturbance.

Another reason bass move into deeper water has to do with light penetration in the shallows. Bass have fixed-pupil eyes, which cannot contract or dilate to accommodate to various light intensities. Whether very bright light is uncomfortable to bass is not conclusively known, but it clearly amplifies or accentuates their presence, making them more conspicuous. This probably not only goes against their instinct to hide from larger predators but also, when the tables are turned, makes them less effective predators. Bass are left with only two choices: Retreat for deeper (and darker) water or, if no deep water exists, find seclusion in the shaded water found beneath expanses of matted weeds or toppled trees.

How Deep Is Deep?

As we've seen, bass are schoolfish and in most lakes and reservoirs they spend most of the year away from the shorelines and in the depths. The perplexing question is, how deep is deep? There is no correct answer, for depth is always relative.

In an expansive southern flatland impoundment, deep water may be an old stream channel winding across the bottom where the water is ten feet deep. Ten feet is certainly very deep water if 95 percent of the reservoir averages only five or six feet deep. As a result, in such an impoundment, bass will probably inhabit the stream channel much of the year. Unless, that is, the water is extremely clear and is as brightly illuminated at ten feet as at five feet. Then, they will probably congregate along certain portions of the channel, perhaps where there is a forest of standing timber. In the absence of such cover—here's one of the "exceptions to the rule" —schooling instincts may be repressed as individual bass scatter widely for small patches of lily pads or hiding in any other tiny bit of shade.

Conversely, in a canyonland reservoir in some southwestern state, where the depths plunge, perhaps, to several hundred feet, ten feet would be classified as very shallow water and probably only infrequently see bass activity. In such a body of water, bass would probably elect to spend most of their time in depths ranging from 15 to 40 feet. But all of this depends upon water and weather conditions as well as other localized influences. During periods of reduced light penetration (e.g., during the hours of dawn and dusk, or even after dark), the fish might move considerably shallower, depending upon the particular forage they are tied to. And during a periodic cold front, they might move much deeper, perhaps to 60 feet or more.

In all of this, the thing to keep in mind is that bass generally go as deep as need be to feel safe, reduce being too obvious, and enhance their abilities as efficient predators.

These generalizations about bass seeking deep water, avoiding bright light and forming schools do not always apply to fish in many newly created manmade lakes and reservoirs. Although such newly created bodies of water constitute only a small percentage of the bass-fishing water available in this country, for the sake of your complete education as an advanced angler, they should be mentioned here. The exceptions to the rules, in this case, take a little explanation to understand, so I'll momentarily digress.

The early years in the life of any lake or reservoir provide very exciting shallow-water fishing. For the first five to ten years or so, the floor of the impoundment is abundantly endowed with high levels of various nitrogen compounds, which foster extensive aquatic growth and a very prolific food chain. Hoards of baitfish and small panfish provide ample food for the ravenous young bass, and their populations soar. Because the life-sustaining nitrogen compounds and the subsequent food chain are both widely dispersed over the reservoir's area, so too are the bass, and they continue to put on weight at a rapid pace.

During these youthful years of an impoundment's life, the shoreline plugger experiences fast action and is able to load his stringer on almost every trip. The bass are not yet overly large, averaging two to three pounds, but they seem to be almost everywhere. Because such waters are abundantly supplied with vegetation, flooded brush and standing timber, a continual process of organic decay creates tannin-stained or at least slightly murky water, and this sharply reduces light penetration. The bass feel relatively safe under these conditions, and since the shallow-water covers are teeming with food, the fish often delay their customary post-spawning movement into the depths. Instead, they continue to seek refuge in and around the existing shallow-water cover, which not only offers hiding but easy eats; in this situation, they are easy targets for anglers. Predictably, such an impoundment soon receives the reputation of being "hot," and voluminous amounts of national publicity in the outdoor magazines prompt anglers to flock to the site in droves. But like all good things, the fun is short-lived.

After about ten years—sometimes more or less, depending upon the individual body of water and its limnological characteristics—the fishing action begins to taper off for the plug-pitcher. He begins to notice that tireless casting to the shallow weeds and stumps is resulting in fewer and fewer strikes. Instead of catching upwards of 30 bass a day or more, he may now be getting only a few. The bass, of course, are still in the impoundment in plentiful numbers, and larger than ever. But the angler has failed to adapt his fishing to the changing personality of the water as it progressively continues to age.

One of the many changes a lake or reservoir experiences as it grows older is the gradual depletion of the life-sustaining nitrogen compounds originally in the terrain over which the body of water was constructed. A major result is that the most productive fishing areas become progressively fewer in number. As the food supply decreases and becomes concentrated in a few areas, and as the water characteristically begins to clear somewhat, the behavior of bass in an aging impoundment also changes. They are no longer roamers; nor are they widely distributed over most of the impounded area. They begin schooling or at least loosely grouping in certain areas near the depths. Soon they will spend most of their time *in* the depths and the once-true description, a "bass in every bush," rapidly becomes so much history. As the easy catches for the unskilled masses of anglers become rare, the national publicity will slowly dwindle, and in all likelihood the angler who must have visible, shallow-water cover to cast to will give up on this impoundment.

Bull Shoals Reservoir in Arkansas is a prime example of the phenomenon of reservoir aging. During the first 15 years of the reservoir's life the name Big Bull was on the lips of every bass angler across the nation. Catches were simply phenomenal. Today, of course, 40 years later, that is no longer true. Old-time anglers have forgotten Big Bull even exists, and the younger generation is not likely to read about the lake in a sportsman's magazine. The water is clear now, the food chain has long since subsided to barely self-sustaining levels, and the bass spend nearly all of their time in the depths. Consequently, excellent strings of bass are still caught at Bull Shoals from time to time, but never by the shallow-water shoreline plugger. Those catches are logged by grizzled, old deep-water hounds who have learned far more about bass behavior than just the basics.

The Nature of Structure

To return to the main thread of this discussion, we have established that for the most part bass live in schools in the depths, and that in any given lake or reservoir there are only certain locations where those schools may be found at any given time. We'll now add to our growing knowledge still another tenet of bass behavior: *Bass live on or very near the bottom.*

The actual depth bass will go to will vary from time to time due to weather and water conditions. But regardless of whether the bass are in 12, 15 or 25 feet of water, they will nearly always be *on the bottom.* There are two exceptions to this rule: (1) bass may be found at various levels in and around cover when the water is less than 8 feet deep, and (2) bass may suspend at arbitrary depths when they follow surface-swimming schools of baitfish in midlake regions. Both situations are discussed in later chapters.

Schools of bass don't live, however, on just any type of bottom. Most often, they are found in conjunction with some type of *structure.* Structure is any bottom condition that presents a noticeable difference from surrounding bottom conditions. As noted in Chapter 2, spawning bass like bottom materials consisting of coarse sand, gravel, shell, rocks, clay, or marl, but are usually averse to heavy concentrations of mud or silt. The same is basically true during their deep-water lives throughout the remainder of the year.

There are many types of structure that bass in any given natural lake or manmade reservoir may be using at any given time. It may be an underwater hump or island that juts up from the floor of the body of water, a long underwater bar, or perhaps a point of land that juts out from the shoreline and then extends underwater for some distance. Other structures might consist of the edge of a weedline where the water rapidly drops off into the depths, a series of underwater stairstep ledges or rocky outcroppings, a place where the bottom composition changes from sand to clay, or perhaps a stream channel winding along the floor of the body of water. These are all classified as *natural structures.* Not all of them are present in every body of water, but most lakes and reservoirs usually have some of them.

One of the best ways to grasp the idea of underwater structure is to take an occasional drive through the country. Stop now and then along the side of the road and survey the surrounding terrain, trying to envision the entire area suddenly flooded with water as it would be if a natural lake or manmade reservoir were suddenly created there. This mental image will give you a picture-window view of the water's otherwise hidden

Envision this valley suddenly flooded with water and a lake created, then pick out features that might attract bass. The most obvious are the drop-off, brush piles and, in the background, what would become a swampy area of standing timber.

personality. Now, search for places where the terrain exhibits radical changes of one kind or another. Note the ridgelines and how they slope at different angles. These, when underwater, will usually be the points jutting out from the shorelines. Note the flat-bottomed areas and see if you can find humps. These will be the submerged islands rising up from the floor. Are there any elongated mounds spanning sections of the flats? These will be the bars and saddles. Do you see any depressions, cuts or slices in the landscape? These will be the "holes," which are often bass magnets of the first order. Are there any creeks, brooks or streams meandering through the terrain? These too will hold many bass during much of the year. Are there any steep banks, bluffs or cliffs? Bass will probably be along these sheer walls during the winter months. What about cover such as brush piles, small clumps of standing trees, trees toppled by high winds, rock piles, or other structural formations that seem to be situated in open pastures or fields or on hillsides? These also constitute radical changes in the bottom and would probably hold bass.

Moreover, as you are visually examining different types of terrain in the countryside, continually quiz yourself. If the area really were inundated, where would the deepest water be? Where would the bottom be hard and where would it be soft and muddy. When bass move out of deep water during early spring, with thoughts of spawning, what areas in the land before you would likely attract them? After you've found what would probably be the spawning grounds, can you find locations female bass would use as holding stations? Do you see any types of structure extending from what would be the shoreline all the way into what would be the

This is what the floor of one lake actually looks like (it was drained to perform maintenance on the dam). The most striking feature is the winding stream channel on the bottom.

deepest water in the immediate area? Examples might be a long sloping point, a small brook trickling down from the highlands, rows of stumps on a steep hillside, or rock slides. These configurations, and many others, as we will see later, will probably be the very best bass structures in any body of water.

In addition to natural structures, artificial bodies of water often possess various *manmade structures,* which also cause radical changes in the bottom. You probably will see many manmade structures in your imaginary lake as you drive cross-country. An old building foundation is one example, or perhaps the supporting concrete pillars of a small country bridge crossing a small river. Are there any county or township roads winding across the terrain? These will nearly always be constructed of very hard gravel, chunk rock and other materials; if they're somewhat elevated and surrounded by soft marshy ground, they will attract bass

In this newly created lake in the process of filling, the long sloping ridge in the foreground will soon be an underwater point; just behind it, a hump will soon be an underwater island.

during all seasons but especially at spawning time if they are located near the shallows. The same applies to abandoned railroad spurs. The ties and rails may have been removed, but the limestone bedding is certain to be still intact. Are there any fence rows, borrow pits (where sand, gravel or fill dirt were removed for construction purposes), drainage culverts or ditches along roads, or utility poles? Junk piles of scrap building materials such as bricks and concrete slabs often hold amazing numbers of bass. All of these, and more, which men have created and discarded, constitute manmade structure, and bass will use them as religiously as they do weedbeds, felled trees, bars, points, and drop-offs.

The reason for this exercise in identifying structure—either natural or manmade—is that *bass, during every month of the year, are highly object-oriented.* In other words, they like to get next to something, in contrast to other species such as walleyes that dote upon open-water habitats often

In addition to natural structures, bass also are attracted to manmade structures. Here, on a new lake beginning to fill, note the small country bridge and old roadbed. When eventually covered with ten feet of water, bass may use this structure as religiously as a weedbed or stump field.

entirely free of cover or structure. If you can locate structure, you're well on your way to finding the bass in any body of water.

Bass Movements

The place where a school of bass rests in deep water is called a *sanctuary.* But only in rare circumstances can bass be caught when they are in this resting area, for a variety of reasons. The sanctuary is usually a very small area where bass, when resting, are schooling very tightly. Because a sanctuary is likely to be in very deep water, pinpointing its exact location can be next to impossible. Additionally, because of the depth, precise presentation of lures is a precarious venture at best, as various "controls" that must be exercised over the lures are lost. And finally, schooling bass in a sanctuary are rather inactive and can seldom be tempted into biting or provoked into striking.

The angler's saving grace, as noted earlier, is that a school of bass will occasionally *migrate* from its sanctuary to some other area a short distance away, usually located in somewhat shallower water. And during the course of this migration the bass can be caught by numerous methods because they are now in a highly active state and the shallower water makes lure presentation much easier.

A study conducted several years ago by two scientists associated with Southern Illinois University emphasizes several of the points already mentioned about the migration habits of bass. In this study, a large number of spawning bass in the shallows were temporarily stunned with electroshocking equipment. The fish then were outfitted with identification tags and carefully released back into the water. Subsequent shocking programs to recapture tagged fish were carried out during following months.

The study revealed that after the spawning period only one to two percent of the originally captured bass were back on the shoreline at any given time. What this means is that after spawning has been completed, over 98 percent of the fish spend the majority of their time away from the shallows and in deeper water. In addition, 96 percent of the bass that at some time or other left the depths and migrated toward the shallows were recaptured within 300 feet of where they were initially tagged. This confirms the "home range" tendency of bass, briefly described earlier. Unlike some other gamefish species that are classified as migratory and engage in seasonal shifts of location, often covering long distances (e.g., salmon), bass migrate for relatively short periods of time and over short distances within their home range.

It should be noted that when bass migrate from their sanctuaries they do not simply fan out and disperse. Nor do they generally travel in a haphazard manner or in random directions. Instead, they usually travel in an orderly fashion as a group and along types of underwater "highways," or migration routes, following "signposts" consisting of structural variations to their destinations.

During the warm-water months of late spring, summer and fall (and sometimes throughout the year in the warmest, southernmost states), bass movements within the home range may take place two or three times each day. Migrations frequently occur during the early morning hours, sometime around noon, and again during the evening. A migration may last as long as two hours or be as brief as 20 minutes. During the cold-water months of late fall, winter and very early spring, however, migrations often occur only once a day or once every other day, usually around noon, and they frequently last only 30 minutes.

Additionally, and this is critically important, the season of year determines the migrational characteristics. During the cold-water months, bass tend to migrate from their sanctuaries in a somewhat vertical plane as they move from the depths toward the steeper shorelines; also, the distance of the migration may be very short. During the warm-water months (water temperature above 50°), however, bass generally migrate on a more horizontal plane as they move from the depths toward shallow shorelines. You

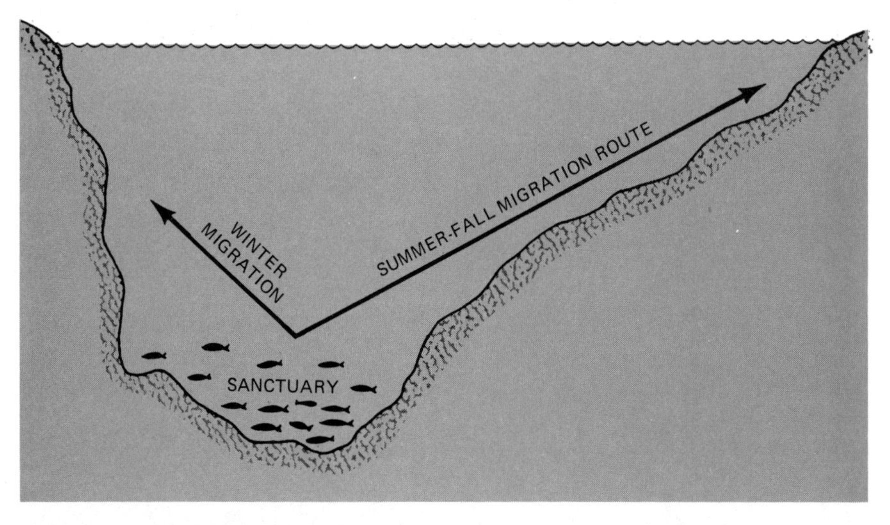

Bass migration characteristics are dictated by the seasons and related water temperatures. When the water is warm, bass typically travel long distances on gently sloping structures. When the water is cold, their migrations are much shorter, sometimes almost vertical, on steep structures.

may have already experienced this phenomenon yourself, noticing that your best catches during the colder months of the year seem to come from the steep shorelines and related structures, which rapidly drop off into the depths, while your best catches during the warmer months come predominantly from gradually sloping shorelines, which extend far out into the lake or reservoir. (Chapter 4 goes into more detail on when and where bass migrations occur; Chapter 13 covers the movements of bass in rivers and streams.)

It should be noted as well that bass schools do not always migrate simply because they are hungry and in search of food. This should be obvious because it is inconceivable that every bass in every school in a given body of water would be hungry at exactly the same time. If this is

If you keep a log indicating the times of day bass were caught you're sure to note similarities between your catches and those made by your pals who were on the water the same day. This confirms the belief that bass have distinct periods of activity and inactivity.

the case, then why *do* bass migrate several times a day? Well, that is a question no one has conclusively answered. All we really know is that at certain, somewhat predictable times nearly all of the many schools of bass in any given lake or reservoir seem to simultaneously begin climbing out of their sanctuaries and traveling to their destinations. Further, it is during these periods of movement that they are most frequently caught by anglers.

This, again, is something you may have already noted during your fishing experiences. If you keep a logbook, indicating when and where you've caught your bass in the past, you'll begin to note striking similarities and coincidences. And if you compare your records with those of your angling buddies, you'll probably discover that on any given day your peak periods of action have been quite the same. If you encountered most of your fish from, say, 7 to 9 A.M. on a given day, and then again from 3 to 4 P.M., and your buddy was on the water in another boat and likewise caught fish that day, it's a good bet that most of his bass came aboard during roughly the same time periods.

CHAPTER

4

Learning To Read Structure

Buck Perry is known as the Father of Structure Fishing for it was he who, decades ago, first described the behavior of bass as they periodically migrate back and forth between their deep-water resting areas and associated shallow-water destinations.

In this chapter, I'll be discussing a number of Perry's original concepts and findings about bass habits and looking at recent refinements that can be applied to specific situations where unique, localized conditions prevail. In order to utilize much of this information, however, anglers must know how to read maps and use electronic depth sounders, for these are the "eyes" that allow us to see below the surface of the water to find where bass are living. These are critically important skills because, as any guide, professional tournament angler or other expert will testify, being able to "find the fish" is 90 percent of the effort.

Reading Maps

Show me a consistently successful bass angler and, regardless of how or where he likes to fish, I'll show you an angler with a tacklebox jammed full of maps. I'll also show you a fisherman who looks upon maps as more valuable in the day's work ahead than any particular lures or baits or secret tips gleaned during predawn strategy sessions or picked up from the current boathouse scuttlebutt.

At the outset, it's worth stating that an accurate map, in addition to helping you find bass, can help you find yourself when camp is lost. This safety feature takes on its greatest significance when fishing many of today's manmade reservoirs. These huge impoundments often sprawl for 40 or 50 miles and are characterized by interconnecting river systems, long creek arms and mammoth bays that may easily confuse an angler and cause him to lose his bearings at the first wrong turn. More than once I've become so engrossed in my fishing that approaching darkness suddenly caught me far from the launch ramp and I had no idea where in the dickens I was. This is when I pull out my map, orient myself, then follow river channel marker buoys until I see the welcome sight of marina lights winking in the distance.

Before we examine specialized fishing maps, let's review the old stand-bys—the government agency charts—because on occasion any angler may want to use the two together for even more efficient fish-finding. The most popular of these have been the U.S. Geological Survey topographical maps (called *topo* maps for short).

A topo map shows the land contours and formations that existed in an area when the map was prepared. They are most useful to anglers in regions where lakes or reservoirs have been created *after* the maps were compiled; in such cases, a topo map provides a picture of the underwater features of a body of water. Overall, topo maps are considered quite accurate because the required land measurements are obtained by a combination of aerial photography and surveyors actually walking the area with their transits. However, it's important to realize that changes in terrain—from either natural or human causes—that may occur after a map is compiled will not be shown on it.

Topo maps are available in different scales, and consequently represent terrain areas of different sizes. Since, as an angler, you are most interested in what small or restricted bottom areas look like, it's best to obtain topo maps with the smallest scale possible. In most cases, 20-foot contour intervals are standard, but sometimes 10-foot intervals are available; now and then you'll really strike it lucky and find maps with 5-foot intervals.

Contour lines, of course, enable cartographers to present a visual picture of what a landform looks like. Depending upon the spacing interval between the lines, it's easy for an angler to differentiate between flat, gradually sloping and steep underwater terrain features, or to locate abruptly defined features such as drop-offs. Topo maps also show the locations and configurations of stream channels, riverbed routes, and manmade structures (roads, bridges, building foundations) that were present when the maps were prepared. In addition, different colored inks indicate the location of forestlands, meadows, and open fields at the time a map was compiled.

For purposes of distributing topo maps, the U.S. Geological Survey has divided the country in half, the Mississippi River being the dividing line. If you're interested in maps of lakes that are somewhere east of the Mississippi, contact the U.S. Geological Survey, Map Distribution Center,

1200 South Eads Street, Arlington, VA 22202. For maps of areas west of the Mississippi, write to the U.S. Geological Survey, Federal Center, Denver, CO 80225.

Whichever office you contact, at first, send no money. Maps have to be ordered by quadrangle number, and either of the two USGS offices will send you a free index listing maps available for the region you request, along with an order form and price list (most topo maps cost about $2). Since the largest reservoirs may well overlap several quadrangle surveys, it may be necessary to purchase two or more maps and tape them together in order to have a chart showing the entire body of water.

Also, because topo maps typically show the land contours *before* a lake or reservoir was created, it's usually necessary to draw in the shoreline of any now existing body of water. You can do this by first contacting the agency that created or presently manages the waterway and finding out the maximum pool elevation (in feet above sea level) of the lake or reservoir. With a felt-tipped pen, then simply trace the numbered contour line that corresponds to the maximum pool elevation and you'll outline the entire shoreline perimeter of the lake on the map.

To determine water depths within a lake's basin and related creek arms and embayments, a bit of mental gymnastics is required because on topo maps contour lines are labeled with the elevation from sea level. To determine the actual water depth at a particular contour line, subtract the sea-level value on the map from the pool-stage value given to you by the agency that built the lake, and insert that number for future reference. For example, if the pool stage for the lake is 350 feet and the sea-level elevation

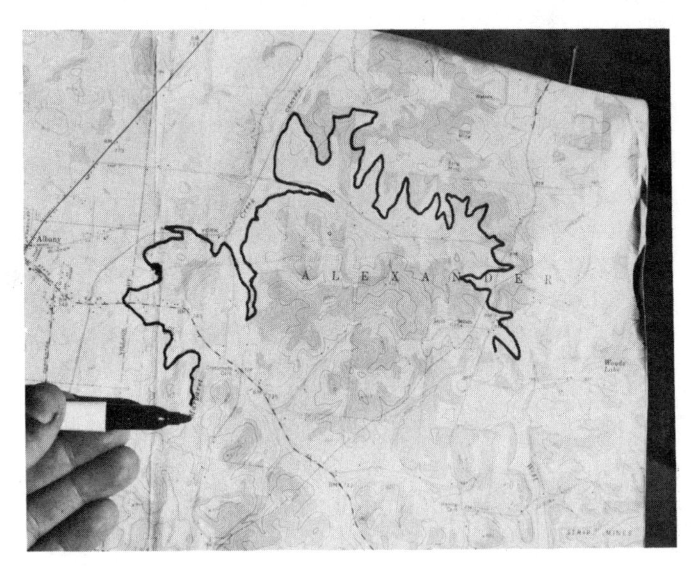

When adapting topo maps to bass fishing, it's usually necessary to determine the pool elevation of the now-existing body of water and then draw in the shoreline.

of the contour line you're looking at is 325 feet, the water depth at that particular location is 25 feet.

A type of contour map very similar to a topo map is a hydrological chart (often called a *navigation map*). Occasionally, these are not as accurate as topo maps. This is likely to be the case with hydro maps of a manmade lake compiled years after the lake is completed and with maps of natural lakes that have existed for thousands of years. In such situations, the maps generally are based only on aerial photographs and sonar soundings.

Hydro maps are usually available from whatever agency is presently charged with managing a particular body of water, such as a state department of natural resources, the Army Corps of Engineers, a watershed control (flood control) agency, or hydroelectric power company. For example, the Tennessee Valley Authority (Maps and Engineering Records Section, Knoxville, TN 37902) can provide excellent navigation maps of all TVA-controlled waters. Other sources of hydro maps include the National Ocean Survey (Map Distribution Division, Riverdale, MD 20840) and the U.S. Department of Commerce (Oceanic and Atmospheric Administration, Washington, DC 20036).

There are several major drawbacks to both topo and hydro maps, one of which has been noted already. Although such maps are initially quite accurate, they are reverified only infrequently, usually every 15 to 20 years. And, since lakes, reservoirs and navigable waters are not static things, but have living and ever-changing personalities, it is impossible for such maps to be precisely up to date at all times. In loose-terrain regions, or where bodies of water are continually subjected to significant amounts of wind, wave action over the years may partially obliterate some underwater terrain features and/or create new ones.

Illustrations of such underwater landforms periodically altered by nature include sandbars, shoals, reefs and submerged islands. And, stumps or trees on the bottom will gradually rot away. If any noticeable current runs through inundated stream or river channels on the bottom, a type of underwater erosion also may take place. This eventually may alter the appearance of the channels themselves or of adjacent structures previously held in place by root masses.

Further, siltation occurs to some extent in every lake and reservoir, so that the basin configuration slowly fills in as a result of sediment settling out of the water. This, along with the annual buildup of decayed organic matter sinking to the bottom, causes a lake or reservoir, over a long period of time, to become shallower and shallower. To remedy this in navigable waters, dredging operations may occasionally be undertaken. These can create countless types of underwater ridges, channels and well-defined edges.

Periodic landslides near steep shorelines—where the soil has slipped or where boulders or entire rock facings have tumbled into the water—create points, underwater stairstep formations, drop-offs or other bass-holding features where none previously existed. Sometimes just the opposite happens. For example, at one lake I fish there used to be a drop-off shelf, along a certain steep shoreline, that always produced smallmouths. Then, a tornado uprooted trees on an adjacent hillside and a landslide subsequently took place. Where the drop-off once was is now only a gradual underwater slope, and I haven't caught a smallmouth there since.

All of this makes a good case in favor of every serious angler having a depth sounder, not only to find structures shown on a map but also to more precisely determine their outlines and dimensions as they currently exist. Pronounced differences between what the map indicates and current conditions should be marked on the map.

An easy way to avoid some of the drawbacks and inconvenience of standard topo and hydro maps is to use the specialized *fishing maps* now being compiled by some private map companies. These companies are in

Maps specifically designed for fishermen are inexpensive, yet excellent investments. Not only are they more accurate than standard topo and hydro maps, they're usually waterproof and show far more of the kinds of underwater details anglers are interested in.

the business of taking conventional topo and hydro maps, reverifying the underwater terrain features, and publishing the updated maps more often than do governmental agencies. In addition, these maps cover entire lakes. This in itself eliminates the time and hassles involved in ordering different quadrangle surveys, drawing in the shoreline, trying to figure out depths from contour lines and pool elevations, then awkwardly piecing together the individual maps to form a coherent view of a body of water.

Another benefit of these fishing maps, which are produced exclusively to help advanced fishermen, is the additional information, only rarely shown on governmental maps, that most include. A case in point are maps of the many lakes and reservoirs created before 1960 that were cleared of standing timber, stumps, brush and similar cover before their dishpan-shaped basins were allowed to fill. This procedure left much of the bottom, and countless shorelines, almost entirely denuded and barren of ideal bass habitat. Also, irregular bottom contours ordinarily sought by bass for use when in deep water were obliterated by bulldozer blades. Consequently, the boat slips, dock pilings, catwalks, concrete breakwater walls, rubble riprap, mooring posts and similar manmade objects created *after* the building of a lake—and the making of maps—often constitute not only the bulk of fish-holding cover in certain areas but the very best. Maps showing these objects are not only convenient but sometimes vital to fishing success.

In the case of lakes not cleared before being filled, many of the new fishing maps even show the locations of cover such as weedbeds, flooded forests, underwater stump fields, clambeds, rock piles and fencelines. When knowledge of such features is combined with the contour lines and water depth values on the maps, these charts become literally worth their weight in good catches.

Another distinct advantage that fishing maps have over regular topo or hydro maps is that most are made of plastic-coated or other specially treated paper, so they are impervious to weather and water. Because of this feature, these maps won't be reduced to a mushy glob of papier-maché if they are rained upon or dropped in a wet boat bottom. When some of my new maps have blown overboard, I've simply retrieved them, shaken off the excess water, and gone back to fishing.

Since these new maps have only recently hit the world of bass fishing, they are currently available only for the largest, most popular and well-known lakes and reservoirs. Although many of these maps are now being stocked at local marinas, tackleshops and bait stores near their respective bodies of water, ordering them directly from the various map companies is the most reliable way to obtain them. They generally cost $2 to $5 when ordered direct. A listing of the companies now distributing specialized fishing maps, and a brief description of what they offer, follows:

Structure Graphics Company (917 Pyramid Drive, Valley Park, MO 63088) sells extremely detailed contour maps of 19 bass lakes in the Ozarks (Arkansas and Missouri) as well as of waters in Illinois, Oklahoma and Texas.

The Alexandria Drafting Company (417 E. Clifford Avenue, Alexandria, VA 22305) has available eight map directories published in atlas form. These are so detailed that even individual underwater bushes and hedgerows are shown! Most of the maps are for midwestern and southeastern waters.

The Permaguide Map Company (2427 Ninth Street S.W., Canton, OH 44710) offers plastic, weatherproof contour maps primarily of Ohio waters but also for lakes in Florida and Georgia.

Lakes Illustrated Company (Box 4854, Springfield, MO 65804), perhaps the biggest of the fishing map distribution companies, is collaborating with tournament angler and tackle manufacturer Tom Mann to produce excellent charts for bass anglers. At the present time, this company has detailed contour maps of 150 lakes in 20 different states, and each map is virtually indestructible.

Marine Surveys Company (650 Industry Avenue, Anoka, MN 55303) offers 56 maps compiled by Al and Ron Lindner, founders of *The In-Fisherman.* These maps are of lakes—in Minnesota, Wisconsin, Illinois, Iowa and California—that the Lindners have personally mastered, as professional guides, when fishing in tournaments, or in conducting on-the-water seminars. Not only do each of the maps show the hot spots they've found but on the back of each map there is a detailed narrative as to how the fish in that particular lake migrate during the seasons, exactly where to find them during every month of the year, and which lures and techniques are best.

There are several things to keep in mind when you are using any type of contour or fishing map. First, it's wise to spend a little time studying a map before actually taking it on the water. In particular, you should become familiar with the map *legend.* This is a small block somewhere on the face of a map that indicates how bottom structures and other features are represented on that particular chart.

The dry terrain surrounding a body of water will usually be shown in yellow (or sometimes green or brown). The water itself may appear as various colors in different regions. Very shallow water is usually shown in white, moderate depths are indicated in light blue, intermediate depths in light green, and the deepest water in a lake in dark blue.

Inundated stream channels and riverbeds winding along the floor of a lake are shown as solid blue lines or black dotted lines. Old roads are indicated as parallel dashes. Building foundations now covered with water are black squares. Drowned railroad spurs are represented by single lines with perpendicular cross-marks. Swamps are presented with symbols that look like rising suns, and submerged timber, stumps and brush may be indicated by either single black dots or "puffball" marks.

Reading a map is easy if you go slowly and survey only small areas at a time. After a bit of practice, you, and anyone else, can use a contour or other fishing map and a compass to travel to any on-the-water location with no more difficulty than you would experience using a common road map to travel from one town to the next.

The contour lines on a map, of course, indicate both depth and how rapidly or slowly the bottom depth changes at a particular location. Lines

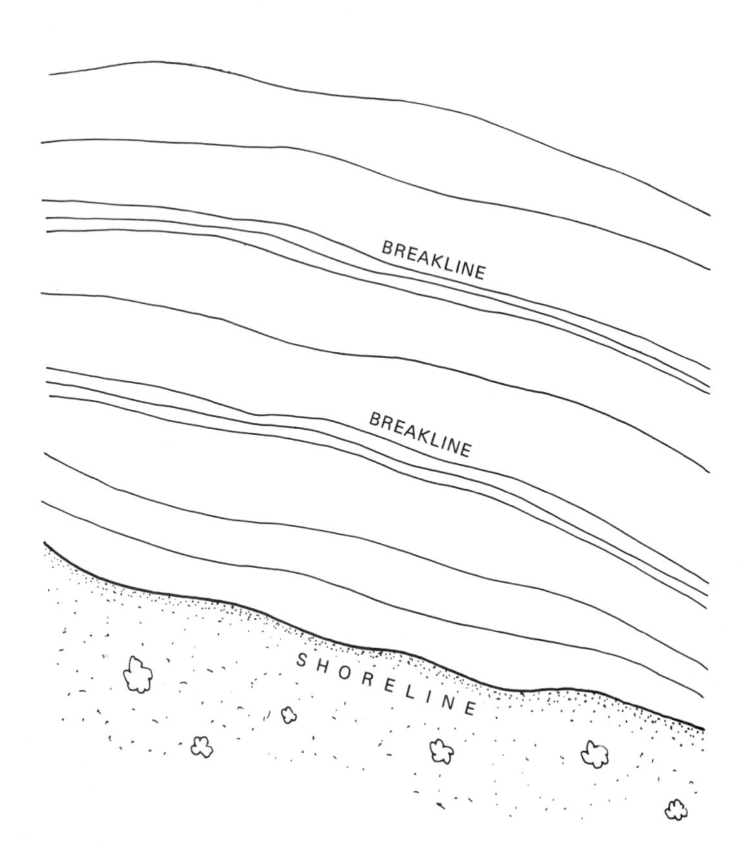

Chart 4–1. *Mapmakers use contour lines to indicate changes of depth. Where the lines come close together, the water depth drops off sharply in breaklines.*

very close together indicate a very rapid change in depth. In some places, contour lines may be so close together as to appear to form a single, heavy black line, which represents an abrupt drop-off. Conversely, the farther apart contour lines are spaced, the more gradual the underwater slope. This is one of the keys to understanding which bottom structures bass may or may not elect to use during the course of their migrations from the depths.

Chart 4–1 shows a section of shoreline as it might appear on a map, with contour lines drawn in. As you can see, several widely spaced contour lines just beyond the edge of the shoreline show how the bank begins to taper away gently underwater. Then there are several contour lines very close together, indicating a rapid change in depth. Next comes another gently sloping section of bottom and then still another drop-off. Nearly every body of water will have a similar shoreline configuration as the bottom slopes, either sharply in places or gradually, into the depths. The actual drops, where the contour lines are close together and run for some

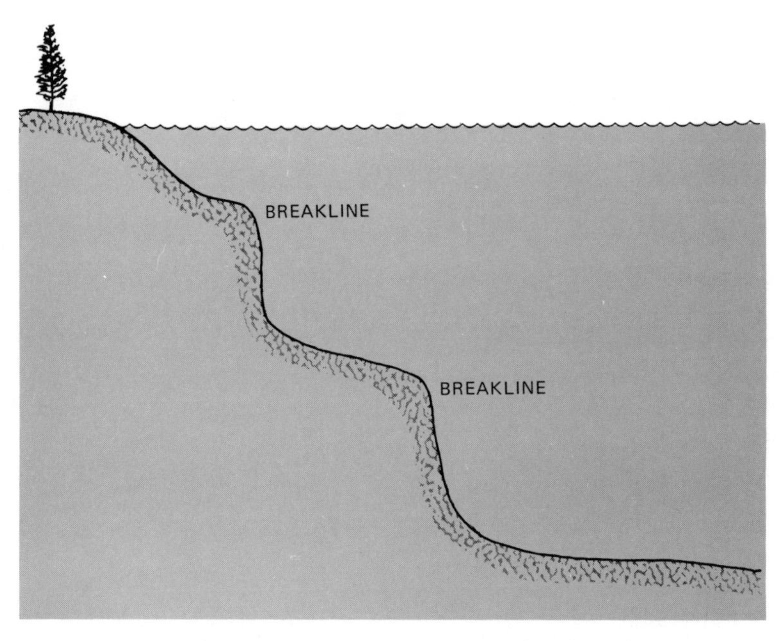

Chart 4–2. *This underwater side view of the same shoreline illustrated in Chart 4–1 shows the two drop-offs separated by gently sloping shelves.*

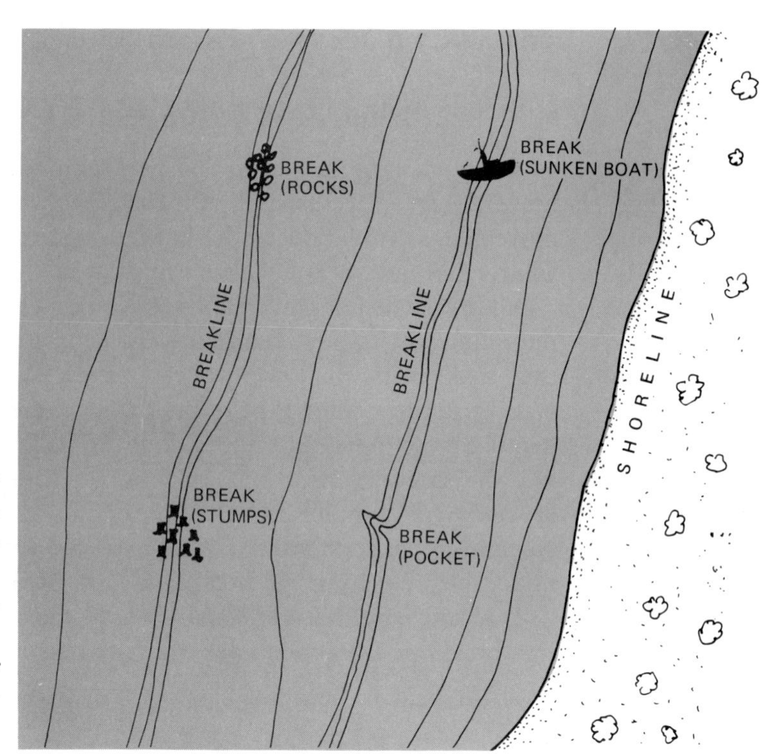

Chart 4–3. *Breaks, or changes on breaklines, are generally where most bass are caught. Breaks can be natural features, such as rock piles, or manmade objects, such as discarded slabs of concrete or even an old sunken boat.*

distance, are called *breaklines* by advanced structure fishermen. Every body of water will have at least one breakline but usually two or three and sometimes several more. Further, these breaklines commonly extend around the entire lake, regardless of its size.

Chart 4–2 shows a side view of the shoreline configuration and breaklines shown in Chart 4–1.

Any interruption in the smooth contour of a breakline is called a *break,* and these interruptions may take on many appearances. As illustrated in Chart 4–3, breaks may be sharp indentations, pockets or ditches, but they may also be structural features such as a cluster of stumps, pile of rocks, jumbled logs or clump of brush. A classical structure-fishing tenet is that in most cases, *the largest bass in most bodies of water will be caught at breaks on breaklines.*

The breaklines shown in Charts 4–1 and 4–2 are rather straight-line affairs and are meant only to represent a single piece of shoreline. Actually, breaklines may take on many other forms, too. They will still, on maps, be represented as contour lines that run close together for some distance, indicating rapid changes in depth. But they may meander in close to the shoreline or wander far away from the shoreline toward midlake areas, and in so doing they will take on the appearances of long bars, points and other structures.

Plotting Bass Movements on Maps

In Chapter 3, we saw how bass periodically leave their sanctuaries and move toward various destinations. Now we are going to follow their movements in relation to the bottom contour shown on a fishing map. Charts 4–4 and 4–5 illustrate a typical bass migration route.

After bass depart from their resting area en masse, the first "signpost" migrating bass come to is called a *contact point.* This is the first association they make with shallower water as they leave the depths. Usually the contact point is some type of breakline where there is a rapid change of depth, for example, the edge of an underwater shelf that drops off steeply into the sanctuary area. Bass seldom rise from the depths of their sanctuary and make contact with the edge of a breakline, however. Rather, they customarily make contact at some specific location where there is some noticeable change in the breakline. At a break!

Typically, a school will usually stop at the contact point (a break on the first breakline they encounter) for a short while before proceeding on to

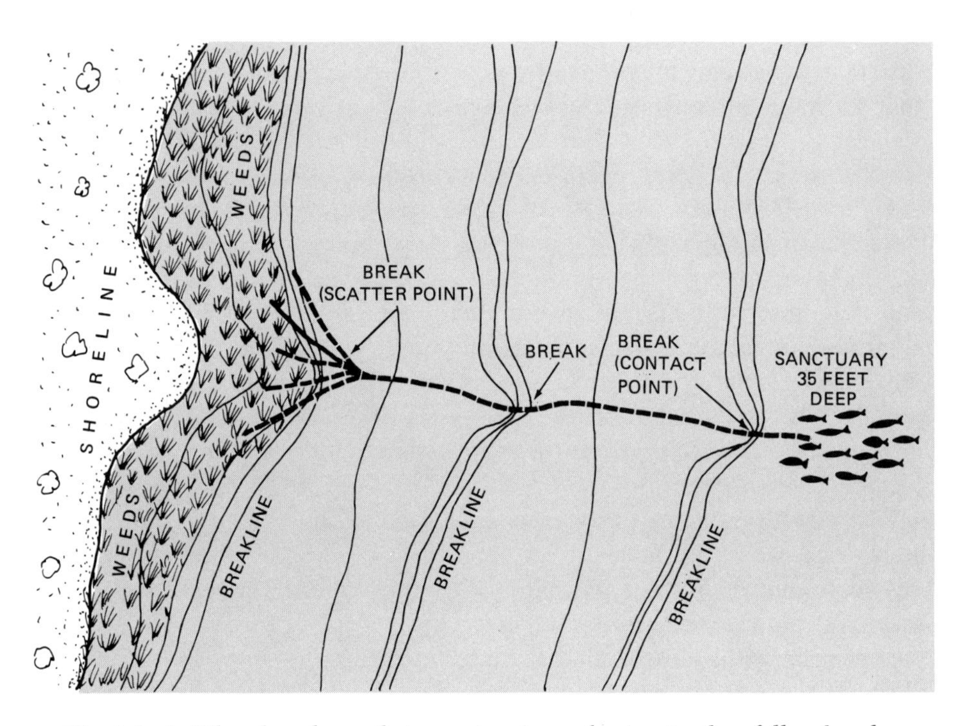

Chart 4–4. *When bass leave their sanctuaries and migrate, they follow breaks on breaklines, until they reach the scatterpoint where they disperse.*

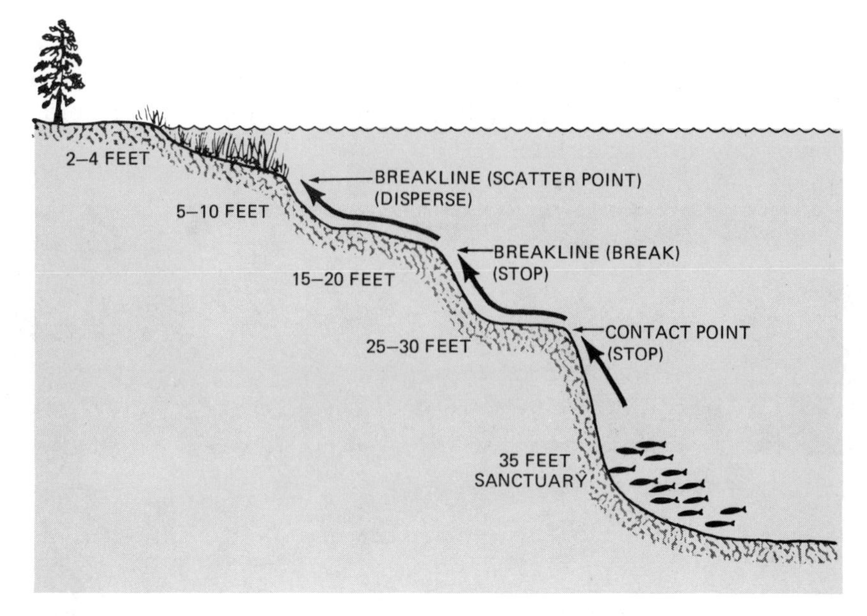

Chart 4–5. *An underwater, side view of how bass typically migrate on structures and pause at various breaks.*

the next signpost. This pause takes place probably because the fish need to acclimate themselves to the venture into shallower water, making sure that all is safe and right with the world before going onward. In fact, as we shall see later, if the school consists of very large fish and the water is crystal clear, they may go no farther than the contact point due to their shyness and distrust of the bright shallows before them.

Let's assume, however, that the school of bass consists of 20 fish averaging three pounds apiece and due to existing water and weather conditions they intend to "go all the way." The next signpost, or stopping place, in their migration past the contact point will undoubtedly be another breakline. And again, they will not usually contact that breakline just anywhere, but where there is a break.

The very last breakline at which the bass continue to school is called a *scatterpoint.* From this location, the school disperses. They no longer have the darkness of the depths to afford safety, so it is now necessary for individual fish to find their own hiding places in and around weeds, rocks, standing timber and brush. These offer concealment and provide suitable ambush sites at various depths ranging from two to eight feet deep, depending upon the nature of the cover.

Anglers can catch bass at all of these locations along their migration route (contact points, breaks on breaklines, scatterpoints, and cover formations they disperse into and around) either by eliciting feeding responses or by provoking strikes. As mentioned before, bass do not migrate only when they are hungry; but when they do migrate, they generally are in a very active state and can therefore be rather easily tempted into biting or forced into striking at lures.

Chart 4–6. *A classic bass migration situation, shown in this aerial photograph with a contour map overlay, is a long shoreline point that extends underwater.*

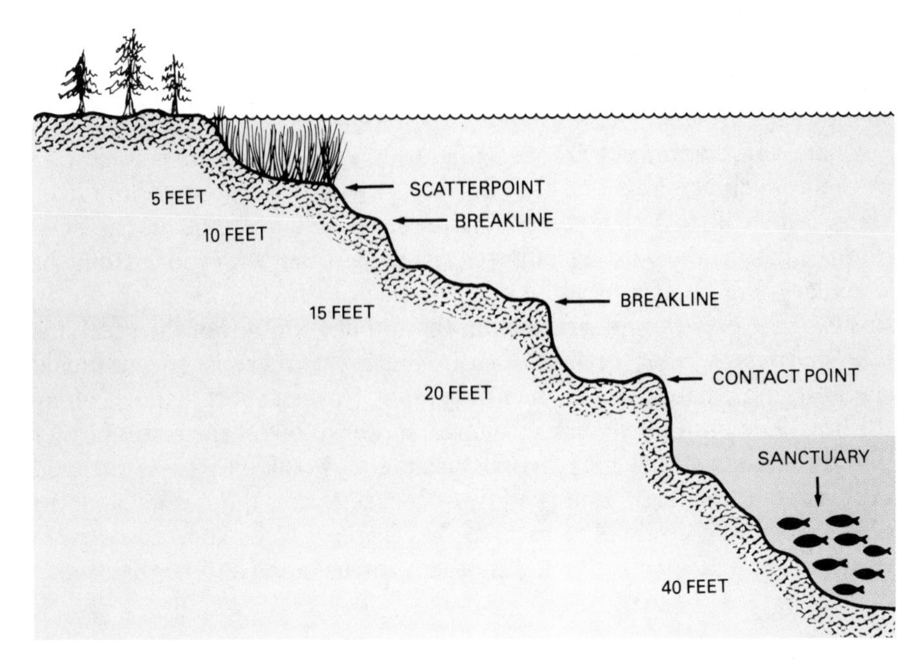

Chart 4–7. *Here is an underwater, side view of the same point, showing the rapid changes in depth that bass associate with during their travels.*

After an indeterminate amount of time in the shallows, the bass begin drifting back toward their sanctuary. And unless they are spooked by a careless angler and make mad dashes for the safety of the depths, they will usually follow the same migration route that led them toward the shallows. They can be caught during this return migration, too, but an angler has to work fast because the fish will not be pausing as long at the various breaks on breaklines as they did when venturing toward the shallows.

One of the most classic migration situations in lakes and reservoirs—and perhaps one of the easiest for anglers to find and master through the use of contour maps—is that of a long, sloping point jutting out from the shoreline and extending for some distance underwater. Charts 4–6 and 4–7 show two views of what such a point might look like, with the breaklines and breaks labeled.

Despite the discussion and examples presented so far, bass migrations are not always cut-and-dried, straightforward sojourns. Indeed, the route may be very crooked, slanting off at various angles because the intermittent breaks along the way—the signposts—may not all be uniformly situated as they lead from the depths to the shallows. Upon contacting a break on a breakline, the fish may have to travel a short distance to either the right or left, following the breakline or contour change until they reach the next signpost, which directs them further into the shallows. Another thing that may be perplexing is that bass sometimes move from their sanctuary to an adjacent deep-water area, rather than heading for the shallows.

Chart 4–8 diagrams a crooked migration route, with the bass resting in their sanctuary area in about 35 feet of water. Adjacent to the deep water is a shelf (breakline) extending for some distance. The first association the bass make with a shallower structure when they move from the sanctuary will be at a break (contact point) on the breakline (shelf). In this case the break or interruption in the smooth contour of the breakline is a sharp protrusion or knob. From the break there is no additional signpost immediately before the fish, so they travel a short distance along the breakline until they come to such a marker to direct them still farther into the shallows. This next signpost is another break on a breakline, and in this case the interruption is a pile of rocks. Again, there is no signpost directly before the school of bass, so they again travel a short distance to the right until they come to one, another protrusion on another breakline.

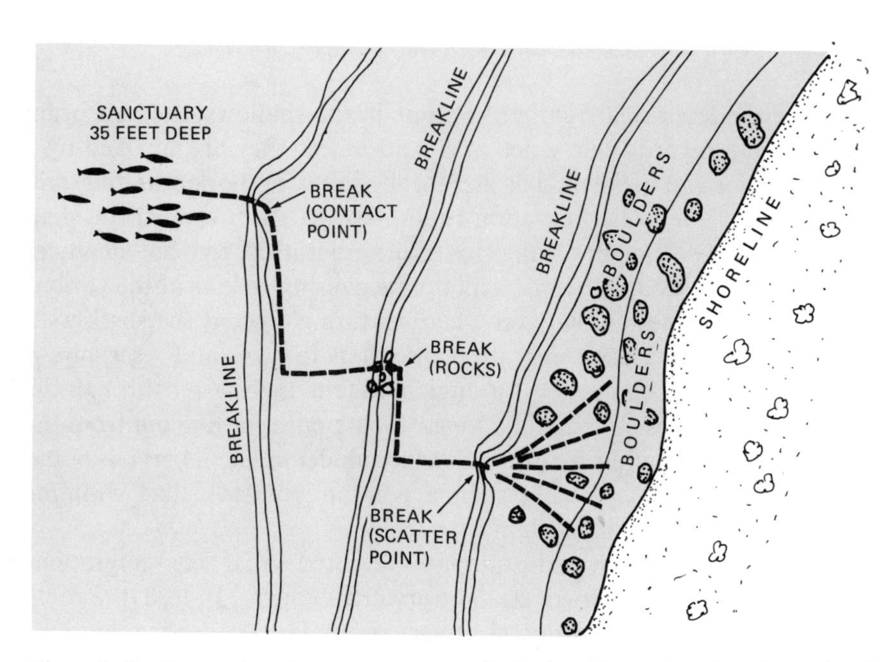

Chart 4–8. *Bass migration routes are crooked when the various breaks on breaklines do not occur in a straight line perpendicular to the shore. In such cases, a school of bass must travel to the right or left along a breakline until they reach the next break to guide them to still shallower water.*

Since the fish are now fully into the shallows, this final break serves as the scatterpoint and they subsequently disperse among boulders in the shallow shoreline water.

All of this may be an oversimplification of bass migrations and we'll be taking another look at bass movements later in this chapter. But the point to be made here is that schools of bass generally move in a well-disciplined manner, following "route markers," and these signposts may not always lie in a straight line as they lead from the depths to the shallows, or from the depths to adjacent deep-water areas.

Because bass migrations take place only during certain times of day, when a good migration structure is located, anglers often have to wait for the fish to move!

Of course, working the contact point, the various breaks on breaklines and the vicinity around a supposed scatterpoint is likely to be futile if the bass have only recently completed a major migration and are resting once again back in their sanctuary area.

Many advanced structure anglers, having located the site of an ideal structure that has produced fast action in the past but seems to be void of fish at the moment, park and wait for the next migration. This strategy can pay off, especially if the angler does not know when the last migration took place (if the previous migration took place six hours ago, another one might begin in only minutes). Other enterprising anglers, however, upon checking their favorite structures and concluding that no migrations are presently taking place, use this slack time to search for additional structures which may provide even better movements when the bass begin to climb from their sanctuaries. And still others, while waiting for the fish to move, search for *straggler* bass.

Stragglers are lone fish that have somehow become separated from their schools. They usually head for the nearest cover—a submerged brush pile, felled tree or pile of rocks. These fish constitute the occasional bass caught now and then by perpetual shoreline pluggers tirelessly working down the same bank, mile after mile, with no idea where the bass are or should be. The purposeful straggler-angler, on the other hand, may or may not find an occasional lone fish to add to his stringer, and it doesn't really make any difference to him. He is simply biding his time, waiting for the bulk of the fish to move. About once every hour, he'll take a break from his straggler fishing to check out a nearby migration route where he may have had success before, hoping the fish have begun to travel from the depths. If they have, he'll entirely forget about stragglers and concentrate upon working the large school. And he may, if he's in the right place (which this book is all about), load his boat with whoppers in only 20 minutes' time.

Using Depth Sounders and Graph Recorders

Depth sounders are probably this century's greatest boon to bass fishing; every serious angler should own one if he wants to advance to the rank of expert. There are three main types and all operate either from a pair of dry-cell batteries or from the 12-volt battery onboard boats.

The first is a simple *needle-gauge* depth sounder. This is the least expensive type, costing an average of $60. It merely indicates the depth of the water beneath your boat.

The most expensive type of depth sounder is the *graph recorder,* which can cost upwards of $500 and which actually draws a permanent picture of the lake, from the surface to the bottom, showing all depths and structural formations as well as the presence of the fish themselves.

A majority of anglers favor the middle ground, however, using a third type of depth sounder called a *flasher,* which costs anywhere from $150 to $250. A flasher unit possesses a clocklike face that is marked in various increments indicating depths. Scales covering different depth ranges are available; the one any particular angler buys depends largely upon the types of waters he customarily fishes. A bass angler who lives in the Southeast and plies his trade on flatland reservoirs will undoubtedly want a flasher unit with a 30-foot scale that gives high resolution and definition in shallow water. In the Midwest, where an angler fishes highland lakes, a depth sounder with a 60-foot readout scale would probably be more appropriate, while an angler who fishes the deepest canyonland reservoirs of the Southwest would do best with a 100-foot flasher unit. A 100-foot unit cannot display as much detail of bottom structures as does a 30-foot unit, but it does show a greater expanse of bottom.

The heart of a flasher depth sounder is a probe, or *transducer,* mounted on the hull of the boat, that transmits a "cone" of sound waves into the water. At the same time, a high-intensity neon bulb whirls at a constant speed behind the calibrated face of the depth sounder. The sound wave discharges are regulated to fire about 24 times per second at zero on the dial, which gives a constant surface reading. The bulb also fires 24 times per second at the point on the dial that indicates the depth, which is determined by the length of time it takes the sound waves to reach the bottom and return to the transducer. Although the bulb is rapidly firing, it appears to the human eye as an almost constant light.

Through the use of a depth sounder, an angler can determine the exact water depth beneath his boat and he can also determine the bottom composition and the location and dimensions of various types of structures and cover formations. For example, if the band of light indicating depth on the face of the depth sounder is very wide and bright, this means

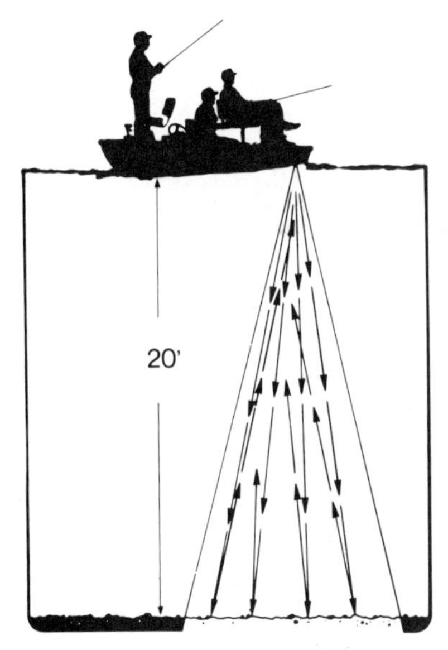

GRAVEL OR HARD CLAY:
GOOD REFLECTIVE BOTTOM
CONDITION WITHIN CONE AREA

Pattern A. *The constant zero reading on a flasher depth sounder indicates the water surface. In this pattern, the wide band of light at 20 feet indicates a hard bottom and strong return signal.*

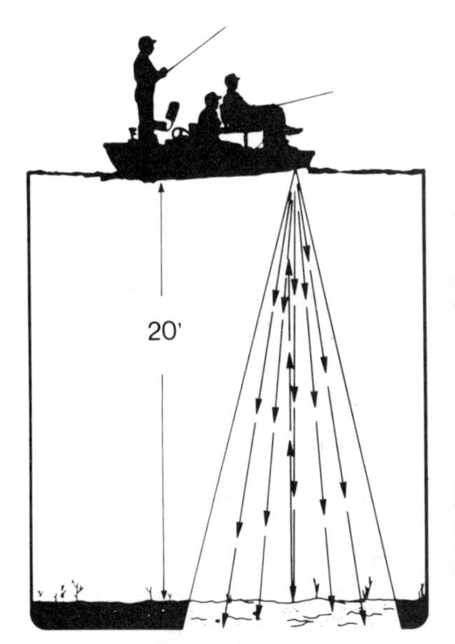

SOFT MUD/DECAYING VEGETATION:
MOST SIGNALS ARE ABSORBED
BY SOFT BOTTOM CONDITION

Pattern B. *The thin band of light at 20 feet indicates a soft bottom that is absorbing much of the signal.*

the bottom composition is hard (such as gravel, rock or sand) and is allowing a strong return signal to bounce back to the boat (Pattern A). Conversely, if the band of light is thin and weak, the bottom is soft (such as mud) and is absorbing much of the signal (Pattern B).

Individual spikes (thin bands of light) appearing between the constant surface light and the bottom signal indicate the presence of something. Learning to determine what, by interpreting the signal pattern, can take a good deal of practice. As shown in Pattern C, a mass of very thin spikes near the surface probably indicates a school of baitfish such as shad, but it could just as well be a school of panfish such as crappies or white bass. Somewhat below these thin spikes, particularly if they are signals interrupted by baitfish, you may see a number of wider bands of light representing a school of bass following the forage. Spikes near the bottom may indicate resting bass, but they may just as well be big rough fish such as catfish or carp, or even boulders or stumps.

The most dramatic signal pattern occurs when the recorder passes over a steep drop-off (Pattern D). Suppose you're surveying a lake area, reading a constant 20-foot depth and then pass over a sharp drop-off where the depth plunges to 100 feet. The depth sounder face will light up like a

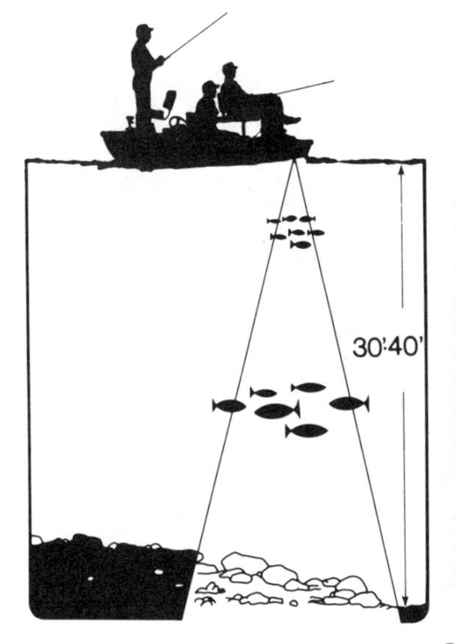

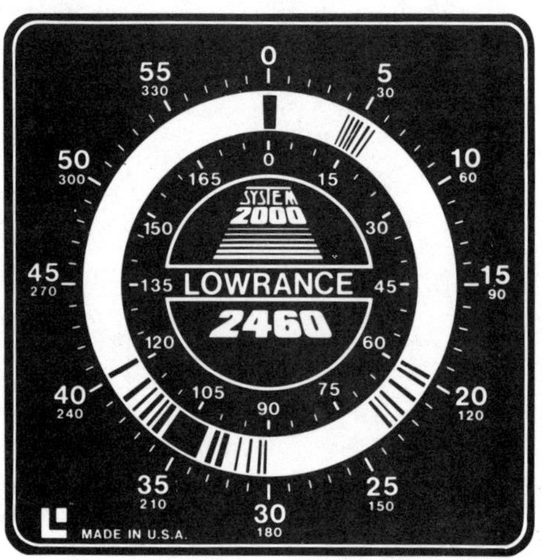

SIGNAL WIDTH INDICATES SIZE OF FISH

Pattern C. *Thin spikes near the surface generally mean baitfish or panfish. Mid-depth signals of varying widths indicate fish of different sizes. Likewise, a broken-up bottom signal occurs when the bottom is littered with rocks of different sizes.*

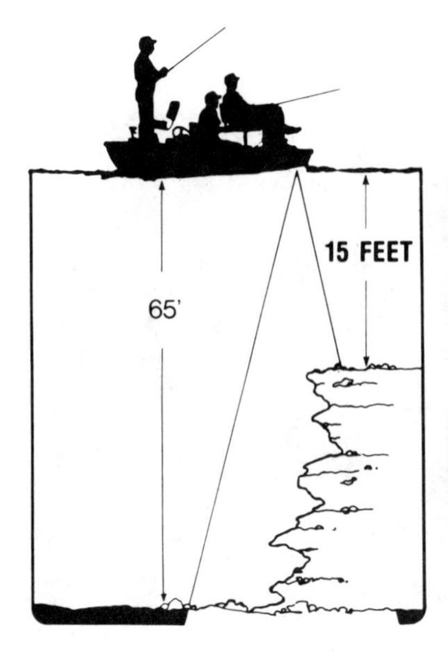

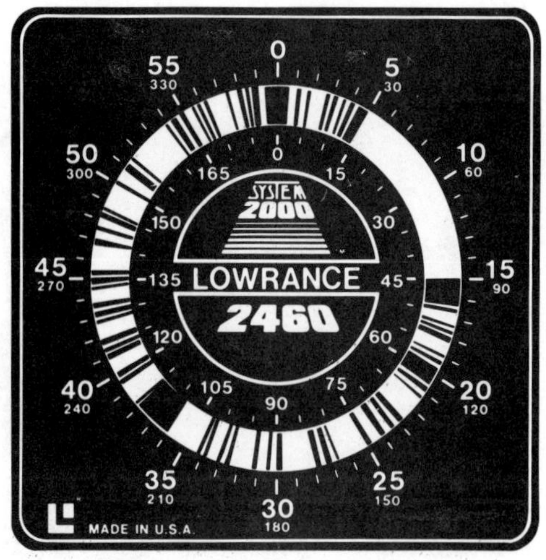

STEEP, ROCKY LEDGES

Pattern D. *When a depth sounder passes over a rocky drop-off, the dial lights up like a Christmas tree.*

Christmas tree, but soon you will be reading another constant single-band signal, this time at 100 feet.

Other signals often encountered by bass anglers using flasher depth sounders are illustrated in Patterns E, F and G.

Many serious anglers, especially when working from bassboats, like to use two depth sounders in conjunction with each other. One depth sounder, mounted on the steering console and commonly having a 100-foot scale, is used for monitoring bottom conditions while traveling at fast speeds. A second unit, perhaps with a 30-foot scale, is mounted on the bow, with the transducer attached to the lower leg of the electric trolling motor. This unit gives anglers "eyes to the bottom" once they are "on structure" and attempting to slowly bird-dog a breakline or other feature.

Also, many anglers like to turn up the gain dial on their flasher units to receive an echo reading—a separate, second picture of the bottom. All this really amounts to is increasing the strength of the signal so that the first signal shows a bit more detail; if the gain is not increased, very small details might not be amplified enough to be discerned.

Full instructions come with flasher depth sounders and it's wise to spend as much time as necessary studying them so you can use the unit proficiently.

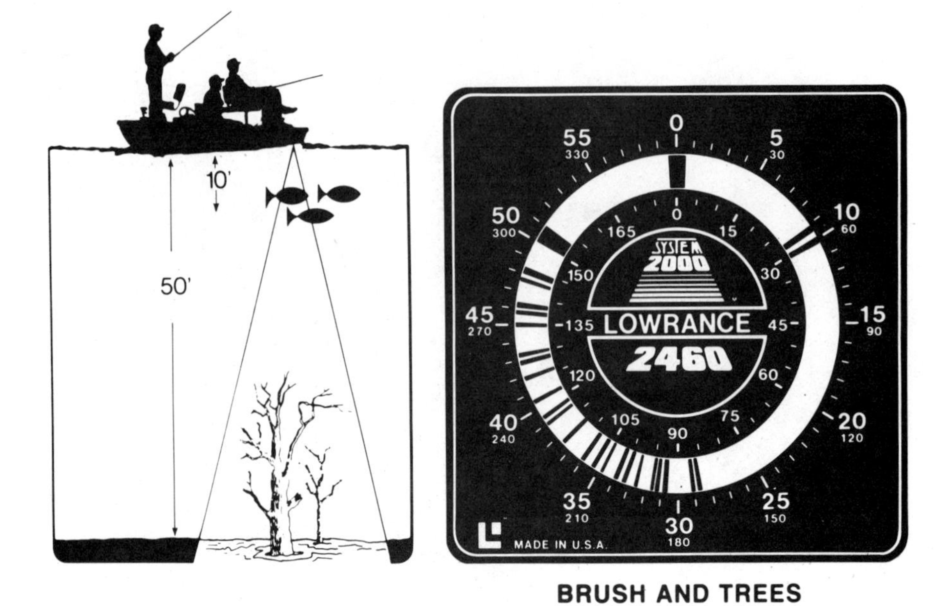

BRUSH AND TREES

Pattern E. *The wide band at 50 feet indicates the depth, over a hard bottom, while the many random spikes just off the bottom indicate a treetop. Also note the fish suspended above the tree branches, and how the depth sounder records them.*

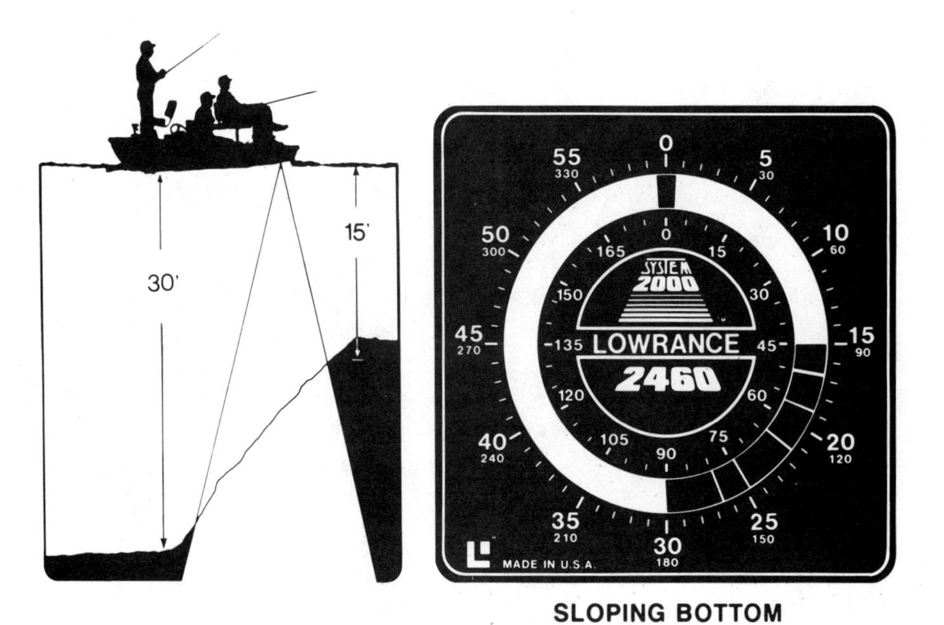

SLOPING BOTTOM

Pattern F. *A continually sloping bottom, where the water depth drops from 15 to 30 feet, is recorded as an almost constant, descending band of light.*

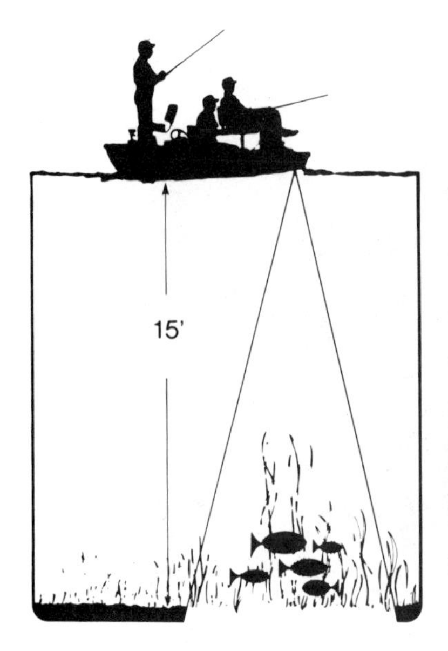

WEEDS RETURN THIN SIGNALS

Pattern G. *Weeds have a tendency to absorb depth sounder signals, causing them to register as very thin spikes.*

Many anglers like to "read" lake areas quickly with one depth sounder mounted on their steering consoles. For slower, more methodical work, they then move along under the power of an electric motor while using a second, bow-mounted unit. Anglers here are following a winding stream channel through a grove of timber.

Truly expert bass anglers also make use of graph recorders, such as this digital display model by Lowrance. These units produce a permanent record of underwater features, so you can later study the chart in detail.

Very advanced anglers (guides, tournament pros and other experts) also make use of graph recorders, which are guaranteed to increase anyone's fishing knowledge by leaps and bounds. Graph recorders have several advantages over flasher depth sounders.

With a flasher unit, everything from the surface to the bottom is displayed in the form of flashing lights, which not only must be interpreted correctly but are seen sometimes for only fractions of a second. Consequently, you must keep your eyes glued to the dial to be sure you don't miss something.

Graph recorders, in contrast, actually draw a picture of bottom structures. Not only do you not have to constantly watch the unit, you also have a permanent record that can be studied over and over again and even referred to at a later date. Furthermore, there is little guesswork in trying to interpret what the graph is trying to tell you, as the pictures produced clearly differentiate trees from rocks, stumps from weeds and all the rest. Fish (commonly referred to as "hooks") show up as crescents, their size proportional to the size of the fish.

Probably the biggest frustration in using a graph recorder occurs when you "mark" a bunch of big fish right beneath your boat but are unable to get them to bite. Of course, if you were not using a depth sounder, you

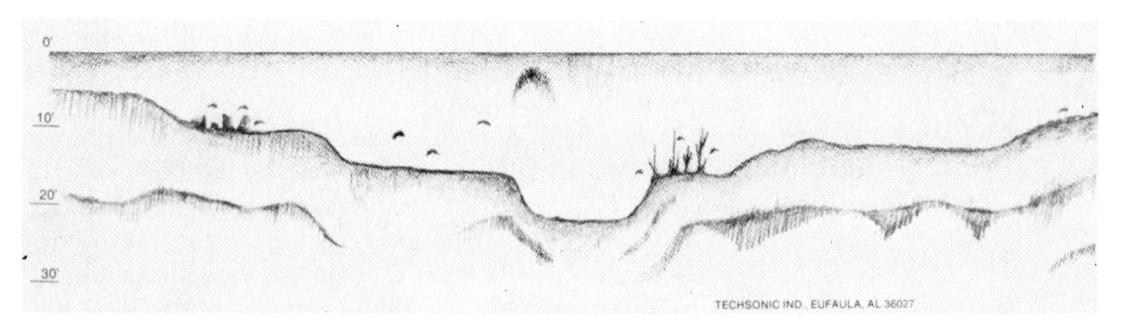

Graph recorders that offer high definition and resolution show you exactly *what's beneath your boat. This read-out strip represents a portion of a flatland reservoir with an old river channel winding along the bottom. Note the stumps in the shallows, which are holding several bass, the bass suspending in the trees along the edge of the old channel. That big crescent near the surface, just over the suspended bass, is probably a school of shad.*

might believe that no bass were present. But to actually see them and not be able to catch them has a very sobering effect upon even the most accomplished expert. The reason for this unfortunate situation, as explained earlier, is that bass in deeper water often are in a very inactive state.

Without going deeply into electronic technicalities, those graph recorders best suited to bass fishing have these features: A gray (or white) line adjustment dial that separates the bottom from near-bottom objects such as weeds or fish; a paper-speed adjustment, which allows you to have a fast paper speed in shallow water for maximum detail and a slow paper speed in deep water; a depth-range selector, which serves the same purpose as the various depth scales available in flasher models; and an interference rejection dial to prevent other electronic devices onboard from causing static blips on the paper. Furthermore, the most useful models have a high-frequency, high-power, peak-to-peak capability. This is simply a fancy way of saying the unit sends out a signal strong enough to penetrate deeper water and has sufficient resolution and definition to project clear pictures in both deep and shallow water. In other words, such a high-quality unit can separate fish and bottom objects from each other and represent both as sharp images rather than as the blurred and sometimes indistinguishable images typical of less sophisticated models.

In concluding this section, I should emphasize the importance of studying a contour map thoroughly before you go fishing. In this way you can formulate a game plan, knowing in advance which areas of the lake are most likely to see bass activity, and in those respective areas which bottom structures are most worth investigating.

Having arrived in the general area you intend to fish, and now beginning to locate structures indicated on your map, one of the best ways to determine any bottom feature's exact conformation (remember, contour maps are not always precisely accurate) is by dropping marker buoys overboard as you motor over them while watching your depth sounder or graph recorder.

Factory-made markers are available through tackleshops and fishing-tackle mail-order houses, but you can also make your own at little cost. I simply use a brick-size piece of styrofoam wrapped with 50 feet of cord that has a two-ounce weight tied to the end to hold the marker in place. You can also use discarded outboard oil bottles to serve the same purpose.

It's a good idea to have at least six markers on hand as you begin dropping them overboard at intervals to outline the dimensions of the structure you intend to fish. This gives you a good picture of what the structure actually looks like. Then, on subsequent outings, after you're already familiar with the structure's exact features, you may not have to drop all of the buoys. On a long, sloping point, for example, you may need to set out only one marker, at its tip. On a long underwater bar, two markers may suffice, one at each end.

Commercially manufactured marker buoys come in many sizes and shapes and are widely available through tackle dealers.

You can make inexpensive markers from blocks of styrofoam or discarded outboard oil bottles wrapped with cord.

Almost any angler who is just learning advanced structure fishing experiences a combination of difficulty, exasperation and even boredom when working deep contours and breaks, especially if his previous fishing has involved many years of perpetual shoreline plugging in which there are always numerous targets, such as weeds and stumps, to cast to. Suddenly, he's in open water with no targets (none that he can see, anyway). The use of marker buoys helps to alleviate some of this initial sense of feeling lost and also keeps his enthusiasm alive.

More Insight on Bass Movements

We've examined several different kinds of structure and how bass use them. But the many structures that exist in any body of water far outnumber the inhabiting schools of bass. Therefore, the bass have a choice and will select those structures that possess a combination of ideal characteristics. By classical structure-fishing standards, *to qualify as ideal structure, a given bottom contour or feature must extend all the way to the deepest water in the immediate area.*

Here, an angler has outlined the dimensions of an offshore structure (a submerged hump) he intends to fish, which will allow him to present his lures accurately.

For example, Chart 4–9 diagrams two points extending from the shoreline. Both have deep water nearby containing schools of bass. But, as the bass in View 1 begin to climb from their sanctuary, they would be confronted with a wide flat containing no signposts (breaks on breaklines) to guide them to their destinations. As a result, the bass probably would not select this area as a migration route.

In contrast, the shoreline point in View 2 extends far out, all the way to the deepest water in the area. Upon rising from their sanctuary, then, the bass would not be faced with an open, endless flat. Rather, a signpost —the tip of the point (breakline)—occurs right near the deep water, and the bass would make contact wherever there was a break. As you can see, there are also other signposts in the form of shelves (breaklines), which would attract bass farther into the shallows; closer inspection might reveal certain portions of those shelves to be littered with stumps, rocks or other breaks.

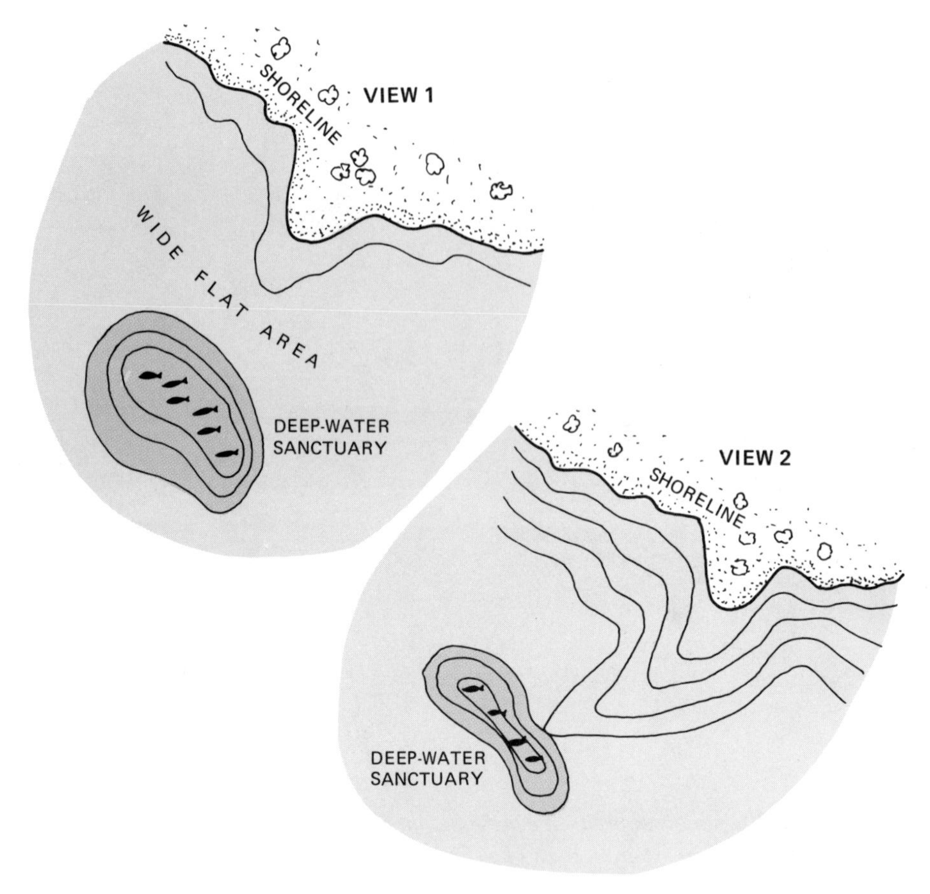

Chart 4–9. *Bass migrations are most likely to occur where appropriate structure extends from the shoreline to their deep-water sanctuaries, as shown in View 2.*

As we've seen, migrating bass head for breaks and an angler can expect to catch most of his bass at breaks on breaklines. But that poses an interesting and often perplexing question. What if there are a number of breaks on the same breakline? The rule-of-thumb answer is this: *When a breakline possesses more than one break, migrating bass will make contact with the one that is the sharpest, steepest or most pronounced.*

Chart 4–10 gives a visual representation of what I'm trying to explain here. A long, three-fingered point extends offshore. For simplicity, I've drawn in only the breakline farthest from the shore, but each of the three fingers of the point lead all the way to the deepest water in the immediate area. Which finger are the bass most likely to make contact with as they begin entering the shallows?

Obviously, fingers A and B slope gradually into the depths; according to the rule, the fish would probably make contact with finger C, which is very abrupt. You could, I suppose, fish all three fingers. But realize that

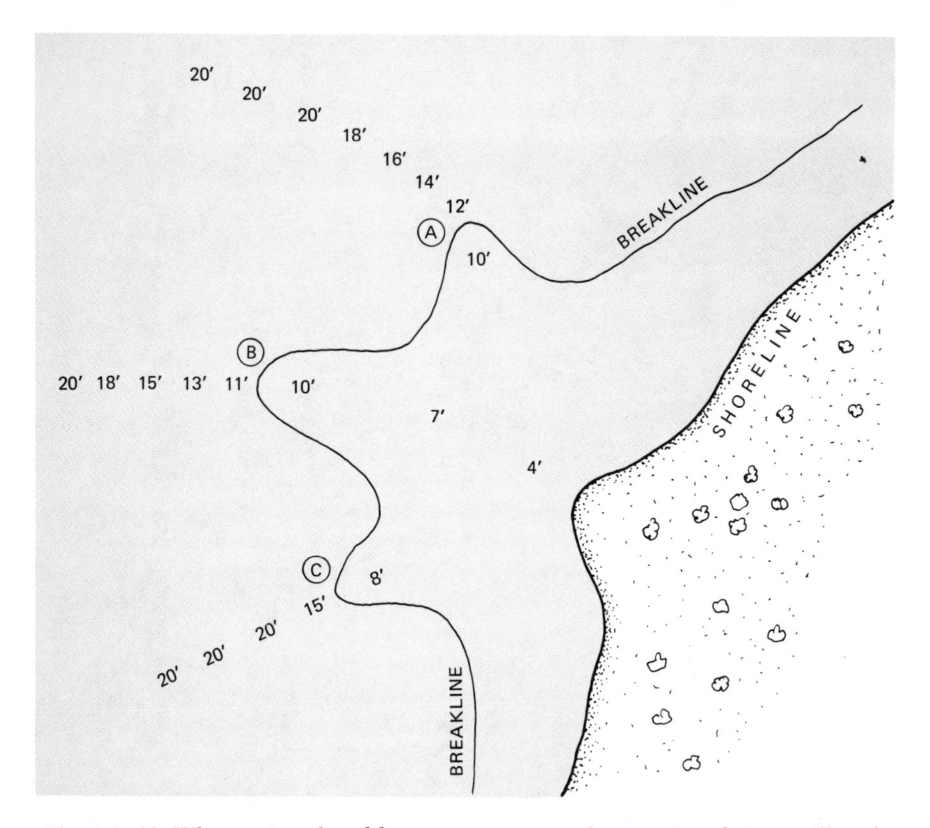

Chart 4–10. *When a given breakline possesses more than one break, bass will make contact with the sharpest or steepest one (Finger C) as they move into the shallows.*

if time is short and you've got several dozen other places to try as well, you may be wasting precious time working unproductive water. This is especially likely in the case of large points of land that take a lot of time to fish thoroughly with various lures to see what the bass want on any given occasion. Such considerations separate the expert from the amateur: The amateur fishes everything, but the expert concentrates on a specific high-probability area, then quickly moves on to another high-probability area. Consequently, it takes the expert far less time to home in upon his quarry and begin adding fish to the live well.

To briefly review some of the things discussed so far, take a look at Chart 4–11, which is marked with various types of contour lines, structures and depths. Before reading further, see if you can determine which structures bass would be most likely to use for migrations, and why.

Location A shows a long breakline in the form of a sloping shelf. This would be an ideal migration location because there is a break on the breakline, in the form of ditch, where the break drops off immediately into the deepest water in the area. And there are additional breaks, or signposts, in the form of rocks and then stumps, that would allow migrating bass to find their way into the weedy shallows.

Location B is a nice-looking point extending out from the shoreline and dropping off steeply at its tip. However, it does not extend all the

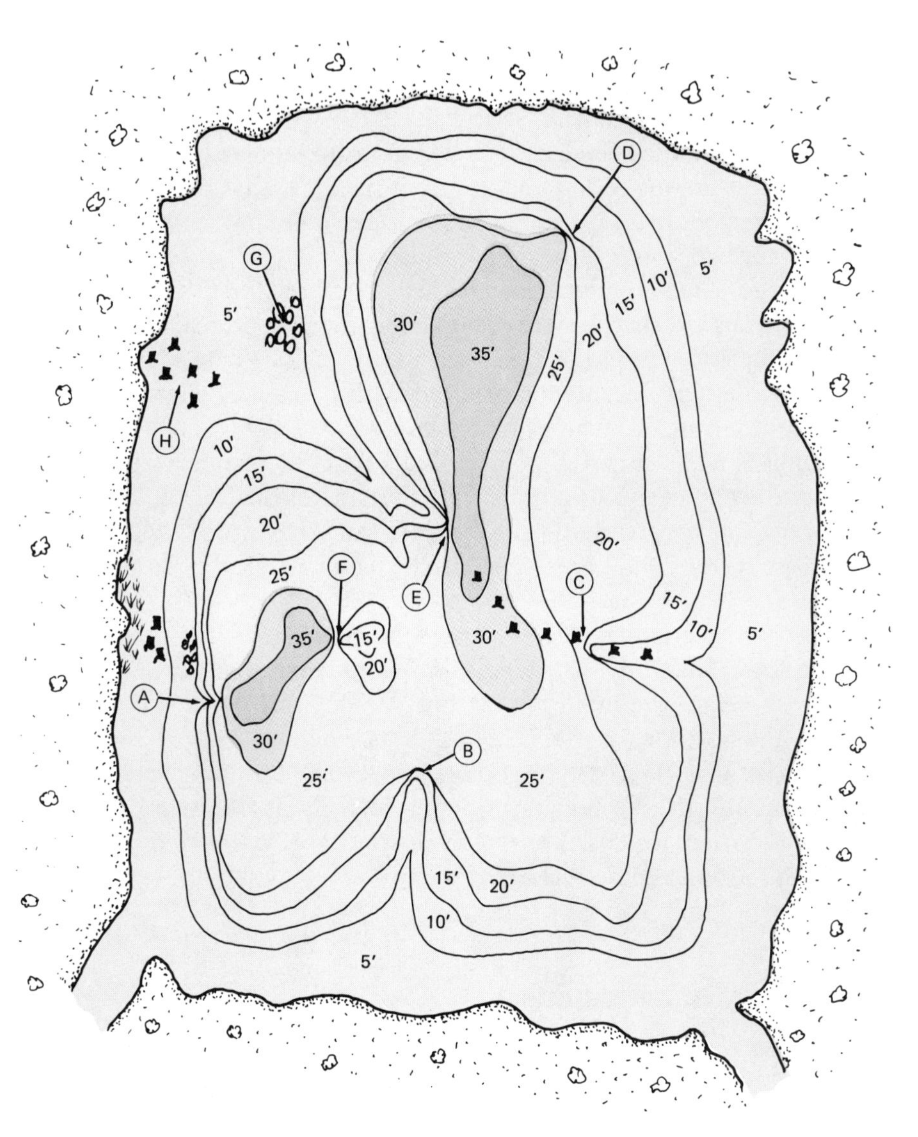

Chart 4–11. *Here is a hypothetical lake situation to test your knowledge. Based upon what you've learned so far, which are the most likely places to find bass?*

way to the deepest water in the area. This location might hold a straggler bass or two at its very tip, but if time was short I wouldn't waste much time here.

Location C is another nice place, an underwater bar or sloping ridge. This structure does not extend all the way to the deepest water in the area, either. But in this particular case there are additional breaks in the form of stumps that extend across the flats to the deep water. If the stumps are still present, this location would be an excellent bet as a migration route, but keep in mind that stumps eventually rot away. Once they do, the migration route would be interrupted and any bass traveling in this area would go no farther than the last break.

Location D is a nice break on a breakline. And an occasional straggler fish might be adhering to this contour, so it would always be worth a cast or two (or maybe three) if you happened to be in the immediate vicinity. But there are two things that would probably not attract a school of bass or encourage a major migration on this structure. First, although the breakline drops off sharply into deep water, there is no real connection with the deepest water in the area. Second, the inshore side of the breakline consists only of a gently sloping flat with no radical changes in the bottom contour and no significant cover.

Location E looks super! A point extends from the shoreline with two fingers at the end of the structure. Note that one of the fingers, however, consists only of a very gentle slope, while the other drops sharply into the deepest water in the area. The steeper point would be the one bass would use.

Location F is another ideal structure. In midlake, a hump sticks up from the floor. The west side is where bass would make contact and they'd probably travel to the hump's crest but not descend down the gradual slopes to the north, east or south.

Locations G and H would be good places to pick up straggler bass that failed to reunite with a school, moving up the point at Location E, during the return journey to its sanctuary. Such wayward bass would probably hide in and around these rocks and stumps.

Find Superstructure!

With a topo map or hydro chart an enterprising bass angler can quite easily find bass-holding structures. He can also find structures with a flasher depth sounder or graph recorder. Yet if he combines the use of a map and depth sounder, it's possible to go one step further in the systematic elimination of barren water by finding *superstructure.*

By definition, superstructure is a particular, smaller segment of a much larger structure. If bass are using the structure at all, likely as not they'll be congregating around superstructure. In a sense, this is ground we've already covered because it's basically the same as finding a break on what may be a very lengthy breakline.

But superstructure may exist in many other forms as well. For example, take what happened when my pal Bill Parsons and I were recently casting plugs on Minnesota's Lake Vermilion. We were after smallmouths that were schooling in midlake areas where sunken islands jutted up from the bottom to within ten feet of the surface.

Some of the islands were enormous, but the bass were not randomly scattered around them; instead, they tended to group tightly wherever there were piles of broken rock dotting the tops of the islands. The islands themselves were therefore the enticing structures we found on our map, but once on location it was then necessary to use our depth sounder to find the superstructure that was holding the fish.

This situation proved to be one of the greatest learning experiences either of us ever had. We could cast off the left side of the boat and not get a nibble, then cast off the right side to a part of the submerged island where there was a rock pile and immediately have our arms yanked with vicious strikes. In previous years, long before I could appreciate the significance of superstructure, I might have made only a few random casts at such an island and then moved on, not realizing there were probably plenty of bass nearby but clinging only to certain parts of the structure.

The essence of finding superstructure, then, is finding something different about an overall much larger structure. It's a skill that can be practiced even when fishing shallow water cover.

I've seen many professional bass guides go for superstructure when fishing those vast swamp areas found in conjunction with many shallow flatland reservoirs throughout the South. To their paying clients, the apparently never-ending stretches of jungle-like cover, weedbeds and other growth look pretty much the same. Such a profusion of seemingly ideal cover gives the impression there should be a bass wherever one casts, but in reality that is seldom the case. Suddenly, the guide brings the boat to a halt and tells his clients to begin casting at stumps and tree trunks that look exactly the same as the thousands they've already bypassed. And the clients begin catching bass!

What the guide doesn't say is that these particular trees and stumps are *different* because they are standing along the edge of a ditch. The water here averages eight feet deep, compared with only three feet deep almost everywhere else. Given the choice of so much cover, the fish have become

The author admires a brace of handsome eight-pounders. In this swamp, all the trees look pretty much the same for miles, but these beauties came from trees along the edge of a superstructure ditch where the water was significantly deeper than everywhere else.

selective in their choice of holding stations and opted in favor of the very best the area has to offer. They've chosen superstructure!

I've seen virtually the same situation in open, midlake areas when expansive carpets of vegetation blanket the surface on enormous shallow flats. This is particularly common in the Kissimmee chain of lakes in Florida, but also in the midlake moss beds at Toledo Bend, the grass flats on Santee-Cooper's Lake Marion and elsewhere. As is often the case, you fish hour after hour without success and eventually begin to conclude you're dealing with union bass that have gone on strike.

Then, in a particular spot that looks the same as a dozen others you've already tried, you hook a big fish. Its frantic thrashing on the surface almost makes your hat lift off your head. After clipping the fish onto your stringer you make another cast and another bass wallops your lure!

"It's about time," your pal shouts as he wrestles with a big fish of his own. "The bass have finally started to bite."

That may or may not have been the case. Maybe the fish did indeed just begin to move and now are active. But also, maybe they have been feeding all along and the two of you have now finally found them. But what was it about that place that attracted the bass? Again, the answer is probably superstructure and often it may have nothing at all to do with the weeds but with the bottom composition beneath all that greenery.

Perhaps there is a 50-acre expanse of lily pads. The bottom is almost entirely mud, but in one small area it changes to clay. In a situation like this, you can bank on the bass congregating near the clay. Other times, a change in the weeds themselves may be the telling clue. In that same 50-acre expanse of lily pads, there may be a tiny place (superstructure) where thick pencil reeds occur, and this "noticeable difference" may attract bass, causing them to group in relatively tight quarters.

The same phenomenon often applies to rocks as well. I find it rather difficult to believe that bass would consistently use one type of rock over another—for example, sandstone instead of granite—but the sizes of the rocks can be significant. It's not that bass prefer big rocks or small rocks, but that they seem to have a penchant for whatever rocks happen to be different from the prevailing size. Find a shoreline where a majority of the rocks are the sizes of basketballs, look for a brief stretch of pea-gravel and you'll probably find bass. Similarly, if there is a long bank strewn with small rocks or broken shale, a single large boulder somewhere is probably the home of the biggest bass using the bank at that time.

This knowledge of superstructure is invaluable to the angler who subscribes to the principles of deep-water structure fishing. It's doubly valuable to the angler randomly looking for shallow-water stragglers while waiting for bass schools to migrate. Add it to your arsenal of growing bass savvy and it will pay off handsomely.

CHAPTER

5

Bass In Natural Lakes

As their name implies, *natural* lakes are created by nature, generally through glacial activity thousands of years ago but also in some cases through volcanic action and even earthquakes. This differentiates them from *manmade* lakes or reservoirs created by humans, typically for specific purposes, such as flood control, water supply, generation of hydroelectric power, and/or recreation. Since manmade bodies of water are created over previously dry land, they're classified according to the predominating features of the original landform (flatland, highland or canyonland). Natural lakes, however, are classified according to their geological ages. And it is this single feature—geological age—that determines which bass species reside in a particular lake and how they live and move and feed, if indeed the lake in question is even capable of supporting bass in the first place.

Natural lakes generally are classified as *oligotrophic, mesotrophic* or *eutrophic.* Roughly speaking, these terms refer to the relative age of lakes. Thus, along the continuum of chronological age, oligotrophic lakes are the youngest. They may, in fact, be thousands of years old, but are considerably younger than mesotrophic (middle-aged) lakes, which are *tens* of thousands of years old, or eutrophic lakes, which are still older.

It's difficult, if not impossible, to place each and every lake in a specific category because portions of a lake often age at different rates. This aging process, known as *eutrophication,* involves the gradual filling in of a lake basin caused by the buildup of decaying plant and animal matter, shoreline erosion and sedimentation; as a result, the body of water becomes progressively shallower. As a natural lake becomes older, and shallower, certain species of plants and animals begin to vanish, as the habitat no

Most natural lakes were created by glacial activity and are classified according to their geological ages.

longer is conducive to their needs, and other species subsequently take their places. These changes are accompanied by dramatic shifts in the food chain and successive plant life.

A quick overview of the three types of lakes will show why, for the purposes of this book, we can largely forget about the two extremes—the youngest and oldest:

Oligotrophic lakes are the deep, cold, infertile lakes that commonly speckle the northern Canadian provinces and are home to lake trout, walleyes and northern pike. The only bass found in oligotrophic lakes are smallmouths, and even they do not begin appearing until quite late in an oligotrophic lake's life, about the time the body of water is beginning to reveal the first hints of becoming a very early mesotrophic lake.

Finding smallmouths in late-stage oligotrophic lakes is relatively easy

Natural lakes age through a process known as eutrophication, in which sediment and decayed organic matter gradually fill in a lake's basin. In time, certain fish populations disappear and others begin taking their places.

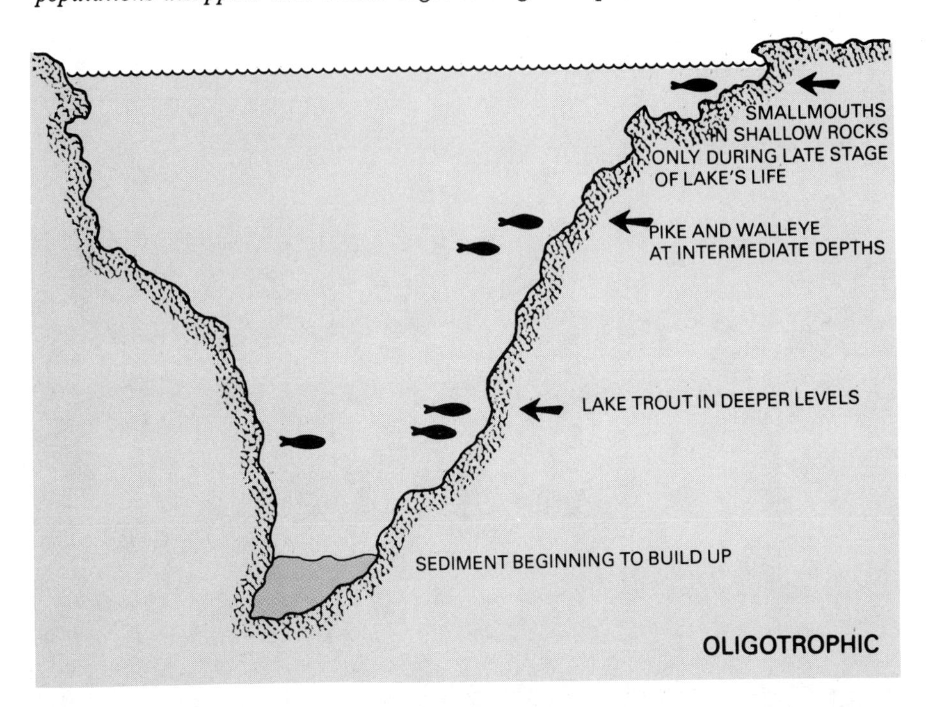

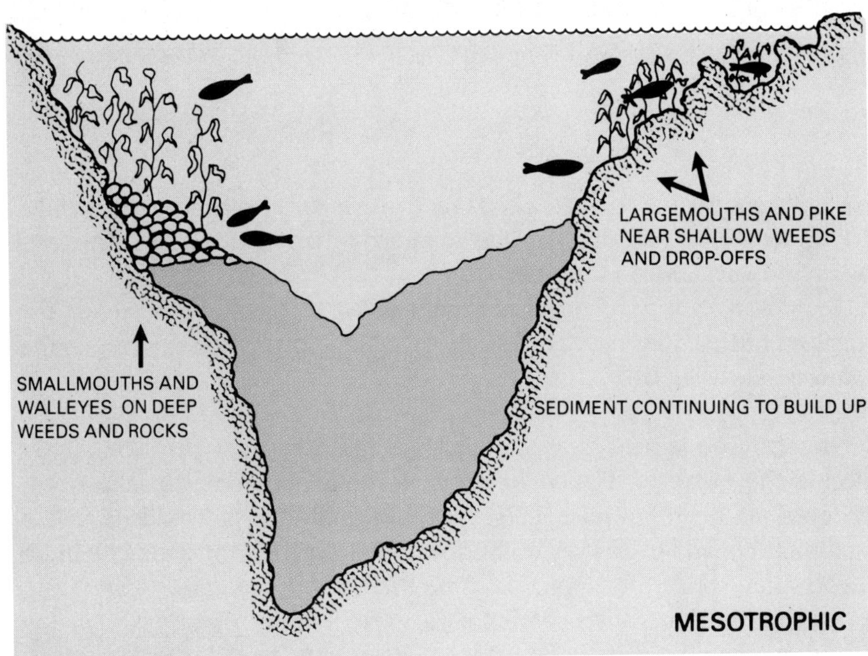

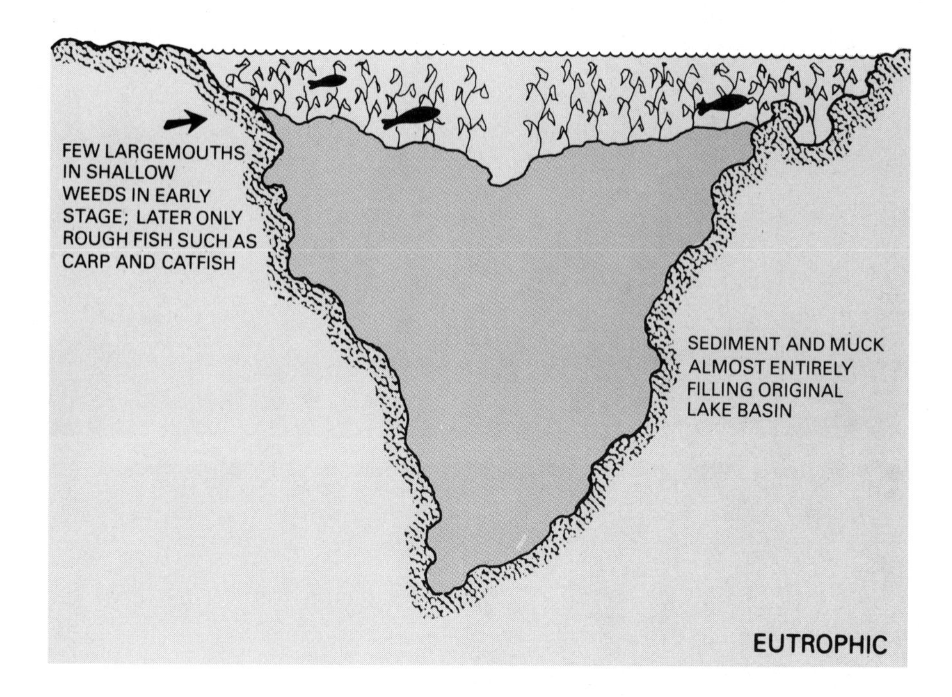

because throughout the year the fish will be in very shallow water (generally, less than 12 feet deep) around shoreline boulders and other rocky cover.

Eutrophic lakes are shallow, warm, marshy lakes that occur primarily in the middle and southern sections of the country. They are inhabited mostly by rough fish and scavengers such as carp, bowfin, catfish and gar. The only bass found in eutrophic lakes are largemouths, and they reside in such lakes only during the earliest eutrophic stages.

Finding largemouths in early-stage eutrophic lakes is also relatively easy because they too will be in shallow water (the depths have long since filled in), usually around weedbeds.

Mesotrophic lakes are not only the most numerous natural lakes across the United States (most are located in the northern border states) but also the most difficult to study and interpret because they contain a wide variety of bottom structures and types of cover. In fact, just as we categorized all lakes into three groups—young, middle-aged, or old—we can further classify mesotrophic lakes themselves as being young, middle-aged or old.

Largemouths are the predominant bass species in eutrophic lakes. Look for them in shallow water, especially around weedbeds.

Young mesotrophic lakes generally have smallmouths as the dominant bass species, with only a smattering of largemouths in the water and then only in the shallow embayments. Middle-aged mesotrophic lakes may have both largemouths and smallmouths in relatively equal numbers in a wide variety of locations. And old mesotrophic lakes may have large-mouths as the predominant bass species, with smallmouths only minimal in number and found only in the lake's deeper and colder regions.

Predator-Prey Relationships

When some signal stirs feeding impulses in bass, they can be ferocious predators. Yet they're always at the mercy of the prey they feed upon. Similarly, the prey is highly dependent upon still smaller life forms, all the

Mesotrophic waters are the most numerous natural lakes of interest to bass anglers. Both largemouths and smallmouths may be present and found in a many locations within such lakes. It's sometimes helpful to further classify mesotrophic lakes into young, middle-aged or old. In general, as a mesotrophic lake ages, the proportion of largemouths to smallmouths increases.

way down to plankton. Consequently, all manner of complex interrelationships may exist among the inhabitants of a given body of water. If their prey shifts location, for example, bass must follow, unless the prey ventures into the habitat niche of some other predator species, in which case bass generally will avoid the area and find themselves some less favored prey item.

In this section we'll take our first glimpses at predator-prey relationships, a fascinating topic that will periodically recur in later chapters. At the outset, it's important to emphasize that the particular prey species bass are tied to determines where they are most likely to be found and which lures or live baits are likely to prove the most productive. So, although a knowledge of the lower life forms in a body of water may seem rather far removed from the subject of bass fishing, it's closer than you think.

Your local fish and game agency is a good place to start learning about prey species and predator-prey relationships in your favorite fishing grounds. Biologists at the agency undoubtedly monitor the population levels of gamefish, panfish and forage in various lakes in the region. In many cases, gamefish may also be subjected to harmless stomach-content analysis, which can help unravel predator-prey relationships.

An intriguing and particularly relevant phenomenon is the seasonal variation in the composition and productivity of the food chains in most bass waters. This variation has a direct impact on bass fishing throughout the year, and helps explain an apparent paradox that befuddles many anglers.

If you'll recall from Chapter 2, during late spring and early summer, the body metabolism of postspawning bass increases dramatically as the

Advanced bass anglers understand that predator-prey relationships determine where bass will be found and which representative lures are likely to prove most productive in a particular body of water.

water continues to warm. This triggers increased feeding activity. Why is it, then, that as midsummer approaches—when the water is warmest and the bass hungriest—fishing action for most anglers tapers off and the so-called "dog days" arrive? An explanation for this is relatively simple, although few anglers are aware of what is really happening.

During the early spring, a lake's food chain has not yet fully developed. The appetites of prespawning bass begin to stir, but food is not yet abundant enough to satisfy them. Consequently, bass are both eager and gullible, and pounce on almost any offering. Soon after spawning, when the bass's attention returns to feeding, the food chain may still be relatively unproductive, and the angler once again enjoys easy success.

As time passes, however, the food chain rapidly proliferates and bass become far more selective and cautious. Now, enormous schools of shad or minnows may roam near the surface, a chorus of frogs sing through the night hours, and hoards of insects flit about shallow-water abodes, all testifying to a food chain in high gear. With so much food readily available, a bass needs only to yawn as an inappropriately chosen lure swims by or a live bait is sloppily and unnaturally presented. During these months, you *really* have to know your stuff in order to dupe bass into biting upon something made of plastic or metal.

After the first few hard frosts of autumn, however, everything begins swinging back in favor of the angler as he now heralds the arrival of good fall fishing. He may sincerely believe the dog days are over and the bass have once again begun feeding, but actually his new-found success can be attributed to something entirely different.

The arrival of cold weather, particularly in the northern states, usually sees a massive die-off of shad and other baitfish species. Frogs and crustaceans begin burrowing into bottom muck for winter hibernation. Young-of-the-year panfish have grown so large they no longer constitute easy pickings. The cold air has even erased most of the insects. The only thing that hasn't yet begun to wind down is the body metabolism of bass. Their systems are still in high gear, and they now have an instinctive compulsion to put on fat stores to sustain them through the upcoming cold-water winter months.

As there is again a marked absence of food, the bass no longer exhibit the selectivity that characterized their feeding patterns months earlier and they once more become quite responsive to lures or baits. The fish may even exhibit a high degree of competitive feeding. Countless times, I've begun cranking in a nice bass that struck a lure and seen two or three other fish chasing the first, trying to grab the plug away. This phenomenon may explain why anglers sometimes catch two bass on the same lure on the same cast.

Bass in the Weeds

Weeds of various species are found in all waters from the smallest farm-pond to the largest manmade reservoir. They play an especially important role, however, in mesotrophic natural lakes because bass living in such lakes generally must share the water with still larger gamefishes.

In most manmade lakes, on the other hand, bass typically "rule the roost." In other words, they're at the very top of the food chain and can pretty much roam at large, with little concern for their safety.

The situation in mesotrophic natural lakes, where bass often are simply an intermediate species in the food chain, is definitely more dangerous. One minute the bass are predators; the next minute, if they're not careful, they may be someone else's prey! The dominant predator species in many waters of this type is the northern pike, but in others the chain pickerel, musky and, to a certain extent, even the walleye will feed upon bass if and whenever the chance arises.

Little wonder that bass head for the weeds in such threatening circumstances. In and around weeds, bass can capitalize upon their predatory advantage of feeding by ambush. Yet at the same time, because of their almost truncated body shapes, they can move quickly to elude elongated species such as pike, which are far more efficient predators in open waters.

Curiously, there also seems to be a little-understood behavioral instinct in predatory gamefishes that causes them to "respect" each other's territorial feeding grounds. In certain weedbeds, for example, I've seen anglers catch bass, and only bass, for a time, followed by a half-hour lull in the action; when the action picked up, nothing but walleyes were caught—in the same exact location. Several hours later the walleyes had long since vanished and bass were once again prowling the weeds. From a human perspective, it seems as though each species held offshore, waiting for the others to finish feeding and leave, whereupon they themselves moved into the area to capitalize upon the available forage. Such "species acknowledgment"—whatever its cause—occurs most often when two gamefish species tied to the same food supply are of nearly equal size and therefore do not pose much of a threat to each other.

Conversely, if a school of big northern pike moves into a region inhabited by bass, the bass seem to recognize the disparity in size and react accordingly. This is exactly what occurred during one of the BASS Classic tournaments staged several years ago in the Alexandria Bay region of upstate New York. Here, a widening in the St. Lawrence River takes on many features of a natural mesotrophic lake, including the presence of such typical shoreline vegetation as cabbage weeds and coontail. The weeds are thick and commonly exist in narrow bands or ribbons somewhat

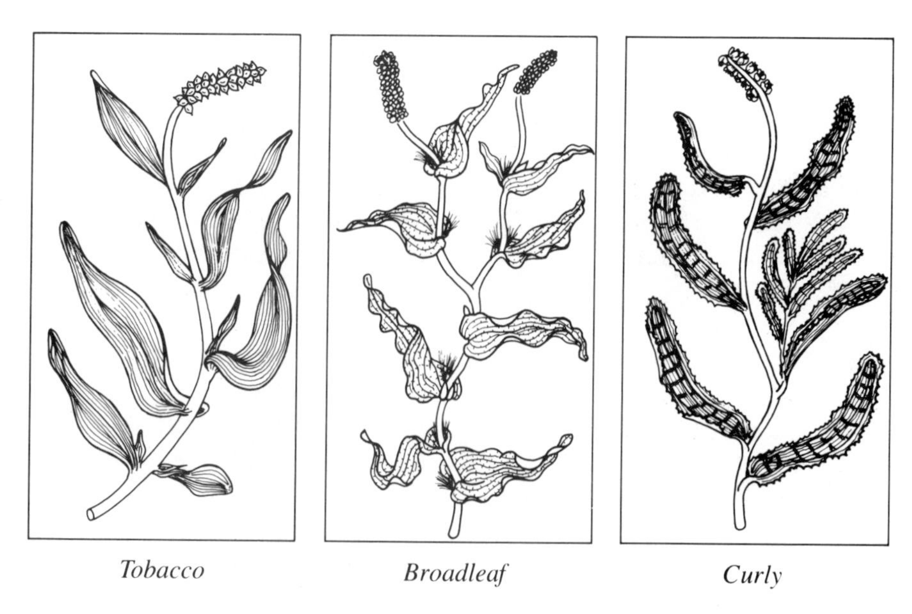

In natural lakes, cabbage weeds are the most attractive to bass; astute anglers should learn to identify the three species.

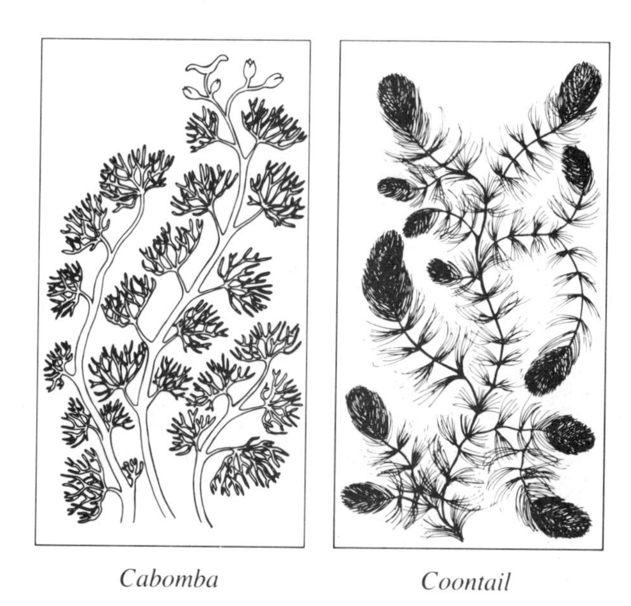

If cabbage weeds are absent from a natural lake, bass are likely to be found in cabomba weeds and coontail.

away from the river banks. In other words, extending out from the bank is an open channel of water for eight or ten feet, then the band of weeds, then the open water of the main river complex. The contestants fishing this Classic tournament quickly learned that if they wanted to catch bass they absolutely had to fish the *inside* weedline closest to the banks. If they cast their lures along the outside, deep-water edges of the weeds, they'd get nothing but pike.

This example is not an isolated case. Indeed, in many mesotrophic lakes bass are found in the shallows and in the weeds. Moreover, they often must content themselves with using only selected areas of weeds where they are least likely to encounter larger predators. This, then, is another exception to the general rules and illustrates again that specific, localized conditions may deviate from classical structure-fishing tenets.

To many anglers, weeds are weeds and that is that. Yet in mesotrophic lakes, certain species of weeds are far more attractive to bass than other species. Advanced anglers know how to identify the favored ones. From my experience, bass will choose cabbage weeds (*tobacco cabbage, curly cabbage,* or *broadleaf cabbage*) over all other species. If these are absent or very sparsely distributed, bass will go for *cabomba weed*, followed by *coontail.* Find any of these species in a mesotrophic lake and you've found your bass. Besides their favorites, bass periodically use lily pads and reeds, and sometimes even cattails, depending upon the movements of their forage, season of the year, and competition from larger predators. Other weed species, which are more prevalent in manmade lakes and reservoirs, will be covered in the next chapter.

Several factors influence the position of bass *within* weedbeds. Adapting your fishing techniques to take these factors into account can lead to exciting bass action. First, the angle at which the overhead sun strikes a heavily matted weedbed will determine how accessible the bass are to an angler's lures. In other words, if the sun is on your back as you are casting toward a weedbed, its slanting rays will reach far back underneath the leading edge and the bass on that side of the weedbed will be much deeper within the weeds. On the other hand, if you cast to the weeds with the sun in your eyes, as uncomfortable as this may be, you'll invariably see much better success; the near edge of the weeds will not be as brightly illuminated and bass will therefore be closer to the outside edge and more likely to see your lure.

The wind also can influence the position of bass in specific weedbeds, particularly during midsummer months. When the wind is howling, bass tend to vacate the weeds and take up positions in open water on the downwind sides of the vegetation, provided larger predators don't pose an immediate threat. The reason for this is that the strong wind literally "blows" baitfish out of their weedbed hiding places into open water where the waiting bass gorge upon them. An insightful angler therefore knows to forget about all other areas of a weedbed when the wind is gusting and

When fishing large, matted weedbeds, cast with the sun in your eyes because, in this position, the bass will be close to the outside edges of the weeds nearest to you.

concentrate his efforts on the downwind side, using lures that closely represent the forage in that given lake.

When the wind is not blowing with such intensity, there are still other specific weedbed locations where bass are most likely to be found, or rather where they're likely to be in a high state of activity. They seem to be the most active when they are relatively near the surface or at some mid-depth in the weeds or alongside the edges. Conversely, when they sink to the bottom, they're usually inactive and not responsive to lures.

Good advice, then, when fishing weeds, is first to work the surface water, perhaps with a topwater bait, spoon, spinnerbait, buzz-bait or, if conditions allow, a shallow-running plug. Then work the mid-depths, pumping a spinnerbait or weedless spoon up and down. I use jigs and plastic worms, too, which sink to the bottom, but I don't really fish the bottom. I use such weighted lures only to serve as a reference as to how deep the bottom is, and on the retrieve "jump" them upwards to entice bass holding at the mid-depth levels.

I'm referring here, of course, to sites where the weed growth is not so thickly matted as to prevent the presentation of lures. If prolific midsummer weeds lie like vast, impenetrable carpets across the surface, you have

If bass do not have to contend with offshore predators, they like to position themselves in open water on the downwind sides of weedbeds during windy weather. The gusting wind literally blows baitfish out of their hiding places and toward the waiting bass.

When bass rest on the bottom in weeds, they're generally inactive, but when suspended in the middle of the weeds or near the surface, they're quite responsive to lures. Therefore, shallow-water spinners and similar lures are good baits to try first.

only two alternatives: Fish potholes, channels, slots and other openings in the weeds, or fish the edges. When you fish openings in weedbeds, don't cast right into the middle of them. Any bass watching the opening for an easy meal might be spooked if a heavy lure suddenly splashes right down on top of them. Instead, cast a lure such as a plastic worm or weedless spoon about five or six feet beyond the hole so it gently splats down on top of the matted weeds. Then slowly slither the bait to the edge of the pothole and let it crawl down one side and up the other.

When fishing the edges of weedbeds, move your boat in close and cast

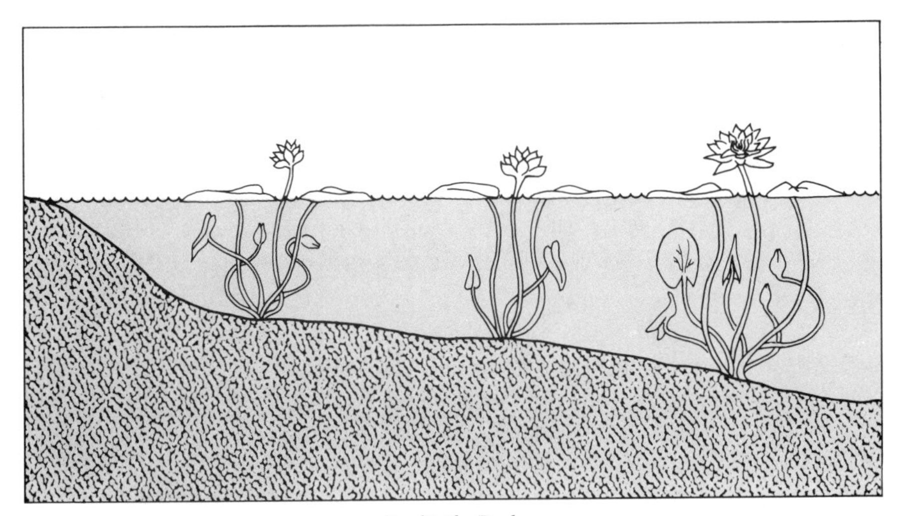

Bad Lily Pads

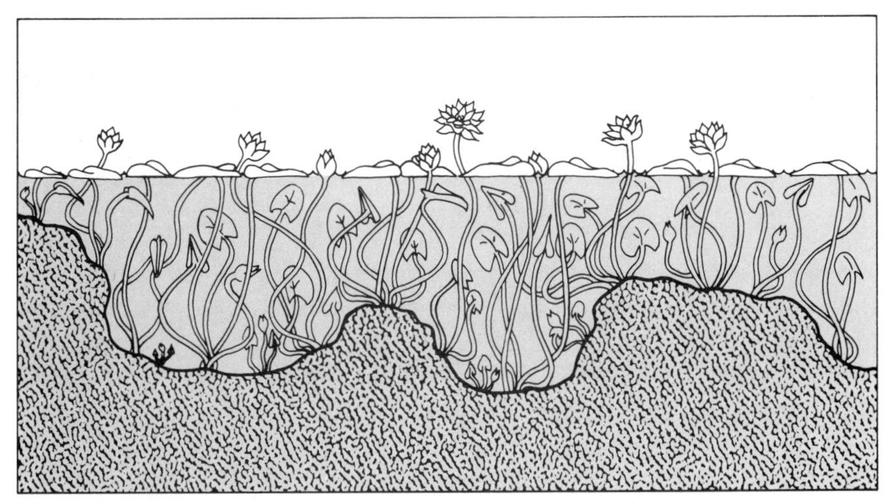

Good Lily Pads

Don't fish thin beds of lily pads (top). Choose thick pads situated over irregular bottom contours (bottom); they provide better action.

parallel to the edges; this keeps lures in the productive fish zone for the entire length of the retrieve. If you stay back some distance, casting to the edge of the weedbed and retrieving your lure perpendicularly to the boat, your lure quickly leaves the fish zone and the remainder of the retrieve will be through unproductive water.

Another rule of thumb about weedbeds—one that pertains specifically to late-fall fishing—is to fish only *green* weeds, as opposed to those that are turning brown and dying. As the cover begins to die and fall into a dormant stage, two things happen. The cover becomes quite thin and no longer offers the same concealment as when it was thick and green. Perhaps more critical, the weeds, due to the curtailment of photosynthesis, stop giving off oxygen; as they begin to decompose, they actually consume oxygen and release carbon dioxide, making the weeds unsuitable as bass habitat. As a result, bass begin congregating in weeds that still are green (at least, for the time being), and anglers feverishly race around the lake searching for these short-lived hot spots.

There are two keys to fishing lily pads in natural mesotrophic lakes. First, if the water is very clear, fish the largest pads you can find, as they offer bass the best concealment. If the water is murky or off-colored in some other way, find beds of small "dollar pads." Second, fields of lily pads growing over irregular bottom contours are vastly more productive than pads found over smooth, flat bottoms.

With regard to reeds, bass distinctly prefer thick-stemmed types. Fields of reeds can grow in many configurations—close to banks or in midlake areas, and in both shallow water and at mid-depths. If time is short and you're searching for optimum conditions most likely to attract bass, look for thick fields of thick-stemmed reeds situated close to drop-offs where the water depth beneath the reeds averages two to five feet.

The Crawdad Connection

I first began realizing the importance of crayfish to bass one winter when going over my logbook of catches in previous years. In addition to noting weather conditions, water conditions, depths at which bass were taken, and types of lures that proved most successful, I've also recorded the stomach contents of fish killed (although, nowadays, a majority are released). A few calculations with these last data uncovered several revelations, which I call the "crawdad connection."

Of all the bass I've taken in various types of natural lakes during the past decade, 18 percent had no food in their stomachs whatsoever, 12 percent contained food remnants that couldn't be identified, and 27 percent had food that consisted of various species of baitfish or panfish. Here's

In natural lakes, reeds in midlake areas can be hotspots of the first order.

the shocker: A whopping 53 percent of the largemouths and smallmouths possessed material that, in various stages of digestion, could positively be identified as crayfish!

The logical conclusion from this finding is that artificial lures duplicating a crayfish's appearance should undoubtedly be the most effective. I decided to investigate the matter, especially when one final tabulation showed another crucial finding.

Approximately 75 percent of the bass that had crayfish in their stomachs were *over* 2½ pounds in weight, whereas 85 percent of the bass that had baitfish or small panfish in their stomachs were *under* 2½ pounds in weight! This suggests that not only should crayfish-resembling lures be the very best for hooking bass in general, but they should consistently yield larger fish.

My initial excitement was dampened somewhat when I saw from the logbook records that crayfish-type lures seldom had fared well at all. The only thing to do was study the critters themselves, to see if there was an explanation for the paradox.

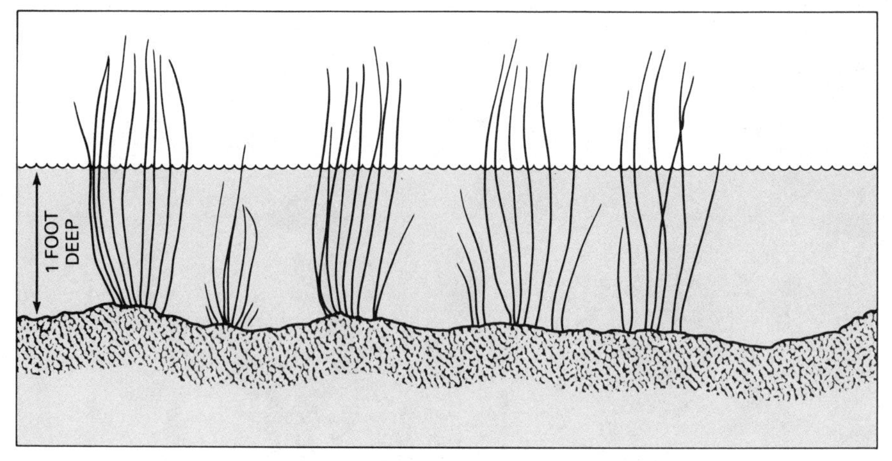

Bad Reeds

Sparse clutches of reeds in shallow water (above) seldom attract as many bass as thick-stemmed reeds (below) situated along drop-offs.

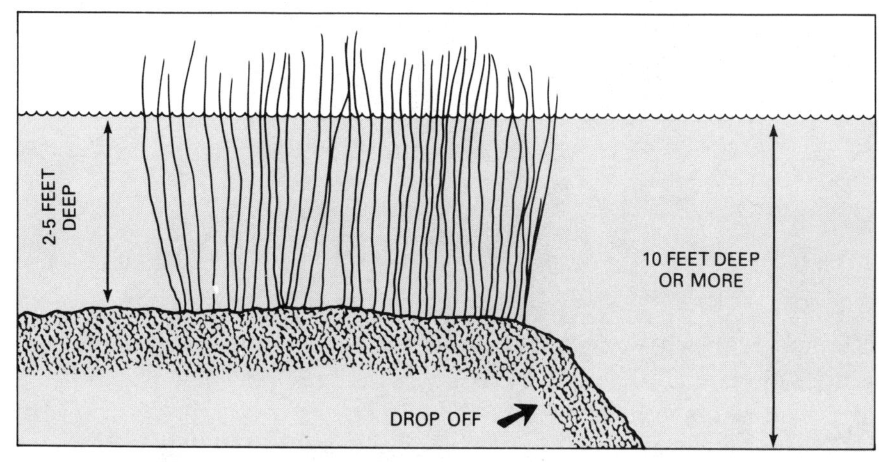

Good Reeds

Incredible as it seems, there are more than 100 species of crayfish on the North American continent, all of them true crustaceans and therefore very closely related to the lobster. Seventy belong to the genus *Cambarus*; these average one to five inches in length and are the overwhelming favorites of both largemouth and smallmouth bass.

Also sometimes called *crawdads,* members of the *Cambarus* clan possess a wide variety of colorations that generally reflect the unique chemistry of the water they inhabit. In one lake they may be brownish olive or dark green, while in a sister lake just across the road the majority may display a pale amber or even black hue. One color feature that all crayfish display, however, is a tinge of orange or red highlighting the sides, the edges of the large front pincers, and other joints in their many segmented appendages. Consequently, just any lure that vaguely resembles a crayfish may not be nearly as productive as another that is a closer facsimile of those inhabiting the water where the angler is fishing.

Crayfish usually live three to five years, and mate an average of eight times. The spawn consists of a cluster of about 200 eggs, which the female holds under her abdomen with small legs, called pleopods, until they are ready to hatch. In late-stage oligotrophic lakes and early-stage mesotrophic lakes, most crayfish like to hide in and around various rocky formations (crevices, crannies, holes and the like). But in those lakes beginning to reveal signs of aging—middle-aged mesotrophic through middle-aged eutrophic lakes—crayfish begin burrowing into the silt, muck and mire covering the former rocky cover.

The all-determining element in a crayfish's life cycle, however, is the percentage of lime in the water, as this influences how rapidly the *chitin* in the shell hardens, and therefore how often the shell must be shed as the crayfish continues to grow. When a crayfish *molts,* or sheds, its shell first splits along the back; then the creature humps up through the opening

In natural lakes, crayfish are a key link in the predator-prey relationships involving bass. More than 100 species are known to exist in North America, many differing widely in size and coloration.

while simultaneously withdrawing its legs; finally, the tail is brought forward and then out of the old shell.

A crayfish that has just molted is quite vulnerable to predation because its shell is soft. In natural lakes with a high lime content, crayfish populations tend to molt more frequently than they do in more acidic lakes. As a result, alkaline lakes have relatively high populations of crayfish in the vulnerable soft-shell stage, when they are favored prey of bass.

It is possible to determine the lime content of a natural lake with a commercially manufactured pH meter (see Chapter 8). It's just as easy to merely note the species of trees surrounding a body of water, as they are good indicators of the soil and mineral composition, which determines the water's pH.

For example, aspens, alders, and especially cedars dote on very alkaline soils. Lakes ringed by these species are likely to have high lime levels and high populations of soft-shell crayfish. You can expect good bass action with lures that resemble crayfish in these waters. On the other hand, the presence of lakeside pines, spruces and aspens, of various types of moss growing on spongy rock-strewn ground, or of exceptionally clear water year-round all indicate acidic water, with correspondingly lower soft-shell crayfish populations. Although bass in such lakes may occasionally feed on crayfish, they are more likely paying most attention to other prey. Crayfish-type lures won't get much rise out of the bass in these lakes.

But there is much more to it than that. According to a recent study by Dr. Allen Keast of Queen's University in Ontario, and still other research findings presented at a predator-prey symposium conducted by the Sport Fishing Institute, most fish species are *generalist* feeders when young. This is particularly true in those regions of the country where there is a marked difference in the seasons and the populations of different prey species peak at specific times. However, most gamefish species also tend to become more specialized in their dining habits as they age and grow larger. The preference that the largest bass exhibit for crayfish, especially those in the vulnerable soft-shell stage, over some panfish or baitfish species illustrates what scientists refer to as the *expended energy principle.*

Briefly, larger bass that have become sedentary in their lifestyles seem to be able to instinctively "weigh" the food value of a prey item in relation to how much energy must be spent to capture it. As it turns out, crayfish are much higher in protein and other nutrients than are baitfish and panfish, and they are considerably easier for bass to catch, especially when they have recently molted. The typically rapid response that crayfish evoke from bass simply represents the bass's instinct to get the most nutritious food with the least amount of expended energy, or effort.

Particularly for larger, more sedentary bass, crayfish represent a highly nutritious, easily caught food source. Their preference for crayfish over other prey thus illustrates the expended energy principle—that is, getting the best possible food with the least amount of effort.

I remember talking once with several scuba divers who had been watching smallmouth bass on Ontario's Lake of the Woods. Schools of emerald shiners would occasionally venture so close as to almost brush against the noses of the big brown fish. Now and then one of the bass would quickly dart forward in a futile attempt to seize a minnow, but usually it was just a tad faster and more adroit than the bass and managed to escape. Understandably, the bass concentrated their feeding energies on crayfish, sometimes in rather ingenious ways.

For example, these Lake of the Woods bass seemed to stand vertically in the water with their heads pointing directly downward as they rooted around in jumbled rock piles on midlake reefs. This activity often flushed crayfish from their hiding places, whereupon the bass would quickly flare their gills; like a piece of fluff being swept up into a vacuum cleaner hose, the hapless crawdad would literally be sucked into a fish's mouth from as far as ten inches away. There was no muss, no fuss, and only a minimum of energy had to be spent in order to acquire the highly nutritious food.

None of my initial investigations into the life and times of crayfish really explained my consistent lack of success with artificial lures that looked like crayfish. The "crawdad connection" was still a mystery that cried out for a solution. After many years of trial-and-error experimentation, I finally stumbled upon not one but several solutions.

The first clue in the trail of evidence became obvious when I noted that most crayfish-lookalike lures on the market are floating-diving plugs painted to resemble crayfish. They do indeed bear a striking resemblance to crayfish, but they do not *move* the way crayfish do. They are clearly phonies to any discerning bass.

Crayfish, you must realize, are strictly bottom-dwelling creatures whose movements fall into two categories: crawling and swimming. Crawling—their most common method of locomotion—while not very fast can occur in any of three directions (forward, backward and sideways). Swimming—which crayfish do when they are alarmed and trying to escape—is always backward. A crayfish swims by making repeated, pulsating strokes of its abdomen; this results in a stop-and-go skipping movement across the bottom that generally covers a distance of less than two feet on each lunge forward. With each spurt forward, the quick abdominal strokes create little clouds of roiled bottom sediment.

There are many representative types of crayfish lures on the market, but knowing how to rig and fish them so that they move like crayfish is important to success.

One way to simulate this movement of crayfish is to place a ½-ounce sliding sinker on the line just ahead of the plug to quickly take it to the bottom and keep it there. Then, retrieve the lure with an erratic stop-and-go movement, allowing the diving plane on the nose of the plug to dig into the bottom and kick up sediment. Another option is to use jigs exclusively, which perhaps more closely mimic crayfish movement than any other lures.

In studying the habits of crayfish, I also learned that they are basically nocturnal creatures. They prowl around during the low-light periods of dawn and dusk, and even after full dark, but spend the bulk of the bright midday hours deep in hiding. It's logical therefore to assume that bass become accustomed to this daily rhythm of their favorite forage and adapt to it. I do know my best bass catches on crayfish-lookalike lures occur during the early morning and late evening hours; during midday almost anything else seems to work better.

Two other bits of crayfish lore are worth relating. According to biologists, the vast majority of any given lake's crayfish population will be found at depths *shallower* than 20 feet. And, crayfish like very high oxygen levels, which means they are frequently found in greatest abundance on windswept banks and particularly in midlake areas on reefs, shoals, sunken rock-capped islands and similar places very common to natural lakes. These two insights explain why smallmouths are typically found around shallow, rocky cover in late-stage oligotrophic lakes. It also explains why, in older mesotrophic lakes, when smallmouths and largemouths are beginning to appear at the very top of the food chain, that bass tend to congregate on structures away from the shorelines. In both cases, the bass are found *where* their favorite food occurs in abundance *when* the reduced numbers of still larger predators, such as pike, make that food accessible.

It's under these conditions—older natural lakes in which bass are approaching or at the top of the food chain—that classical structure-fishing tenets described in Chapter 4 become most relevant. Of course, during early spring the bass will seek out protected shallow-water haunts to engage in their spawning rituals. But as the early summer months approach, the fish may not always be forced to remain in the shallows but can move somewhat offshore, living most of the time in deep water but periodically migrating upon shallow structures.

In such natural lakes, bass may use long shoreline points; drop-offs; *outside,* deep-water edges of weedlines (there are few larger predators to force the bass to the inside edges); and especially midlake structures such as bars, reefs, shoals, humps, saddles and similar configurations. Of the

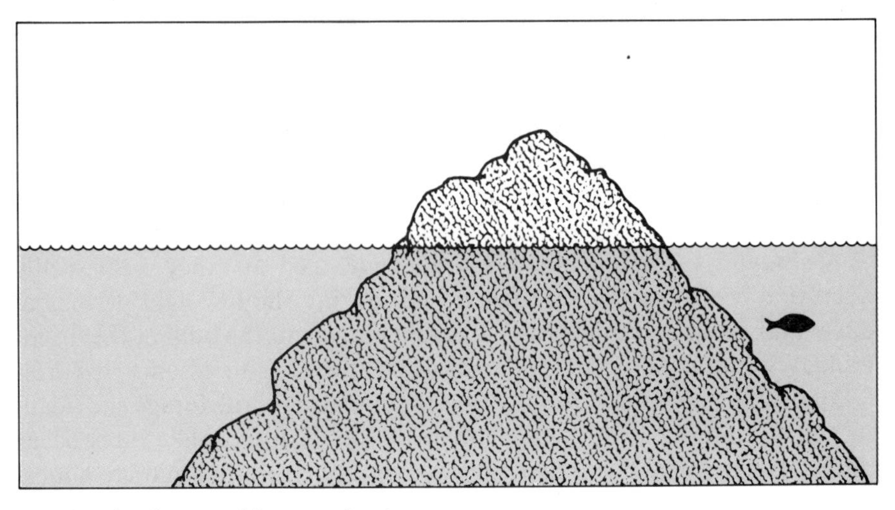

Visible islands are seldom productive.

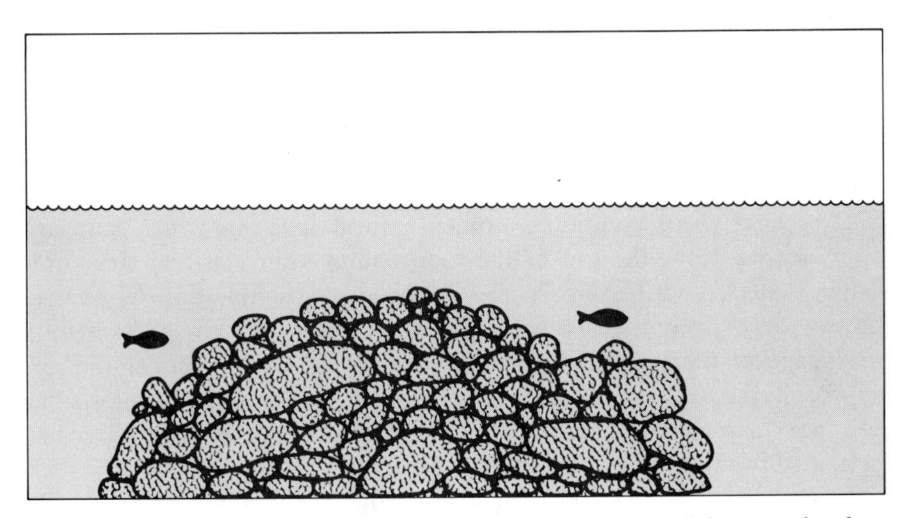

Submerged rock island has good water depth and pronounced features, but bass are not overly attracted to round, smooth rocks.

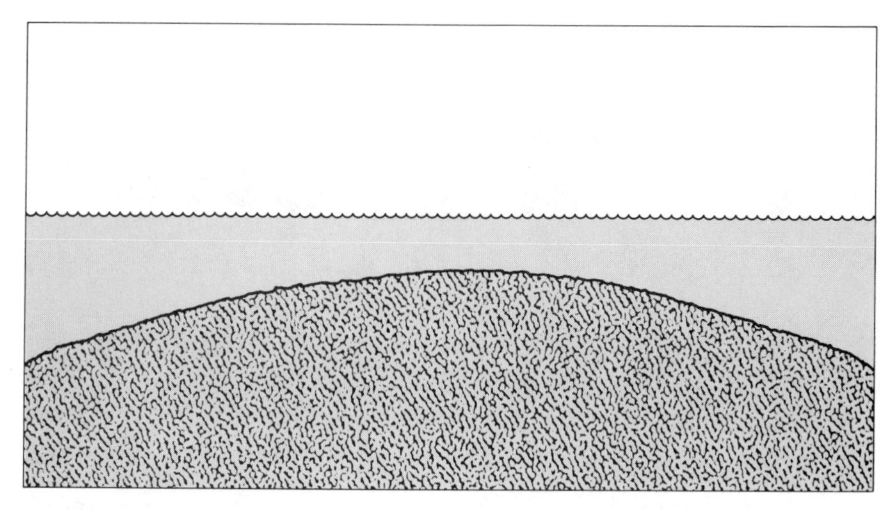

Submerged bar tapers too gently and is too shallow; not likely to attract bass.

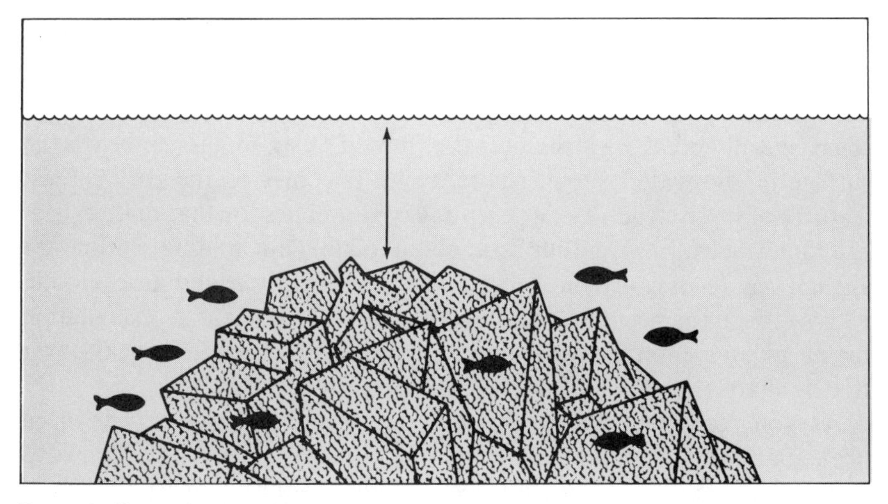

Best of all: good water depth, angular rocks, sharp-breaking features.

In older natural lakes, bass often congregate in midlake areas where rocky bottom cover often harbors huge crayfish populations.

many structures that any angler may chance upon, some are much better than others. Gently tapering structures, and those that visibly poke above the surface of the water, are only sporadically productive. Far better are steep, sharply breaking structures that top off at six to ten feet below the surface of the water. Furthermore, when it comes to the rock-capped features of these structures, or even rocky shorelines for that matter, bass just don't seem very enthusiastic about taking up holding stations or engaging in feeding around rocks that are uniformly round and smooth. I know it sounds peculiar, and nobody really has a scientific explanation for the phenomenon, but time and again bass distinctly prefer rocky cover that is sharp, slablike and angular in appearance.

As you read the coming chapters on lures, live baits and assorted presentation methods, keep in mind our discussion about the "crawdad connection." It's not a guaranteed way of filling your boat with fish (there is none). But it is indeed another important piece that fits nicely into the picture-puzzle lives of bass.

CHAPTER

6

Bass In Artificial Lakes

No two bodies of water are exactly alike, and experience acquired on one is not always applicable to fishing another successfully. Each bass water has a personality all its own; each can be considered a separate, living thing with its own unique water chemistry, bottom structure, plant growth, fish populations, and aquatic life. As these and other features differ from lake to lake, so will the required fishing techniques. This inherent diversity is most evident in manmade bodies of water.

It wasn't until about 1940 that anglers began realizing the vast recreational potential of manmade impoundments, which were created originally for flood control, water storage, and irrigation, and later for generation of hydroelectric power. The Army Corps of Engineers has designed and built many of the nation's reservoirs, but local municipalities, private utility companies and state fish and game departments have long been involved in reservoir construction as well. Today, an estimated 11,000 reservoirs of various sizes speckle the North American landscape, more than 1,500 of them sprawling over 500 acres or more.

The vast majority of these reservoirs were created by damming a major river system and allowing the water to back up and inundate previously dry land. Historically, largemouths have been the principal gamefish species stocked in such waters, because of their adaptability to a wide variety of water chemistry and terrain conditions. In those cases in which smallmouths and spotted bass existed in the original river system, and continued to thrive in the resulting reservoir, supplemental stockings of these species often have been undertaken. In some cases, walleyes, striped bass, hybrid bass (offspring of mated white bass and stripers) and northern pike have also been stocked, providing anglers in certain locales with a veritable smorgasbord of fishing action. In most reservoirs, however, the largemouth is the premier species and occupies the very pinnacle of the food chain. Finding itself in such a situation—under no threat from larger predators—the largemouth is able to roam just about anywhere it pleases, subject of course to certain water conditions to be discussed in Chapters 7 and 8.

Exactly how largemouths or other bass species live and move and feed in a particular reservoir depends chiefly upon the character of the river system dammed and the features of the dry land subsequently covered with water. Based on these characteristics, manmade lakes are commonly classified as *flatland, highland* or *canyonland* bodies of water. Keep in mind, however, that as in the case of natural lakes, few manmade reservoirs fall precisely into one category, as they may reveal composite characteristics of more than one lake classification. In fact, biologists sometimes even go further in their classification of reservoirs to include *hill-land, lowland* and *plateau* categories. For the bass angler, however, an in-depth knowledge of *flatland, highland* and *canyonland* waters should provide the necessary foundation to find and land bass in manmade reservoirs.

Flatland Reservoirs

Flatland lakes and reservoirs are commonly found in the Midwest and South where the topography of the country is quite flat and consistently at or below sea level. Generally, a flatland reservoir is created by building a very long dam on a major river and permitting the water to back up and flood stands of southern hardwood, former farmlands, prairies, marshes, lowland swamps, and similar terrain. The created impoundment may possess a tremendous variety of cover above and below the water's surface. Stump fields, grass beds, matted expanses of weeds, standing or felled timber, brush, boggy islands and other types of junglelike growth may seemingly be everywhere. In other impoundments, cover may occur only in the shallow headwater region and various embayments and creek arms, with the depths near the dam being relatively open water.

Flatland reservoirs are basically shallow, averaging four to ten feet deep near the headwater region and 20 to 30 feet deep near the tailwater region of the dam. These reservoirs do not have steep shorelines or high bluffs overlooking the water; instead, the shorelines taper very gradually toward the midlake areas. In many cases, a flatland reservoir may be only five or six feet deep a hundred yards away from the bank.

The uniqueness of flatland reservoirs is twofold: First, the deep water is mostly above the bed of the river that was dammed to form the impoundment. Second, although there may be gradual rises or depressions

Flatland reservoirs built over level terrain are often so shallow that anglers can wade-fish in search of their quarry.

here and there, the main riverbed and the beds of associated feeder streams constitute the major bottom contours. With the exception of these beds, most of the rest of the reservoir floor consists of expansive flats.

In flatland reservoirs, individual bass may be caught almost anywhere that natural or manmade cover occurs, but schools of bass are usually found only in the riverbeds. Bass in a flatland body of water will use the riverbeds (depending on the season of the year) as their primary sanctuary areas, and their migrations will usually only be to adjacent or connected structures or cover.

Of course, during the spring the bass schools break up. Males and females alike may simply travel from the riverbed structures to nearby shallow flats for spawning, but they more commonly like to follow feeder stream channels into the shallows, particularly if they lead into large embayments. This, then, is one key to finding spring bass: Shallow embayments that have "active" stream channels running through them will contain far more fish than other embayments that are simply catch basins for rising water levels during rainy periods.

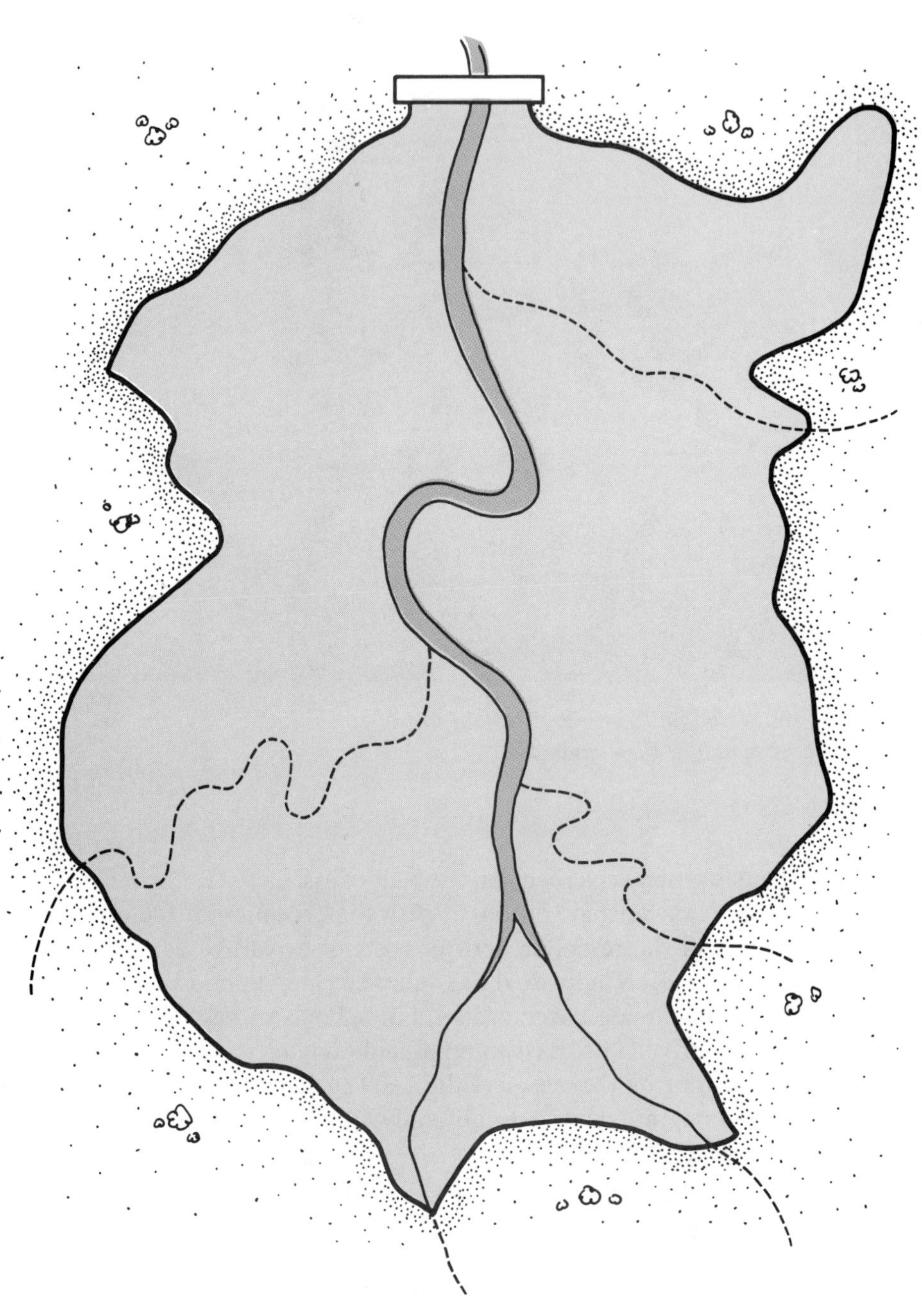

Flatland reservoirs are generally quite wide and saturated with cover. Random fish may be taken around the cover, but schools of bass exclusively related to the old riverbed and related stream channels, which offer the deepest water and also the primary change in bottom contour.

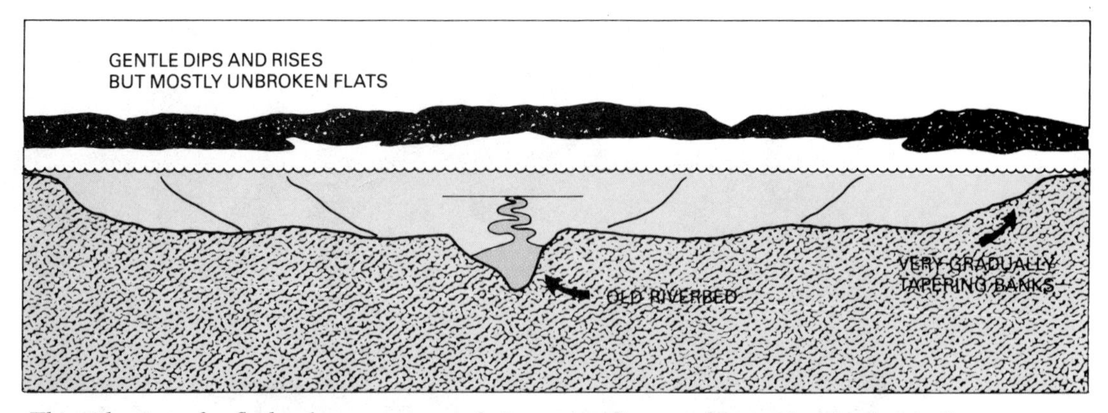

This side view of a flatland reservoir reveals its personality: gently tapering banks, shallow water, and an old riverbed that seldom meanders in close to the banks.

There are two other types of spawning locations that I nearly always find productive in flatland waters. One is an old roadbed, which is most often composed of hard-packed sand, clay or gravel (there may even be concrete or asphalt roads with a light covering of silt that has settled from the water). And the other is an abandoned railroad spur left intact when the reservoir was flooded. Both features are quite common in flatland reservoirs and are usually clearly marked on maps. If not, the shoreline may reveal where they enter the water, and you can trace their routes with a depth sounder. Roadbeds and railroad spurs that run near the main channel are the best bets of all, since the bass do not have to travel far from their schooling areas to find them.

In flatland reservoirs, spawn-spent bass may immediately retreat to a nearby stream channel and hold there for several weeks. Or, in their movements away from the spawning grounds they may stop to hug the bases of trees or brush cover. These stopovers are only for brief periods, however, as the bass continue toward the depths to re-engage in schooling activity. Now is a time when many anglers begin experiencing light stringers. Rather than follow the fish to their various summer, fall and winter homes, they continue to plug the standing timber in the shallow swamp areas, the weedbeds and other visible cover. They may catch a bass here or there, but the action is sporadic at best. Instead, they should be working cover leading away from the spawn sites to the stream channels, the stream channel contours themselves, and then later those structures found in conjunction with the main riverbed.

The first association a school of bass has with shallower water when it migrates from the depths of the riverbed or the feeder stream channels (they'll be in the riverbed during the summer and winter, and in the deeper

Prime places to look for spawning bass in a flatland reservoir include cover-filled flats adjacent to the main riverbed and also those embayments that have active stream channels running through them.

stream channels in the fall) will be the edge of the channel itself. This location serves as the contact point and also the first (and sometimes only) breakline. Since this breakline may be extremely long and uniform, the bass will make contact with the edge of the channel at some location where there is a break. This may consist of several stumps situated on the edge of the channel, a felled tree, a pile of rocks or some other type of superstructure. If, beyond this break, there exists nothing but expansive, unbroken flats, the fish will probably go no farther. You'll either catch them at the break along the edge of the channel or not at all. But if intermittent structural signposts lead from the channel to, perhaps, a nearby weedbed, the bass may continue their migration somewhat farther.

Another type of structure that may be productive, particularly during the fall months, is a sharp S-bend in a deep stream channel (a bend in the main riverbed could be as much as a mile long). Due to the washing effect of the current, the bass may rest in the outside, undercut portion of the bend and migrate up the inside bend where a shoal is created by fine sand settling out. Again, the fish may go no farther than the edge of the channel, or they may follow signposts to some nearby area. Still another type of structure—a genuine hot spot during the summer and winter—is a *channelpoint.* This occurs where the old riverbed loops in close to shore and

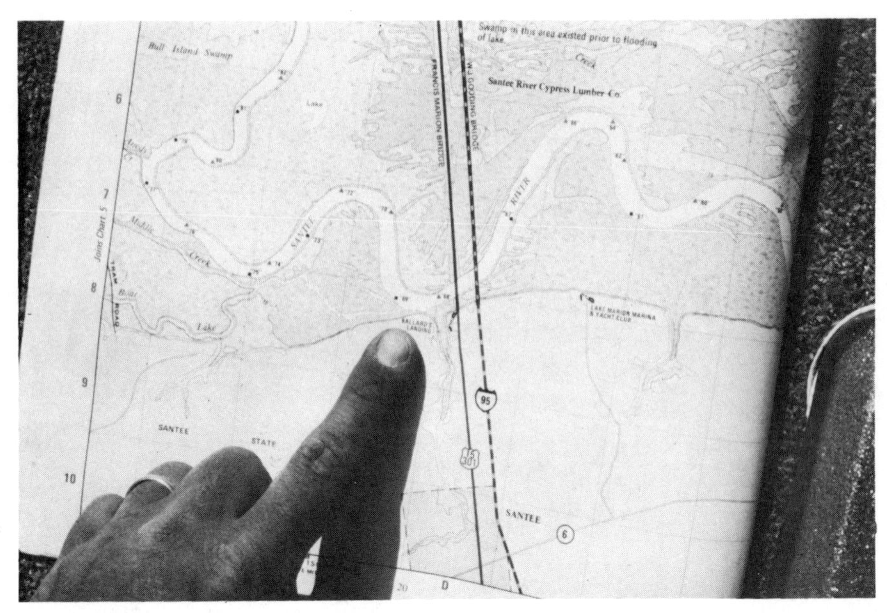

On a bottom contour map, here is what a channelpoint looks like, where the old riverbed loops in close to a tapering shoreline point. Such a rare hotspot is worth searching for.

a tapering point of land simultaneously extends all the way to the edge of the channel—a classic migration situation.

Yet another hot spot in flatland reservoirs, which originally was identified by the legendary Buck Perry, is a *delta.* Deltas are elongated ridges that sometimes are found along the edges of stream channels and riverbeds. They're found predominantly in regions of former agricultural operations, having been created by farmers plowing bottomlands right up to the edges of streams and rivers, and generally they are covered with stumps, trees and brush.

Carefully studying a bottom contour map may also reveal junctions where two stream channels join. This situation gives birth to underwater points, ridges, saddles, humps, hogbacks and similar features that are highly attractive to bass. It also gives rise to two concepts I named many years ago as *off-structures* and *on-structures.* These concepts are invaluable to anglers trying to pinpoint the whereabouts of schools of bass during summer, fall and winter, not only in flatland reservoirs but also in highland reservoirs and the shallower headwater regions of canyonland reservoirs.

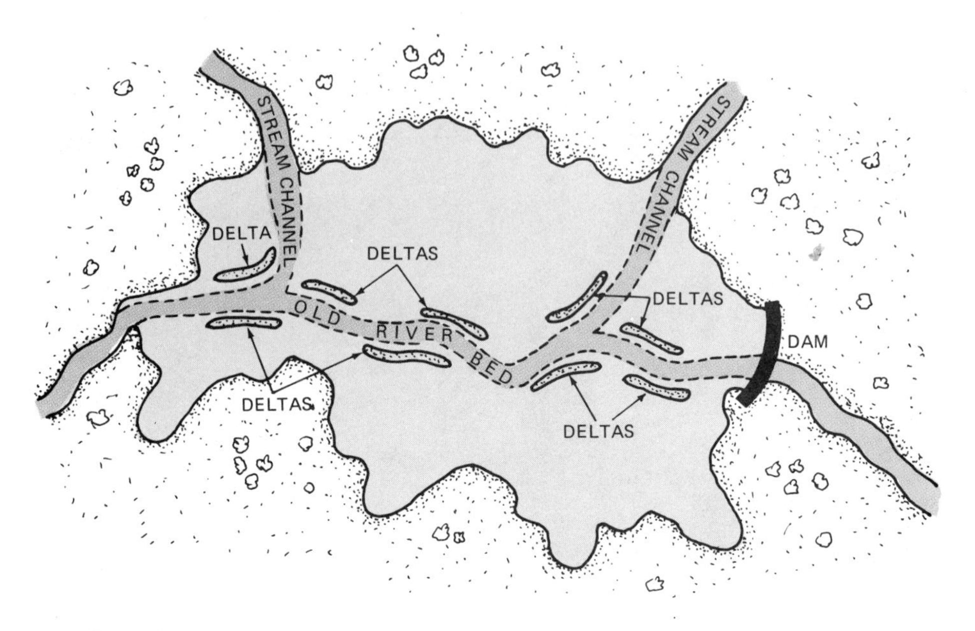

Deltas are shown by contour lines.

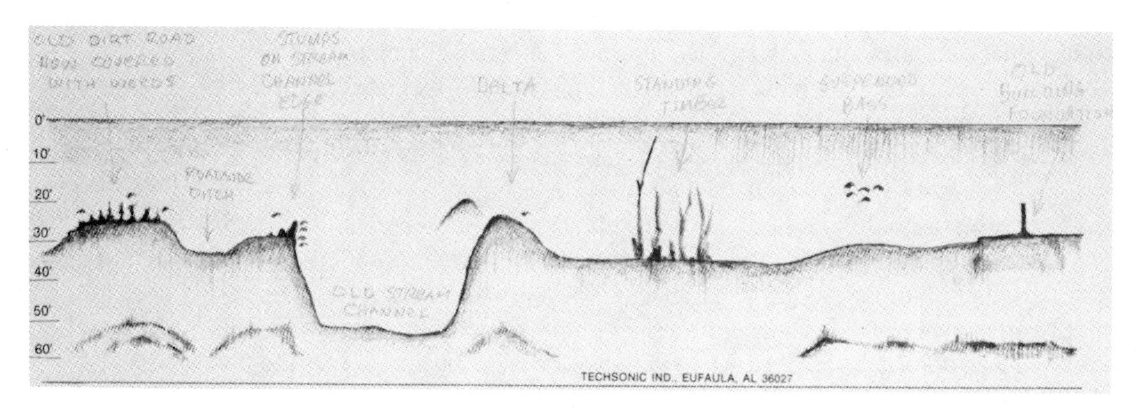

This readout strip from a graph recorder shows the floor of a flatland reservoir with an easily recognizable delta on one side of an old stream channel. Other features shown that are typical of flatland reservoirs include an old roadbed, roadside ditch, standing timber, and an old building foundation.

As the terms suggest, on-structures are those structures that are in some way connected to the shoreline; off-structures are those that are detached from the shoreline and consequently found in midlake regions. An example of an on-structure is the channelpoint described earlier. An off-structure, however, might be a bar, shoal, reef, hump, sunken island, underwater ridge or rock pile. It can even be a weedbed, but whatever the feature it is away from the banks of the lake.

The important distinction between these two types of structure is that *bass customarily use on-structures during the spring and fall and off-structures during the summer and winter.* Of course, there are exceptions to the rule, most of them having to do with the available water depth adjacent to the structure in question; an off-structure that is quite shallow, for example, would probably be used during the fall rather than the winter.

As noted already, during the summer, fall and winter, most big bass in flatland reservoirs will be relating in some way to the main riverbed or associated structures. But it's worth noting that in late fall bass often migrate again. During this period, which may last up to four weeks depending upon local weather and water conditions, I have found bass exhibiting *false-spawn* behavior; that is, they temporarily leave the main riverbed area and head once again in the direction of former spawning areas used the previous spring. They don't go all the way, however, but only to those cover-filled locations where they temporarily held at the end

During summer, fall and winter, bass in flatland reservoirs (and also in portions of highland reservoirs) make religious use of off-structures and on-structures.

of the spring spawn (the mouths of embayments and creek arms, and along the edges of cover-filled flats adjacent to the riverbed or stream channels). During false-spawn movements, schools of bass briefly disperse and generally can be found in loose groups of three to six fish.

So far, we've been discussing natural features in flatland reservoirs that attract schools of bass. Homing in upon such places should always be a serious angler's first priority because of the fast and exciting action that awaits. When fishing for school bass, it's entirely possible to catch a large fish on every other cast and limit out in mere minutes.

Nevertheless, as noted in Chapter 4, sometimes you have to wait for the fish to move—engage in a migration—before they can be caught. And during this waiting period it may be worthwhile to concentrate upon straggler bass. In flatland reservoirs, stragglers often can be found in various natural structures and cover formations that are detached from riverbeds or channels, or are in other quite shallow regions—that is, in locations avoided by schooling bass. In addition, flatland reservoirs invariably are teeming with manmade features that are highly attractive to straggler bass.

I particularly like to work submerged building foundations and old farmponds. Those ponds are actually "holes" on the bottom of a reservoir, and they're well worth investigating. Also, don't overlook old roadbeds, especially where bridges (now underwater) cross tiny brooks or where ditches or culverts border such roads. Other manmade features that often attract stragglers are the rocky rubble or riprap in causeways (highway foundations) that border or cross flatland reservoirs, and the slab rock used to protect the dam facing at the deeper end of the impoundment. There are others, too, but they warrant special treatment in coming chapters.

Because the primary purpose of many flatland reservoirs is to facilitate flood control and the related drainage of terrain upstream from the impoundment, water levels are adjusted to accommodate periodic rainfalls. Typically, as rainfall swells feeder tributaries, they in turn dump into the reservoir and the water level rises until the lake reaches maximum holding capacity, whereupon the gates of the dam are opened and the water level allowed to slowly recede. In many cases, the dam gates are even opened ahead of time in anticipation of a heavy rainfall.

Whatever the actual sequence of events, however, the best bass fishing takes place when the water level is slowly rising. Under these conditions, bass (both schools and stragglers) begin migrating much shallower than usual and seem far more aggressive and responsive to lures. Some anglers believe this is due to the sudden profusion of additional food washed into the water, which triggers more active feeding responses.

Conversely, when the water level is falling, fishing action generally takes an abrupt nose dive. The bass move much deeper than usual and into temporary holding stations until the water level stabilizes. They can still be caught now—make no mistake about that—but you'll have to work very hard for them.

Another feature that exists in some flatland reservoirs, but rarely occurs in highland or canyonland impoundments, is the presence of shallow swamp habitat, particularly in the deep South states. Often, these swamps are hundreds of acres in size and characterized by almost impenetrable cover in the form of standing timber and floating weedbeds. In swamps in southern flatland reservoirs, the most common weeds favored by bass are elodea, hyacinth, hydrilla, milfoil, lily pads and moss. The standing timber commonly found in swamps is cypress, willow, tupelo and black oak.

Swamp bass are fairly predictable in their feeding schedules, compared with bass in other waters. High noon is far and away the most productive fishing time. When the sun is directly overhead, the extensive vegetation

An ideal location for straggler bass is the riprap of causeways and dam facings.

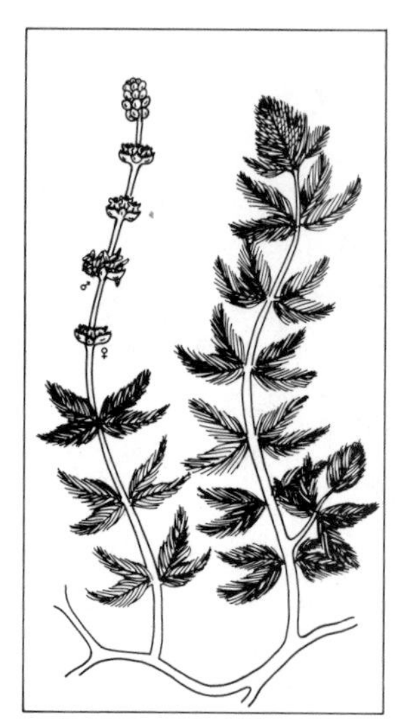

Milfoil

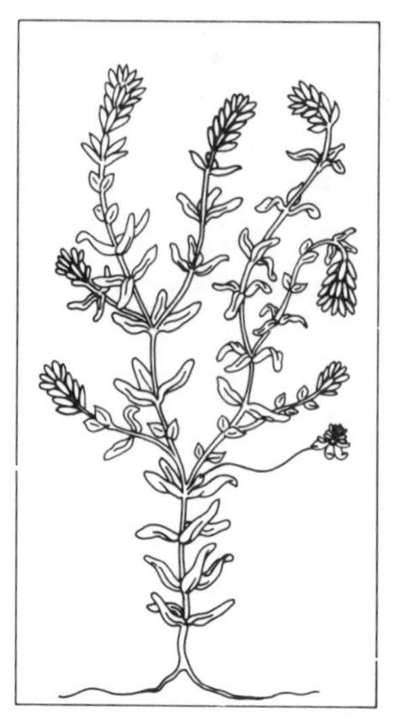

Elodea

The weed species common to flatland reservoirs that bass use most include milfoil and elodea. In certain waters, there may also be extensive mats of hyacinth and lily pads.

releases more oxygen into the water than at any other time and this vigorously stirs the food chain into action: Tiny microorganisms and insects first exhibit heightened activity, followed by baitfish and panfish, and, finally, bass.

Finding bass in swamps also is fairly easy. The key word to keep in mind is *superstructure*! In flooded stands of timber, for example, try to find something different—a ditch, hole or even an edge where two different species of trees such as cypress and willows border. The same thing applies to fishing matted expanses of weeds. Look for some type of irregular bottom contour, hump, edge or other feature that distinguishes a small area from the larger overall mass of weeds.

When water levels fluctuate in flatland reservoirs, knowing bass anglers often head for the swamps *en masse.* During slowly rising water levels, search for bass in the locations just described, although they may be a bit shallower than usual. During falling water levels, however, there is one place and one place only worth fishing—the stream channels on the floor of the flooded swamp.

Likely as not you'll find gobs of bass there stacked up like cordwood. These channels serve as the only deep-water retreats bass have available when the plug is pulled, so to speak, and the water level begins dropping. In fact, not only bass but all manner of swampland aquatic creatures from catfish to bluegills to alligators will make a beeline for the deeper stream channels until the water level stabilizes and once again eventually begins to rise to its former level.

Huge swamps occur in many flatland reservoirs, especially in the deep South. Here, the best fishing action occurs during midday; if the water level is falling, head straight for the old stream channels wandering through the swamp.

Such stream channels are easy to find by first locating them on a map and then using a depth sounder to trace their routes as they meander through the swamp. Indeed, many times you can even visually spot an old channel's course by simply looking for narrow avenues winding through stands of timber and weedy flats.

Lastly, predator-prey relationships between bass and their forage are far more diverse in flatland reservoirs than in natural lakes. As discussed in the previous chapter, in natural lakes bass forage heavily on crayfish, and to a lesser extent on various minnow and panfish species. In flatland reservoirs, bass also will forage upon crayfish, whenever the opportunity arises. But they're even more closely tied to threadfin shad, gizzard shad, small catfish, bluegills, sunfish and assorted swamp creatures such as frogs, freshwater eels and small snakes. Knowing which prey bass are tied to in specific waters is invaluable in locating bass and then trying to elicit feeding responses or provoke strikes with representative offerings. These topics will be described in detail in later chapters.

Highland Reservoirs

Highland reservoirs are found in hilly or mountainous regions, and the vast majority are located in the eastern half of the country. They generally are constructed by building a dam between rather steep mountain ridges and permitting river water to back up and flood a series of associated gorges and valleys.

Even an untrained observer can note a number of radical differences between a highland and a flatland body of water. A highland reservoir usually does not possess much weedy cover, except perhaps fringing the shorelines for short stretches, in the backs of coves and embayments, in the backs of feeder creeks, and in the headwater region. Standing timber, however, may be profuse from one end of the lake to the other, the particular species depending on both the soil types and elevation of the region; hardwoods and pines are the most common.

The bottom, or floor, of a flatland reservoir may be composed primarily of muck and other soft materials, whereas that of a highland reservoir usually is quite hard and clean, containing sand, gravel, rock, silt or a combination of these materials. Lacking the rich, fertile bottom materials that give flatland reservoirs a variety of water colors, highland impoundments are generally quite clear.

Although the most obvious deep waters—and prime bass locations—in a flatland lake are found over old riverbeds and associated stream channels, such is not the case in highland reservoirs. These reservoirs typically are so deep, often 200 feet or more, that the old river channel is simply too deep to be used by bass, except in the shallowest headwater region. Even many of the feeder creek channels from the midway part of a highland reservoir down to the dam end of the lake may be too deep for bass, except where they are close to the shorelines.

In contrast to the flat, or gradually tapering, shorelines of flatland reservoirs, the banks of highland impoundments are typically steep and sharp-breaking. Bluffs, cliffs, sheer rock walls and similar features often cause the water to be quite deep close to the shoreline in many places; underwater, ledges, outcroppings, stairstep rock formations and drop-offs may plummet into 60 feet or more of water.

From my experience, bass behavior in highland reservoirs is far easier to figure out than bass behavior in flatland lakes, simply because in highland waters the excessive water depths offer bass far fewer options. In other words, during any given season of the year, perhaps as little as only 10 percent of the water contained within a highland impoundment is suitable as bass habitat. Learn that 10 percent and you'll hit paydirt.

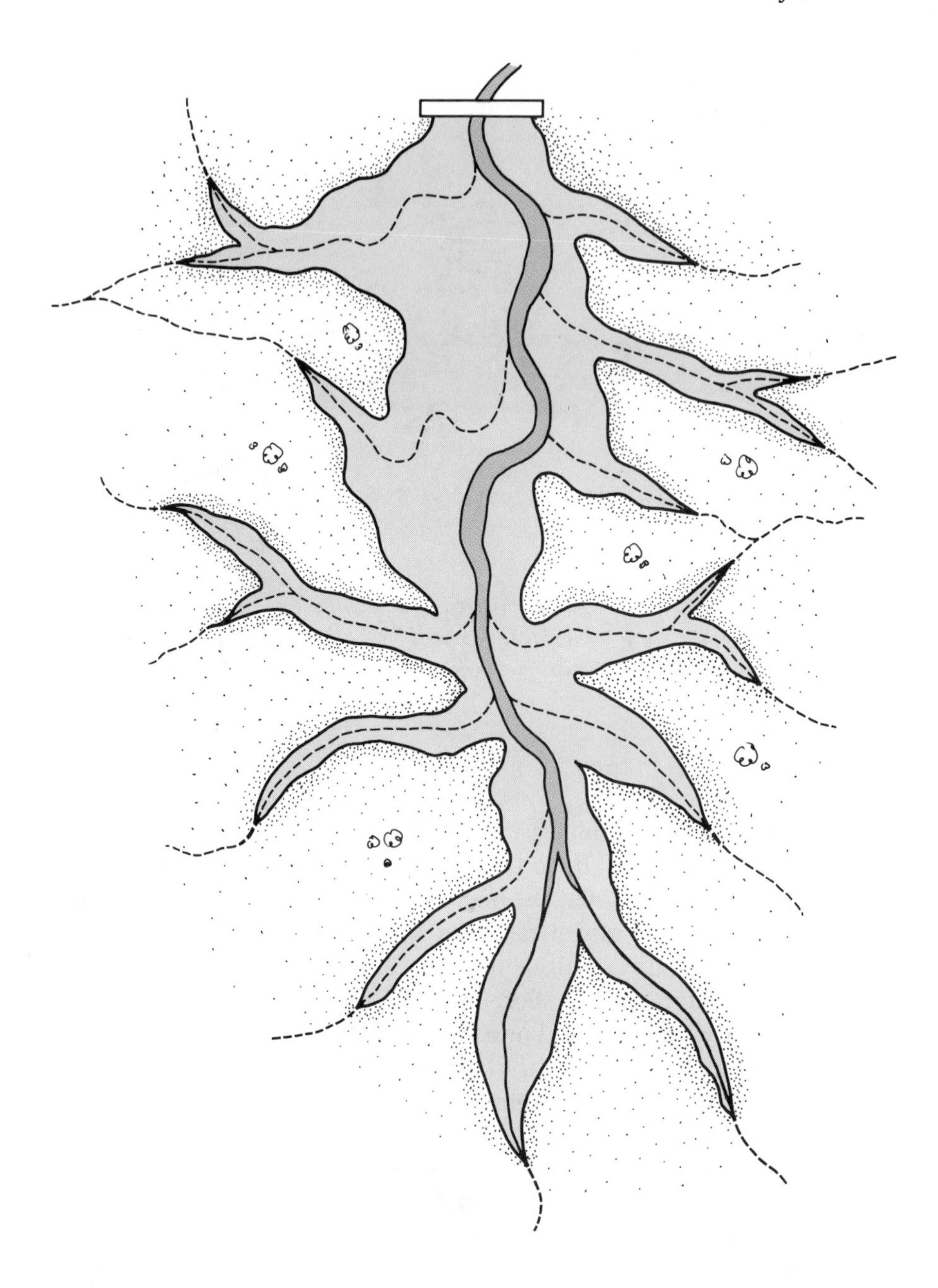

A highland reservoir typically has irregular shorelines, characterized by high bluff banks and many narrow feeder creek arms. Toward the dam end of the lake, the old riverbed and associated stream channels on the bottom may be too deep for bass, which tend to congregate in only a portion of the lake.

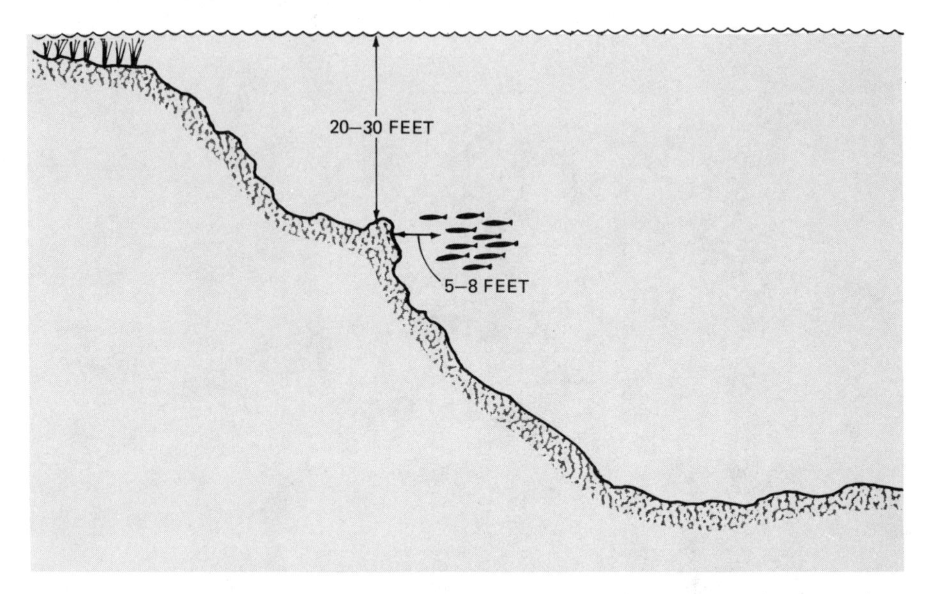

Since the old riverbed in a highland reservoir is usually too deep for bass, they commonly find sanctuary in holes at the bases of shoreline drop-offs, or they may suspend off the edges of deep breaklines where there are rocky outcroppings.

During the spring spawning period, for example, many coves, embayments and creek arms will be too deep and cold to promote bass mating. Likewise, during the summer, the main river channel will be so deep and cold that bass will not travel far from the main banks. Instead, their sanctuary or resting areas will be in holes, gulleys and other deep-water locations often found close to shoreline drop-offs and underwater ledges.

Also during the summer, and into the fall and winter months, highland reservoir bass spend a good deal of time suspending themselves at arbitrary mid-depths in standing timber. Typically, they migrate from deep water to shallow water not on a horizontal plane but rather on a vertical plane as they move up and down within the branches of the trees. During the summer months, large numbers of bass also chase schools of baitfish in midlake regions. Then, during the late fall and throughout the winter they're back in the trees again, and also engage in vertical migrations along very steep shoreline rock walls where the water may be 50 feet deep or more.

The discussions of the migration behavior of schooling bass in Chapters 3 and 4 are most applicable to highland reservoirs. Here, migrating bass typically make use of on-structures such as shoreline points, breaks on

Highland reservoir bass love to suspend in standing trees, where their daily migrations are more vertical up through the branches than on a horizontal plane.

breaklines, and superstructures. But in the shallower headwater region of a highland impoundment, bass also may use off-structures during the course of summer and winter migrations.

The water level in highland reservoirs is manipulated primarily to create hydroelectric power and drawdowns are much more dramatic than they are in flatland reservoirs. While the water level in flatland lakes may fluctuate from three to five feet, in highland reservoirs the level may fluctuate from ten to as much as 25 feet. In addition, highland reservoir water levels often are manipulated on a daily basis, and frequently are brought way down to a winter-pool stage.

The frequent and large fluctuations in the water level in highland reservoirs have a tremendous impact upon bass location and bass activity. For example, when water is being "pulled" to generate electricity, bass throughout the lake exhibit a frenzied desire to begin feeding. If you look at the surface of the water very closely, especially in creek arms, focusing upon bits of leaves and other debris, you'll even see it traveling in a

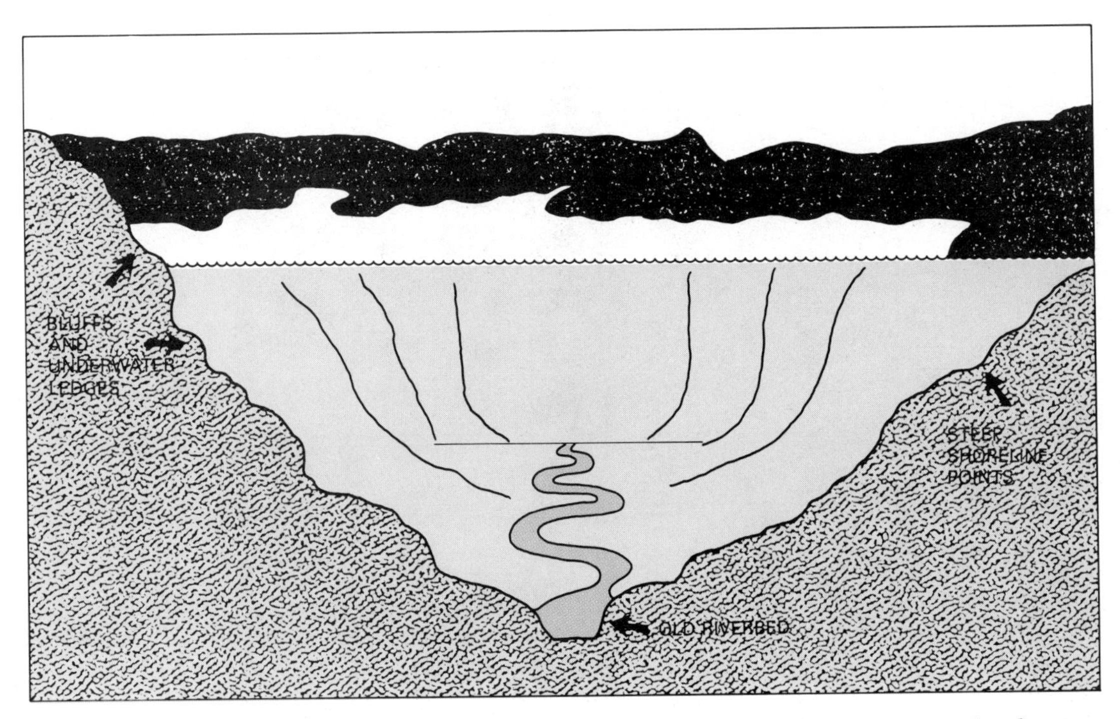

This cross-sectional view of a highland reservoir reveals the presence of underwater drop-offs and ledges, as well as steep shoreline points, where classical bass migrations often take place.

downstream direction, even though the dam site where they're pulling water may be 30 miles away. This sudden presence of "current" is like a tonic to bass that may have been previously lethargic and for a period of several hours they customarily go on a feeding rampage. It's worthwhile to find out from the agency operating a particular highland dam when water will be pulled through the turbines to generate electricity; then, call your boss and fake the biggest illness you can think of in order to go fishing.

A slightly different situation occurs when a highland reservoir is being brought down to the winter-pool stage. At first, the receding water level turns bass off and causes them to retreat into deeper holding stations. However, once the water level has stabilized, action begins to pick up again and may even surpass all previous success any angler has enjoyed. The simple explanation is that after removal of such a massive volume of water, the fish are far more concentrated than at any other time of year. Since this occurs at a time of year when bass are schooling anyway, numerous schools may actually find themselves joining each other in select places until literally hundreds of fish are living in tight quarters. With forage levels long since depleted—due to the approach of winter—now is when an angler may search long and hard for his bass but, once finding them, crank in a nice fish on almost every cast.

In highland reservoirs there are numerous places where this schooling activity may take place, but I especially like to look for depressions of standing timber where the water is 18 to 25 feet deep. Also check the inside, deep-water sides of steep shoreline points littered with rubble, brush, stumps or timber. And be sure to investigate stream channel junctions, or places where feeder tributaries dump into the main riverbed in the shallower headwater region of the impoundment.

The principal prey of bass in highland reservoirs are shad, crayfish, small panfish and salamanders.

In contrast to flatland reservoirs, which are home exclusively to largemouths, highland reservoirs may contain smallmouth and spotted bass, in addition to largemouths. The information in this section applies to largemouth behavior in highland impoundments; I'll cover smallmouths and spotted bass in Chapters 18 and 19.

Canyonland Reservoirs

Canyonland reservoirs are located predominantly in the western and southwestern states where mammoth concrete dams span relatively narrow gorges and rushing rivers are allowed to back up and inundate vast networks of steep chasms. Such impoundments are generally created to produce hydroelectric power. The water depth in the vicinity of the dam may be as much as 600 feet, and water level fluctuations during power generation periods and winter drawdowns may range from 10 to over 150 feet!

Typical bass cover in the form of weeds and standing timber is virtually nonexistent in a canyonland reservoir, although sparse swatches of sagebrush, manzanita, mesquite, scrub oak, juniper and cottonwood trees may occur, particularly in the backs of coves.

Largemouths are the predominant bass species, although the Florida subspecies has been introduced into many such waters, most notably those in southern California. Their principal forage is shad and crayfish, but in many canyonland impoundments the establishment of a "two-story" fishery permits bass to gorge themselves upon young rainbow trout.

Bass in canyonland reservoirs are almost always confined to shoreline regions containing slides of underwater rocks or gravel that have loosened and fallen from the sheer walls. The water in other locations is too deep for bass.

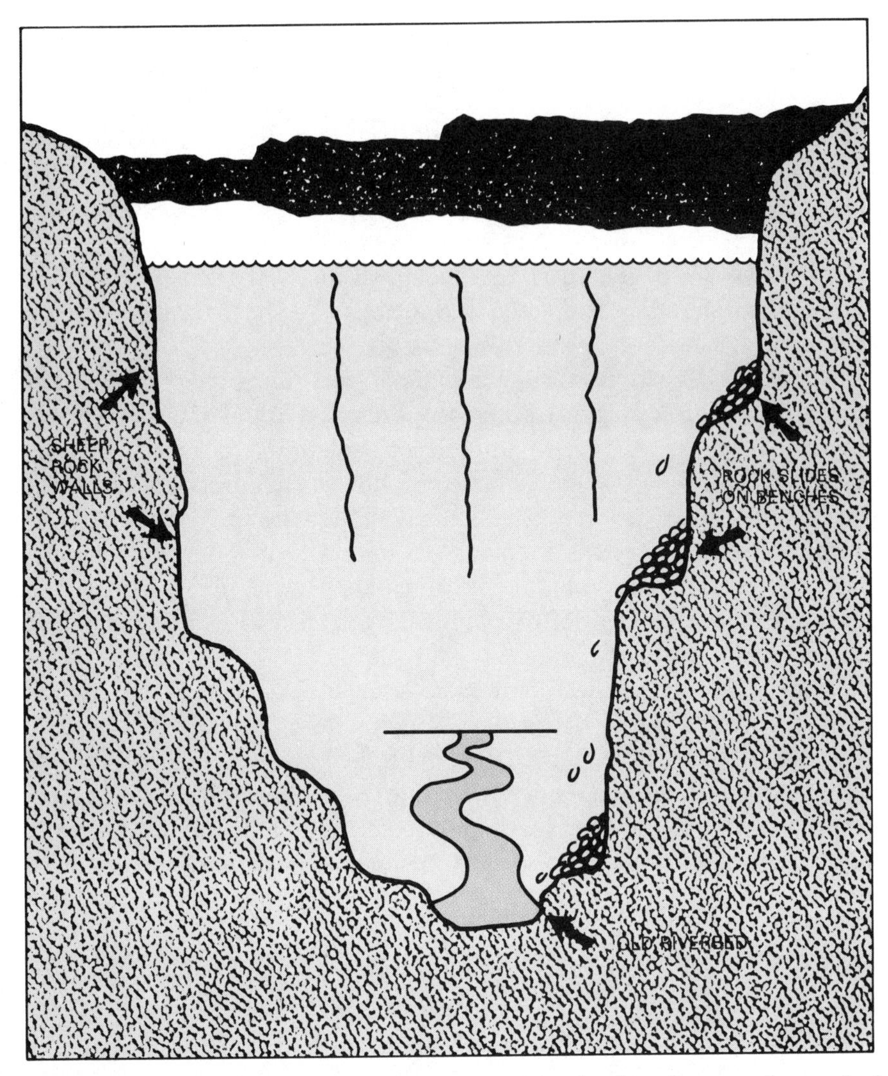

This cross-sectional view of a canyonland reservoir clearly points out the marked absence of cover. Generally, the bass are found shallow, relating to slides, or suspending at arbitrary depths along the sheer rock walls.

Bass in canyonland reservoirs are unquestionably tied to the shorelines because generally the remainder of the impounded water is simply too deep and cold for them. Further, with the exception of the small amounts of woody cover that may be present, the shoreline regions bass favor most are composed of jagged rock walls or *slides.* Slides are slanting underwater structures made up of sand, gravel, chunk rock and boulder slabs that over time have been loosened from the canyon's walls and fallen into the water immediately below.

Spring spawning activity almost exclusively takes place far back in the shallowest areas of coves and feeder creeks, but also sometimes along the main-lake shorelines where relatively shallow shoreline benches or shelves are covered with a thin layer of sediment.

The remainder of the year, bass locate themselves on steep shoreline points, along shoreline drop-offs, and against the sheer facings of steep walls.

Although the locations of canyonland bass are quite predictable, catching them is at times a frustrating proposition. Part of this problem is attributable to the very clear water such reservoirs possess; the other difficulty is that the most active fish are found in shallow water. As most experienced anglers are well aware, clear, shallow water requires a quiet, careful approach, long casts, spiderweb lines and tiny lures. However, offsetting the difficulty encountered in landing canyonland bass is the highly aggressive behavior often exhibited by the fish when water is pulled through the turbines at the dam.

During major drawdowns, however, when the water level may fall as much as 150 feet, the only course of action is to look upon the water as a brand new reservoir, treating it as though the now-exposed banks where you previously caught bass never even existed. Wait until the water level stabilizes before you go fishing, though, because such major reductions in pool levels temporarily disrupt bass behavior and cause them to cease feeding.

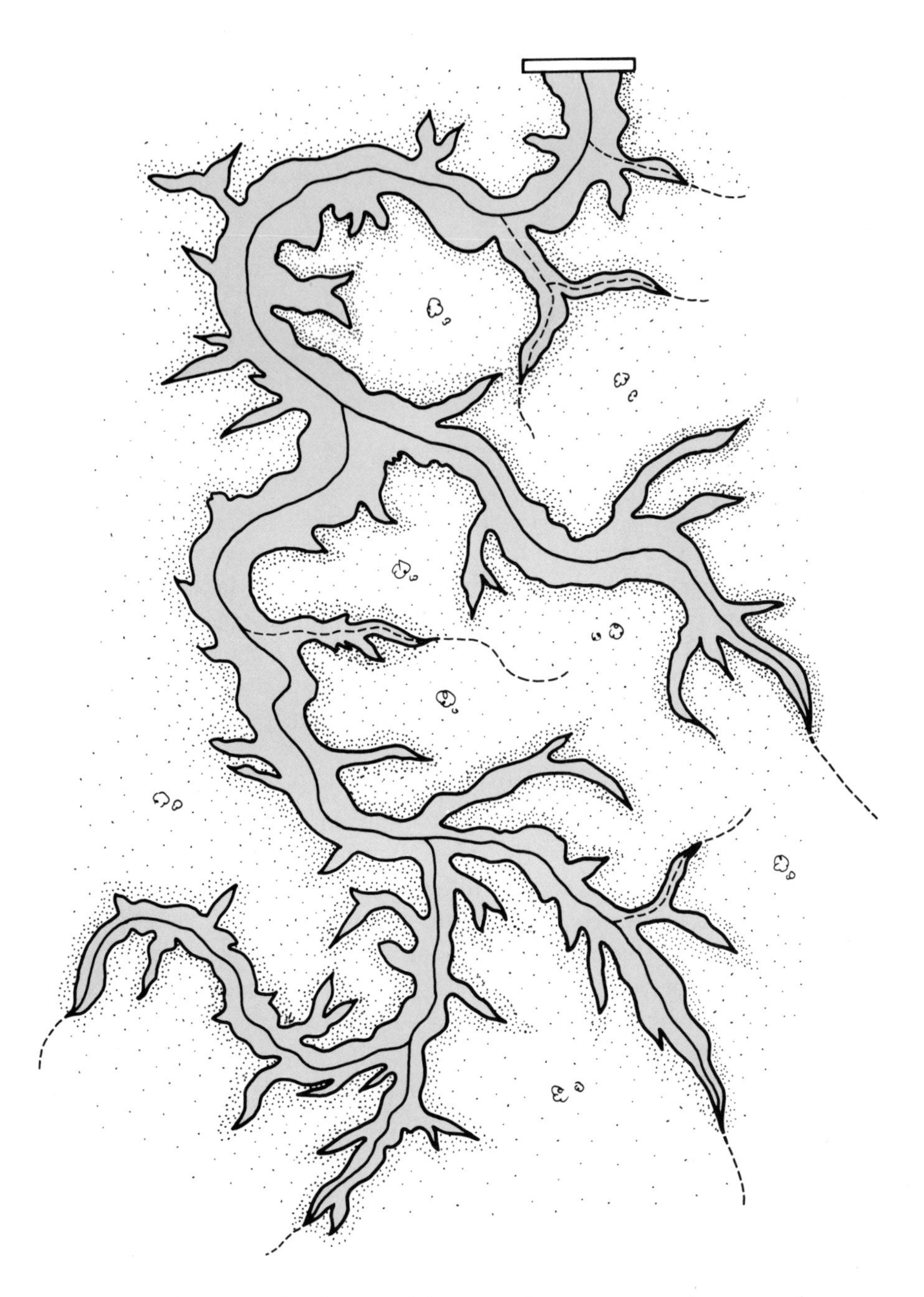

A representative canyonland reservoir has countless narrow creek arms and exceptionally clear water.

CHAPTER

7

How Bass React To Light

As the previous two chapters have illustrated, the behavior and location of bass are largely determined by the particular type of lake in which the fish are living. For example, bass inhabiting an early-stage natural mesotrophic lake will differ markedly in their lifestyles from bass residing in a manmade flatland reservoir. Yet even within specific lake categories, wide variations in water conditions will significantly alter the way bass live, move and feed.

On first inspection, two highland reservoirs may appear identical, but their resident bass populations may exhibit entirely different behavior patterns due to differences in the color, light penetration, oxygen saturation, and pH of the water, and the influence these factors have upon plant growth and the movements of baitfish.

Therefore, what I've said so far about bass behavior in different types of lakes should be looked upon merely as a broad overview. Now it's necessary to become intimately familiar with the water conditions existing in each lake you decide to work, as those specific conditions will determine the location of bass, and in turn the most productive approach to finding them. In this chapter we'll look at how bass react to light. And in the following three chapters we'll consider the effects of oxygen, pH, water color, temperature and general weather conditions on bass behavior.

The degree of light penetration into the depths of any lake or reservoir determines how deep bass will go to find sanctuary, how far they will retreat into the catacombs of thick cover, and to a certain extent how shallow they will move during the course of migrations. Obviously, penetration of sunlight varies from day to day as weather conditions change. It can even vary during a given day as the angle of sunlight striking the water changes. The color, or clarity, of the water also influences light penetration.

As mentioned earlier, because bass have fixed-pupil eyes they cannot accommodate to varying light intensities by contracting or dilating their pupils. Moreover, since they begin life as prey for larger species and eventually become predators themselves, they quickly become averse to bright light and illuminated places. This leaves bass with only two alternatives for locating hiding places: Find seclusion in heavy cover, or retreat into the depths. Since shallow-water, heavy-cover bassing is a specialized undertaking discussed in Chapter 14, this chapter focuses on lakes and reservoirs with at least moderately deep water. And in these types of waters, studies have shown that bass have such an aversion to bright light it may even override their survival instinct!

Studying Bass Reactions to Light

A number of techniques have been used to investigate the effects of light on bass movements. One early study was conducted in Lake Mead, a canyonland reservoir in Nevada, which has gin-clear, very deep, cover-free water. In this study, biologists donned scuba gear and took floodlights underwater in search of bass. They found one school in a sanctuary area about 45 feet deep, just off the edge of a drop-off which plummeted still further into the depths.

(Previous underwater encounters with bass and other fish, by the way, have shown that skindivers can often closely approach large fish underwater, and sometimes even touch them, without the fish registering alarm. They seem to just slowly mosey along, continuing about their normal activity. Poke a finger at them and they may dart a few feet away, only to swing about and return to the immediate vicinity.)

Anyway, when the bright floodlights were switched on in the Lake Mead study, the bass quickly dived for the darkness of the depths. The divers pursued them at a leisurely pace, and eventually the bass went so deep they entered the band of water known as the *hypolimnion,* where they began revealing signs of oxygen deprivation. In other words, they began to suffocate . . . any fate was acceptable, so long as they got away from that damned bright light!

Subsequent to this research, Buck Perry conducted similar studies in the southeastern states, lowering lights underwater and observing bass reactions. His conclusions were very much the same.

During these early studies on light penetration, however, the only type of instrument available for actually measuring light intensity underwater was designed for photographic use and required the user to go underwater to take readings. Therefore, fishermen who had accepted the idea that light penetration largely determined the depths at which bass would most frequently be caught began devising many crude approaches for evaluating underwater light intensity without having to submerge themselves. One such effort was simply to tie a white china cup (a variation of the limnologist's Secchi disc) to a line and lower it over the side of the boat into the depths. When the white cup disappeared from sight, the angler measured the amount of line which had been let out, doubled that figure, and then fished no shallower than that depth. (The measured distance was doubled because light not only had to penetrate through the water down to the cup but had to reflect off its shiny surface and bounce back an equal distance.) A similar technique, still in use today, is to lower a large, slow-sinking white plug into the water and measure the length of line at which it is no longer visible. Again, the measured distance is doubled to give the total depth that light penetrates.

An equally effective method is to measure the bottom depth, using a line with an attached weight, at the outside, deep-water edge of the weedline. Since vegetation will not grow where sunlight does not penetrate, this method gives the maximum depth of light penetration without having to determine when a cup or plug disappears from sight.

These rather crude attempts to measure underwater light intensities did not appeal much to Roland Martin, who for years was one of the most sought-after bass guides on the Santee–Cooper lakes in South Carolina. So Martin—convinced of the importance of light penetration in determining bass location—set about building the very first underwater light meter for use in bass fishing (it was never commercially manufactured, however).

The meter, which he nearly always carried around in a padded suitcase, consisted of a six-volt bulb and a cds light lamp cell, which were placed at opposite ends of a plastic tube that was shaded against extraneous light. The cds cell was connected to a milliammeter that registered the amount of light from the bulb reaching the cds cell through the water.

With this homemade invention, Martin then proceeded to conduct tests on 20 different lakes across the country, comparing light-penetration readings with the depths at which bass were found. The results were startling: If, for example, the degree of light penetration at various depths on any given day were the same at Table Rock Lake in Missouri and Sam Rayburn Reservoir in Texas, the bass in both lakes would find sanctuary at almost exactly the same depths. Further, the shallow-water levels they would move to during the course of a migration would also be approximately the same. These findings, of course, depended upon all other conditions (e.g., temperature, oxygen) being roughly the same.

Having long since accepted the basic tenet that light penetration strongly influences bass behavior, I was meanwhile poring over biology books and research studies, attempting to learn as much as possible about how bass perceive color, which is really only a combination of various wavelengths of light. But I was stymied in my efforts by the lack of a reliable, commercially available instrument that could be used for precisely measuring light underwater.

Fortunately, I was soon able to get further involved with the business of studying bass and their reaction to light as a result of a cooperative venture with an independent testing company in Tulsa, Oklahoma. The company, Fishmaster Products, Inc., was pioneering the development of a light meter for anglers called the Depth-o-Lite. I, in turn, did extensive testing and experimentation, revised some currently held beliefs about bass behavior, and then published my findings as a special feature in *Sports Afield* in early 1973.

The small, battery-operated, handheld Depth-o-Lite offered fantastic amounts of data previously unknown to the majority of this country's bass

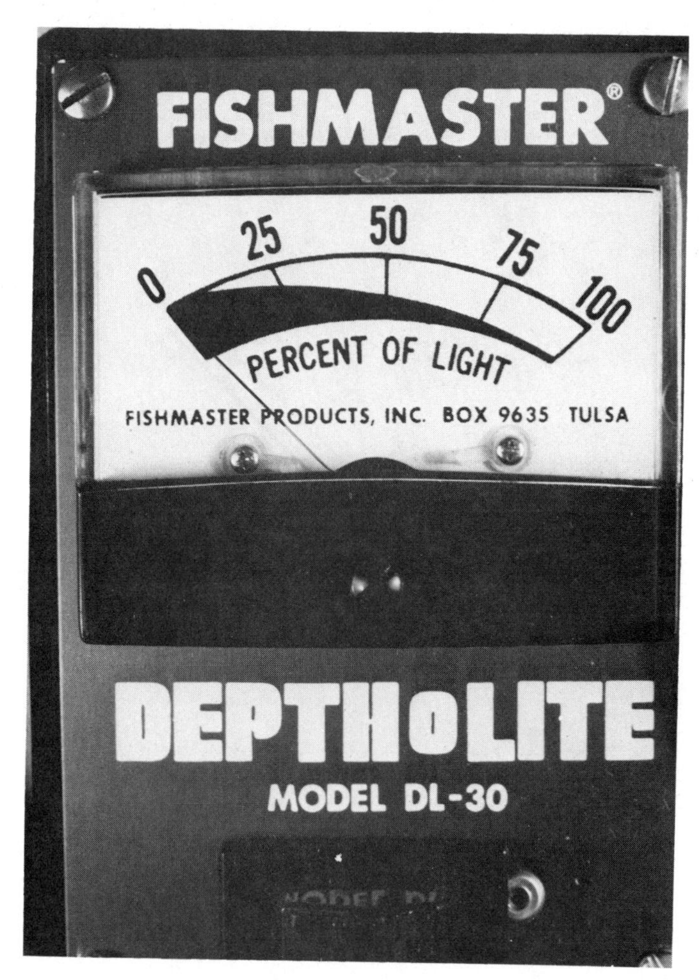

Sophisticated equipment for measuring underwater penetration of sunlight has yielded valuable insights about bass behavior. Although this particular model no longer is available, light-penetration theories still abound.

anglers. The unit looked much like a common water temperature gauge, with a wire that could be unwound from the frame as a sensor probe was lowered to various depths indicated by a color-coding system marked on the wire.

When the sensor is at various depths, the user pushes a readout button and the percentage of light penetrating to the probe registers on a meter. At a depth of one foot below the surface, for example, light penetration on a relatively bright day would be approximately 100 percent. As the depth increases, light penetration gradually diminishes until eventually there is almost total darkness.

Based on my tests with the Depth-o-Lite, I concluded that the depth at which light almost ceases to penetrate and nearly total darkness begins (i.e., light penetration of five to ten percent) generally is the *shallowest* depth at which bass will seek sanctuary, if the body of water goes that deep. How far bass will move inshore during a migration also depends in part on the degree of light penetration. But I am not yet ready to say that

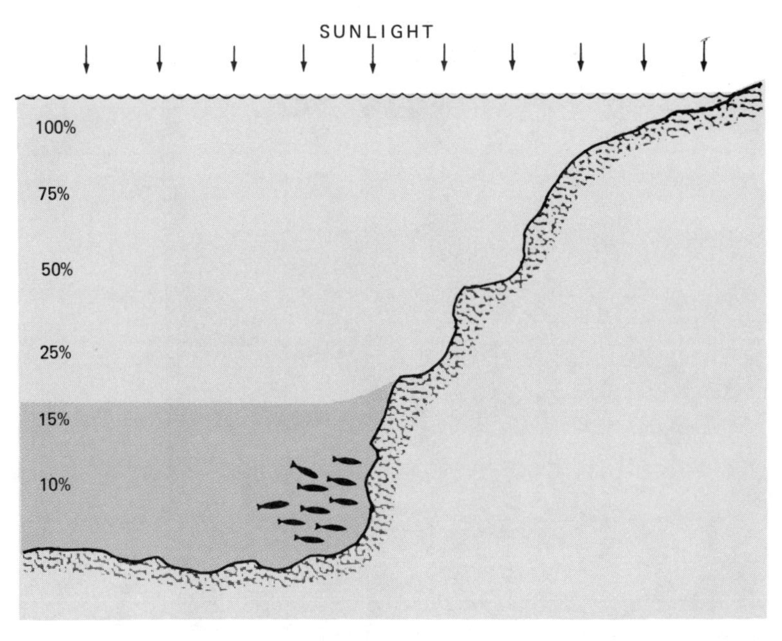

In the absence of heavy cover, sunlight forces schools of bass into the depths. Generally, the shallowest depth at which they'll seek sanctuary is where light penetration is between five and ten percent.

the fish will always move inshore until they reach a certain level of light penetration, whereupon they will go no farther; too many other factors govern their behavior at this stage, such as the cover they are moving into, overhead cloud cover, and water clarity. I will say, unequivocally, that in a majority of cases larger fish (three pounds and over) will rarely move as shallow as smaller fish.

Unfortunately, the Depth-o-Lite (and a similar, competitive meter later marketed by Garcia Corporation) was not commercially successful and has faded into obscurity, although a few tackleshops around the country may still have a few units in stock. The device was simply too far ahead of its time . . . too advanced to be fully appreciated by anglers 15 years ago, many of whom still weren't convinced that electronic depth sounders were anything more than expensive, unnecessary gadgets. Nevertheless, the light-penetration concepts that stimulated development of the Depth-o-Lite can help any angler to quickly home in upon bass no matter where he lives.

Conditions Affecting Light Penetration

The depths to which light will penetrate depends upon existing water color and weather conditions. On any given day when a high overhead sun is pounding the water, light rays will penetrate clear water more easily than muddy, stained or cloudy water. Fine particles of sediment in suspension not only block penetration of light rays but bounce them back toward the surface at various angles. A chop on the water caused by wind ruffling the surface will scatter the rays, too. Heavy cloud cover will screen out much of the light as well, and even rain, fog, smog, haze and similar air conditions will prevent sunlight from penetrating the water.

What is important to keep in mind, therefore, is that bass will seek sanctuary at different depths and travel to different locations when they migrate in response to changes in the amount of light penetrating the water that result from variations in the prevailing conditions. Moreover, those conditions that fishermen find most pleasant may not be the most favorable for bass.

Calm waters, a high overhead sun, no threatening cloud cover, and picnic-type air temperatures prompt anglers to flock to their favorite lakes in droves. The day is grand for fishing, or rather for the fishermen. But it is horrid for the fish! They will live and move at considerable depths, often making themselves inaccessible to the majority of anglers.

On the other hand, the most unpleasant days for fishermen are usually the best days for bass and bass fishing. A dark, overcast sky with wind ruffling the water surface and perhaps a light rain falling leads to greatly

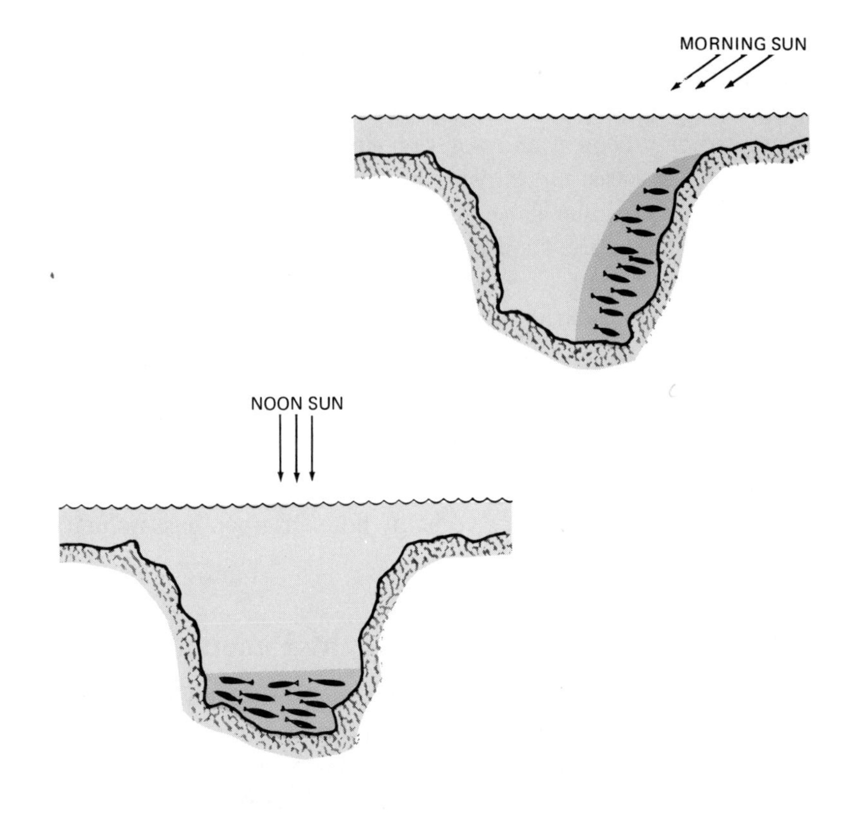

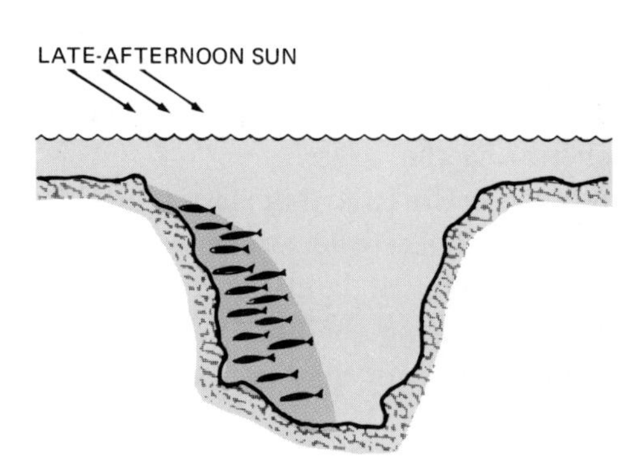

This side view of a river channel on the bottom of a flatland reservoir demonstrates how bass change locations as the angle of the sun changes. During midsummer, when fishing the channel, you'd obviously want to work the eastern side in the morning, then come back along the western edge in late afternoon.

reduced light penetration. This causes bass to seek sanctuary at somewhat shallower depths, and when they move they will often do so upon very shallow structures. The fish are also likely to be highly aggressive and responsive to lures. The paradox is that under such favorable fishing conditions, you're likely to have the whole lake to yourself.

In addition to the general weather conditions, the movement of the sun during the day affects light penetration because the sun's rays strike the water at varying angles. During the morning and evening, light penetration is considerably less on the side of a lake closest to the sun than in the middle or on the opposite side. Thus, migrating bass will move into shallower waters along the sun-side shoreline during these hours.

An obvious strategy suggested by this preference is to fish likely structures on the far eastern side of a lake in the morning and the structures on the far western side during the late afternoon. Should you inadvertently reverse this fishing strategy, during both morning and late-afternoon fishing, the bass would be on very deep structures when they migrated, and your chances of bringing in a good string would be substantially reduced.

This approach can even be applied to fishing bodies of water that do not have significant depths. Let's say you're fishing a flatland reservoir during midsummer and you automatically know schooling bass will be relating to the main river channel. Since the channel may be as much as 100 feet wide, you have to decide to fish one side or the other. Understandably, you'd want to probe the eastern edge in the morning, and come back in the opposite direction along the western edge in late afternoon. Right? Right!

CHAPTER

8

Oxygen, pH and Water Color

Measuring Oxygen Levels

One of bass fishing's most recent technological adjuncts began about a decade ago when an Austin, Texas, scientist invented the first small-scale oxygen monitor for anglers. His name was Dr. Martin Venneman and his brainstorm was dubbed the Sentry Oxygen Monitor.

When I tested the equipment for a special report in *Sports Afield* in 1974, I found the Sentry advanced in concept and spectacular in its accuracy, and I was convinced its use would quickly spread to all corners of bassdom. It was a good guess because within a few months after my article was published, three respected manufacturers of fishing tackle had launched major research projects to develop and market oxygen-measuring equipment of their own.

Venneman's inventiveness was spurred by the results of his extensive testing of numerous waterways with much larger and more sophisticated equipment. He discovered that "at any given time from 50 to 80 percent of the water in any lake does not contain enough oxygen to support fish life!" Shortly thereafter, he began work on a scaled-down version of the larger equipment he'd been using so that anglers could take advantage of his findings.

I'll begin this discussion of how oxygen monitors work and why a knowledge of what I call oxygen-structure fishing is important to anglers with a quote from my original *Sports Afield* article: "Oxygen-monitoring equipment does not guarantee you will consistently be able to find or catch bass. It does guarantee you will not waste one minute of time fishing where no fish can possibly survive." In other words, oxygen evaluation is one more technique the seasoned bass angler can use to systematically eliminate barren or unproductive water. All efforts may then be concentrated in those areas most likely to contain bass.

It should also be mentioned that bass living in rivers and streams are seldom influenced by changing oxygen levels. The ever-present current in such flowing waters generally makes any unfavorable changes in oxygen levels so short-lived that they have no effect upon the bass and do not force them to radically alter their habits or move to other areas.

Oxygen evaluation is most useful to anglers on larger lakes and reservoirs where miles of shoreline twist and turn to form numerous channels,

Using an oxygen monitor does not guarantee you'll find or catch fish. It does guarantee you won't waste time where there are no bass!

bays, coves and other such places which may be subject to wide variations in water temperature, light penetration and, most important, oxygen levels.

All bass species (indeed, every species of fish) must have enough dissolved oxygen in the water around them in order to live. Although bass are quite tolerant (within limits) and very adaptable to changes in many environmental variables, their requirement for minimum oxygen levels is absolute—no compromise, no tolerance, no adaptation. Bass absolutely must have certain levels of oxygen or they will be faced with an immediate alternative: Either move out of the area altogether, or perish!

Optimum oxygen levels for most bass species range from 5 to 13 parts per million (ppm), though they highly prefer and will seek out waters with 9 to 12 ppm oxygen. Of the four bass species covered in this book, small-mouths are an exception to the rule: They prefer waters somewhat less saturated with oxygen, in the range of 3 to 8 ppm. Bass of any species that remain in a lake area where the oxygen level is below 3 ppm will die of asphyxiation. And if they remain in areas with more than 13 ppm, they will experience symptoms of oxygen poisoning.

You may have already witnessed numerous instances of oxygen depletion but never been aware of exactly what was happening. For example, baitfish in a minnow bucket, after several hours, often begin coming to the surface to gulp air. The same can occur with bass kept in a closed live well. In both cases, the fish have simply depleted the oxygen supply in the water and come to the surface in search of oxygen. Adding fresh water or turning on an aerator solves the problem.

Oxygen levels may also become depleted in large sections of lakes and reservoirs, particularly during the summer and fall months. Such reductions result from abrupt changes in barometric pressure, underwater "density" currents, wind direction and velocity, and other acts of Mother Nature. These forces are strong enough to deplete the oxygen even in vegetation-filled areas. The effects of oxygen depletion or oversaturation may last for only a day or two, or they may last for several weeks. This is why anglers should frequently take oxygen readings in those lake sections they fish most regularly, especially if they are experiencing difficulty finding bass.

Most oxygen meters available today are small, battery-operated, hand-held devices. They have an oxygen-sensing probe attached to a metered line that is lowered into the water to various depths. When a button is pushed, a small dial with a needle-type gauge registers the parts per million of oxygen at the depth where the probe is suspended.

To reap the greatest benefit from an oxygen monitor, you should spend a little time, at the very beginning of the first day on the water, determining oxygen levels in various portions of a lake or reservoir. Motor back and forth across the lake, taking oxygen readings here and there and jotting down the numbers on your contour map. Now you're ready to begin fishing, searching for good structure, but only in those areas known to have oxygen levels suitable for bass. You've completely eliminated from consideration those areas found to be incapable of supporting fish life, regardless of how "bassy" they may look.

On subsequent days on the water, you need only quickly reconfirm the oxygen levels at your favorite fishing locations. If something has happened to radically change the oxygen level, you can be pretty sure that the bass have left the area—and so should you. All in all, then, the oxygen monitor is a time-saving boon that can greatly hasten your initial search for good bass structure and tip you off when a once productive site has lost its attraction for bass.

While surveying a body of water for optimum oxygen levels, you

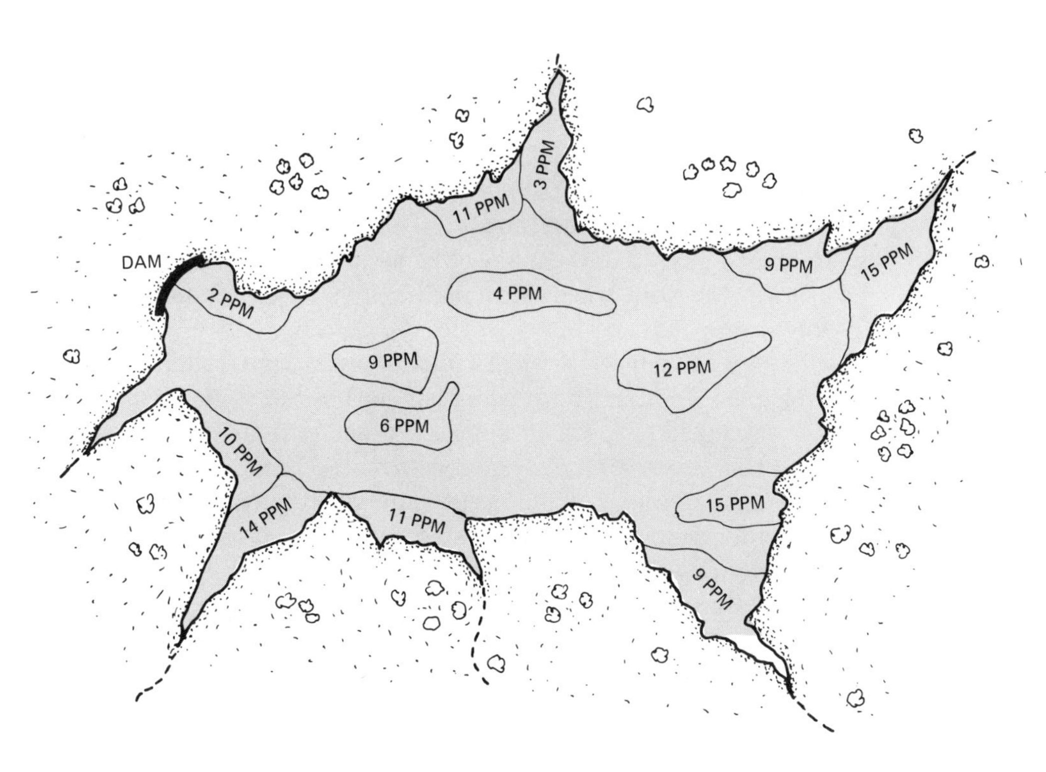

Bass periodically change locations so they always are in water saturated with 5 to 13 ppm of dissolved oxygen. By finding areas on your map likely to hold bass, depending upon the season, then recording oxygen levels, you know which places to fish and which to avoid.

shouldn't ignore the effect of light penetration and suitable structure in determining which locations will draw and hold bass at particular times of year. The point to be made here is that even when light and structure (and perhaps other features as well) are ideal for bass, if oxygen levels are not suitable, an area will be as barren of fish as the rafters in your garage.

To make this perfectly clear, let's look at the hypothetical example of an angler who is fishing a highland reservoir that has an off-structure in the form of a midlake bar. It's a very long bar that runs from relatively shallow water to very deep water—a perfect migration structure—and this bar is the midsummer home of a school of largemouths. They stay in their sanctuary just off the end of the bar where the water is deepest (let's say 50 feet) and several times a day they migrate up the structure toward its shallower portion where the water is 12 feet deep. The bar possesses a number of rock piles at scattered intervals; these serve as the breaks which the fish follow when they migrate. The angler lucks out and takes several nice bass at 12 feet deep during one of the school's migrations. This is understandable, because before fishing the area he took an oxygen reading and discovered the shallow end of the bar to possess 11 ppm of dissolved oxygen. That night, at home, he listens to the wind howling outside; the following morning he unsuccessfully fishes the 12-foot level of the bar for three hours without a strike. He should have taken an oxygen reading first! The wind may have pushed the oxygen-rich water farther offshore or rearranged it in some other manner. Perhaps the 12-foot level now possesses only 4 ppm of oxygen. Since the bar is quite long, the fish may still be using it. But now, when they migrate, they may be coming only to the 20-foot level.

Although the subject of water temperature is discussed in detail in the next chapter, I should note here that during the summer most of the deepest lakes and reservoirs become separated into three distinct layers of water. These are commonly referred to as the *epilimnion* (upper layer), *thermocline* (middle layer), and *hypolimnion* (bottom layer).

The hypolimnion, the layer of water just above the lake floor in the very deepest sections, is generally (there are exceptions, discussed in the next chapter) completely void of oxygen. The upper two layers are most often oxygen-saturated, and temperature variations and other factors determine the depths at which these two layers form. Therefore, for the sake of simplicity in this chapter, I'll consider the upper two, oxygen-rich layers of water as one, called the *oxycline.* An advanced angler consequently uses his oxygen monitor in conjunction with his water temperature gauge to determine the exact depth of the oxycline, for he knows that if he fishes below this level he will be in the hypolimnion, where no fish can survive.

One condition all anglers should be on the lookout for is called an

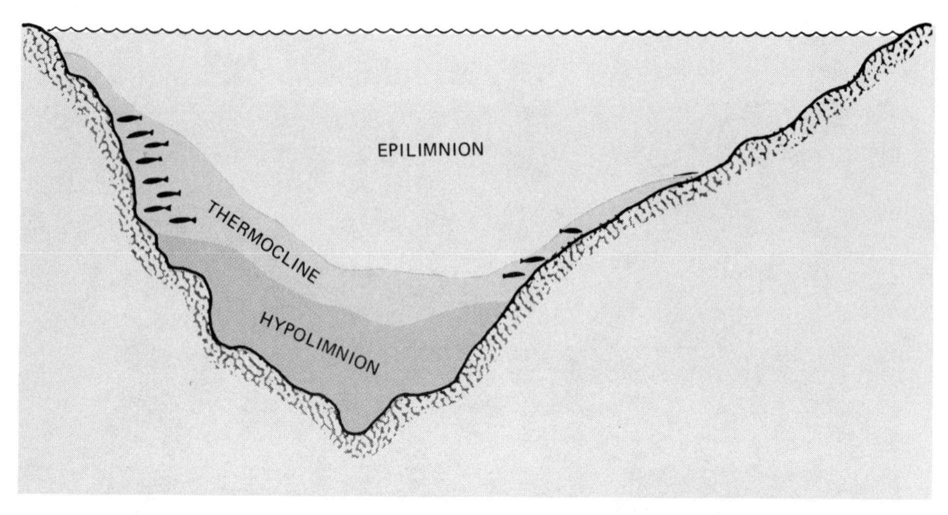

Many bodies of water stratify during the summer but the resulting layers of water are never uniform. They vary in shape and depth, depending upon wind and wave action. The thermocline, due to its colder temperature, contains more dissolved oxygen than the upper epilimnion. The hypolimnion contains so little oxygen bass cannot live there.

oxygen inversion, which is the brief formation of a third layer of water *below* the oxygen-void hypolimnion. An oxygen-inversion layer is usually high in oxygen (8 to 13 ppm) and is most often found near a sharp drop-off or in association with underground springs. Bass may be trapped in an inversion pocket, usually in a fairly confined area. Until wind and wave action cause the inversion layer to dissipate, the bass can go absolutely nowhere, because venturing out of the pocket would mean entering the oxygen-void hypolimnion and perishing. That is something they will not do under normal circumstances.

Only a limited number of inversions occur at any one time in a body of water, and their existence is usually brief. But if you stumble onto such a situation, you may experience the fastest fishing of your life, literally catching a fish on every cast until your arm turns to rubber or until you spook the school. Even if the fish do turn off, however, rest them for a short while and you can usually return to where you left off and begin catching them again.

The one time you don't have to worry much about oxygen levels is during the spring when numerous feeder creeks and tributaries continually pour in large quantities of fresh oxygen-rich runoff water. Perhaps this

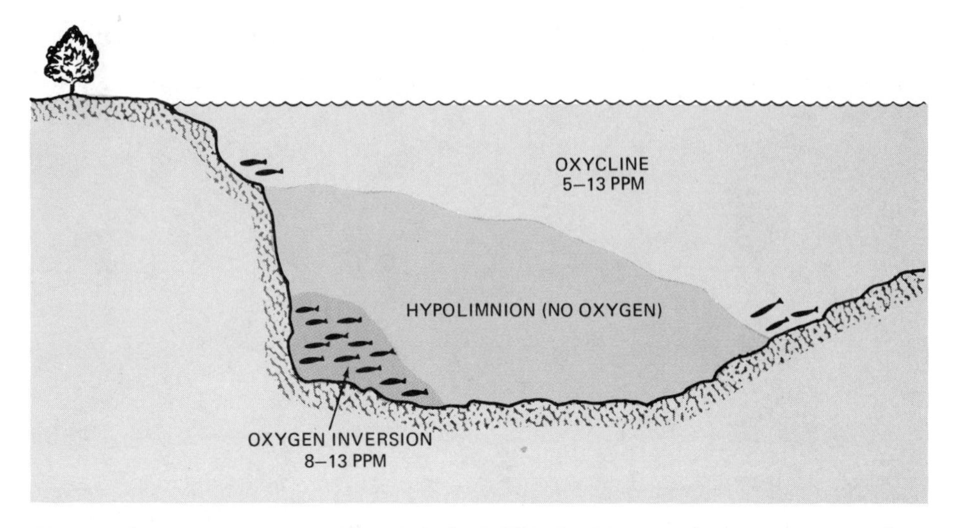

Here is what an oxygen inversion might look like. In this case, the bass are trapped in a confined region, a situation that can offer the fastest action imaginable.

is one of nature's safeguards, assuring that bass will not be forced periodically to abandon their nests. But about the time the spawn is ended and the body of water is beginning to settle down (or complete its spring *turnover,* which is discussed in the next chapter), check the batteries in your oxygen-monitoring equipment. From this time of year through the remaining seasons, frequent evaluation of oxygen levels can play an important role in your level of bassing success.

Try a pH Monitor

The pH of a solution is a measure of its acidity or alkalinity. The pH scale runs from 0 to 14, with a measurement of 7 considered neutral; anything lower than 7 is acidic and anything higher than 7 is alkaline, or basic.

Like all animals, fish must maintain a certain chemical balance in their blood and body fluids if they are to survive. Since the pH of their blood is slightly alkaline—about 7.6—it is not surprising that bass seek out water with approximately the same pH. When the water pH is near this value, bass are best able to withstand stress and utilize the oxygen in the water properly. This is not to say bass will travel extraordinary distances to find an ideal pH; the species are very adaptable and can survive in water with a pH ranging from 6.7 to 9.6. However, given any choice, if there is water within their immediate region that has a pH of 7.5 to 7.9, that is where bass will be.

Dr. Loren Hill—inventor of the pH Monitor—is most responsible for the latest bass-fishing craze sweeping the nation. Many guides and tournament pros are convinced that pH is the *singlemost important water condition to know when looking for bass.*

In 1979, Dr. Loren Hill, chairman of the Zoology Department at the University of Oklahoma, developed the first pH meter that could be used by anglers to evaluate water conditions in their favorite lakes. Dubbed the pH Monitor, the small gauge can be hand-held or mounted on a boat console. A probe is then lowered on a wire to various depths, with the pH of the water at those depths registering on the gauge's calibrated face.

After the pH Monitor was first introduced nationwide, anglers searching for bass generally tested the water in various regions and then fished only those places where the pH was the optimum 7.5 to 7.9. That is still an excellent approach for finding large areas where fishing success is likely to be much better than elsewhere. Since then, however, Hill has pioneered an even more refined approach to locating bass that is more in line with bass movements on structure and how shallow (or deep) those movements may take place. Furthermore, it's his opinion that an optimum pH is more important to bass than water temperature, oxygen or light penetration. Only after bass have located themselves in water with an optimum pH do other water conditions take over and more specifically determine their behavior.

Hill refers to this new breakthrough as a *pH profile*; learning how to profile a lake is fast, easy and insightful. First, pick an area of the lake you wish to fish, based on an educated guess as to where bass should be at that time of the year. Then, lower the probe of your pH meter into the water; take the first reading at the surface and subsequent readings at one-foot intervals all the way to the bottom. After recording these values, you'll discover a *pH breakline* at some particular depth—that is, a point where

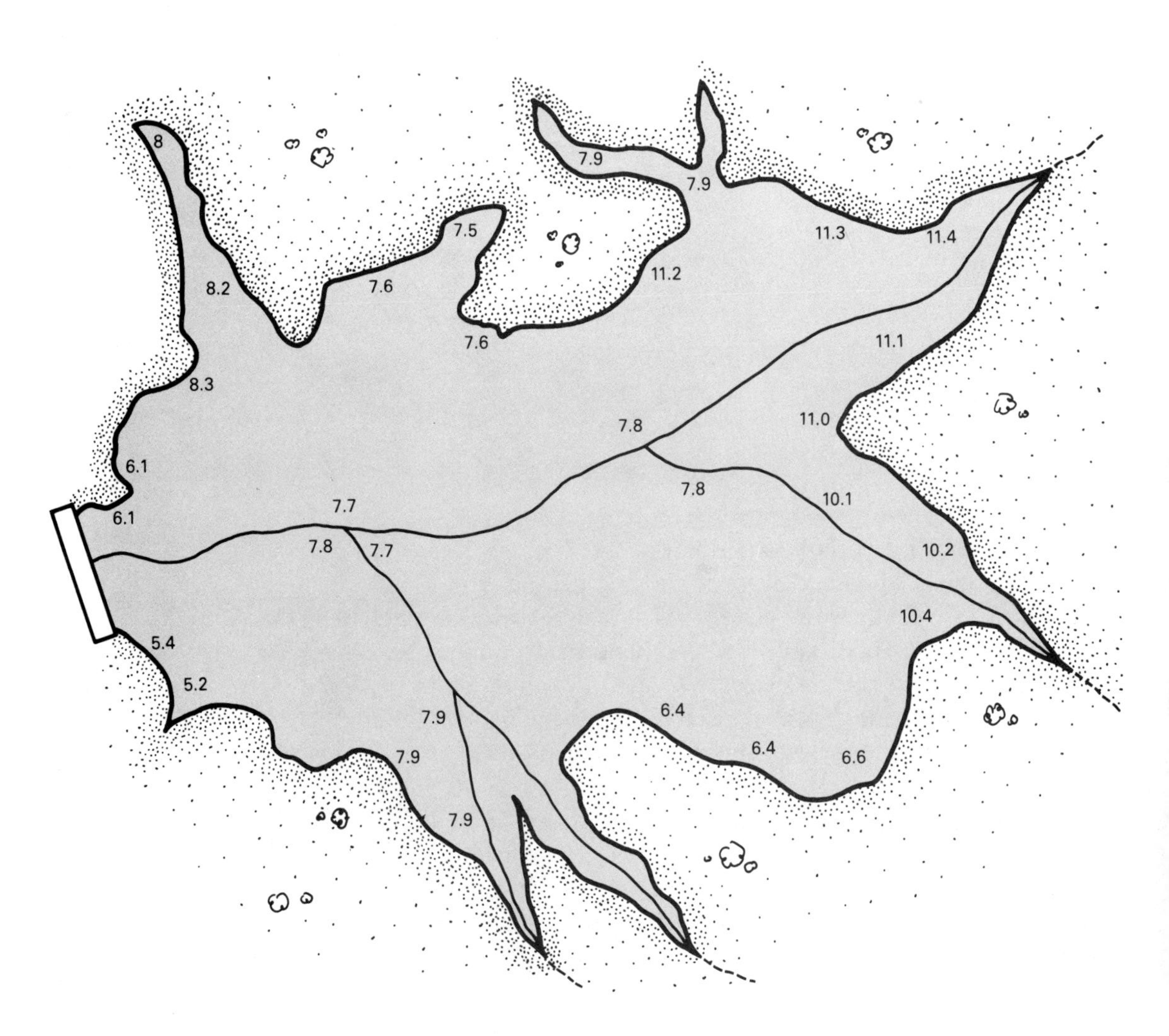

By taking random pH readings and jotting them on your map, it's easy to home in upon specific locations that are most attractive to bass. In this particular case, the pH is ideal where feeder stream channels dump into the main riverbed. If the time is midsummer, this information could be the most important clue to catching your bass.

the pH changes rapidly. For example, readings may fluctuate back and forth by one-tenth of a unit, and then suddenly, at some specific depth, you'll note a full one-unit change in pH. (This change may not seem significant, but in actuality it is. The pH scale is logarithmic, so pH 8 is ten times more alkaline than pH 7, and pH 9 is 100 times more alkaline than pH 7.) Table 8–1 shows an actual pH profile; note the sharp break in pH between water depths of four and five feet.

Hill is firmly convinced that in any lake the pH breakline is the depth at which a majority of bass will be the most active. Theoretically, therefore, if the pH breakline happens to be six feet deep in the particular region you're fishing, working that specific depth "should" reward you with far more bass than working significantly shallower or deeper water.

Like oxygen levels, the pH can vary widely in various locations of a lake. Furthermore, the pH may change on an almost day-to-day basis. Rainfall is one of the most common causes of pH changes, especially in many northeastern states where "acid rain," with a pH as low as 5, is prevalent. In other regions, even the runoff water after a rain may cause a pH shift, depending upon the acidity or alkalinity of the surrounding soils. Other things that periodically cause pH changes include photosynthesis by plant life in the water, decay of plant and animal matter, and even foreign substances (e.g., sewage or chemicals) released into the water.

At the present time, the only commercial pH device designed for fishermen is the pH Monitor, available from the Lakes Illustrated Company (Route 3, Mt. Vernon, MO 65712). More still needs to be learned about behavioral reactions of bass to pH changes, but even at this point I'm convinced a pH Monitor will greatly help anglers catch more fish.

Consider Water Color

The color, or clarity, of the water in any given lake or reservoir always has an important influence upon the success of a bass angler. It determines, in part, how deep bass seek sanctuary, how shallow they travel during migrations, the ease (or difficulty) they have in capturing food or striking at lures, and subsequently which tackle may be most appropriate.

Stable water colors, which remain pretty much the same year-round, result from the chemistry of the water and the physical composition of the bottom materials in a particular lake. In the rockbound, infertile natural lakes of the far North and the canyonland reservoirs of the desert Southwest, the water is typically quite clear. Conversely, southern flatland reservoirs, which are nearly always highly fertile, may have a variety of water colors ranging from cloudy green (the result of algae bloom) to brown/black or stained (the result of tannin being released into the water by decomposing brush, felled trees and standing timber). The presence of certain types of clay or iron ore deposits may leave the water with a distinct red or rust color. Very shallow waters with soft mire bottoms (e.g., eutrophic natural lakes) may take on a muddy brown color throughout the year.

Unstable water colors, which often persist only for a short time, may catch the angler entirely off guard. These are caused by high winds, heavy rains, water runoff from higher ground or increased current velocities all of which roil the bottom sediment. Unstable water colors are nearly always muddy brown or cloudy.

Although some water colors are not ideal for fishing, an anxious angler need never cancel a fishing trip because of the water color. He may, however, in the case of unstable water colors, have to use other angling

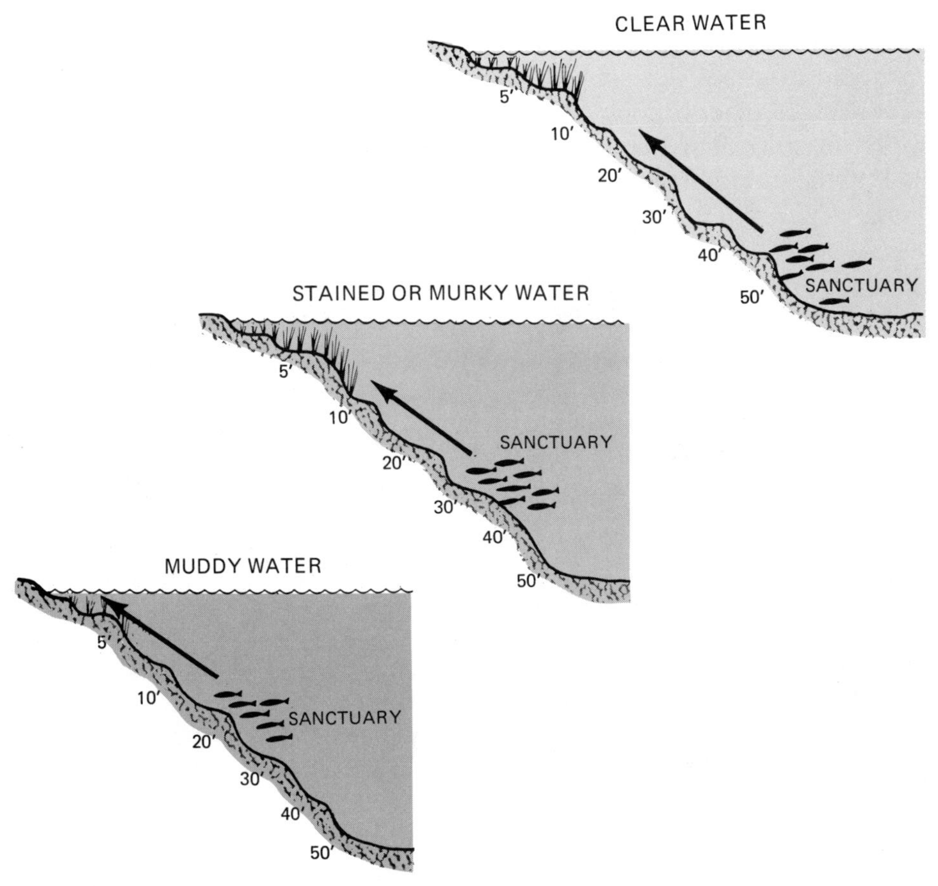

Water colors may be either stable or unstable. In either case, the color of the water commonly influences how deep bass will seek sanctuary, and how shallow they will travel during migrations.

strategies than he originally had planned. I have taken big bass from water of all colors—from those so clear I could see a dime on the lake floor at 25 feet, to those so muddy the lake looked like a giant chocolate milkshake. But the colors I consider ideal are those that are at neither end of the clear/muddy spectrum but somewhere in between.

Slightly murky, milky, or stained waters are probably the very best. Under these conditions bass are not overly spooky, an angler can use heavy tackle if existing cover conditions warrant such gear, and he can expect bass to migrate to quite shallow levels.

Sparkling clear water with a preponderance of heavy cover is the most difficult of all to fish. In such water, bass generally stay quite deep, they migrate shorter distances and for only brief periods, they are very restless and uneasy because of the bright illumination, and contact with them can usually be made only through the use of cobweb lines and small lures.

It's usually in an angler's best interest to eliminate from consideration those locations in a body of water that do not exhibit water colors favorable for fishing. And he should do this before he ever slips his boat into the water and begins searching for suitable structure or evaluating other water conditions. Fortunately, a large percentage of the lakes and reservoirs in this country are so enormous there is rarely a time when an angler cannot find the exact water color he wishes to fish in.

One way to find ideal water colors is by simply driving around a lake. If the lake is too large to make this practical (some reservoirs are more than 60 miles in length), the next best bet is to inquire at a local marina or fishing camp. The operators of these facilities and their employees continuously keep tabs on water conditions. This initial investigation on your part may later save countless hours of randomly searching for good water coloration by boat. But keep in mind that while water color is usually stable for several days or perhaps even weeks at a time, it can change overnight.

When winds lash your favorite lake and heavy rains fall, the shallower headwater areas will be the first to show a muddy appearance. Better-colored water can usually be found if you move farther down the lake toward the tailwaters, as the deeper water near the dam is seldom affected by brief changes in the weather.

One prime place to find bass after torrential rainstorms is some type of "edge" where you can see a distinct change in the water color, usually where muddy water adjoins clear water. This may be along the main banks of the lake, several yards out from the shoreline, or it may be where a small rushing feeder stream dumps into the lake. In either case, the newly created edge is a type of structure along which bass like to position themselves, gaining an advantage over baitfish that suddenly find themselves exposed and in the open.

TABLE 8–1. pH Profile, Jeremy Creek Arm, Acton Lake

Depth (feet)	*pH*		*Depth (feet)*	*pH*
Surface	7.9		7 feet	6.9
1 foot	7.9		8 feet	6.9
2 feet	7.9		9 feet	6.9
3 feet	7.8		10 feet	6.9
			11 feet	6.8
4 feet	7.8	} pH Breakline	12 feet	6.8
5 feet	7.1	}	13 feet	6.7
6 feet	7.1		14 feet	6.7

After a torrential rainstorm, an excellent place to find bass is along a water color "edge," where clear water meets cloudy water.

CHAPTER

9

Water Temperature: Key To Bass Behavior

The lake types and water conditions examined in the past few chapters are largely responsible for determining *where* bass are most likely to be located within a given body of water. But once you've found the critters, you've got to get them to chomp down on a hook. So, from here on, we're going to be looking at the many aspects of actually "catching" bass. And it is *water temperature* that governs their activity levels and the types of behavior they can be expected to exhibit.

In this chapter I'll discuss—and refute—three bass-fishing tenets that a majority of anglers have accepted as gospel for decades. One states that the hypolimnion is devoid of oxygen. This may be true at certain times of year, but at other times the hypolimnion may actually have higher oxygen levels than the other water layers. A second fallacy is that bass seek out certain water temperatures where they feel most comfortable. This is pure bunk. And still another claims that water temperature always determines how deep bass will go. This, too, is entirely untrue. All of these myths, I'm sorry to say, have been and still are given big play in the outdoor magazines.

Early-Season Lake Choices

The month was March and the location was Burr Oak Lake in southeastern Ohio. Sleet-driven winds were tormenting me and my partner Billy Williamson, who was a study in contradictions. One moment he'd be gazing forlornly across the slate-gray water where cakes of ice danced like an armada of white ships, his teeth chattering and his nose dripping. Yet now and then he'd peer over the sidewall of our aluminum boat and jiggle the cord stringer. That would immediately bring a splashing ruckus from

Here, a diehard bass angler's attire leaves no doubt as to how cold it is. The day before this picture was taken by the author, cakes of ice still floated on the lake. Most fishermen don't realize how long it takes the water to warm in spring.

the two 5-pound bass we had on the snaps and in an instant Bill's dejected frown would turn into the widest, warmest grin imaginable.

"This is what Webster would call a bittersweet experience," my pal then remarked. "Half of me is pleading to go home to defrost, yet the other half is calling me a dummy for even considering throwing in the towel."

Across America's heartland countless other anglers face the same quandary every spring and, of course, it is indeed possible to get out too early. I'll never forget the time spring-fishing fever manifested itself to such extremes that my eyes became glassy and my speech slurred. An hour later I was poised in the bow of my boat, wielding an oar to break through shoreline ice in an attempt to reach open water. After six hours without a nibble, I gave up the vigil and charted a nonstop course for the nearest cafe and a hot bowl of soup. Other times I've seen unusually warm, shirtsleeve weather in March, verily raced to some lake or another, and still scored ZIP.

The thing most anglers fail to realize about early-spring fishing is that no matter what the weather is like, water temperatures rise only one degree at a time—over agonizingly long weeks. And it is water temperature, not air temperature, that reigns supreme over early-season fish behavior. Even after the last of winter's ice has disappeared and been followed by a full week in the seventies, the water temperature may still be only around 38° or 40°.

This very slow warming of the water is known as the *spring turnover,* but this is an erroneous term. After the sun's rays melt the previous winter's ice, they next begin warming the surface water. Since this warm surface water has a lighter density than the much colder water directly beneath, it stays right on top. The only way deeper water is able to warm up is by *conduction,* the downward transfer of heat from one water molecule to the next. As we all know, heat would much rather rise than fall, and this is the reason why the water takes much longer to warm in the spring than it takes to cool during the fall. So the term *spring turnover* is really a misnomer, because the water doesn't really turn over as it does later in the year.

It stands to reason you shouldn't expect to find bass mauling lures or engaging in chase-and-catch feeding behavior this early in the season, and don't expect to fill a washtub with a lot of fish. The cold water has caused their body metabolisms to slow to a crawl over previous months, making them very lethargic. Anglers can indeed catch bass in early spring, but to cash in on the action it is necessary to select the right lake, then fish in the right places.

The best possible choice is a small lake that's quite shallow, as it will tend to absorb maximum quantities of sunlight during the day. On a shallow lake, the wind also does a better job of mixing the warm air with the cold water, raising the water's temperature more quickly than generally occurs on a large, deep lake. In fact, this phenomenon holds so consistently true that in states located north of the Mason-Dixon line I often spend all of February and March working the farmpond circuit. Then I switch to either a eutrophic natural lake or a flatland reservoir, reserving my mesotrophic lakes, highland reservoirs and canyonland reservoirs for much later in the year. Obviously, all of this is not such a critical concern for anglers living in the mid-South states, and it's rarely of any concern at all for those residing in the deep South.

If you have more than one lake to choose from, remember that a clear lake will undoubtedly warm much faster than one of the same size that contains off-colored water. It's a simple physical principle that sunlight can more easily penetrate clear water than milky, sandy or muddy water.

After you've selected a small, shallow, clear-water lake as the best prospect for early-season bass fishing, next give careful thought to where in the lake the bass are likely to be most active. Typically, the tailwaters of lakes and reservoirs, near the dam, are much deeper than elsewhere and therefore the slowest to warm. So begin exploring the headwaters, or upper end of the lake, where feeder tributaries and creek arms first give birth to the shallow but ever-enlarging lake system.

In early spring, there's no need to be on the water at the crack of dawn, nor much to be gained by fishing until evening darkness sets in. Later in the season, the hours of dawn and dusk are indeed prime fishing times because of reduced sunlight penetration. But shortly after the ice melts in early spring, just the opposite applies. Now, after a long winter of relative dormancy, periods of direct midday sunlight, for reasons only the bass can explain, seem to offer the best action. So concentrate your fishing efforts during the hours of 10 o'clock in the morning until about 4 o'clock in the afternoon.

Another key to successful early-season fishing is to work the shorelines, bays and coves situated along the north and northwestern banks of the lake. These regions are sheltered from the prevailing wind and therefore are protected against winter's last bitter assaults. Also, north and northwestern banks receive longer periods of daily sunlight exposure than southern and southeastern banks and this, too, accounts for water temperatures that are remarkably warmer—perhaps by as much as 12°—than those in other portions of a lake.

In some cases, targeting a specific bass species can be the secret that adds more weight to your stringer early in the season. This is the strategy Bob Parkinson and I employ when we make our annual early-spring pilgrimage to lakes in the White River drainage on the Missouri–Arkansas border. There, Bull Shoals, Table Rock, Taneycomo and Norfolk contain all three bass species; before casting the first lure we take water temperature readings to determine which species is likely to prove the most cooperative.

A dashboard-mounted water temperature gauge of the type shown here, which gives constant readouts, can be used to find the warmest regions of a lake, which usually are the best for early-season fishing.

For example, if the temperature is around 45°, we know we'll do best trying for smallmouths. If the water is around 55°, we know smallmouths are gradually going off their feed in preparation for spawning, so we try for spotted bass. If the water is around 60°, we know smallmouths are actually spawning and spotted bass are beginning to go off feed, which leaves largemouths as the target species. In a nutshell, just remember that smallmouths are the first to become active in early spring, followed by spotted bass, and then largemouths.

Keeping warm is essential to successful early-spring fishing. It constantly amazes me how warm it can be on dry land and yet how the temperature feels as much as 25° cooler when you're on the water. With a few minor exceptions, I dress for a spring-fishing outing exactly the same as I do when I plan to sit in a duck blind or maintain a long watch on a deer stand. But, above all, *perseverance* is the keynote: Until the water temperature rises still higher a slow, methodical approach over long hours is imperative.

Summer's Elusive Thermocline

The warming water of spring triggers the spawning behavior of bass, as described in detail in Chapter 2. And the water will continue to warm through the summer months to the point where surface temperatures may often approximate air temperatures, soaring as high as 80° or even 90° in certain areas of the country.

As the top layer of water warms much faster than the deeper, colder water, a point is reached at which the transfer of heat downward from one molecule to the next ceases. This leads to the formation of the three layers of water mentioned in the last chapter: the *hypolimnion* at the very bottom, the *thermocline* in the middle, and the *epilimnion* on top. Sometimes these layers are well defined, but usually they appear only as fluctuating zones.

Water stratification and the resulting formation of a thermocline do not occur in every natural lake or manmade reservoir. Usually these phenomena take place only in deep, clear-water lakes and reservoirs at least 30 or 40 feet deep. Thus, summer stratification is more characteristic of mesotrophic natural lakes, highland reservoirs and canyonland reservoirs than other waters.

In those shallow lakes and reservoirs with an average depth of perhaps no more than 15 feet, where thermoclines do not form, heavy cover usually screens out some of the sun's penetrating rays, so water temperatures in the shallows don't become exceedingly high. In midsummer, for example, the water temperature under heavily matted lily pads or hyacinth may be as much as 15° cooler than that of adjacent water of the same depth where there is no vegetation.

In waters in which stratification takes place, the thermocline is the middle layer of water that separates the upper warm water from the lower, very cold water. Within this layer, or zone, the temperature changes rapidly, often as much as 0.5° F or more with each foot of depth. Anglers can easily determine the upper and lower limits of the thermocline in a lake with a handheld, battery-operated water temperature gauge, which has a sensing probe attached to a metered line. Table 9–1 records the actual water temperatures in Burr Oak Lake in southeastern Ohio. In a stratified lake such as Burr Oak, a sharp decrease in temperature over a relatively short distance indicates the location of the thermocline. The data reveal a 10-foot thermocline from 20 to 30 feet deep; note how the water temperature abruptly drops 13° within this narrow depth range.

It should be repeated, however, that the upper and lower limits of a thermocline often are not constant but rather may drift upward or downward from day to day, and even from hour to hour, during the summer.

Most thermoclines average 7 to 10 feet thick, are found at depths of 20 to 35 feet, and range in temperature from 55° to 70°. However, this is only the norm. At Lewis–Smith Reservoir in Alabama, where the depth may drop from 5 to 300 feet just a few yards from the shoreline, I once found a thermocline that had a lower limit of 70 feet.

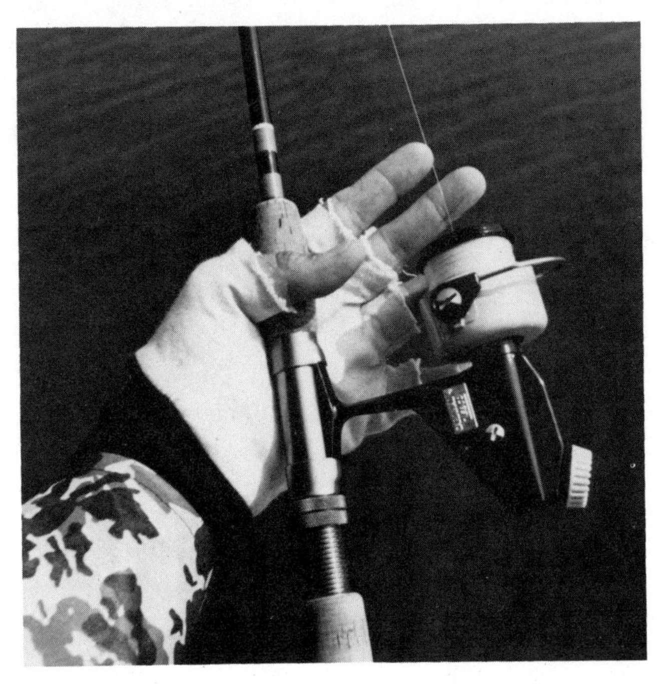

Keeping warm adds to bass-fishing success and enjoyment. Dress the same as you would if planning to sit in a duck blind. Fingerless gloves keep hands warm yet allow you to handle tackle.

In shallow lakes, where no thermocline forms, weedy cover protects the fragile environment from "burning out." Under the matted vegetation, the water temperature may be 15° cooler than it is in similar waters without vegetation.

In all of this, the important thing for bass anglers is that when stratification occurs in a lake, fish often will be found in greater abundance within the thermocline than elsewhere. Moreover, bass within the thermocline generally will exhibit more active behavior than bass located elsewhere. There are two reasons for this: First, the upper layer of water, or epilimnion, usually has so much light penetration that bass activity is discouraged; second, the hypolimnion is usually void of oxygen. That leaves the thermocline, where there is a favorable combination of reduced light penetration, ample oxygen and desirable pH.

Although the thermocline is generally the best depth for the bulk of your fishing efforts, there are always exceptions to the rule. For example, you might discover a long structure leading all the way to deep water that looks as though it might have good migration possibilities. A thermocline, we'll say, exists from 20 to 30 feet deep and so you decide to begin fishing at that depth. But no strikes come. You move deeper and begin catching good fish at the 45-foot level.

At this point, you might well ask, "How could this be? How can bass possibly exist below the thermocline, where there is no oxygen?" It's a question that often befuddles even the most experienced anglers.

For years fishing experts and even a few biologists stalwartly proclaimed that the hypolimnion contained no oxygen and that fish in this layer of water would survive only a few minutes. But biologists have recently begun to realize that at certain times during the year, the hypolimnion may possess much more dissolved oxygen than the thermocline itself. And further, this seldom-fished layer of water may be chock-full of bass!

The reason for this phenomenon takes a bit of explaining but is not overly difficult to understand. When a lake is stratified, there is little or no mixing of the various layers, and therefore there is no way for the lower layer to receive oxygen from the upper layers via rain, wind and wave action or as the byproduct of photosynthesis. This is how the upper two layers receive practically all of their oxygen. But while the hypolimnion receives no oxygen at all from these sources, this does not mean the lower layer is dead, at least, not all of the time.

You must remember that when ice-out first occurs during late winter, there is no stratification to separate one layer of water from another. As a result, the entire body of water will temporarily undergo an oxygenation process as strong winds lash the surface, feeder streams gush forth with spring rains, and a profusion of plant growth gets underway. Under normal conditions, therefore, the deeper portions of any body of water are fairly well saturated with oxygen at the time stratification occurs. And since the lower layer of water is much colder than the surface (averaging 15° to 25° lower), it can quite easily retain its prestratification oxygen load for some time (cold water will retain more oxygen than warm water). As the season wears on, and as the stratification of a lake's waters becomes more pronounced, the hypolimnion will gradually lose its oxygen. But at the very outset many fish will be down in the hypolimnion and be perfectly contented, thank you.

The gradual loss of oxygen from the hypolimnion, while the thermocline and epilimnion continually replenish their oxygen supply, is due to several factors. For one, there is almost no plant life—and hence no photosynthesis—at great depths, since beyond 30 feet at the most, even in very clear water, there is too little sunlight to support it. Moreover, the fish present in the hypolimnion, of course, consume part of the oxygen.

Every angler should own a water temperature gauge. They're reliable, inexpensive, and allow you to determine quickly if stratification has taken place in your favorite lake.

TABLE 9–1. Water Temperature Readings, Burr Oak Lake

Depth (feet)	*Temperature (degrees F)*	
Surface	78	
5	78	
10	76	
15	75	
20	73	Thermocline
25	66	Thermocline
30	60	Thermocline
35	59	
40	58	
45	56	
50	54	

And the rest is gobbled up in time by the oxygen-consuming decay of dead plants and fish that sink to the bottom and slowly decompose.

It's worth noting that in infertile mesotrophic lakes in the northern states bass often are able to live in the hypolimnion for most of the summer. There is simply not enough decaying organic matter to consume the large quantities of oxygen present in the deeper water at the time stratification occurs. However, just the opposite is true farther south, particularly in the Gulf States region. Here, the oxygen initially in the hypolimnion is rapidly consumed because the high fertility of many man-made reservoirs creates vast quantities of decaying organic matter.

This information about lake stratification suggests several strategies that will help you in locating bass. First, it's wise to determine whether those lakes or reservoirs you plan to fish during late spring, summer and fall experience stratification. Those waters that do not stratify, of course, can be fished using the locational tactics discussed in previous chapters. Those that do stratify—and this is something you can determine in five minutes' time with a water temperature gauge—*generally* should be fished within the upper and lower limits of the thermocline, simply because this layer usually has the best combination of light penetration and oxygen level for bass. Above the thermocline, there's too much light for bass; below it, there's too little oxygen. However, remember the two exceptions to the rule when the hypolimnion may contain enough oxygen to support bass activity: during late spring in clear, fertile bodies of water, and during

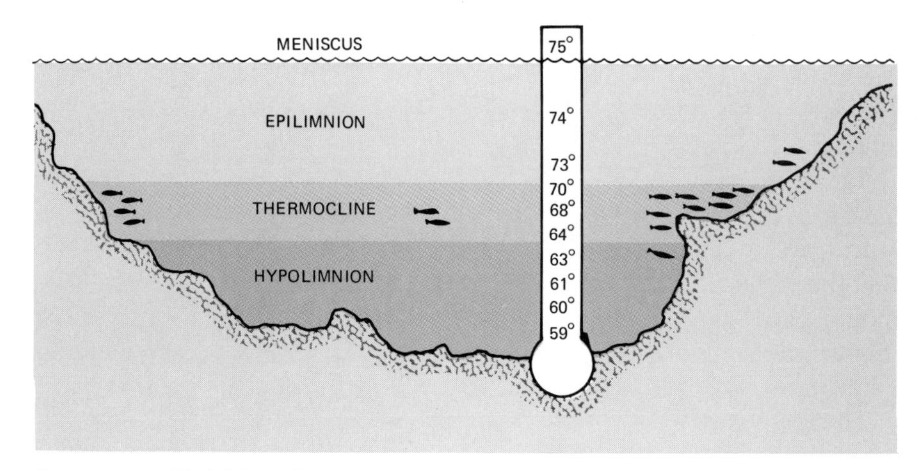

In most stratified lakes, the greatest number of bass, and the most active bass, will be found within the thermocline.

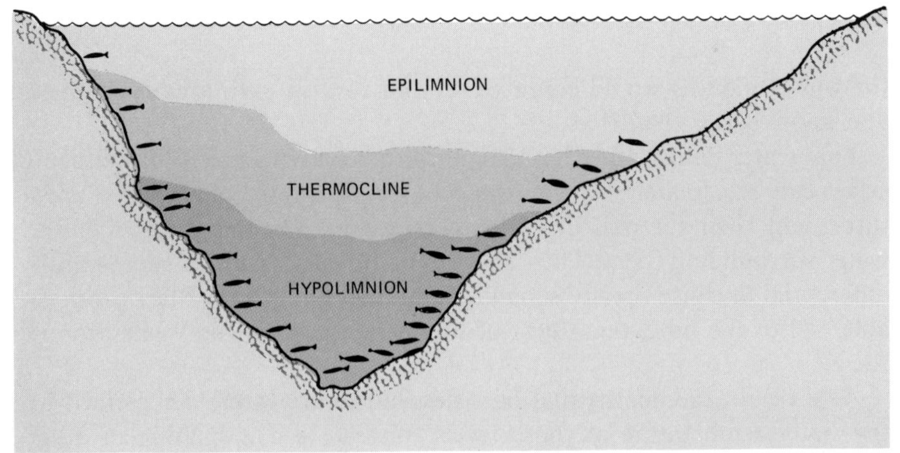

At certain times of year, and in certain types of lakes, bass may be found in the hypolimnion. This is particularly true in deep, infertile lakes where there is an absence of vegetation.

all months of stratification in infertile northern lakes. In these two situations, you may well do better fishing deep into the hypolimnion than restricting your efforts to the thermocline.

Now that we've seen—contrary to popular opinion—that the hypolimnion can contain both oxygen and bass under certain conditions, let's examine another myth that has hampered the bass-fishing efforts of many anglers. This one states that bass "prefer" certain water temperatures, that during the summer months they seek out cool water where they can be "comfortable," and that during the winter months they seek out warm water, again where they feel comfortable. Nothing could be further from the truth! Sure, bass do indeed move into the depths during the summer and they gravitate back toward the shallows during the fall, but water temperature has little to do with it.

Tackle manufacturers who make electronic water temperature gauges have fostered the mistaken notion that bass "prefer" certain water temperatures over others. On their instruments they plaster guidelines stating that the preferred temperature range for largemouths is 68°–75°, for smallmouths is 63°–68°, and for spotted bass is 65°–70°. I shudder at the thought of how many hundreds of thousands of anglers have been misled by these guidelines.

The truth is that *bass do not favor one water temperature over another.* Nor will they travel great distances, as some would have us believe, to find water temperatures they supposedly prefer. If that were true, those locations in lakes or reservoirs where industries discharge warm water during the winter months would contain every bass in the entire reservoir. And you know better than that.

That water temperature has little influence on where bass locate themselves can be explained by their physiology. They are cold-blooded creatures, and their internal body temperature is the same as that of the water surrounding them. Thus, there is no internal/external temperature differential to cause them discomfit. In human terms, they "feel comfortable" all of the time, regardless of the temperature of the water around them.

As a result, the depths that bass descend to are rarely determined by the water temperature at those levels. Instead, a combination of other factors—the degree of light penetration and water stratification, oxygen levels, and pH—seems to be most important in determining which waters are most attractive to bass.

(I might mention in passing that trout, salmon, and some other *cold-water* fish species seem to be more sensitive to water temperature than are bass and other *warm-water* species. Even with these fishes, however, some scientists are coming to believe that it's actually the higher pH associated with cooler water, rather than lower temperature itself, that is important to their physiological well-being.)

Although water temperature has little to do with *where* bass are found, it exerts a powerful effect on their metabolic rates and, in turn, their *level of activity.* Thus, the guidelines accompanying water temperature gauges actually represent temperature ranges within which the respective species can be expected to exhibit *maximum activity.* At temperatures below the range needed for maximum metabolic rates for any given bass species, the fish will not feed regularly nor actively, and lures or baits must therefore be presented at very slow speeds because the fish are somewhat lethargic. As their metabolic rates increase, spurred by increasing temperatures, the fish require more frequent replenishment of food stores. They also become more active when they feed—in fact, they are more active in everything they do. Under these conditions, faster lure speeds will be more productive than slower ones.

Monitoring water temperatures, then, gives you some idea as to which types of lure presentation will prove most effective. If you're fishing a 25-foot-deep underwater bar, and your temperature gauge says the water at that depth is only 55°, use a very slow retrieve, or perhaps even switch to live baits that can be worked slower still. On the other hand, if you're working the tip of a shoreline point that's only 10 feet deep, and the temperature at that depth is 76°, you can probably expect to get the best action by cranking in your lures almost as fast as you can turn the reel handle.

The Fall Turnover

The approach of the fall and early-winter fishing seasons brings a predictable restlessness in many anglers, especially those who live north of the Mason–Dixon line. Looming in their immediate future is the end of another year of piscatorial pursuits. This is the time when any angler worth his Jelly Worms finds himself electronically charged with anticipation. He knows there remain only fleeting weeks for one final hurrah before winter storms begin sweeping down from the northland, making it prudent to exchange spinning rods for shotguns and rifles.

Even those who reside in Sunbelt states may begin feeling a sense of urgency as occasional frost-glittered mornings hint of still more severe weather to follow. A few hardy souls may continue to brave the elements and pursue the black bass species throughout the cold-water months. But the physiology of largemouths, smallmouths and spotted bass dictate a gradual winding down of their body metabolisms and activity levels as water temperatures slowly begin to recede from their summer levels.

For a while, however, the bass are as restless and anxious as those anglers trying to dupe them. For the previous three or four months, stability has pretty much characterized their watery worlds; their daily behavior and locational patterns have been rather consistent and reliable. Yet now, a sense of change is being felt.

Midday air temperatures still may climb beyond 80°, but when the searing sun dips below the horizon at dusk, an unmistakable chill in the air becomes evident. This chill, which precipitates a degree-by-degree lowering of the surface layer of water, is the signal to bass that their aquatic communities are about to undergo a radical alteration in both appearance and composition, the so-called *fall turnover.* This brief phenomenon serves to prepare all manner of fish species, vegetation, and other aquatic and terrestrial life for the period of relative winter dormancy that nature has decreed for upcoming weeks.

The fall turnover, and more importantly how it affects bass behavior, actually is quite easy to understand. As the surface water slowly cools, its molecular structure becomes denser, and therefore appreciably heavier, than before, causing it to sink to the bottom. As a result, the warmer, lighter water lying beneath is forced to the surface, subsequently is cooled, and the cycle repeats itself.

The effects of this homogenizing of previously stratified water layers from top to bottom are many:

- Any thermocline that may have previously existed is quickly destroyed.

- For a brief period of time, the water temperature is fairly uniform at all depths.
- The water itself may reveal a temporary turbulent coloration as silt, sediment, decayed organic matter and other bottom debris is swept up and recirculated by the maelstrom.
- Many types of emergent and submergent vegetation begin to wilt, turn brown and lay over while certain other types of life (frogs, turtles, insects and minute zoological organisms) begin to disappear.

Bass react to these changes in several ways. On the one hand, the gradually cooling water can so upset their metabolic regularity that active feeding behavior may become sporadic. Yet there are sure to be periodic reversals in this as occasional Indian summer days seem to breathe new life into the water, promoting temporary bursts of feeding activity that must be experienced to be appreciated. Also, once the thermocline has dissipated, bass are free to roam through depths they may not have used in earlier weeks.

In short, fall bass fishing can be as unpredictable as any angler might ever come across. It's as though the fish are confused, wandering aimlessly, trying to understand and adjust to the day-by-day, fluctuating characteristics of their environment. Summer schools of bass are gradually breaking up, scattering widely, few of them exhibiting predictable behavior from one hour to the next. The fish seem to instinctively sense the necessity for engaging in many last-minute activities, such as putting on weight and finding new homes, that will sustain them through the upcoming cold-water period. Yet they seem indecisive about satisfying these needs, their behavior changing from day to day and sometimes even moment to moment.

Hence, fall fishermen must be *versatile* if they are to enjoy any measure of success. Make no mistake, the inflexible diehard who perpetually pitches plastic worms into brushpiles or crankbaits along rubble shorelines will take a few bass, now and then. But his catch ratio will appear pale and insignificant compared with that of the angler who commands many types of tackle, lures and presentation techniques.

Perhaps the secret to successful fall fishing, however, is having the guts to take a devil-may-care approach to finding bass—a more or less random strategy that you probably wouldn't consider at other times of year. This can pay off because in the fall bass are widely scattered, both in terms of the depths at which they are holding and in terms of the types of cover or bottom contour they cling to. So, ply waters from two to 25 feet deep. Fish clean bottoms as well as those littered with brush, stumps, logs, gravel and slab rock. Fish weeds, bushes and felled shoreline trees. Fish boat docks, rubble riprap along dams and causeways, and concrete bridge and retaining wall structures. Fish inundated roadbeds, ditches, stream channel bends, humps, saddles, channelpoints, islands jutting up from the bottom, drop-offs and reefs.

In other words, *if it looks good, fish it.* But only briefly! Don't expect to find a bonanza of bass at any single location. Likely as not, you'll pick up two bass in one place, another somewhere else, and still another yet elsewhere—none of them doing the exact same thing in the same types of places. Moreover, keep in mind that this fleeting transition time—with its topsy-turvy water and unpredictable fishing—can be counted upon to quickly wane as the cold-water season rapidly approaches. Depending on the latitude, the fall bassing season may last only a few weeks during which time water temperatures can be expected to plummet from 10° to 40°.

Winter Bass

As late fall blends into winter, bass move into their cold-water homes and become far more predictable in their behavior. They begin to group into much larger schools than at any other time of year, largely because places suitable to supporting them during the upcoming weeks of semidormancy are relatively scarce.

Since most lake vegetation is now either dead or dying, bass begin making a transition to *woody cover*—brush, standing timber, stump beds, and downed treetops. Strangely, for reasons that biologists cannot explain, winter bass seem to have a preference for such woody cover even in the deep South where weeds may remain green throughout the winter. Once the fall turnover is completed, and particulate matter in suspension has settled out, the water in most lakes becomes very clear.

There are several key places to search for bass during the winter, places where they can be caught right up until ice begins forming on lake surfaces.

In flatland reservoirs, shallower highland reservoirs and the shallowest headwater regions of canyonland reservoirs, the old riverbed winding along the floor of the impoundment, along with its associated feeder tributaries, become magnets of the highest order. Pay particular attention to the edges of these channels where there are deltas, ridges and saddles peppered with woody cover.

In deeper highland reservoirs, canyonland reservoirs and mesotrophic lakes, late-season bass tend to migrate vertically along steep banks, as discussed in Chapter 3. If you can find drop-off ledges, standing timber and stumps along these sheer shorelines, you've hit paydirt. Shoreline points that drop off steeply at their tip ends may also be hot spots, especially, again, if they have stumps and trees in evidence.

From my experience, in all of these types of lakes and reservoirs, winter bass seem to favor depths of 12 to 20 feet. When the water temperature ranges from 40° to 50°, rarely do I ever find them shallower or deeper.

One thing that must be emphasized, however, is that not all bass in a particular body of water will be doing the same thing at exactly the same time. For example, bass living at different ends of a lengthy manmade reservoir may exhibit entirely different behavior on any given day of the week. This is simply because in the shallower headwater region, the temperature may be 45° with the bass in their winter homes, whereas at the much deeper tailwater section near the dam, the temperature may be 55°, with bass still experiencing fall turnover conditions.

What all of this means is that bass anglers who are having exasperating difficulty catching fish at one end of a lake, due to whatever conditions, might easily find their luck reversed if they head for the opposite end of the lake and ply different tactics on bass regimented to an entirely different lifestyle.

A similar ruse is to concentrate on larger lakes during the chilly times. As small waters are the first to warm in the spring, they also are the first to cool late in the year. Larger lakes and reservoirs are much slower to reveal the effects of the changing seasons and thereby offer good bass action long after small bodies of water have succumbed to winter's ravages.

Finally, I should say a few words about mid-winter fishing around warm-water discharges. There are thousands of such facilities across the country—most situated throughout the Midwest—and they offer some of the most unique bass fishing imaginable.

Basically, an industry along the banks of a major body of water takes in cool water for the purposes of cooling condensors, or heating it to produce steam to generate electricity, and the resulting warm water, or *plume,* is discharged back into the lake or river. This discharged water frequently has a temperature as high as 75° to 85° and therefore substantially warms the immediate area around its discharge location.

In the immediate vicinity of the discharge, for example, the water temperature may be as high as 80°, with bass there exhibiting a high level of activity. Yet 200 feet away, the water temperature may be only 60°, with bass there only mildly active, and 500 feet still farther away the temperature may be only 35°, with bass there being almost comatose.

In some locations, stratification occurs around discharge points, and bass may suspend close to the surface, at least in the warmest sections.

And sometimes bass exhibit unnatural migration tendencies by moving into the warmest areas of plumes to feed ravenously upon baitfish, then dropping back into colder water where they either cling to edges or sink to the bottom. The wind also plays havoc with fishing strategies around warm-water discharges by pushing the warm water one way for a few hours, or days, then doing a complete reversal.

One thing is certain, however. If there is a warm-water discharge facility on one of your favorite bodies of water, it can offer excellent bass-fishing opportunities throughout the winter months. Since each and every discharge situation is unique, trial-and-error experimentation is a must. Measure water temperatures before each day of fishing, making sure to take readings in various areas as well as from top to bottom. With this "profile" in hand, then concentrate upon the warmest water you find. Generally, this will be within five or six feet of the surface.

As fall begins yielding to winter, bass shift locations. At this time of year, they will be congregating on steep banks, in moderately deep water; as soon as weeds begin dying, bass can increasingly be found in and around woody cover, such as standing timber and stump beds.

CHAPTER

10

How Weather Affects Bass

Bass are extremely sensitive to abrupt changes in their environments, much more so than many other species, and they react accordingly, often in a negative manner. In fact, if one word could be used to describe the environmental circumstances they like most, that word would have to be *stability.*

This is why I always recommend keeping track of weather conditions and, if at all possible, going fishing after a three-day period of stable weather. This is one of the most important pieces of advice this book has to offer.

Don't make the mistake, however, of thinking stability necessarily means calm, settled weather. In the context in which I'm using it here, stability refers to *consistency.*

Therefore, a three-day stable weather pattern could mean three days of clear skies and gusting winds, or three days of overcast skies and steady rainfall, or three days of muggy weather under a scorching sun, or three days of cold weather. What is important is not the specific character of the weather but the fact that the particular type of weather occurs without interruption for at least three consecutive days.

This three-day period gives bass time to acclimate themselves to the changes in their environments that ushered in the period and to begin a slow and steady recovery to their former levels of activity. Hence, beginning with the *fourth* day after a change in the weather, fishing "should" be terrific. And it should stay that way, at least until such time as the weather once again changes abruptly.

Pray for Rain

The weather—even three-day stable weather patterns—varies widely in terms of cloud cover, amount of solar radiation able to penetrate that cloud cover, air temperature, wind velocity, and so on. It stands to reason that some weather patterns afford much better bass fishing than others.

Personally, I pray for rain. Indeed, I've been diligently summoning help from the rain gods for more than 30 years.

It all began when I was a youngster living in northeastern Ohio. My brother Jeff, then age 7, and I, age 9, used to sneak into nearby Silver Lake to catch bass. It was, and still is to this day, a private lake surrounded by very lavish estates. I remember that along one stretch of shoreline was a boathouse and adjacent to it a concrete retaining wall from which protruded wooden boat slips, and that's where the bass fishing was best.

Anyway, when we were barefoot tykes, the keeper of the boathouse was a cantankerous old goat. It was his job to watch over the expensive sailboats moored nearby while simultaneously maintaining the exclusivity of the lake by keeping out the local riff-raff. And true to his responsibility, not a summer went by in which the old man didn't kick Jeff and me out at least a couple dozen times. But we'd be right back several days or a week later, each clutching a spincast rod and a Maxwell House coffee can filled with nightcrawlers, duly flinging the baits out from the docks and then waiting patiently for our red and white bobbers to duck under.

The secret to tapping Silver Lake's impressive bass population, we learned in due time, was to *pray for rain.* You see, the watchman had rheumatism that began flaring up after several days of foul weather, and so he remained sequestered in the warmth of his boathouse office, not wanting to venture out into the damp mist and drizzle merely to hassle a couple of sopping wet, runny-nosed kids.

It became a matter of routine, therefore, that when it was sunny and bright we stayed home and mowed lawns to finance our addiction to fishing, and after a couple of days of rain we charted a nonstop course for Silver Lake.

Looking back, we caught tremendous numbers of bass on those rainy days, yet we didn't have enough angling knowledge to realize how conducive rainy days were to superb bass fishing. At that young age, we didn't associate the rain itself with the activity levels of the fish. As far as we were concerned, rainy days provided good opportunities to catch bass simply because we could fish undisturbed without some old fart shaking his fist at us and threatening to call the sheriff.

Today, three decades later, I still pray for rain, a primary reason

Rain is like a tonic to bass. It adds oxygen to the water and homogenizes pH levels. The overcast generally associated with rain also allows bass to use shallower water.

being the solitary fishing inclement weather affords. On a sunny, bluebird day, almost any lake you can name will sprout wall-to-wall boats. Yet add just a little drizzle and an overcast sky to the picture and those boats will thin themselves out by about 75 percent. Now, add a gentle, steady rain and the soft murmur of distant thunder—*a glorious bass day* —and you might as well be in some wilderness heaven because the entire lake is yours alone!

There are other obvious, and also not so obvious, reasons why rainy weather provides much better bass action than some other types of weather. The decreased boat traffic during rainy spells means there're fewer outboards churning the shallows and blatantly disrupting the activities of bass schools that have recently migrated into skinny-water haunts or of stragglers waiting in ambush around cover. It also means you can throw a crankbait alongside any particular stump as late as 10 o'clock Saturday morning without having the dejected suspicion that half a dozen other plugs have already been there ahead of you.

But aside from these fringe benefits, rain acts like a tonic that invigorates lethargic bass, entices them out of the depths to prowl the weedlines and rocky shores, and encourages them to begin feeding heavily. In effect, bass are fooled by rainy weather. Cloud cover and raindrops pelting the surface diminish underwater light intensity, thus making wary bass feel more at ease by simulating, all day long, the same dimly lit conditions that ordinarily exist only during the hours of dawn and dusk.

Falling rain also adds oxygen to the water, which has an energizing effect upon the body metabolism of bass. Some biologists even contend that rain (and the associated effects of wind) changes the pH of the water by pushing, pulling, rearranging and homogenizing various layers of water and lake regions so fish are more inclined to move and become active rather than remain holed up in isolated places.

Of course, you should not base your entire game plan on just plain old-fashioned rain because a particular combination of many factors add up to the heaviest stringers.

To begin with, I'd pray for a light, steady rain, or one that's intermittent, not a fullblown, driven storm that makes one's skin feel like a pin cushion. Along with this, I'd color the sky a solid gray to reduce the amount of sunlight that penetrates the depths. Perhaps I'd even hang a dark thunderhead here and there, but there would be absolutely no lightning to endanger anglers. A light breeze would be blowing as well, not so strong as to hamper proper boat control or accurate casting of lures but just enough to put a mild chop on the surface.

The air temperature would be hot and humid—let's say 85°. The water temperature would be 65° to 80° because that is the range in which bass are most active. And the water color would be slightly milky or cloudy.

Finally, as noted earlier, all of these weather and water conditions would be in their third or fourth day of stability.

These are picture-book-perfect days for bass and any angler who looks upon his sport with more than just passing fancy will want to do anything possible to be on the water. Call your boss and tell the biggest lie you can think of to avoid going to work, reschedule your wedding date, even go as far as to postpone your own funeral!

Cold Fronts Turn Bass Off

Now let's imagine the worst possible bass-fishing conditions so they may be avoided at all costs.

On these horrendous days the sky will be a bluish white, with no clouds visible for miles. The sun, directly overhead, will be relentlessly pounding the water with intense, bright light. Not even a whisper of a breeze will be stirring, and the water will be as clear and flat as a sheet of glass. The temperature of the water will be less than 65°; even more detrimental, the air temperature will have been rapidly dropping for several hours and now will be lower than the water temperature.

What we've been describing is a classic example of a *cold front,* and few other things are as certain to give all fish species, but especially bass, a severe case of shut-mouth.

According to meteorologists, a cold front is defined as a line on a weather map that indicates the leading edge of a mass of cool weather advancing into some other region presently occupied by warmer weather. Sometimes cold fronts can be readily identified, particularly in the East and Midwest, because the difference in air temperature on each side of the front may be as much as 25°. Other times, most notably in the South and Southwest, cold fronts may be almost indistinguishable because the change in the air temperature is but a few degrees; but they are bonafide cold fronts nevertheless and have the same adverse effects upon bass behavior as do more obvious fronts.

Most anglers have heard the term *cold front* before, and they know that it somehow causes bass to become almost comatose. Yet before that happens, fantastic action typically occurs as the leading edge of a front approaches. The reason for this little-recognized activity is that an advancing weather pattern destined to collide with a resident weather pattern of greatly varying air temperature invariably gives birth to, you guessed it, rain! Now, briefly, the bass almost go berserk and seem bent upon suicide. Yet once this stormy weather has passed through, and for perhaps two days thereafter, even those experts who write bass-fishing books may strike out.

Many anglers mistakenly reason that cold air itself turns the fishing sour, but that's not the case at all because it generally takes weeks of consistently cold weather to change the water temperature even a few degrees. Rather, the movements, activity levels and behavior patterns of bass are affected by the significantly increased sunlight intensity that accompanies passage of a cold front through a region.

Let's take a closer look at the sequence of events leading up to and following the arrival of a cold front. From three to five days before the arrival of the leading edge of the front, the sky turns slightly gray and overcast, with a smattering of puffy cumulus clouds here and there. At this time, bass begin using somewhat shallower cover and feeding zones than previously. The next day, the leading edge of the front is closer still, clouds are growing darker, and light breezes begin sweeping through the region like advance guards. The fishing action gets better because the amount of light penetration into the water is retarded even more, allowing school bass to not only move still shallower but remain there for longer periods, and causing straggler bass to move out of the thicker portions of cover to prowl the edges.

The following two days the sky is filled with ominous looking thunderheads, at times the ceiling seems almost black in places, and a distinct mugginess prevails as a blanket of stormy weather lowers itself closer to the earth and prevents surface heat from rising and dissipating. Rain begins falling, sometimes in spits, sometimes as spray when the wind gusts, sometimes as a steady downpour. Although conditions are very gradually turning for the worse, we're nevertheless still in a period of progressing stability. A radical change is imminent, but as yet it has not taken place, and the bass seem to be everywhere.

There are fish on the points, in the weeds, scattered along the rocky banks and patrolling shallow stump fields. Now, only a lone boat can be seen on the water, its occupant resembling a half-drowned cat, yet he couldn't be happier because he's experiencing bass angling at its finest.

The following morning the front passes completely through the region. If the lake is located north of the Mason–Dixon line, dawn arrives with an unmistakable crispness in the air. No matter where the lake is located, the former shroud of low, dark clouds is gone and left behind is a mile-high sky that gives one the impression he can see forever. The bass, which had over a number of days gradually acclimated themselves to the stability of decreased light levels, and progressively moved shallower and shallower, are now suddenly and unexpectedly faced with dazzling brightness.

Like moviegoers who wince when they first emerge from dark theatres, the fish find themselves confused—disoriented. Their instinctive reaction is to seek the safety of dark or shaded water. Some of the fish accomplish this by diving for the depths in a state of panic and then lethargically lying on the bottom; others bury themselves in the labyrinth of dense cover.

In either case, the shock of the radical change entirely disrupts any fish's state of being, causing it to cease all former activities, fall into a sluggish state, and undergo a long and gradual recovery period.

Yet, curiously, most of the anglers who stayed home during the inclement weather now begin thinking that since the weather has cleared, it is a splendid time to go fishing again. And, predictably, they catch nothing.

Just as predictable, savvy anglers are now staying home to catch up on odd jobs. They know that in due time they'll be able to schedule fishing outings with far better chances of success.

I'll never forget the time Steve Matthews and I traveled to Bull Shoals Lake on the Arkansas–Missouri border and upon our arrival were greeted with a tremendous rainstorm. It took a full day of pleading and cajoling to get Matthews to go fishing, and he later remarked he'd established two personal records: Never before in his life had he gotten so wet, and never before had he caught so many bass in a single day.

Ironically enough, the very next day the front passed through, leaving bright, clear skies; now it was I who refused to go fishing. So Matthews went by himself, to the very same location where we had mopped up the day before. After six hours he finally threw in the towel, having boated only one scraggly looking crappie.

Coping with Changeable Weather

Fishermen who are locked into regimented schedules and who therefore have little flexibility in staging their bass-hunting adventures can still hedge their bets. Advance planning is the key.

Say it's Friday night and you plan to fish all day Saturday. The specific lake you plan to fish is about 30 miles west of your home. That evening, while readying tackle, you tune in a weather forecast and learn that a cold front is moving in your direction and probably will arrive sometime during the night.

In such a situation it would be foolhardy to follow through with your original plans. When you arrived at the lake, you'd find abominable post-cold front conditions and receive little more for your efforts than a sore casting arm. Much wiser would be to select a different lake located 30 to 50 miles *east* of your home.

Indeed, many expert anglers who know that weather characteristically moves across the country from west to east commonly drive eastward 100 miles or more during the late-night hours, with some particular lake in mind, so they can fish in rainy weather under cloudy skies, at the leading edge of a cold front.

Of critical importance is deciding where, exactly, to fish on a given body of water. Perennial advice from many writers is to concentrate upon embayments, coves, creek channels and shorelines located on the lee side of a lake. The reasoning, so it goes, is that such regions are protected from the prevailing wind and therefore are calmer; in addition, boat control and casting accuracy are easier to attain in leeward locations. In theory, it's sound advice; in practice, it's a real bummer.

Rain and associated winds exert their greatest influences upon bass—stimulating their metabolism and galvanizing them into action—on the *windward* side of a lake. Only the bass themselves can confirm why this is so, but the most logical explanation has to do with the effect unsettled weather has on their prey.

In those places where the water is choppy, schools of baitfish are unable to maintain their equilibrium and tight-schooling tendencies. The hapless prey is at the mercy of the elements, and as their schools become disjoined, individual prey members are catapulted one way and then another. Bass, with predator instincts second to none, move in to capitalize on the forage's vulnerability. The same fate awaits crayfish that are dislodged from hiding places as weather-created water currents agitate bottom mire and sweep across gravel shoals and rocky bars.

To be sure, no one should venture into risky areas where fishing may become a hazardous proposition. But, after taking account of the risks, you can do no better than explore eastern and northeastern lake areas that are fully exposed to the brunt of an approaching frontal system. In addition to bassy-looking bank configurations, shoreline points and rubble riprap, be sure to check primary breaklines (deeper, secondary breaklines won't be used much now), underwater ridges, and especially midlake weedbeds; sweeping gusts of wind hitting one side of the weeds has the effect of literally blowing the forage out of their hiding places within the cover into open water on the other side where bass may be stacked up in large numbers to take advantage of the sudden profusion of free eats.

Admittedly, however, there are certain times when any angler finds himself with no choice in planning his fishing. The most common example occurs when an angler is on vacation, from home, and suddenly is faced with post-cold front conditions. The only alternatives are trying to find at least a few cooperative fish or chalking up the outing as a total disaster and going home early. Sometimes I've done that very thing—packed up and headed home, scowling and cussing my bad luck every mile of the way—but at other times I've salvaged the situation with a little ingenuity.

The first possibility is switching to another bass species, or another body of water. If you've come for largemouths, consider trying instead for either smallmouths or spotted bass if one or the other inhabits the same lake. The latter two species generally live in deeper water than largemouths, where light levels are usually lower, and they therefore are not quite so adversely affected by cold fronts.

Or, if you've been fishing a lake or reservoir, try shifting your efforts to a nearby river. Because all rivers have a current, they always have more particulate matter in suspension, and hence greater water color, than lakes. Consequently, bass behavior is not so adversely affected by the dazzling bright light that shocks fish in typically clearer lakes and reservoirs after rainy weather has ceased and the frontal system has moved entirely out of the region.

If neither of these options are feasible, at least revise your fishing tactics. After a cold front goes through, remember that most bass streak for nearby deep water—25 feet to sometimes 50 feet or more—and become quite inactive. This state of affairs calls for cobweb lines, tiny lures, perhaps even live bait, a much slower retrieve, and diligent perseverance.

Under the same conditions, straggler bass that do not abandon the banks will retreat for the darkest, heaviest cover they can find. Now is when your casting skills become vital. You should land at least a few fish by deftly tossing your offering far back under overhanging tree branches and into the tiniest imaginable potholes in matted vegetation. Another tactic that may pay off is to work jigging spoons deep within the crowns of drowned trees on the bottom.

However, never expect more than sporadic action under such cold-front conditions. You'll get one fish here, another there, then completely bomb out at the next dozen locations. It's likely to continue that way, too, for at least the next three to five days before the action can be expected to slowly pick up again.

Soon, day by day, the sky will begin revealing creases of light gray that are slowly blending themselves into solid overcast. Just be patient, you know what's coming. You've been hoping for it all along. *Rain.*

Bass When It Sizzles

It was Lake Conroe, in Texas. The air temperature was a blistering 105°. The water temperature, the warmest I had ever seen in 30 years of chasing bass around the country, was an incredible 92°. Hell, I'll drink coffee that's cooler than that.

Despite these seemingly unfavorable conditions, Bill Bartlett and I were enjoying good, if not excellent, bass fishing. One reason, I believe, is because the weather and water conditions had been the same for a week. In other words, we were in a prolonged period of *stability.* Also, we were restricting our efforts to the heaviest, matted carpets of weeds we could find, beneath which my water temperature gauge said the water was a "cool" 80°.

There's a certain temperature, believed to be about 82°, at which the body metabolism of bass peak, and then as the temperature continues to increase, they quickly wind down in their activity levels. Fortunately, it's rare for the water temperature to climb much higher than critical point throughout an entire lake. There may be places where the water is absolutely torrid, and bass in those areas will be relatively inactive. But there are sure to be countless other places where the temperature is not so high, due to a variety of factors; bass in these locations can provide the caliber of fishing all anglers dream about.

When the water temperature begins nudging the 80-degree mark—which is quite common in the southern latitudes but quite infrequent north of the Mason–Dixon line—move downlake toward the tailwaters or dam, where the water is significantly deeper no matter what the lake classification and where cooler water is sure to be found. Get out your water temperature gauge and determine the depths of the thermocline, as the bass will congregate in it. On bodies of water that are not deep enough to be stratified, check maps or consult with marina personnel or perhaps a local fishery biologist in an attempt to learn the locations of springs or sinkholes. Finally, as my friend Bill and I did at Lake Conroe, diligently probe shaded cover, not only weedbeds but also the shade afforded by underwater ledges and outcroppings, and even docks.

Water increases in temperature just as slowly as it decreases, and up to a point, bass seem to adapt fairly well to increasing water temperatures.

Indeed, several other factors that we've discussed—light penetration, pH, oxygen levels, season of the year—affect their behavior much more significantly than does warm water.

CHAPTER

11

Go Fishing When The Fishing Is Best

Although few anglers have unlimited time for fishing, most do have some latitude about when to work their fishing outings into otherwise cramped schedules. By carefully selecting the specific days they go fishing, and the specific hours each day they indulge their sport, busy anglers can maximize the harvest reaped from limited time on the water. This is so because bass are more active, and hence easier to catch, at certain times of certain days than at others.

Except in the cases of river and stream bass, bass spend the majority of their time in a rather inactive state, either resting in schools in deep-water sanctuaries or hiding in very heavy cover. And anglers who fish for bass during these times are not likely to enjoy as much action as those who are on the water when the fish are in a hyperactive state, either migrating on structure or prowling the perimeters of cover.

All living creatures possess mysterious, internal biological clocks that govern various types of behavior. These timing mechanisms operate involuntarily due to a combination of forces that affect every living creature from the lowest insect form to man himself. Scientists have discovered that the activity levels of various organisms can be charted in calendar form with a fair degree of accuracy. Using these calendars, any angler can therefore schedule his bassing trips to coincide with peaks in bass activity.

For example, let's say Joe Angler is accustomed to rising early in order to be on the water at dawn's first light, and he usually calls it a day and heads home around 4 P.M. On one particular day, however, he consults a fish-activity calendar and discovers that a period of major activity is supposed to begin around 5 P.M. and last until about 7:30. If Joe adheres to his standard routine on this day, he may miss out on the best action the day has to offer. Better that he sleep late in the morning, or spend the morning catching up on household chores, and plan to stay on the water later than usual, until dark.

Solunar Tables

In February 1926, a New York stockbroker by the name of John Alden Knight was feeling restless and decided to set his work aside for a week of Florida bass fishing on Lake Helenblazes, which is the source water for the St. John's River. His guide was Bob Wall, reputed to be one of the state's foremost anglers, but by 11 A.M. on the first day both anglers had lashed the water to a froth and caught only a few "popcorn" bass. Finally, Wall suggested they break for lunch.

As they munched sandwiches, few words were spoken. Knight, especially, was hot, tired and discouraged. And though curious, he didn't bother to inquire why Wall continued to check his watch every few minutes. Then, however, Wall said something that was very puzzling.

"In one hour the moon will be down. And that is when we'll start catching some big bass."

As they sipped the last of their coffee, Wall explained that when the practice was still legal, his grandfather had been a market hunter and fisherman in southern Georgia, and that men who earned their living by harvesting fish and game for sale were not given to wasting valuable time: They'd learned to take advantage of those times each day when the pursuit of fish or game was likely to prove the most productive. One of the many facets of this art, as passed on to Wall by his grandfather, was to be afield or on the water only when the moon was either up or down. Translating this homespun aphorism into more scientific terminology, *up* refers to when the moon is crossing the meridian of longitude overhead, *down* to when it crosses the meridian on its return trip underneath the planet. And during these times, in contrast to all others, substantially greater numbers of fish and game were sure to be encountered.

At first John Knight skeptically dismissed the matter with a chuckle and a wave of the hand. But Wall continued to explain his theory anyway, describing the series of charts he had devised that allowed him to determine the exact position of the moon during any time of any given day. He added that his tables had enabled him consistently to put clients into big bass action over the years, and in his opinion were most responsible for his being the most sought-after guide in the entire state. Knight's ears perked up.

As predicted, the fish began hitting shortly after high noon, and within two hours the anglers succeeded in boating nine bass that weighed an incredible 78 pounds. Then, and Wall predicted this as well, the action quieted again. The bass, Wall said, would not go on another major feeding binge for about 12 hours, so they might as well reel in their lures and head for the dock.

That Florida bass trip had a revolutionary impact on John Knight, so much so that he promptly resigned from his job and launched a full-scale investigation of moon phases and their effect upon living creatures.

Knight's research findings over the years startled the outdoor community, including fish and game biologists. In attempting to account for the apparently well-ordered way in which all creatures exhibit distinct periods of activity, Knight suspected the controlling influence of some common, external stimulus. He then sought to identify the nature of the stimulus and to predict the probable times when it exerted its greatest influence.

Bob Wall believed the moon was the sole governing factor or stimulus. Knight's research revealed it was not the moon's influence alone that regulated the activity of creatures, but the combined influence of both the sun and moon. The term *Solunar Tables* was subsequently coined—from *solar* (pertaining to the sun) and *lunar* (pertaining to the moon)—to refer to charts that indicate time periods during which the gravitational effect of the sun and moon exert their greatest influence on animal activity. As we all know, these forces are indeed strong, as they daily regulate the ocean's tides throughout the world. Today, hundreds of thousands of sportsmen so religiously believe in Solunar Tables that they are regularly published as a syndicated feature in more than 175 major newspapers and a dozen national magazines.

Following his initial investigations, Knight began fishing almost daily and keeping meticulous notes. In compiling his figures and notations some two years later, he discovered that when the weather exhibited radical changes in barometric pressure, air temperature, sunlight intensity, and/or frontal conditions in a particular region, fish activity was minimal or at best unpredictable. But on the great majority of other days, during which conditions remained *stable*, the periods of peak fish activity and the oceanic tide times approximately coincided. The practical spinoff of Knight's discoveries is that an angler can use a knowledge of tide times (solunar periods) to ensure he is on the water during those times when fish *should* be exhibiting their greatest activity during any given day.

John Knight was baffled as to why solunar periods so strongly influenced creature behavior, and finally relegated this natural phenomenon to the storehouse of mysteries that have eternally puzzled mankind. The remainder of his work saw him focus upon the accurate prediction of *when* the solunar effect exerted its influence.

Looking at Solunar Tables on a daily basis, you will note that various fish-activity periods arrive each day approximately one hour later than the

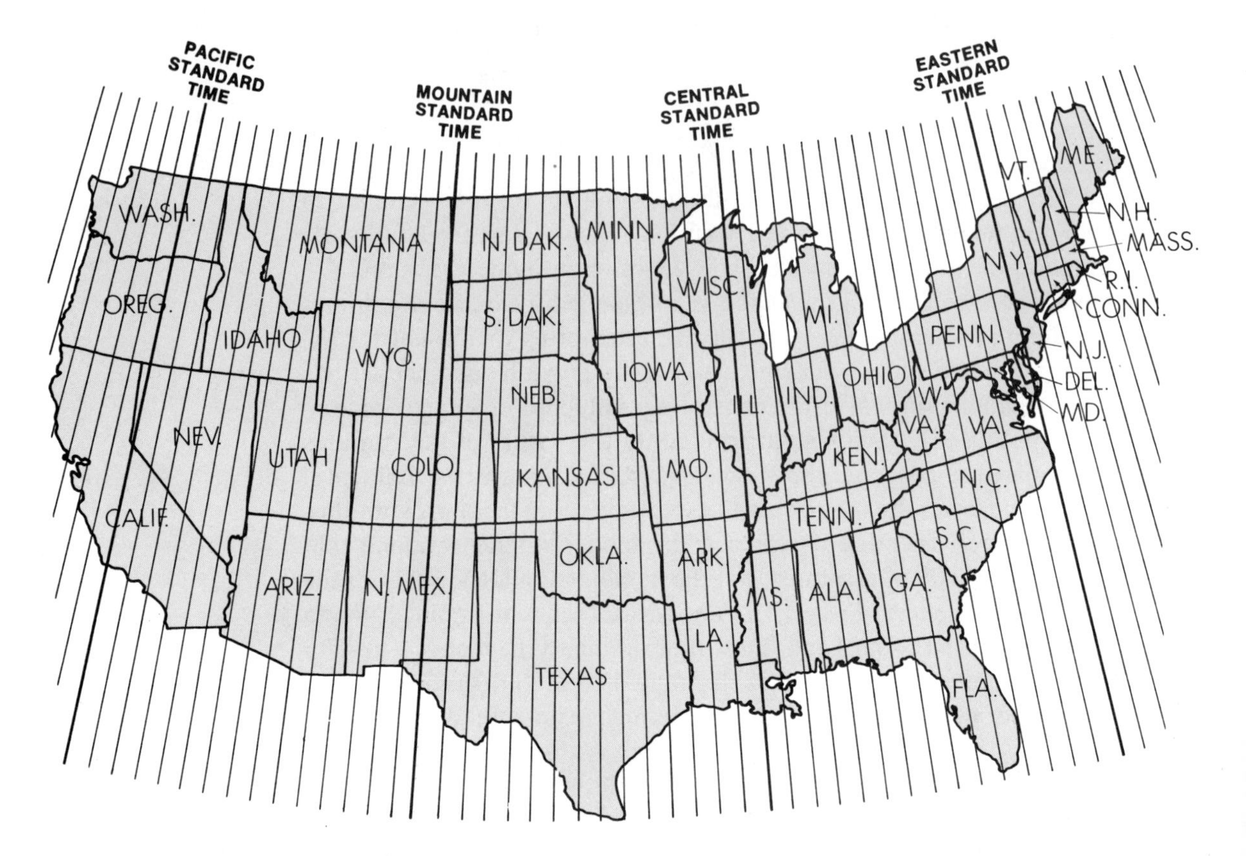

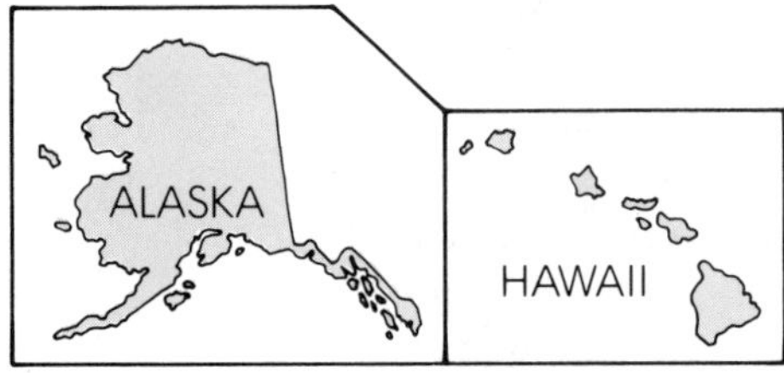

Chart 11–1. *Shown here is a typical monthly Solunar Table. Each vertical line represents a time-zone difference of four minutes, so, depending upon where you live, you either add or subtract the appropriate length of time from the table shown, to determine major and minor periods of bass activity.*

Date Day	AM Minor	AM Major	PM Minor	PM Major	Date Day	AM Minor	AM Major	PM Minor	PM Major
1. Sun.	2:55	**9:15**	3:25	**9:40**	16. Mon.	2:30	**8:40**	2:50	**9:10**
2. Mon.	3:55	**10:00**	4:10	**10:25**	17. Tues.	3:25	**9:40**	3:45	**10:10**
3. Tues.	4:40	**10:50**	5:00	**11:15**	18. Wed.	4:20	**10:35**	4:50	**11:05**
4. Wed.	5:30	**11:45**	5:55	**....**	19. Thurs.	5:25	**11:45**	5:55	**....**
5. Thurs. ...	6:20	**12:10**	6:55	**12:40**	20. Fri.	6:20	**12:15**	7:05	**12:50**
6. Fri.	7:15	**1:05**	7:40	**1:25**	21. Sat.	7:30	**1:20**	8:05	**1:50**
7. Sat.	8:05	**1:55**	8:30	**2:15**	22. Sun.	8:25	**2:15**	9:00	**2:45**
8. Sun.	8:50	**2:40**	9:15	**3:00**	23. Mon.	9:25	**3:15**	9:55	**3:40**
9. Mon.	9:35	**3:25**	10:00	**3:45**	24. Tues.	10:20	**4:10**	10:45	**4:30**
10. Tues.	10:20	**4:10**	10:45	**4:30**	25. Wed.	11:10	**5:00**	11:40	**5:25**
11. Wed.	11:05	**4:55**	11:30	**5:15**	26. Thurs.	11:55	**5:45**	....	**6:10**
12. Thurs. ...	11:45	**5:35**	....	**5:55**	27. Fri.	12:25	**6:30**	12:40	**6:55**
13. Fri.	12:10	**6:15**	12:25	**6:35**	28. Sat.	1:10	**7:15**	1:25	**7:40**
14. Sat.	12:50	**6:55**	1:05	**7:25**	29. Sun.	1:55	**8:05**	2:15	**8:30**
15. Sun.	1:40	**7:45**	1:55	**8:15**	30. Mon.	2:45	**8:55**	3:05	**9:20**
					31. Tues.	3:35	**9:40**	3:50	**10:05**

day before. This is because a "moon" day is nearly one hour longer than our 24-hour "earth" day. In each day there are usually four solunar periods (two minor periods and two major periods), exhibiting different degrees of fish activity. Generally, a major solunar period lasts from two to three hours and is followed by a six-hour lapse in fish activity; then a minor solunar period of about 45 minutes takes place. After still another six-hour lapse, another major period can be expected to occur, and then still another time lapse followed by another minor period. Because the "earth" day is an hour shorter than a "moon" day, however, there will be an occasional day that has only three solunar periods. Chart 11–1 shows a typical monthly Solunar Table.

After extensively studying Solunar Tables and experimenting with them, I've come to several conclusions. Foremost, I've discovered that bass anglers often fall into the trap of relying too heavily upon the tables while forgetting the importance of other factors that influence how bass live and move in various bodies of water, at different times of year, in accordance with existing water conditions. In order for Solunar Tables to aid consistently in bettering your fishing results, they must not be looked upon as a cure-all but only as another tool to be used in conjunction with your repertoire of bass-angling skills. They are only a forecast of the periods of activity—based upon the gravitational influences of the sun and the moon—that may be expected to occur on any given day, when weather and water conditions are stable.

The history and research surrounding the development and verification of Solunar Tables have been presented here only briefly. For a more detailed account of how and why Solunar Tables work, I suggest you obtain a copy of John Knight's book *Moon Up, Moon Down.* As to the tables themselves, monthly charts are published in many newspapers and magazines. You can also purchase them in annual booklet format (as well as Knight's book) from Mrs. Richard Alden Knight (Box 207, Montoursville, PA 17754).

Computerized Actiongraphs

Denny Gebhard, Jim Halverson and Don Lomax all live in Minneapolis, Minnesota; all are computer experts by trade; and all go fishing whenever they have spare time. This explains why one day in late 1971 they were fooling around with an IBM Data-Sorter, feeding the complex circuitry some very specific fishing-related information. They were mostly curious as to whether the computer, having digested complex tide-prediction formulas obtained through the U.S. Department of Commerce, would burp data agreeing with the Solunar Tables or perhaps come up with a different pattern of predictions.

The computer predicted that the best times to go fishing were during the hours of dawn and dusk, which is not in complete harmony with Solunar Tables but is indeed in agreement with the experience of countless anglers for generations. More intriguing though, the results suggested that computer analysis of massive amounts of data pertaining to the factors that determine fish activity might yield more consistently accurate predictions than do Solunar Tables.

The amount of data fed into the computer by the three Minneapolis anglers during the next two years was almost staggering. And the machine responded by drawing graphs that plotted fish activity, on the vertical axis, against time of day, on the horizontal axis. Gebhard, Halverson and Lomax promptly dubbed their brainstorm the *Actiongraph.*

As shown in Chart 11–2, daily Actiongraphs are cross-marked to identify each hour of each day; they also are fully adjustable for time-zone differences (including standard or daylight saving time). On each daily graph, the further the curve moves above the horizontal time axis, the greater the degree of creature activity predicted for that time period. Unlike Solunar Tables, Actiongraphs do not always predict two major and two minor periods of activity each day. Often, there is only one major period in a day, followed by several minor bursts of creature activity.

Gebhard, Halverson and Lomax used tide-predicting formulas in developing their Actiongraphs because, like John Alden Knight, they were convinced that tidal activity is related to the activity of animals. An Actiongraph, however, is not simply a tide table but rather a measure of the strength of the gravitational forces exerted upon the earth by the sun and moon on an hourly basis. Denny Gebhard believes this makes Actiongraphs more accurate than Solunar Tables.

"The method used by earth's creatures to sense gravitational attraction," Denny explained to me, "is still unknown. But the fact that they do react to it in their normal daily patterns is fairly well accepted. It's been thought that simply by observing the tides it is possible to figure out when the gravitational effect peaks or bottoms. This is partly true, but there's a lot more to it than that.

"First, the gravitational attraction is stronger some days than others. When the moon and sun are in conjunction or opposition (lined up with the earth), the force is strongest and the tides are the highest. But the gravitational attraction varies widely throughout the day. Usually the tides do not reflect this variance accurately enough to explain why fish and game seem to react at some times and not others.

"Second, there is usually a lag between the pull of gravity and the movement of the tides. Depending upon the size and shape of the body of water, and the distance from the equator, the tides can lag several hours. Interestingly enough, and this is something that will blow the minds of bass anglers and other freshwater fishermen, it's a proven fact that inland bodies of water such as lakes and reservoirs reveal daily tidal fluctuations the same as the oceans of the world! It's just that they are much smaller bodies of water and as a result the tidal fluctuations are so small that anglers never notice them.

"In any regard, by using a computer, we can avoid studying the observ-

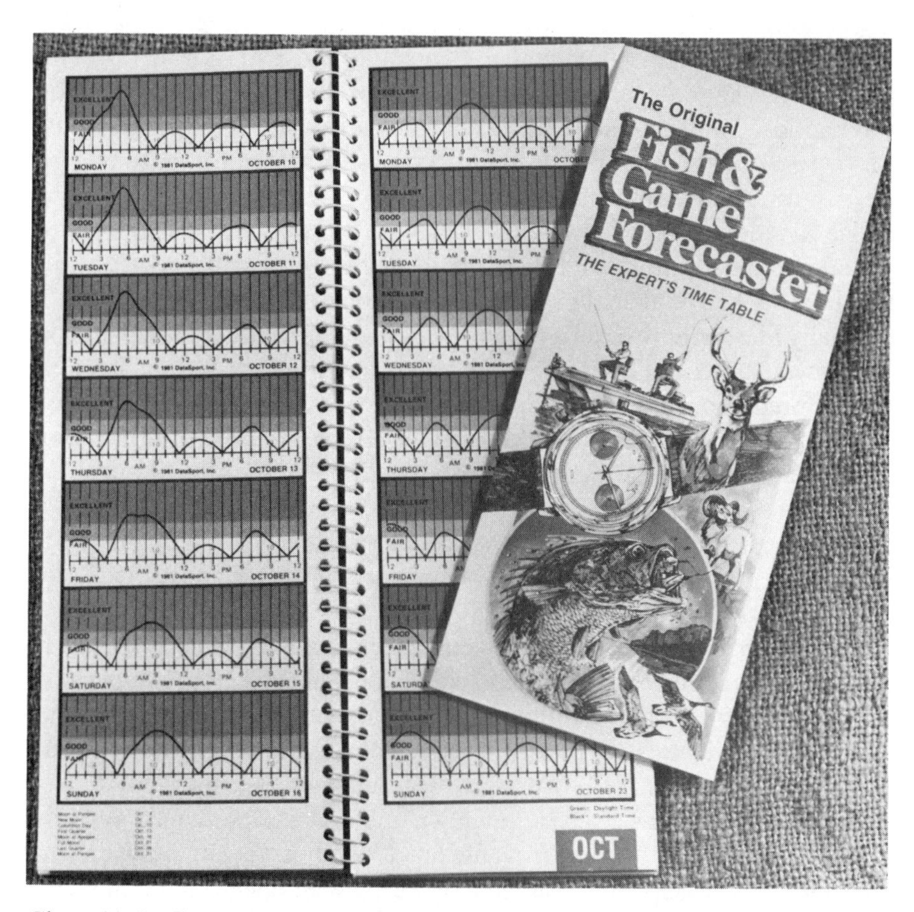

Chart 11–2. *Computer-generated Actiongraphs, based on tide times, sunrise and sunset schedules, and other data related to animal behavior, display when during the day and to what extent bass activity will peak.*

able effects of the gravitational force [tides] and go directly to an evaluation of the force itself," Gebhard concluded.

In addition to the tide-prediction formulas, other data were fed into the computer in the hope of evaluating or at least taking into consideration as many possible factors that, in various proportions, may influence the behavior of fish and game. It has long been known that light has an influence upon fish activity, so sunrise and sunset schedules were stored in the computer's memory bank. Next, the results of 20 research reports dealing with organisms and their biological clocks were programmed into the computer. The data from fish-movement studies (both long-distance migrations and home-range travels) also were added to the continually growing body of data, making the graphs more accurate than the earlier ones.

"Although we consider our Actiongraphs to be extremely accurate . . . ," Denny Gebhard commented, "an angler must still know how and where to fish, and he must take the time to analyze things that can override gravitational influences such as localized weather and water conditions. All these matters taken into account, however, if a guy has only part of the day to fish, we think an Actiongraph can help him make the right choice."

Actiongraphs appear monthly in many major newspapers and are available in a booklet that includes daily graphs for the entire year. What I especially like about the Actiongraph book is that it contains adequate log space so an angler can keep track of his personal results versus the Actiongraph's predictions; do this for just one year and you will be a confirmed believer. Write for a copy of *The Original Fish & Game Forecaster,* distributed by DataSport, Inc. (7601 Washington Ave. South, Edina, MN 55435).

Doug Hannon's Moon Clock

Within the elite fraternity of expert anglers and fishing scientists responsible for much of what we've learned about bass behavior in the last decade, I consider my friend Doug Hannon the most maverick-minded of all. And this is exactly why he has come up with so many more new ideas in recent years than just about all other bass researchers combined.

"To me," Doug says, "hand-me-down angling tradition is always suspect! I know it may sound arrogant, but I don't care. The only way to continually increase your learning is by keeping an open mind and being willing to explore new areas that may in time throw a lot of previously held beliefs out the window."

Just one of Hannon's many current endeavors toward this end has to do with the lunar influence upon bass. The elaborate records he has maintained over the last ten years reveal many interesting findings.

"I charted an unbiased sample of 307 big bass I caught, ranging in size from 5 to 16 pounds, against the time of the lunar day they were caught. Not surprisingly, more of the fish came aboard during major and minor periods than other times."

Most anglers would have stopped right there, with the assurance that gravitational influences do affect bass behavior. But since Hannon's data

Doug Hannon lands one of 307 bass he recruited for a study that produced amazing results. Further research revealed that 73 percent of all world-record fish were caught during the three days on each side of dark and full moons.

was based only on his own personal catches, mostly in the state of Florida, he wanted to see how other random catches nationwide stacked up.

So he went to the International Game Fish Association record book and began comparing record fish against the part of the lunar month they were caught. No one had ever done this before, and his findings were startling.

"The three days each side of the dark and full moons, plus the day of each half-moon, represented about 54 percent of the month," Doug told me, "yet held 73 percent of the world records caught during a ten-year period from 1970–79. More dramatically, the few days surrounding the full moon each month held 41 percent of the world records!"

In his research on bass behavior, Hannon studies only big fish, and with good reason. As he explained, "The overall behavior mannerisms of the species as a whole can be quite diverse, and this is compounded by the fact that little fish will lie to you. They are so unpredictable that catching a bunch of them some particular day, then trying to extrapolate from that experience some kind of insight, is a monumental mistake.

"Big fish, on the other hand, are not nearly so whimsical. Their great sizes alone can be attributed to their having long since learned to follow very prescribed rules of behavior for successful feeding and rapid growth, which is a key element of survival in the world of predators and prey. The paradox is that once you understand these rules of bass behavior, the lunkers are actually the easiest bass to catch! Study the giants exclusively and you'll learn more about any particular fish species than in ten lifetimes devoted to catching the little squirts."

Hannon has packaged his insights about lunar influences on bass into a little device that he calls a *Moon Clock.* Made of durable plastic, and therefore impervious to water and weather, a Moon Clock allows you to determine in an instant, for any day of any month, whether the overall fishing action is likely to be excellent or otherwise, and exactly when peak periods of big-bass activity are likely to occur. Keep in mind, though, that the Moon Clock—like the other fishing aids we've discussed—will not transform a novice into an instant expert. But as an already accomplished angler, you can expect one to dramatically increase your fishing success. Moon Clocks are available from Tern Corporation (9259 Park Boulevard North, Seminole, FL 33543) and also in many tackleshops and baitstores.

Another must item for every serious angler is *Hannon's Field Guide for Bass Fishing,* which details much of Doug's research and in particular emphasizes seasonal patterns regarding bass location and lure choices. The book is available from Atlantic Publishing Company (P.O. Box 67, Tabor City, NC 28463).

CHAPTER

12

Fishing With Live Bait

An angler who finds bass "biting" is very lucky indeed, because bass do not feed continually or at every opportunity. When the water is warm (above 55°), bass probably will feed three times a day, with each foraging session lasting anywhere from 20 minutes to about two hours. When the water is cold (below 55°), bass may feed only once a day, or once every other day, with each foraging session probably lasting less than an hour.

Under the best circumstances, then, bass are actively feeding only about six hours a day; under the worst, they may skip feeding altogether for 12 to 24 hours. An angler who ventures forth in the hope that bass are biting faces rather unfavorable odds. Indeed, the odds are so bad that most guides and tournament pros forget about trying to tempt bass into biting; instead they concentrate on trying to elicit or provoke spontaneous strike responses. These, as we will see in coming chapters, are entirely different from feeding responses.

Nevertheless, when the water temperature is below 55°, anglers may be able to tempt nonfeeding fish into biting upon natural baits. So before delving into the complexities of how bass strike, we should first look very briefly at their feeding habits.

Bass are Class-A predators and seldom show interest in potential food items unless they are exhibiting some sign of life. But except for this fetish, bass select their menu from a wide range of prey species, some of them more or less abundant in particular waters or at certain times of year.

Bass commonly forage on frogs, tadpoles and other amphibians, eels, small snakes, aquatic and terrestrial insects, and even birds and mice upon occasion. But tops on their list of preferred items are crayfish (see Chapter 5) and smaller fish, including baitfish species such as threadfin and gizzard shad, golden or emerald shiners, fathead and bluntnose min-

Doug Hannon at his 5,700-gallon tank where he studies bass behavior.

nows, and the young of panfish or other gamefish, to name only a few.

Doug Hannon, who invented the Moon Clock described in the last chapter, has done an extensive amount of research on bass-feeding behavior. In his backyard on the banks of Keystone Lake in Florida, Hannon has built a 5,700-gallon aerated tank for his "wet pets," a number of bass up to 12 pounds in weight. They subsist mainly on a diet of shiners which Doug catches himself. Since the bass are confined, Doug can observe firsthand many of their feeding mannerisms. Much of what Doug has learned I have confirmed to my own satisfaction in my larger, 3-million-gallon experimental bass lake where more natural habitat conditions prevail.

"Bass go through a ritual before they start looking for food," Doug recently explained. "The first sign is what I call a 'gaping reflex' in which the bass appears to be yawning. I believe this is like a jogger who does stretching exercises to limber up before running, only with a bass it is to quicken its reflexes. Bass also commonly erect their dorsal fins prior to feeding, but so far we aren't sure why."

It is interesting to note that none of the bass species feed by actually closing their mouths on their prey. Rather, they quickly open their mouths while simultaneously flaring their gill covers and expelling water through the gills. This creates a suction effect, allowing them to inhale their prey.

Additionally, feeding bass are not likely to chase far after an escaping tidbit. This may contradict those exciting episodes, described by some of our more romantic outdoor writers, in which a V-wake rapidly closes in on a surface lure across the pond. Actually, the top speed of any bass is only about 12 miles per hour, and they can sustain this speed only for short distances. As a result, bass seldom engage in chase-and-catch feeding, particularly of larger fish. They like to ambush their prey—quickly and decisively—expending the least possible energy in the pursuit of food.

Curiously, bass and their prey often hover side by side without incident, occasionally even brushing against each other with swimming tails and fins. The instant any bass begins "yawning," however, or erects its dorsal spines, every potential prey in the immediate vicinity goes on full alert. Some make mad dashes for the safety of cover, while others freeze in position. Then, in less time than it takes to read this sentence, some biological mechanism triggers the bass's feeding desire and the nearest minnow disappears. Or, even more commonly, some hapless minnow swims too close to the shadowy edge of thick cover, and suddenly a gaping mouth darts from the darkness and inhales it with no muss, no fuss, and little expenditure of precious reserve energy.

Similarly, a bass occasionally may bulldog through a field of lily pads in hot pursuit of a frog scampering away for its life. But nine times in ten, the frog will be placidly sitting on the edge of a pad and then suddenly, without warning of any kind, disappear in a ball of foam.

By the same token, a bass can expel a food item (or a lure) just as quickly as it can take in food, simply by reversing the suction process and blowing the food from its mouth. If the fish discovers or even slightly suspects a counterfeit, it's instantly gone—often without the angler even suspecting how close he was to landing a prize.

The work of Glen Lau Productions, which makes underwater films of gamefish behavior, emphasizes the importance of fishermen being able to "feel" what is going on below the surface. In some filming sessions, anglers presented a variety of lures to bass that had been located by camera-equipped skindivers. In many instances, a frustrated diver would surface and holler at one of the anglers casting lures, "Why the hell didn't you strike? A big bass had your lure entirely in his mouth and then finally blew it out!"

The incredulous reply was nearly always, "I didn't feel a thing."

Fortunately, this type of incident can generally be avoided by using one of the sophisticated rods made of boron, graphite or composites, which are available today. These give anglers far greater sensitivity or feel to what is happening to their lures than is possible with hollow fiberglass wands. Yet experience is equally important, and this is why even the most accomplished experts will occasionally "miss" a fish.

In Chapter 5, I described how water temperature regulates body metabolism, and how body metabolism in turn influences feeding behavior. When the water temperature is cold, all bass species will be quite sluggish. They will feed, to be sure, but only infrequently and with little energy and enthusiasm. As a result, when the water temperature is cold, an insightful angler knows he will have to work his lures very, very slowly.

Indeed, when the water temperature is below 55°, most artificial lures are very ineffective. The usual variety of plugs, spoons and spinners are designed to be cast, retrieved and imparted with various types of action. And generally these manipulations can be implemented or controlled only through the use of at least minimal speed. The trouble is that under cold-water conditions, even these quite slow speeds may be too fast to interest sluggish bass.

Some lures, however, do not fall into this category because they can be worked effectively at speeds ranging from very, very slow to dead stop. These include soft polyvinyl-chloride lures, such as plastic worms, and hard lures, such as jigs which may be dressed with grubs, some variation of pork rind, or perhaps a natural bait such as a live minnow. During cold-water conditions, an angler using artificials should stick exclusively to these types. Their use is discussed in detail in Chapter 14.

Backtrolling With Leeches, Crawlers and Minnows

The second category of offerings ideally suited for cold-water fishing is live baits. Nightcrawlers and live minnows are used the most, simply because they are so widely available. But crayfish and leeches also account for their share of bass, as do salamanders—a very special type of bait to be discussed in the next section.

When I refer to the use of live baits, don't imagine the rudimentary practices of novices who suspend some creature beneath a huge bobber, out in the lake somewhere, and allow it to "soak." For the most part, these well-meaning but inexperienced anglers are wasting their time because they're relying upon the blind luck of an occasional fish coming to them. An advanced bass angler, however, realizes that he must search for the fish, and he keeps searching until he finds them. In a sense, he becomes a hunter.

Bill Binkelman of Milwaukee, Wisconsin, and later Al and Ron Lindner of Brainerd, Minnesota, must be credited with substantially refining the use of live baits during the last several decades. Their methods—known variously as *backtrolling, Lindy-rigging,* or, simply, *rigging,*—have long since become standard practice among modern anglers, so the techniques described here are ones they pioneered.

The most widely accepted, and recommended, tackle for backtrolling

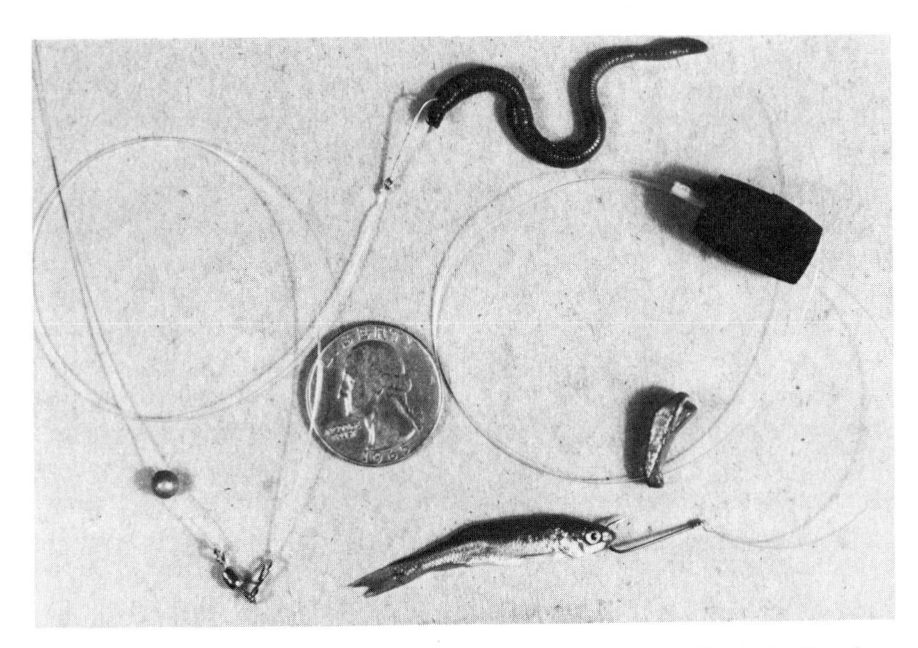

Backtrolling with Lindy-rigs is the most effective way to present live baits. Note here the shoe-shaped sliding sinker, how the nightcrawler is hooked once through the nose, and the barrel-shaped styrofoam bobber. The sinker takes the bait down deep, but the bobber keeps the bait from dragging in bottom mire.

is a medium-action, very sensitive spinning rod with an open-face spinning reel loaded with 6- to 8-pound test premium grade monofilament line. To rig this tackle for bass, thread the line through a sliding sinker of sorts. Those shaped like a shoe are highly favored because of their ability to ride over rocks and other obstructions on the bottom without snagging. The size (weight) of the sinker depends not only on the depth of the water you are fishing, but also on any current or wind that may be present. What you want is to be able to maintain contact with the bottom, but just barely so. Quarter-ounce sinkers are the most widely used, but feel free to go lighter, or slightly heavier, as conditions dictate. With the line threaded through the center hole in the sinker, now tie on a very small swivel. To the other end of the swivel, tie one end of a four-foot length of monofilament, and to the terminal end of the line, a size 8, long-shanked Aberdeen hook. The swivel prevents the sinker from sliding all the way down the "leader" to the hook. And the center hole in the slip-sinker allows the line free travel whenever you desire. This is important because under cold-water conditions bass are usually very spooky and the slightest resistance on the line may cause them to drop the bait. Using a sliding sinker, a bass can inhale your offering and not feel any resistance during the time it takes to wind in any slack and set the hook.

This particular system allows an angler to present his live bait right on the bottom and at speeds ranging from very slow to dead stop. No casting is involved, however. Instead, the angler trolls with either an outboard or an electric motor. Also, he invariably trolls in reverse gear, with the boat going backwards, because the transom of the boat pushing into the water causes the boat's speed to be greatly retarded, compared with that going bow forward; even then, the motor may have to be shifted frequently into neutral to further slow the speed of the bait or even bring it periodically to a complete halt. It's also easier for an angler to make precise course corrections and even turn on a dime when his boat is moving backwards. This is important when an angler has his eyes glued to a depth sounder —one hand on the tiller handle, the other holding his rod—and attempts to work a breakline edge, weedline, breaks or superstructure features of large structures.

Conventional bassboats can be used for this kind of work, with an angler sitting in the bow and maneuvering his craft with a foot-controlled electric motor. But aluminum V-bottom boats operated from the stern are preferred by many for backtrolling because of their higher capability for

As its name implies, in backtrolling the craft is run in reverse. Note here the homemade rubber flaps that prevent choppy water from coming over the back of the transom.

precise maneuvering. Since the water may be choppy from time to time, many anglers fashion splash-guards, from thick rubber sheeting, which are bolted upright onto the transom and prevent water from splashing into the back of the boat.

In backtrolling, the first order of business is to open the bail of the spinning reel and allow line to pay out as the bait and sliding-sinker rig sinks to the bottom. When it hits bottom, you'll feel a distinct "thunk." Now, do *not* turn the reel handle to engage the bail. Instead, curl your index finger around the slack line and hold it lightly. You can now place your motor in reverse gear and begin slowly dragging the lure over various bottom features where you might expect to find bass, in accordance with the type of lake, season of the year, existing water conditions, and so on.

As you try different depths, it will periodically be necessary to take in a bit of slack line, or let a little more out, but for all practical purposes you'll be fishing almost directly beneath the boat at all times. Do not allow a long line to pay out far behind the boat as in speed-trolling, an entirely different technique which is discussed in Chapter 15.

In backtrolling very carefully and slowly across a structure, your first indication of a "bite" may take on many forms, depending on the water temperature, the activity level of the bass and other factors. Sometimes you don't feel anything at all but merely see your line twitch or jump sideways. Other times you'll detect a very obvious bump. Other times you may have the strange sensation of "nothing" on the end of your line, as though your line was cut; this usually means a bass has picked up the bait and is swimming upward or toward you with it. Still other times, you'll feel a very slow, steady weight or resistance.

Determining when to strike therefore requires a bit of trial-and-error experimentation. I usually begin the day "hitting them quick." In other words, when I sense a bass has taken the bait, I immediately lower the rod tip, engage the reel's bail, take up any slack and strike, all in an instant. If I miss several fish, I'll give them a little more time by lowering the rod tip, paying out slack line and counting to five. If I continue to miss fish, I'll give them a ten-count. As a general rule, the colder the water, the longer you have to let the bass "mouth" the bait. As the water warms, and their metabolisms increase, they become far more aggressive and less coaxing is required.

As mentioned earlier, live baits are most effective when the water is colder than 55° and the bass are somewhat lethargic. This is most often the case during late fall, winter and early spring. Live baits are also highly successful throughout the summer months, or almost anytime the fish are suspected to be on very deep structures. At depths beyond about 25 or 30 feet, it is very difficult to maintain precise control over artificials. But live baits rigged and backtrolled as I've described can be accurately worked to depths of 50 feet or more.

As to the baits themselves, I particularly like to fish with nightcrawlers and can offer several tips to enhance your success with them. First, heat is the bane of crawlers, causing them to wilt, shrivel up and eventually die. So always keep your crawlers in an iced-down cooler with your beer or soft drinks. Another ploy is to soak them overnight in a bucket of ice water. The crawlers won't drown but will absorb water and become so plump and frisky they'll almost jump right out of your hand!

Hook a crawler once, and once only, right through the tip of the nose. This is the dark, pointed end of the crawler; the light, flat end is the tail. A crawler impaled in this manner is able to curl, uncurl, squirm and gyrate across the bottom—just the ticket for bass that may otherwise be sluggish and disinterested.

A little home medicine can improve the effectiveness of crawlers in flatland reservoirs and other bodies of water that have a bottom composed mostly of muck and mire. Dragging a crawler through such a turgid bottom seldom pays off with bass strikes; often, I suspect, a bass can't even see the bait. The remedy is easy. Obtain from your family doctor a discarded hypodermic needle and syringe and use it to pump a bubble of air into the body of the crawler. This will allow the crawler to float upward a foot or so above the bottom mire and seemingly "swim" along in tantalizing fashion in direct view of any bass you encounter.

When backtrolling for bass with minnows, you want to present the bait in a lifelike, natural manner, so hook them once through the lips, not through the dorsal portion of the back as is common in crappie fishing. Try experimenting with different minnow species, and different sizes; some combinations will distinctly out-fish others on certain days.

Leeches are super bass baits that few anglers are familiar with, unless they live in Wisconsin or Minnesota where the baits are extremely popular. They look like black worms with round suckers on their heads. Although leeches like to attach themselves to your fingers when being handled, they are harmless. Place your hook right through the leech's sucking disk so the creature hangs free. Although the best bait leeches are only one to three inches in length, in the water a leech may stretch out to five or six inches and gyrate enticingly.

Leeches are available primarily from baitshops in the upper Midwest, but they can be ordered by mail no matter where you live. Check the classified ads in popular outdoor magazines. During storage, leeches absolutely require ice-cold water. In a refrigerator, store them in groups of two dozen each in any type of small plastic cup. They'll keep almost indefinitely and you don't have to feed them. Change their water once a week, using freshwater from a nearby stream, not chlorinated tap water. One other thing is essential to peace and harmony in most households: Never forget that *leeches like to travel,* so be sure the storage containers have tight-fitting snap-top lids.

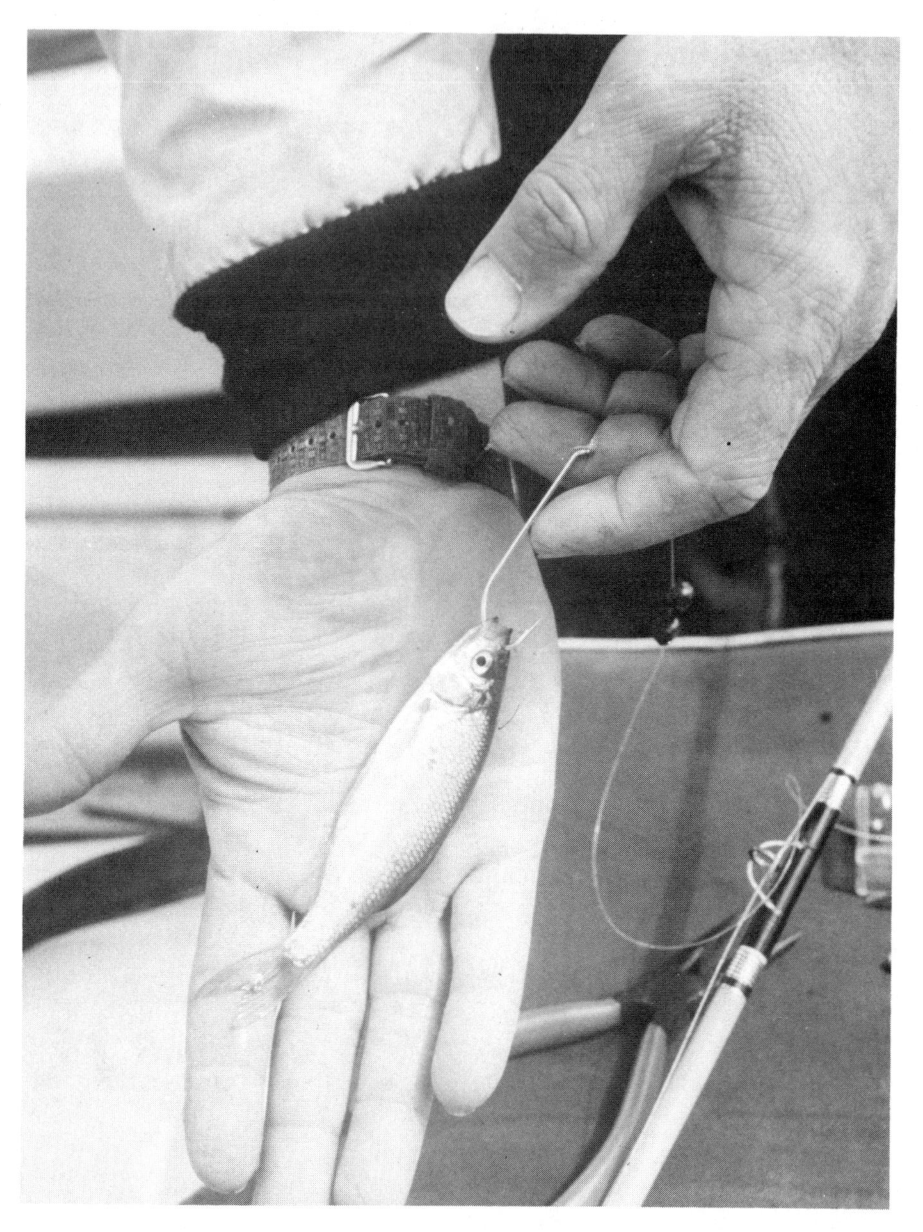

Minnows should always be hooked through the lips so they appear to be swimming in a lifelike manner when backtrolled.

Leeches are excellent cold-water baits. Hook them just once, through the sucking disks located on their heads.

There are two other popular live baits used by advanced bass anglers. One is big golden shiners, used for taking Florida bass, as is discussed in Chapter 20. The other is even more intriguing, and we'll look at that right now.

I Love to Fish with Sally!

"It's weird," Bill Parker muttered as he alternately raised and lowered his rod tip with a steady, bass-coaxing cadence. "I've never fished a bait that you could actually feel scrabbling around on the bottom. Sometimes it seems like the creature is trying to climb up my line like a monkey on a string."

I almost broke out laughing when suddenly Bill's face turned starkly serious and his whole body tensed.

"Something's happening down there!" he gulped. "It feels like a big bass violently shaking his head back and forth, but I haven't even set the hook yet."

"Your sally is going to its great reward," I answered, quickly reeling in my own bait. "Just don't be too anxious. Let the bass run with it."

Seconds later Bill's line stopped twanging up and down and very slowly and purposefully began moving directly away from the boat. Bill engaged the gears of his free-spool reel, leaned forward just a bit, then quickly swept the rod tip back in a wide arc. Almost instantly the bass came topside and wallowed in a spray of water, then dove back for the bottom. It was a dandy fish, maybe six pounds, and as I reached for the net I saw a wide smile begin to etch itself on Bill's face.

This was on Gull Lake in central Minnesota and we were fishing with salamanders, which are probably the hottest big-bass bait you can buy. Every little twitch you see in your line rivets your attention and charges you with excitement because you know anything capable of grabbing a bait that is seven inches long is definitely *not* a little fish.

Depending upon the locale, salamanders may bear a wide number of monikers. Call them mud puppies, waterdogs, spring lizards, chameleons, sirens or simply sallies, but by any name they are pure dynamite when it comes to big-bass fishing.

One reason for their effectiveness is that bass go after salamanders whether they are hungry or not. When bass are hungry and actively feeding, they ravenously devour the creatures because salamanders are highly nutritious, large, and easy to catch and swallow. Yet even when they're not hungry, bass viciously attack and try to kill salamanders at every opportunity, particularly during the spring and early summer. Bass seem to know instinctively that salamanders are bothersome nuisances and highly detrimental to their own kind. Two or three sallies can invade a bass-spawning nest and in a few minutes entirely wipe out all the eggs or newly hatched fry. I've seen spawning sites in shallow, clear water that were nothing short of macabre, fanned-out beds and fry-rearing areas littered all around their perimeters with bits and pieces of mauled salamanders.

These two characteristics of salamanders—being prime food that bass will not hesitate to try and capture when hungry, and being a destructive nemesis that bass will try to kill even when they're not hungry—are super fish-catching features that no other lure or live bait can duplicate.

There are virtually dozens of salamander species native to North America. Nearly all are effective bass baits, provided they are in their aquatic stage of life. Like tadpoles that eventually metamorphose into frogs, most salamander species begin life in water and at some later stage in their development change into land-roving creatures. However, unlike frogs, which bass will eat in any stage in their development, salamanders going from the aquatic to terrestrial stage develop the ability to secrete a distasteful substance in their skin that repels bass. Many scientists believe this transformation takes place when water temperatures rise to a certain level.

So no matter how you acquire your sallies, inspect them closely to ensure they are in their aquatic stage of life as evidenced by three sets of gills along the sides and back of the head. If the gills have disappeared, the amphibians are now in their lung-breathing, land-roving stage of development and they are useless for bass fishing. The best way to store sallies is in a Styrofoam cooler with two inches of water in the bottom and several rocks for the critters to climb upon. The water must be kept cold or the sallies may begin to metamorphose. You can add a tray of ice cubes to the water every day, but this becomes a chore; instead, store the cooler in an old refrigerator in your basement or garage. Feeding sallies isn't necessary unless you plan to keep them more than a month (I've kept them up to nine months); during long-term storage, occasionally give them some dead or still-alive minnows left over from a previous fishing outing.

The least expensive way to acquire sallies is by gathering them in shallow streams, ponds and marshes, scooping them up with a small dip net on a long handle. Just after ice-out in the early spring, the creatures swarm into these shallow waters to breed. The best time to catch them is after dark, using a flashlight. You'll see them suspended in the surface film of water near weeds. Don't be afraid to handle sallies because they don't bite, and none of the North American species are poisonous.

You can also buy salamanders from mail-order baitshops that specialize in shipping sallies, leeches and such around the country; check the classified ads in sportsmen's magazines.

Salamanders are quite hardy and it takes a bass a good deal of effort to kill one. This means you can often catch several nice bass on a single bait before having to replace it.

But you do have to exercise certain precautions. First, never cast a salamander because repeatedly slapping the bait against the surface of the

Whether you buy your sallies from a bait dealer or catch them yourself, store them in a styrofoam container with just a few inches of cold water in the bottom, then add a rock or two for them to climb upon.

water will kill it. Instead, gently pay out line from your reel so the sally sinks straight down beneath the boat, then backtroll it as described in the previous section. Second, many anglers make the mistake of hooking a sally through both lips, as they would a live minnow. This greatly impairs a sally's ability to open and close its mouth and thereby work its gills. I recommend hooking the sally through the nostrils, which are used only for smelling, not breathing.

When working a sally along the bottom, frequently raise your rod tip. This will prevent the sally from hiding under rocks, logs and other bottom debris, where bass cannot see it, and also causes the sally to move around quite a bit. The combination of a sally's four legs continually going and its whiplike tail (which works just like an alligator's tail) produces a lively enticement big bass just can't refuse.

When you get a bite on a sally, your line almost begins thrumming like a banjo string. This is usually the first evidence of a bass trying to kill the bait before attempting to swallow it; it's generally best to give a bit of slack line so the bass doesn't feel resistance and drop the bait. Wait until you see the line beginning to move away before reeling in the slack and attempting to set the hook.

If you run out of salamanders, or don't want the inconvenience of caring for these live baits while on a fishing vacation, consider using sally lookalikes made from plastic or pork. Plastic salamanders are made from the same materials as plastic worms and they can be rigged and fished exactly the same way. Pork rind sallies are equally effective, with most anglers preferring to rig these baits in conjunction with some type of leadhead jig.

Salamanders made from pork rind are excellent choices when live sallies are not available. The best way to fish them is as a dressing on a leadhead jig.

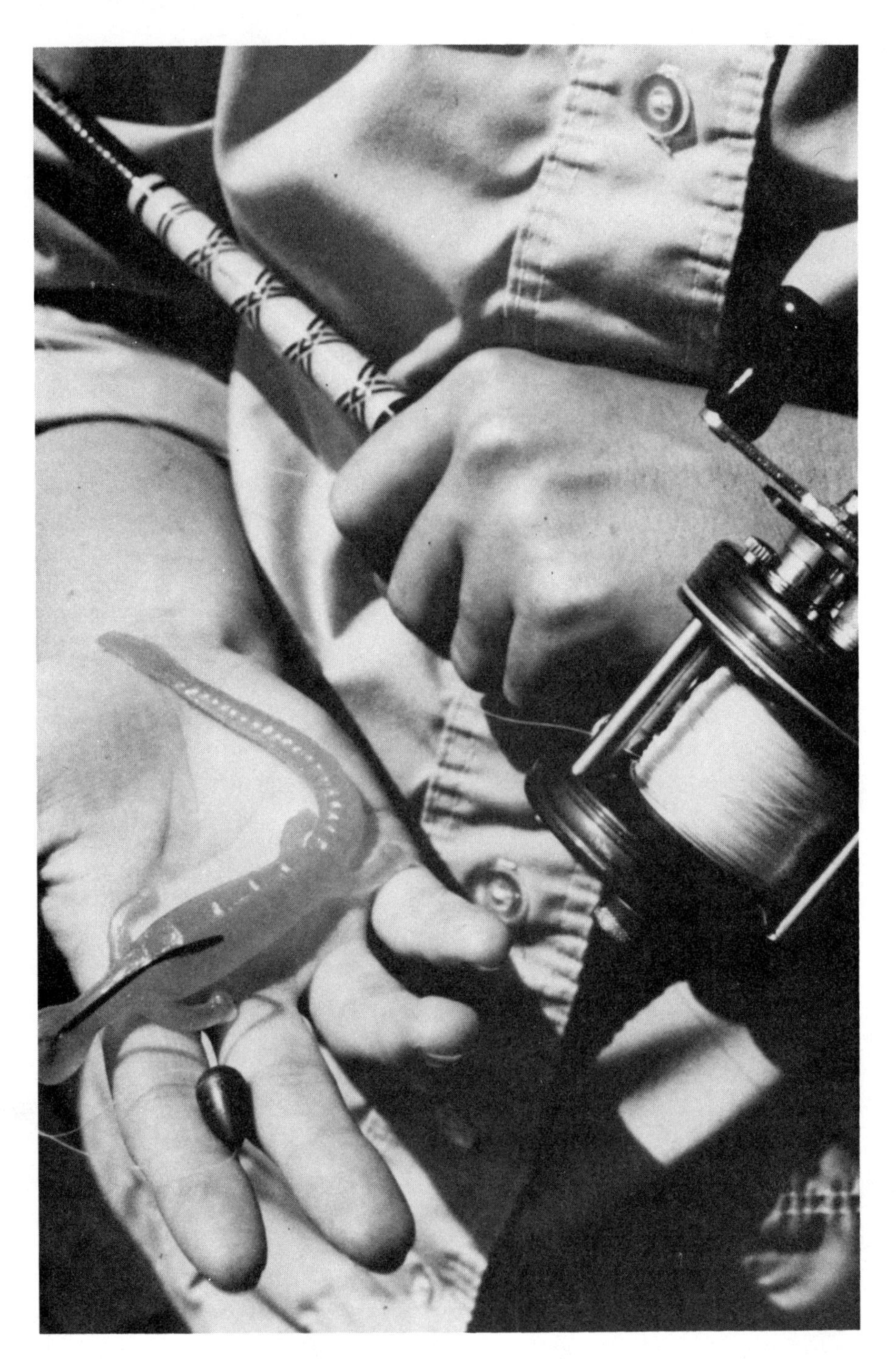

Plastic salamanders are superb spring baits. Rig and fish them exactly as you would plastic worms.

One advantage artificial sallies have over live ones is that you can cast the offerings, which means you can present them to bass in places where it is too shallow, or too choked with cover, to backtroll a live bait. But don't attempt to let a bass run with a phony sally, as you would a live one, as they'll quickly discover it's not the real thing and eject your offering. Strike the very instant you feel a bass pick up the lure.

CHAPTER

13

Lure Selection

As emphasized several times already, bass do not feed often, nor do they feed at every opportunity. In other words, they are in an *active*, or aggressive, state of feeding behavior for only a very small part of any given day. Consequently, most of the time most anglers will have far better success if, instead of trying to entice bass into "biting" upon natural food in which hooks are concealed, they concentrate upon what the fish do for those other twenty-odd hours of the day. What they do, of course, is rest or hide —that is, they are largely *inactive.*

A bass of any species in such an inactive feeding state will generally ignore a slow-moving live bait or artificial lure. But take any lure whose depth and speed can be controlled precisely, bring it right past the fish very quickly, giving it only a fleeting glimpse of the lure, and you may provoke it into striking. Hungry or not, some deeply ingrained predatorial instinct commands a bass to strike.

This response is a type of reflex behavior, similar to that of a sleeping dog who snaps at you when you step on its tail. The dog is not hungry and does not desire to eat you. From an inactive state, the dog simply responds involuntarily to a stimulus over which it has no control. Another example of reflex behavior is the familiar knee-jerk response which a doctor elicits when he lightly taps your knee with a tiny rubber hammer.

Bass (and other predatory fishes) can be similarly provoked into involuntarily responding to stimuli. When a fast-moving lure is brought right past the nose of a fish, it strikes instinctively before there is even time to be wary. Exactly how *fast* the lure has to be moving to elicit this behavior depends largely on the water temperature and its related effect on the body metabolism of fish, as discussed in Chapter 9. If an extremely fast retrieve is used when the water is relatively cold, bass will be lethargic and not as responsive as they would be to a much slower speed.

Another factor that is just as important as the speed of lures in provoking strikes is their depth, because bass will seldom travel great distances to take any lure. If the water is 15 feet deep, for example, and bass are right on the bottom, a lure buzzed across the surface would rarely entice them to rise to pick it off (unless they were in an extremely aggressive state of feeding behavior). Conversely, surface lures may be effective at certain times of year when the "bottom" the fish are lying on is only two or three feet deep.

The point to remember is this: To force a bass to strike requires presenting a lure at such a speed and at such a depth that the fish has no time to be wary or carefully inspect it; rather, the lure must be presented in a way that elicits a spontaneous reflex response from the fish. To achieve this, an angler must know the depths at which the various lures in his tacklebox are designed to run. Next, he must be aware of the speeds with which they are capable of being retrieved. Then he must use only those lures that are capable of running at the depth at which the bass are presumed to be, and he must use them at appropriate speeds, depending on the water temperature at the depth he's fishing.

Both the speed and depth of a lure must be in harmony with the existing conditions under which the bass are living for it to provoke a strike. If an angler is fishing at the right speed, but his lures are not reaching the particular depth where most of the bass are holding, the fish won't strike —and he'll strike out. The same result is likely if he works the right depths but uses lure speeds that are too fast or too slow for the conditions.

Unfortunately, a great many anglers overlook the critical factors of lure speed and depth, and the importance of being able to control them. Instead, they base most of their lure purchases on design characteristics such as action, size and color. The truth is that these attributes do not usually contribute significantly to the bass-catching effectiveness of a lure. (The only exception to this might be lure size, which often but not always determines how deep a lure will run on the retrieve.)

Lure manufacturers, of course, are not likely to grant this point. They're in the business of enticing anglers to buy new and different lures each year —lures with different actions, different designs, different sizes than previously available. I know of one company that makes plastic worms in so many sizes, shapes, colors, scents and other combinations that potential buyers have more than 100 different types to choose from. Not only does this unnecessarily confuse anglers, but it's utterly ridiculous in the first place.

To repeat, the foremost consideration any angler should ponder when selecting a lure is the depth and speed at which it can be worked. It won't matter one bit whether you are casting a plug that is green with red dots or red with green dots, if you are free-swimming that lure four feet deep under conditions in which most bass are at 20 feet: You won't catch many fish, if any at all. It won't matter one bit whether the spinnerbait you're using is tiny or extra-large, or has tandem nickle blades or a single copper blade, if you're skittering it across shallow weeds in two feet of clear water while the bass are moving along 18-feet-deep breaklines that day: Count on going home empty-handed. Nor will it matter whether the lure is vibrating, wiggling or wobbling, if the water is quite warm and the lure is not moving fast enough to provoke a strike. Furthermore, I don't care how many famous tournament professionals have endorsed a particular lure, if you're reeling that lure at breakneck speeds and the water temperature is only 45°, you'll have such little success you may seriously decide to chuck fishing and take up golf.

None of this is meant to imply that lure size, color, action and other variables are unimportant. They may well be, on occasion. But they act only as refinements that may slightly enhance your success *after* proper lure speed and depth have been achieved.

For example, let's say you're casting along a breakline drop-off where the edge of the drop is 12 feet deep. You're using a red and white diving plug that runs 12 feet deep, you're retrieving it at a moderately fast speed, and you're catching a nice fish for every 20 casts. Perhaps you can increase your catch percentage to a fish on every 10 casts by switching to a shad-gray plug that runs at the same depth and speed. But change to a shad-gray plug that runs only three feet deep, or reduce the retrieve speed to very slow, and you may discover the bass have suddenly "stopped biting."

To assure quick access to the proper lures for different conditions, your tacklebox should be arranged in speed/depth categories. In one cantilever tray might be an assortment of lures designed to run six feet deep at slow speeds. Another tray might contain lures that run ten feet deep at slow speeds, and so on, with still other trays reserved for lures that are designed for other purposes. In any given tray, you might have a variety of different brandname lures in different colors, sizes and actions. But the one thing every lure in each tray should have in common is that each is assigned a specific task.

So whenever you purchase new lures, ask yourself several questions. For what purpose do I intend to use these lures? At what speeds should they be retrieved or trolled, and at what depths do they run? If you're able to ascertain from the directions on the boxes that the lures run six feet deep and are recommended for various warm-water fast speeds, and you

To make lure selection easier, keep your tacklebox in order. Reserve one tray strictly for shallow-running lures, another for deep-divers, and so on.

know you need some lures for that kind of work, go ahead and buy several in different colors and sizes with the confidence that your purchase is a wise one.

To illustrate the dramatic influence of lure depth and speed controls on fishing success, I'll recount two experiences that stand out in my memory.

Once, Jerry Bartlett and I were at Kentucky Lake, which straddles the Kentucky–Tennessee border. We were fishing for fall bass in about eight feet of water on a long bar adjacent to a rocky shoreline. Jerry and I were throwing almost identical lures—leadhead tailspinners of exactly the same size and action—and we were rapidly retrieving them over the top of the bar. The only difference in the two lures was their color: Jerry's was green and mine was white.

About every third cast Jerry got an arm-jolting strike and was pulling in nice 2½-pound fish with exasperating regularity. I'd made just as many casts, but hadn't gotten a nibble.

Finally, as he lifted still another fish into the boat, I said, "Gimme that lure," and we switched. Jerry continued to catch bass, on the lure I had unsuccessfully been using, and I continued to catch nothing, on the lure he had been previously using!

I wracked my brain, trying to solve the problem. Initially, I thought it was the difference in color that was responsible, then I discovered what was really happening. I was using a Garcia Ambassadeur 5000 baitcasting reel and Jerry was using an Ambassadeur 5500. Big deal, you say? So what?

Well, here's the answer. The Garcia 5000 reel has a 3-to-1 gear ratio, but the 5500 reel has a 5-to-1 gear ratio. Consequently, with each turn of the reel handle, Jerry was retrieving his lures almost twice as fast as mine. Quickly, I reached for another rod with a similar high-speed reel on it, tied on a *yellow* tailspinner lure, and three casts later socked the hooks into a good fish.

Another time, with Nick Ansely, I was catching good bass and Nick was fuming because of his lack of success. This was at Santee–Cooper, in South Carolina, and we were fishing breaks on breaklines (stumps along the edge of the old Santee River bed). I was throwing leadhead tailspinners again, and so was Nick. Both lures were the same size, color and action, and we were using identical rods, reels and lines. By the time I had put six fish into the boat, Nick hadn't received a strike. Can you figure out why?

After each cast Nick was retrieving his lure at the same speed as I, but he was doing so the very instant the spinner hit the water. I was allowing my lure to sink all the way to the bottom before beginning my retrieve. I was catching bass for no other reason than because I was fishing 15 feet deeper. After I explained this to Nick, he caught a 12-inch bass on the very next cast, then three casts later boated a hefty six-pounder.

I am hoping—I am confident—that you now possess enough knowledge about bass behavior that you will never again purchase another lure *solely* because its manufacturer has painted it with some stunning new color or given it a special wiggling action, or because some tournament pro won a contest with the lure at some faraway lake, or for any other reason not directly related to its depth and speed capabilities.

With the importance of lure speed and depth firmly established, let's begin to consider additional features incorporated into lures that may render them more effective under certain conditions.

Color, Size and Action

The eyes of both man and bass possess what biologists call *rods* and *cones.* Rods are light-intensity receptors, while cones are nerve endings that distinguish colors. As humans, we possess a large number of cones, and thus have precise color discrimination, but only under conditions of bright light. We possess far fewer rods, and this is why our visual acuity begins to fail as the light intensity recedes. As dusk yields to full darkness, our depth of field (how far we can see) rapidly diminishes and our once-sharp object-definition begins to blur. Since we always need light in order to have color, with the transformation of dusk into full darkness, colors change to shades of gray and then black.

Bass possess fewer cones in their eyes than man, and so we can infer that their color perception is not quite as advanced as ours. In clear water, they can perceive a wide range of colors, but they don't see them in exactly the same way as we do. To simulate how bass see colors, look through a piece of light yellow cellophane such as the kind used to wrap candy.

On the other hand, bass possess five times as many rods in their eyes as man, thus enabling them to feed or strike very easily when in deep water or after full dark. But while bass can easily see when light intensity is low, they are quite myopic. The lenses of our eyes are flat and we can adjust them for either long-range or short-range viewing of objects. Bass, on the other hand, possess nonadjustable, round eyes, making them very near-sighted. But this is usually of little consequence to them because, as noted earlier, bass generally do not live in open-water habitats in which they would need to see forage from long distances. Instead, they're primarily muggers that like to wait in dark alleys to ambush, at close range, hapless prey that perchance amble by.

All of this makes a good case in favor of precise lure presentation when working various types of cover or structure. When bass are actively feeding, they simply may not be able to see your offering if it is some distance away. And if bass are not actively feeding, and provoking spontaneous strikes is the only way to catch them, your lure must be closer still! The farther away a lure is presented, assuming it's still within a fish's visual range, the more time the fish has to evaluate it—and a basic tenet of provoking a bass into striking is to *not* allow it this opportunity.

In considering *lure color,* remember that color results from the combination of various wave lengths of light. Furthermore, certain wave lengths are able to penetrate only to certain depths (depending mostly upon the degree of water clarity). So it stands to reason that bass are able to see some colors better than others under certain water conditions in which light intensity varies. What all this boils down to is that a colored lure may take on entirely different appearances to bass when fished at different depths or in water possessing various degrees of color or turbidity.

For example, the wave lengths of light that combine to make the color red are the first to be absorbed as light intensity diminishes. Even in relatively clear water, a lure that appears to be red near the surface will gradually appear to turn light gray as it descends into deeper water. Descending still deeper, it will turn dark gray, and then almost black. In muddy water, the wave lengths making up the color red are filtered out even more quickly, to the extent that only five feet below the surface red may appear as dark gray.

So in certain instances a lure may not appear to be the same color to bass as it is in your tacklebox; this is especially likely for lures used during the hours of dawn or dusk, in very deep water, or in water that is muddy, murky or stained. The irony here is that an angler who catches a few nice bass at 20 feet deep with a fast retrieve, using a red plug, may think to himself, "These red lures are really hot stuff!" Yet in all truth he's misread the situation entirely. First, it was almost exclusively the depth and speed

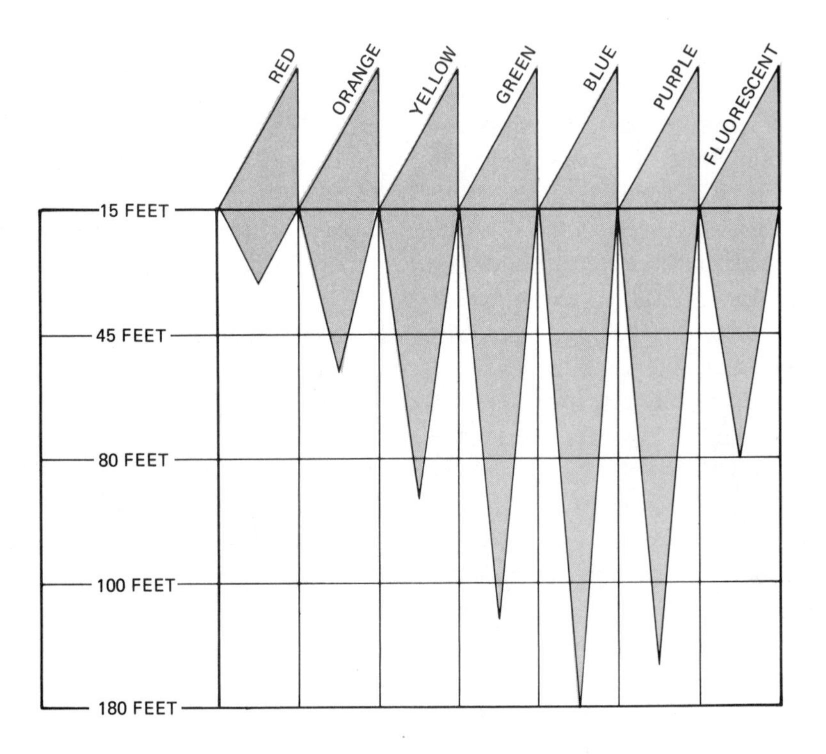

Depths to which various colors retain their integrity in clear water.

he was employing that accounted for the bass. And secondly, the lure he was fishing at that depth was not perceived by bass as red at all but as black.

Down deep it is a dimly lit world of dark blues, greens and blacks (technically, black isn't a color, but simply the total absence of light). And the colors at this end of the spectrum (including fluorescent colors, due to their optically brightened, highly reflective values) not only can be ascertained most easily but retain their original appearances in deeper or darker waters. Scientists claim, in fact, that if a bass were able to live in extremely deep water, it could accurately distinguish dark blue colors at a depth of 180 feet.

This obviously brings us to the million-dollar question: "Do bass prefer, or respond better to, one color more than another?"

Even though there have been controlled experiments in which bass have shown a decided preference for red in clear, shallow water, some scientists believe that variables other than color *per se* may offer plausible explanations as to why bass often seem to "take" certain colored lures more readily than others. One such influence is not the specific color itself but rather the *contrast* that a color reveals when seen against cover or bottom materials. We'll look at this subject in the next chapter, and in even more detail in Chapter 21. Another influence has to do with a type of *adaptation* that bass may theoretically make to the color of the particular prey they are most closely tied to. If bass are gorging themselves every day on emerald shiners, it seems reasonable that plugs of similar size and color would be more effective than something radically different. But, and this is the frustrating part, bass are notorious for throwing out the rule book and doing something entirely contradictory.

Here's another thought to ponder seriously. All of us have probably at one time or another had the experience of casting, say, a blue plastic worm with success. As an experiment we tie on an orange worm or some other color, fish it at the same speed and depth, and draw a blank. So we tie on the blue worm again, and BAM! With this experience locked in our memory banks, guess which color worm we're likely to tie on first when we go fishing again?

What I'm getting at is that I firmly believe a good deal of the success an angler has in fishing particular colors has to do with his faith in those lures (after, of course, he has attended to the matter of speed and depth control). This may sound altogether unscientific, but the truth is that anglers place varying degrees of confidence in various colors, and even in certain types of lures, as they rummage through their tackleboxes looking for "old faithful." Perhaps the color an angler prefers was first recommended to him by some fishing authority whom he respects. Or maybe the angler coincidentally took a nice string of bass on that particular color one day. Whatever the case, he comes to believe in that color. Actually, the color of the lure may be of little importance under the conditions he's fishing. But if he believes in a certain color, he tends to fish that particular color more precisely, methodically and carefully than some other lure or color he has less confidence in. In most of life's endeavors, a positive attitude has a far greater influence on the end result than most of us ever suspect.

Along these same lines my friend Dick Kotis, president of the Arbogast Bait Company in Akron, Ohio, has conducted a number of interesting experiments. Arbogast has long been a leader in researching gamefish behavior and how fish react to colors, sounds and other variables frequently incorporated into lures.

Dick discovered that dark colors tended to spook bass in clear water, whereas the fish seemed not at all alarmed by more subtle hues. In fact, completely transparent lures produced best of all under conditions of extreme water clarity. As a result, Dick began marketing clear plastic lures. They didn't sell. Anglers were not attracted to lures they could see through, even though bass purportedly were.

As a possible solution to the problem, Kotis then began making the very first chrome-colored plugs ever to be seen by anglers. Chrome is a good substitute for clear, because when fished in transparent waters where bass are skittish it has the same unobtrusive effect. Since anglers could not see through a chrome lure they began buying the plugs and in gin-clear water found themselves catching more bass than ever! Leaves you wondering who is most finicky—bass or the anglers who pursue them.

Your goal, then, in selecting the color of a lure should be twofold. Select a lure with a color that the bass can readily see under the given water conditions. At the same time, avoid colors that contrast so much with the environment that they alarm the fish. In more specific terms, I can offer two practical rules regarding lure color. Under conditions of darkness (stained water, muddy water, deep water, or after dark), use dark-colored lures—black, blue, purple, red. Under conditions of bright light (clear or shallow water) use light-colored lures—white, yellow, translucent red, pale green.

Silver and gold colors, by the way, such as those found on metal lures which have been plated, are classified as neutral colors. They can be readily seen at most depths, yet they do not seem to cause a "fright reaction" in clear-water conditions; hence, they can be used any time.

The one time an angler should strive to make his lures vividly contrast with their surroundings is when fishing after dark, particularly when using surface lures. The paradox here is that many anglers might think contrast, in this context, would mean casting a very light-colored lure, but that is not the case at all. Even on a very dark night, the sky is lighter than the underwater environment. Consequently, a bass looking up at your lure from beneath will actually see a darker lure against the night sky better than a light lure, because the lure's silhouette is more pronounced.

Lure size is still another visual factor that may affect the response of bass to lures. As with color, though, the size of a lure is a secondary concern that comes into play once it's presented at the proper speed and depth.

Some anglers firmly believe that little lures catch little fish and big lures catch big fish. It's a logical assumption because little fish are simply incapable of taking on large prey and large fish need, and are capable of, taking on larger forage. But more important, I think, than the size of a lure is the degree to which it represents, or mimics, the forage the bass are tied to in a particular body of water.

If, for example, bass (both large and small) are feeding predominantly on threadfin shad in a given lake, and 99 percent of those shad average 2½ inches in length, you won't have much success offering a plug that looks like a yellow, seven-inch perch. Similarly, let's say you take home three nice bass for dinner and upon cleaning them discover their bellies packed full of crayfish. It doesn't really matter what you caught those bass on, you know for sure that these particular fish, which likely as not had many types of food to choose from, unhesitatingly decided to take the crayfish. Therefore, an orangish brown jig bounced along appropriate bottom structures to simulate crayfish movements probably would be the best bet for the next day's fishing. And, obviously, tying on a big green surface plug that looks like a frog would be fool's play. Yet, believe it or not, many anglers do this very thing, never taking the time to learn about the forage in the waters they frequent, nor ever examining the stomach contents of the fish they catch.

In the final analysis, then, every angler should have at his disposal a wide range of lure sizes that can be brought into use as specific conditions dictate. In clear water, use smaller lures than usual, to avoid the possibility of alarming the fish. In discolored water, select something larger, to provide a more readily discernible "target" for the bass to home in on. And in water that is neither completely transparent or extremely discolored, which is what you'll find most of the time, lures that closely simulate the natural forage in the lake always are the best bet.

Lure action, another visual feature, should not be confused with *speed.* To demonstrate the difference, tie a wobbling plug to your line and lower it into the rushing current of a river, holding it in a stationary position. Even though you're not retrieving the lure as much as an inch, you'll

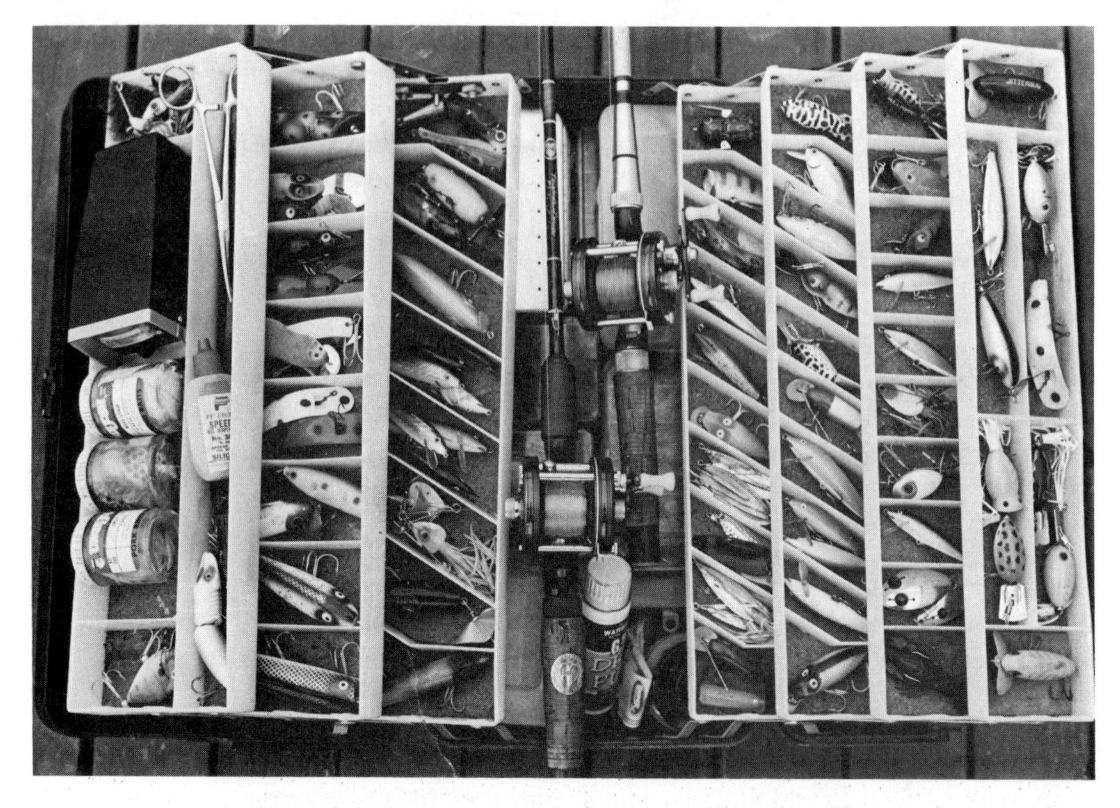

Accomplished bass anglers become lure collectors through necessity because the widest possible selection allows them to be prepared for any situation.

notice it still has action. Of the many factors that enter into successful bass fishing, lure action is probably the least important and yet, curiously, one of the features most promoted by tackle manufacturers.

If and when lure action does play a role in eliciting strike responses from bass, it's my belief this influence has more to do with their sense of hearing than sight. This is especially true in off-colored water where bass use certain anatomical features to detect vibrations given off by prey items moving through the water or scrabbling around on the bottom. This topic is discussed in the last section of this chapter.

Before concluding this section on how bass see lures, I should briefly say a few words about light refraction, which is the deflection from a straight line that light rays undergo when passing from air through the surface of another medium, in this case water. To visualize the effect of light refraction, stick a pencil into a glass of water and you'll see that it appears to be broken or bent at a sharp angle. Because of this phenomenon, bass in shallow water can easily see an angler standing in a boat or on the shoreline, but only if the fisherman is within the so-called "window" of refraction.

If you've spent much time around the shorelines of lakes and other waters, you've probably seen plenty of small bass. And you may have noted that they don't always immediately dart away. Rather, they frequently only move a short distance and then stop. They aren't spooked, yet. What they are doing, very simply, is backing away slightly to increase or expand the angle of refraction so they can have a "better look." Then, just watch them scat!

The tip we can glean from this insight applies primarily to fishing clear or shallow water and it is this: Maintain a low profile, which means staying seated if possible, and make long casts, so that you'll be out of the refraction angle.

Should Lures Smell Good?

When Tom Mann of Eufaula, Alabama, introduced his now famous line of Jelly Worms in a multitude of fruity flavors, he caused quite a stir in bass-fishing circles. Anglers immediately divided themselves into two camps. There were those who threw watermelon-, peach-, and grape-flavored worms (among others) with confidence, but usually with the brims of their hats pulled down over their eyes to conceal their identities. And there were those who simply sat on the sidelines, scoffing and hee-hawing over the absurdity of it all; these angling skeptics may have enjoyed the first laugh, but it's becoming more and more apparent they won't relish the last.

Obviously, no bass ever had an insatiable craving for apple-, strawberry-, or lime-flavored worms. And I can't ever remember having dressed a bass and discovered its belly full of blueberries or persimmons. Yet plastic worms impregnated with such flavors—and various other lures with other scents—have been conclusively proven to be more effective in catching bass than identical—but unscented—lures fished at the same speed, the same depth and in the same location.

It must be remembered that bass spend most of their time in a dark, shadowy world (in the depths or in cover) where they must depend upon all of their senses to locate food or detect sources of potential danger. Vision plays the most important role in this survival. Not only is it the sense bass rely upon most but also the one that triggers the strongest responses. For example, my friend Doug Hannon recently described an interesting experiment, and equally intriguing results. He dunked his plastic worms in gasoline before fishing them. Ordinarily, gasoline is a very noxious substance that repels bass. But in this case, the water was extremely clear and the fish were in a highly active, aggressive feeding state. Consequently, the sight of the worms overcame all other stimuli, and the bass grabbed the gasoline-soaked worms with enthusiasm.

Admittedly, this unusual situation was arranged to demonstrate the degree to which bass rely upon their vision. However, when their vision is impeded, due to conditions such as muddy water or even the darkness associated with night or deep water, bass begin relying heavily upon their senses of smell, taste and hearing. Appealing to these senses also is highly important when bass are not active but have slumped into neutral or inactive behavior patterns.

All fish possess nostrils (sometimes called *nares*) in pairs located on either side of their snouts, just in front of the eyes. Water continually enters the forward nostrils, flows over a series of *olfactory folds* just beneath the skin, then exits through the rear nostrils. Bass also possess taste and smell receptors on their gill rakers and along the sides of their bodies, enabling them to constantly monitor the water about them.

There are several interesting things about the nostrils in bass and other fish. First, the number of olfactory folds differs from species to species. Migratory fish such as salmon, for example, possess far more folds than nonmigratory species such as bass. Furthermore, species that rely heavily upon their sense of smell for feeding purposes possess far more olfactory folds than those that are basically sight-feeders. Catfish, for example, have an extensive number of folds, whereas northern pike have almost none at all. Another discovery that laboratory dissections of various fish species have revealed is that fish acquire more olfactory folds as they grow older. This may partly explain why it is more difficult to catch big fish than small ones: Very simply, they can smell better. In any event, various studies suggest that bass, although not as sensitive to odors and tastes as some other species, can detect substances in the water about them in quite small concentrations, in the range of a few parts per million.

It's not clear which specific tastes and scents are *attractants* to fish, but we do know at least some that are *repellents* to bass. The scent of man has long been thought to repel fish. This scent is caused by the amino acid L-serine, present in human skin and in greater quantity in some people than others, which may inadvertently be transferred to lures and baits when handling them. There also are a wide range of chemical substances —gasoline, motor oil, battery acid, insect repellent, deodorant, and perhaps others—believed to cause adverse behavior in bass.

Many anglers are not aware of it, but bass can be quickly turned off by predator scents, particularly those emanating from the body slime of northern pike, muskies and chain pickerel, and to a lesser extent from the body slime of walleyes and striped bass. Sometimes you can even see this slime on your line or lure. If you hook a big pike, for example, it will undoubtedly try to "roll" in an attempt to cut your line with its sharp gill covers. After boating the fish, you'll notice a clear or milky mucous on your lure and the terminal end of your line. If you continue to fish for bass, I can almost guarantee you won't catch a fish for at least an hour, or until hundreds of casts have removed all the predator slime from your lure and line. This is why it's always wise, after catching a predator fish other than a bass, to cut off several feet of the terminal end of your line and discard it, and to rinse your lure thoroughly by repeatedly rubbing it and sloshing it around in the water next to the boat.

In my opinion, then, plastic worms and other lures need not necessarily smell or taste good to bass, particularly when the water is clear and they are primarily sight-feeding, but they certainly should not smell or taste bad. One reason for impregnating lures, therefore, is to mask any noxious substances that an angler may accidently and unknowingly transfer to the lures he's using. Actually, anglers have been doing this for generations by dousing their lures with vanilla extract, anise oil and other potions.

Then there are the attractants that supposedly appeal to a bass's sense of "good taste." These are the so-called *worm dunks,* which anglers have been concocting for decades by mixing together fish oils, pulverized insects and nightcrawlers, and numerous other secret ingredients. The angler then keeps a mason jar full of the stuff onboard and periodically dips his lure into it.

Since bass anglers have shown such unrelenting faith in masking scents and worm dunks over the years, many companies that sell scented lures have also begun marketing a wide variety of lotions and sprays. Of course, they don't tell you what the secret ingredients are, which makes it extremely difficult to compare different brands or explain why some work and some do not. Unlike the makers of other aids to catching bass, such as pH monitors or oxygen-evaluation equipment, who try to tell you as much as possible, the makers of worm dunks and other potions prefer to shroud their products in an aura of mystery and tell you as little as possible. This automatically leads many anglers to be quite skeptical.

Until more conclusive evidence is available in this matter, I refuse to take sides. Although bass do not have senses of smell and taste as refined as some other species, certain substances may indeed attract them while others are almost sure to repel them. It's also likely that numerous substances can be used to mask those substances that ordinarily may be repellents. But for the moment, I'll leave it to each angler to try a wide range of scent-impregnated lures and add-on scents and determine for himself whether the additional success he enjoys, if any, justifies the price he's asked to pay (some "potions" are presently going for as high as $12 per bottle!).

A couple of other things also merit brief discussion. For one, the addition of flavors, masking scents or attractants to lures makes sense only with certain types of artificials. In the case of hard lures, such as spoons, plugs and spinners, scents probably have minimum effect because the nature of the materials these lures are made of prevents them from absorbing either noxious or attractant odors. Further, since these lures are

There are numerous commercial sprays, lotions, and worm dunks on the market. Some are designed to mask human or other unfavorable odors that may be transferred to lures; others actually claim to attract bass.

designed to be retrieved through the water at relatively fast speeds, they undergo a continual "washing" process.

Soft lures, however, such as plastic worms, salamanders, grubs and pork rinds, are quite porous and will easily absorb odorous substances. This even includes lures such as jigs that may have bucktail or marabou dressings. These types of lures, in addition to being porous, are designed to be worked at speeds ranging from slow to dead-stop. If they reek of some noxious odor, it will dissipate into the water around the lure. Conversely, an attractant substance would exude into the water around the lure and might entice into biting a bass that is not in an active, aggressive feeding state.

Even if you choose not to buy and use various masking agents or attractant substances, don't entirely discount the tendency of bass to eject or avoid a lure that carries a noxious odor. The least you should do is keep in your tacklebox a small tube of concentrated liquid soap, preferably a nonscented "sportsman's soap." Then, each time you switch your outboard fuel line from one gas tank to another, or handle an electric motor battery, or rub insect repellent on your skin, take a few minutes to wash your hands before handling your lures or live baits.

Finally, there is one other matter regarding scents that we should investigate. Scientific studies have confirmed that most fish species release into the water an alarm substance known as *schreckstoffen* whenever the surface of their skin is scratched, whenever they are bleeding, or whenever they have suffered any other kind of superficial or major injury. This alarm substance takes up to a minute to exude into the water, whereupon nearby fish that detect it quickly become frightened and cease feeding or other activity.

Bass will even refuse to accept back into a school former members that have become injured. Once, I saw this happen when watching bass in an underwater observation boat with a glass hull. A bass that had been caught by an angler on the top deck was purposely injured by lightly scratching its skin with a knife. When the fish was released it tried to return to its school, but the other fish would have nothing to do with it, and kept trying to chase the injured fish away, until finally it went off by itself and sought hiding in thick weeds.

Biologists claim that these alarm substances have a deterrent effect only on fish of the same species; they may actually exert just the opposite effect when an unlike species is involved. In other words, an injured bass released back into the water may release a *schreckstoffen* that causes other bass to cease feeding, but an injured bluegill or shad releasing *schreckstoffen* may signal itself as a prey that is disabled and, thus, trigger predatorial feeding responses among previously inactive bass.

This is exactly why fishermen for generations have made a religious practice of clipping the tail fins of bait minnows just before impaling them on their hooks. And some bass anglers I know, when they inadvertently catch a bluegill or other fish, will make a knife slice on the skin of the unwanted species and periodically rub it on their bass lures. Still other anglers, when catching small bass they don't want to keep, may temporarily place them in live wells, to be released later in some other location. Their belief is that, even though the small bass may not reveal any obvious signs of injury, they nevertheless don't want to take any chances of "turning off" still other fish that may yet be in the immediate region.

If you choose not to engage in any of these practices, at least be very careful in handling those fish you do intend to release, for a bass that accidently slips out of your grasp and begins flopping around in the bottom of your boat is certain to have at least very slight abrasions on its skin, causing the release of *schreckstoffen.*

Give Them an Earful

While a bass generally uses all of its senses in combination, the sense of hearing assumes more importance when a bass's vision is impaired. In very dark water, bass may rely almost entirely on the detection of underwater sounds to guide their feeding behavior. Laboratory tests, with bass temporarily blinded, have shown they can pinpoint the exact location of minnows and unerringly seize them without ever using their eyes at all! It therefore stands to reason that under certain water conditions, sound may be an important variable for the angler to consider.

Bass possess ears, but they actually hear with three internal hearing systems, which work in support of one another. Their "ears" are buried deep in their heads and are not open to the outside water. Bass hear by detecting vibrations that are transmitted indirectly from the water through the skin, flesh and bone of the head to the ear. As we have seen, bass, like other fish species, also possess a *lateral line.* This is a series of very sensitive nerve endings just below the skin that detect vibrations. In all fish, the line runs from the head to the tail, and in some species such as bass it can even be discerned as a distinct black line that looks almost like a pencil mark. The third hearing system doesn't really detect vibrations but consists of a gas-filled tube running from the swim bladder to the ear. This organ amplifies the sounds that are picked up by the other hearing systems and transmits them to the ears proper. There, the vibrations are amplified still further by a series of hollow bones before being sent to the brain, where they are classified and interpreted. It all happens within a split second.

Each type of aquatic creature emits a characteristic vibration determined by its shape and method of locomotion. For example, a baitfish swimming at some middle depth, such as a threadfin shad, would send out vibrations different from those of a crayfish scratching along the bottom. Bass become familiar with these sounds, recognizing some as meaning food, others danger, and so on. A lure that gives off an unfamiliar vibration, then, especially when it's not visible to the fish, may spook bass and send them darting for the depths.

Biologists have determined that bass can discern sounds ranging from 20 to about 2,000 cycles per second (cps), but they are most attracted to vibrations of 65 to 75 cps. This intriguing information encouraged George Perrin many years ago to begin studying sounds emitted by various types of lures. Perrin was then top boss at Plastics Research and Development Corporation in Fort Smith, Arkansas, a leading manufacturer of lures under the Rebel name. Using a 36,000-gallon test tank, a frequency generator, an oscilloscope and a graph recorder, Perrin made a startling discovery: The ten most popular lures on the market at that time, although differing markedly in their size, shape, action and materials, all emitted very similar types of sounds and vibration patterns. Consequently, Perrin insisted that all lures marketed by Plastics Research in the future emit vibrations of 65 to 75 cps.

Like every serious bass angler, you undoubtedly own scads of lures put out by many different manufacturers, and it would not be practical to build a test tank in order to monitor their underwater sounds. But you should realize that sound plays an important role in gamefish behavior. And if one particular type of lure seldom pays off, when presented properly, do not hesitate to switch to another. This applies not only to lures made by different companies but even to specific models made by the same company. Modern production techniques, in which tens of thousands of lures are mass-produced with injection molds, can lead to small variations in lures that supposedly are identical. You won't be able to notice these variations with the naked eye, but they are there nonetheless. As a result, a Bagley Balsa-B, for example, may emit a slightly different underwater sound than another Balsa-B that looks identical.

While the shape and action of any given lure play a major role in determining what vibrations it emits, many manufacturers also build in certain sound-influencing features in their lures. Most often, these are hollow chambers, inside the lures, that contain free-floating weights. When the lure is retrieved, the weights bang against each other and against the inside walls of their chambers, creating very audible rattling noises. Time and again, these lures have proven successful in out-fishing similar lures that do not emit such noises.

One possible explanation is that bass are continually on the alert for distress vibrations emitted by various types of forage. Such sounds are not the ones customarily given off by free-swimming, normal forage and indicate some type of injury. Often, such sounds seem to trigger predatory responses from bass, transforming them almost instantaneously from an inactive state to one of frenzied feeding and striking. Perhaps the rattling sounds given off by some types of lures in some way simulates these distress vibrations.

Still other types of lures such as spinnerbaits, buzz-baits and leadhead tailspinners "sound off" through the use of whirling Colorado blades or propellers. Underwater, these lures thump and vibrate. And when retrieved quickly through the surface film, the blades cup air and force it underwater where it is then released, creating a gurgling sound.

Even lures that have traditionally been thought of as being quiet are now known to emit considerable sound underwater. I'm talking here about plastic worms, plastic salamanders, jigs and similar lures. The noise these lures make is a peculiar rubbing or rasping sound, or sometimes a clicking noise as a sliding sinker or jighead taps along the bottom.

Much more research is needed on underwater sound and how it influences bass behavior before sweeping generalizations can be made. For the moment, about all that can be recommended is to use a wide variety of "noisy" lures when underwater visibility is poor. Then, when bass begin showing a decided preference for one type of lure, stick with it.

A few words should also be said about sounds an angler makes during the course of his day's fishing. I remember how, when I was a boy, my father would insist that conversation be held to a minimum when fishing. He believed the sound of our voices would scare the fish. We now know, however, that this is simply a myth.

The surface of any body of water acts like a shield, blocking out 99 percent of all above-surface sounds. While on board boats, anglers can talk as much as they like with no worry about alarming nearby fish.

However, don't scrape your tacklebox against the hull of the boat, and don't carelessly throw your anchor overboard. These and similar actions cause alarming vibrations that penetrate the surface layer of water, sending bass out of the area as though their tails were on fire. One of the greatest culprits that cause bass to quickly turn off is a chain stringer, with several bass on the snaps, banging against the sidewall of an aluminum boat as the fish occasionally thrash around.

Whether or not outboard motors and electric trolling motors spook bass is debatable and probably depends more upon the existing fishing conditions than anything else. Obviously, churning outboard and electric motor props create much louder vibrations and other underwater noises than any lure ever made. And in very shallow, clear water, these noises heralding your approach cannot logically do a lot to improve the fishing. Yet in deeper water, they may have little effect. I may be going out on a limb, but it's my opinion that outboards have little or no effect on bass when they're deeper than six feet. I base this opinion on the fact that I frequently catch fish directly beneath my boat when backtrolling live baits. Electric motors, on the other hand, are typically used in much shallower water. In this case, however, you're usually making casts, either long or short, to cover or structure that is at least six feet away; so again, the motor noise probably causes little disturbance to the bass.

CHAPTER

14

Favorite Lures And Techniques Of The Pros

If you decide to become a professional bass angler and earn a full-time living by following the tournament circuit, it doesn't take many missed meals before you learn some cold, harsh truths about playing the cast-for-cash game. First, you have to find and catch a lot of fish and, of course, the bigger the better. This requires having an intimate knowledge of lake types, water conditions and bass behavior. Second, since you're continually racing against the clock, you simply cannot afford to use any particular lure or strategy that is not a productive investment of your time.

All of this explains why a majority of tournament anglers rely heavily upon a bare minimum of lures. Interestingly enough, Ray Scott, the founder of Bass Anglers Sportsman Society and the singlemost responsible person for bass tournament fishing in this country, has incorporated into his organization's tournament regulations the stipulation that contestants are allowed no more than ten pounds of lures. And this includes the weight of the tacklebox in which the lures are housed! This is no joke. At the end of each day of fishing, when contestants approach the scales to have their bass officially weighed, Scott weighs their tackleboxes as well.

The constraints of time, and regulations, force a tournament angler to choose his assortment of lures very carefully. Foremost, he wants lures that offer as much versatility as possible, since none of the contestants know what lake conditions will greet them upon their arrival. So lures capable of working a wide range of depths from top to bottom, and capable of a wide range of retrieve speeds, are favorites. Just as important, if the pro has any hopes of eating regularly and paying the rent, his selection of lures must include consistent producers that appeal to big fish.

After taking part in dozens upon dozens of tournaments over the years, as both a reporter and at times even a contestant, I've noted a fairly standard selection of lures that seems always to shake out on top. Whether the tournament is on a flatland lake in Mississippi, a canyonland lake in Arizona, or a mesotrophic lake in Minnesota, there are four categories of lures that a majority of pros rely on a majority of the time. These are crankbaits, spinnerbaits and buzz-baits, jigs and jigging spoons, and plastic worms. The specific lures may be made by any number of different companies and, therefore, reveal slightly different design features, but chances are good that a tournament pro's tacklebox of tricks will consist of representatives of these four all-important lure types.

This is not to say that other types of lures are never used. Occasionally, a surface plug, straight-shaft spinner or weedless spoon garnished with a strip of pork rind may find its way into a pro's tacklebox when its applications are justified by unique conditions. But, nationwide, the other lures undoubtedly account for the lion's share of big fish taken by the pros every year. This, therefore, makes them the best bets for casual anglers, too, who may have no interest in competitive bass fishing but who certainly do want to catch fish during their often limited time on the water.

The lures discussed in this chapter will probably add far more weight to your stringer than any other combination of artificials. And while we're at it, let's see how leading tournament pros fish these hot lures to get the most out of them.

Crankbaits

Crankbaits are a specific breed of plugs made from hollow plastic, balsa, ABS foam and, sometimes, wood. The one thing they all have in common is that they are designed to be retrieved at moderate to very fast speeds and in most instances to represent fleeing baitfish or panfish. Most of these plugs float at rest, dive to certain depths on the retrieve, and then exhibit a tight wiggling action as they quickly track their way back to the boat. Because of these characteristics, crankbaits generally are used when the water temperature is warm (60° or higher) and the bass quite active.

Each crankbait has its own narrow range of depth, which depends primarily on the width, length and slant of the clear plastic bill on the nose of the plug. For example, one crankbait, depending on how fast it is retrieved, may run two to four feet deep; another with a longer or more acutely angled bill may dive to six to ten feet; and still another may reach the 12- to 15-foot level. I am not aware of any crankbaits designed to run deeper than 20 feet, so in addition to warm-water situations they typically are used for fishing shoreline cover and relatively shallow bottom structures or contours. The depth range of a crankbait is usually stated somewhere on the package in which the lure is sold.

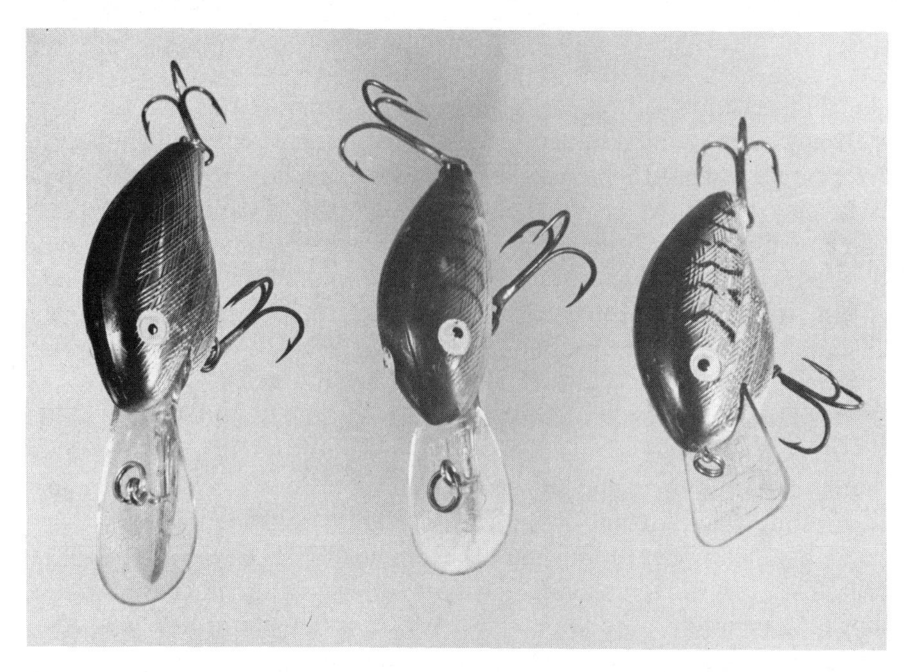

Every crankbait is designed to travel at a particular range of depth on the retrieve. These crankbaits are all exactly the same size, but note the variations in the length and shape of the clear plastic bills, which will take each plug to a different level.

I recommend having on hand at all times an assortment of crankbaits with a variety of depth ranges. Within each particular depth-range category, I also recommend having crankbaits in numerous body designs so you can select one that closely simulates the predominate forage in the lake you're fishing.

For example, if bass in a flatland reservoir customarily feed on panfish such as bluegills, sunfish and crappies, you'll want to rely heavily upon short, blocky, "fat-plugs" or "alphabet lures." Cordell's Big-O, Norman's Big-N, Plastic Research Company's Rebel plugs and the B-series of crankbaits made by Bagley Bait Company would all fill the bill.

On the other hand, if you're working a highland reservoir where bass are feeding mainly upon threadfin shad, you'll want to use crankbaits slightly more elongated in body shape—for example, the Bomber Bait Company's Model-A, Mann's Razor-Back and Pig lures, Bagley's Small Fry series, Bill Lewis Lure Company's Rat-L-Trap and Normark's Shad-Rap.

For working a natural mesotrophic lake where bass may be gorging on bluntnose shiners, emerald shiners, dace or perch, long and slender crankbaits of the slim-minnow design will undoubtedly fare best. Examples of

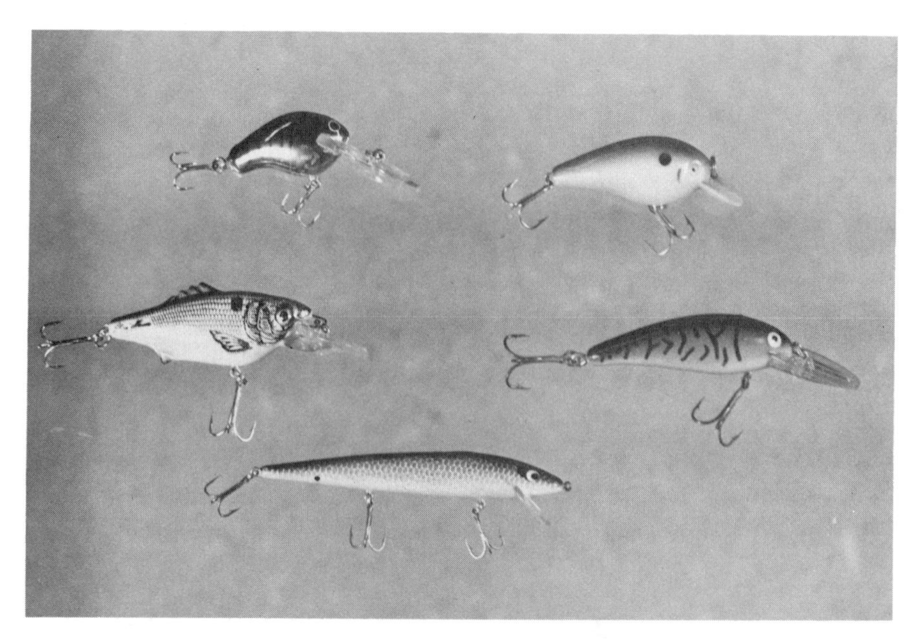

Every expert angler has a wide selection of crankbaits that not only run at different depths but have different body shapes to simulate various types of forage. The two top baits here imitate panfish, such as bluegills and crappies; the two center ones take after threadfin shad; and the lower one might fool bass feeding on bluntnose shiners, emerald shiners or perch.

these are Mann's Hackleback series, Smithwick's Rogues, Normark's Rapalas, Rebel's Minnow series and Bagley's Bang-O-Lures.

Of course, countless other brands are available as well. But regardless of their makers, remember that lures must have the proper depth and speed capabilities, for the given conditions, as discussed in the previous chapter. Only after these prerequisites are met, should lure shape, design and action be considered.

Regarding the color of crankbaits, I usually have the best success with a very few standard hues. Topping the list are shad-gray, mullet-blue, perch, bone, crayfish (brown with orange belly) and chartreuse. Crankbaits are also available in a wide variety of *naturalized* patterns; we'll look at this unique feature of lures in detail in Chapter 21.

Fan-casting is a popular method for eliciting strikes with crankbaits in relatively shallow, warm water, where they are most suited. In this method, an angler saturates the cover with a series of casts in a radial pattern, like the spokes emanating from the hub of a wheel. Once he completes a series of casts, the angler moves his craft and repeats the fan-casting pattern; this allows him to fish the same cover from two or more directions. Only the bass can explain why, but time and again I've seen a fish totally ignore a lure traveling by a stump or other cover at a certain angle, then blast it on the very next cast when the angle of retrieve is changed slightly.

Fan-casting crankbaits in this manner is especially popular with tournament bass anglers who are pressed for time and don't want to risk looking for widely separated schools of bass on deep, midlake structures. So they saturate areas that have shallow cover, machine-gunning crankbaits, searching for stragglers, trying to cover as much water on a given day as possible.

A rather stiff rod with a limber "working" tip is best for crankbait fishing, and watching tournament pros such as Jimmy Houston at work is like observing the inner workings of a well-oiled machine. He casts a fat-plug, for example, several yards past a stump and then retrieves it as

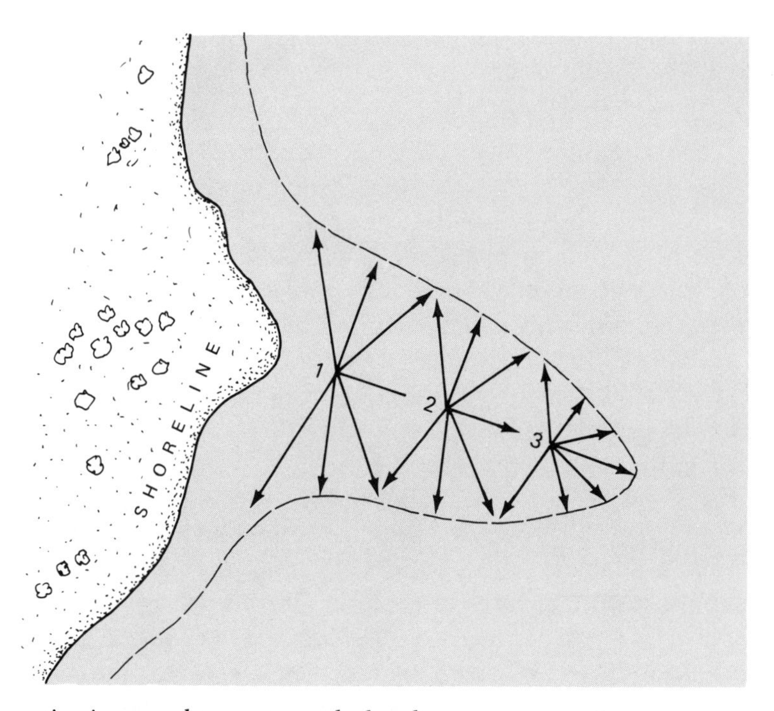

Fan-casting is a popular way to work shoreline points, as well as visible cover such as weedbeds. Each cast radiates from a central pivot point, covering the target area like the spokes of a wheel; then the pivot point is changed so the casts cover a slightly different area. Since fish in very shallow water are likely to be spooky, the author likes to fish the shallows first and then work progressively deeper.

close to the cover as possible. When the lure nears the rod tip, toward the end of the retrieve, he yanks it quickly from the water and sends it on its way to the other side of the stump or the next likely looking spot. The motion is often so fluid that it's difficult to ascertain exactly when the retrieve ends and the next cast begins.

He hopes that if he retrieves his lure past more potential fish lairs during the day than other competitors, he'll elicit the greatest number of aggressive responses.

A bass lying in the shade of a felled tree or some other cover will nearly always hear the rattling or vibrating commotion of an approaching crankbait before he actually sees it. This alerts him. Suddenly, it brushes by his nose! There is no opportunity to take a lengthy look at it or to decide whether he's hungry or not. He reacts and strikes.

Aside from this most popular method of presenting crankbaits, a number of refinements can add more fish to the stringer. Some tournament pros find they can elicit more strikes by varying the lure's speed numerous times during each retrieve. After casting the lure, and cranking it down to the depth at which it is designed to run, they may slow the lure speed momentarily, quickly rip it forward several more feet, slow it again, and so on. Other times, they may allow long pauses in between each forward movement of the lure, so the plug begins to float back toward the surface, whereupon they crank it back down again.

When fishing around boulders and especially woody cover such as stumps, logs and standing timber, some pros use another recent innovation, called *banging,* or *bumping.* In this technique, an angler casts beyond the cover, begins the retrieve, then suddenly moves the rod tip to one side or another, causing the crankbait to actually ram into the cover and just as quickly glance off. Particularly when bass are in an inactive state of behavior, this technique can be so effective it must be seen to be believed.

Another way of fishing crankbaits is *stacking* the lures and *straining the water.* This is used primarily to find the depth at which bass are holding when they are near weedbeds that border very deep water and especially when bass are clinging tightly against steep shorelines where sheer rock walls drop off abruptly into the depths, as in the case of canyonland reservoirs. In this technique, an angler positions his boat close to the weedline or rock bluff and casts parallel to it, first using a crankbait designed to run two to four feet deep. If he has no luck, he ties on another crankbait with a slightly longer bill that is designed to take the lure down to six to eight feet deep. Still no bass? He now fishes the same exact water again, this time with a crankbait that runs at the 10- to 12-foot level. In other words, he systematically works deeper and deeper, until fish are located, and from then on continues working the same productive depth range.

Fan-casting crankbaits isn't restricted to working visible cover or shoreline features. It's also an ideal technique for quickly checking bottom contours in midlake areas such as stream channel bends, breakline drop-offs, ditches, underwater ridges, timbered points, submerged rock-capped islands, and all manner of other structures. Fishing crankbaits in these areas may lead an angler to an occasional straggler fish or two and on occasion to an entire school of bass.

During a day of serious crankbait fishing, an angler will eventually find his lures are no longer tracking a straight course on the retrieve but are veering off to the right or left. When crankbaits operate in this erratic manner, their depth can no longer be properly controlled, which reduces their effectiveness. This veering behavior results from crankbaits repeatedly banging into and bouncing off cover, or digging into the bottom, which alters their running characteristics. In fact, many brand new lures fail to track a straight line on the first cast, due to the vagaries of mass-production techniques.

In any case, frequently *tuning* lures is an inseparable part of crankbait fishing. Tuning is accomplished by using a pair of needle-nose pliers to

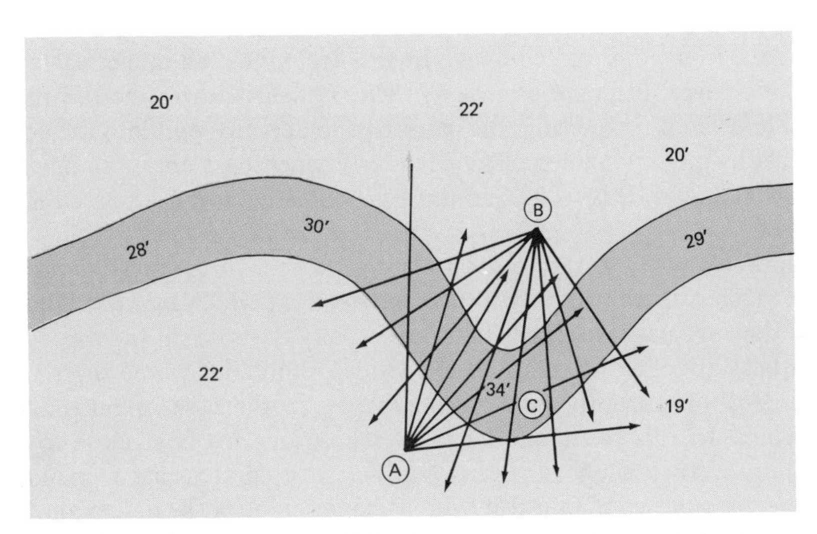

Fan-casting crankbaits across midlake bottom structures is one of the fastest ways of checking them. Here, a bend in a stream channel on the bottom may hold straggler or school bass. By positioning the boat first at location A, *then location* B, *an angler can easily work the entire structure from many different directions.*

bend the wire loop on the nose of the lure to which the line is tied. If the lure consistently angles off to the right on the retrieve, slightly bend the line-tie to the left, or vice-versa if the lure veers off to the left. Be careful not to make radical adjustments; just bend the line-tie a tiny bit, in the direction you want the lure to travel, and you'll correct the problem.

Interestingly, however, many anglers sometimes purposely bend the line-ties far to one side or the other to intentionally untune their crankbaits and make them travel at acute angles to the line of retrieve. They do this when fishing docks, places along the banks where trees have low branches extending out over the water, or shorelines where there are underwater ledges and recessed caves. By bending the line-tie far to the right or left, as the casting direction may warrant, it's possible to make the lure travel

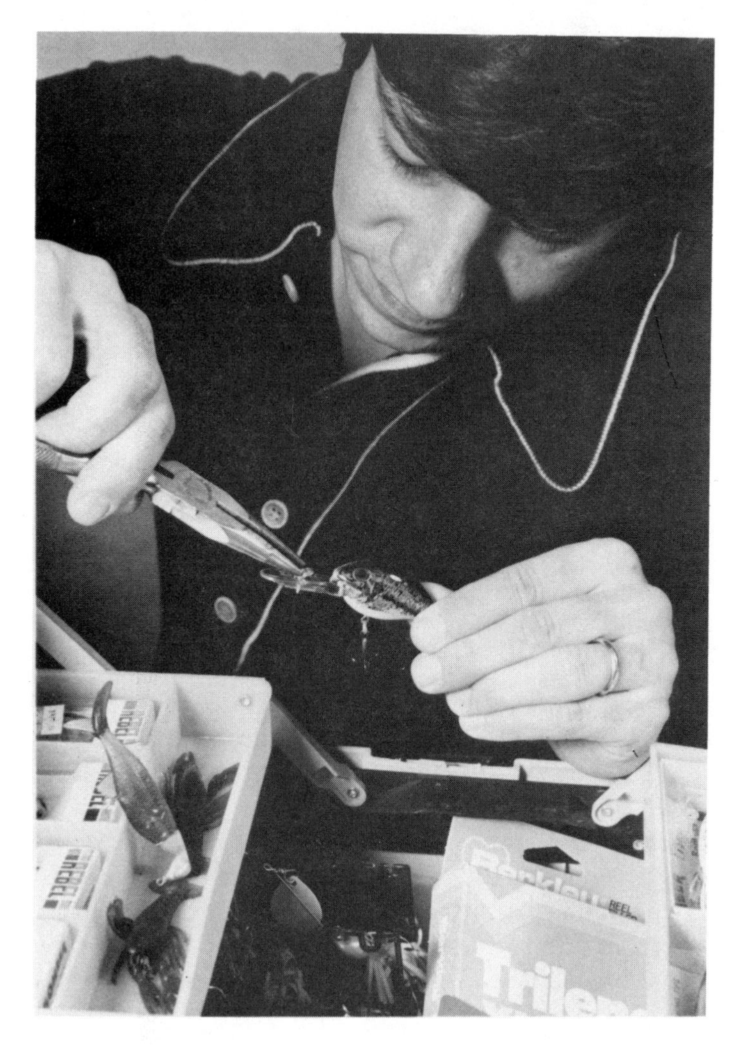

After extensive use, crankbaits may not run true in the water but tend to veer off to one side. The cure is tuning the lure by bending the line-tie slightly—to the left if the bait veers right, and vice-versa.

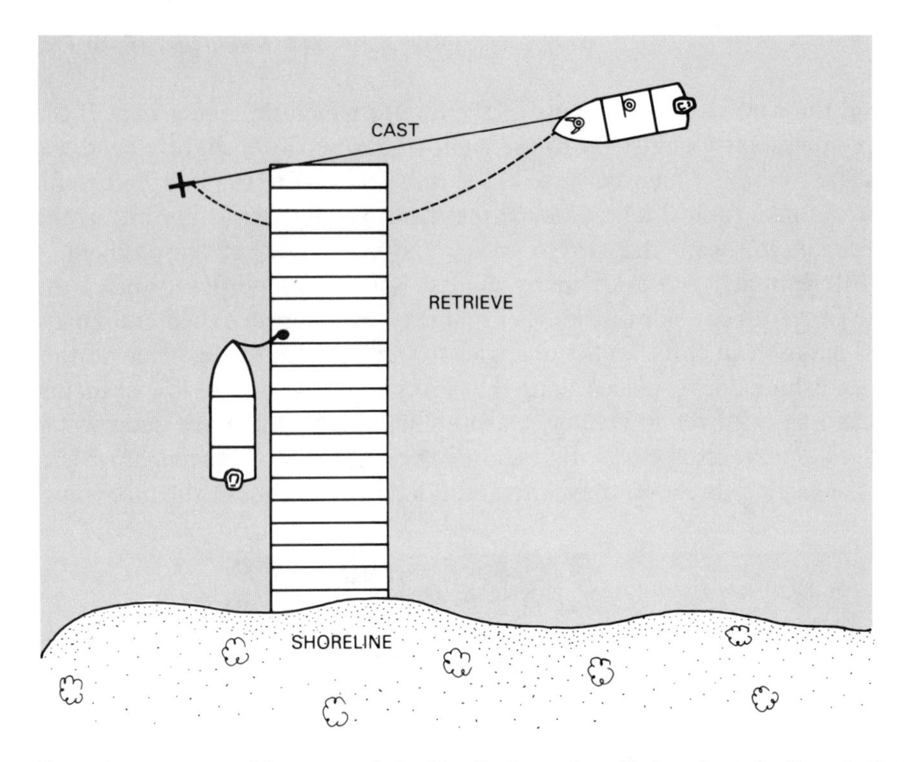

Sometimes, untuned lures are desirable. By intentionally bending the line-tie far to one side, you can make a crankbait swim far back under a dock or overhanging tree branches.

far back underneath such cover in a manner that would be impossible when using a tuned lure that tracks a straight course on the retrieve. And it's far back in these dark hideouts where the largest bass often like to hide during those brief times when they are in the shallows.

Spinnerbaits and Buzz-Baits

Spinnerbaits are among the bass world's most versatile lures. They can be spluttered across the surface, throbbed along at mid-depths, or pumped up and down across the bottom. They can be retrieved at agonizingly slow speeds, or worked so fast your reel almost begins to smoke. With such a wide range of depth and speed controls at your command, these lures can be used virtually every month of the year in which there is open water. Best of all, spinnerbaits can be worked in thick, foreboding places where good judgment tells you not to cast other lures, and it's these very places where straggler bass like to bide their time, undisturbed by less adventuresome anglers.

Spinnerbaits are among the most versatile lures. This is the author's close friend Inky Davis, a bass guide at Santee-Cooper, South Carolina, admiring a 9-pound largemouth.

Most veteran anglers own dozens of spinnerbaits in a wide variety of colors and sizes and have relentlessly pitched these baits over, around and through every imaginable type of cover. So rather than describe the fundamentals of spinnerbait fishing, which are probably familiar to you, I'll pass on a few refinements I've seen many pros use to tip the balance in their favor.

Let's start with the blades adorning such lures. In ultra-clear water, bright nickle-plated blades are notorious for spooking fish; this is the time to switch to spinnerbaits with hammered-brass or copper blades. Conversely, when the water is murky or off-colored in some other way, you need additional "flash" to enable bass to better see the lure; now, do indeed use nickle-plated blades.

Should your spinnerbaits be outfitted with single or tandem blades? I use both, depending on existing water color and temperature, and also on whether submerged cover is present. A *single-spin* (a spinnerbait with one large Colorado blade) sinks more quickly and therefore runs deeper on the retrieve than does a spinnerbait with two, small tandem blades. When cold water requires a slow retrieve, a tandem-bladed spinnerbait is the choice because it can be worked quite slowly without sinking and getting buried in weeds or deep brush. On the other hand, a single blade moves more water than tandem blades (which oppose each other and somewhat negate their water-moving ability), and this makes a single-spin far more effective in off-colored water where a loud, noisy lure helps bass home in upon their target.

Spinnerbaits come in a multitude of solid and contrasting colors. But in a casual poll of several dozen leading tournament pros and full-time guides, I found that the most popular among bass and bass anglers alike are all-white, all-black, all-yellow, all-chartreuse, yellow and black, and chartreuse and black. If among this assortment of colors you include some spinnerbaits with single copper blades, tandem copper blades, single nickle blades and tandem nickle blades, in many different sizes of each, it's easy to understand how an avid spinnerbait angler may have as many as 100 of these particular lures at any given time.

There is a marked difference of opinion among anglers as to whether rubber skirts are better than vinyl skirts, but it's my opinion the bass could care less. From a practical standpoint, however, vinyl skirts remain flexible and lifelike longer than rubber skirts, which have a tendency to fuse together after a while.

One thing all pros agree upon, though, is that reversing a spinnerbait's skirt as it comes from the factory is wise. Simply take the skirt off the hook, turn it around, and push it on backwards. In this manner, the skirt no longer trails out far behind the lure but bunches up, giving the spinnerbait a more compact, fuller-bodied appearance. This can be quite helpful when bass are not aggressively feeding because otherwise they often have a tendency to just grab the very end of a long, trailing skirt, thereby missing the hook.

On those days when bass are *short-striking*, most pros do not hesitate to use a trailer-hook, which is sometimes also called a *stinger.* This is a second hook, usually a long-shanked 4/0 Sproat with a wire weedguard, that is merely slipped over the spinnerbait hook. Some anglers like the hook point riding up, while others prefer it facing downward. In either case, some type of "keeper" arrangement must be engineered to prevent the trailer hook from falling off during the cast. I've found the easiest remedy is to use a center-punch to make ¼-inch-diameter circles from plastic coffee can lids. I keep a little envelope of about a hundred of them in my tacklebox. One of these little disks can be impaled on the spinnerbait hook, the stinger slipped into place, and then a second keeper-disk im-

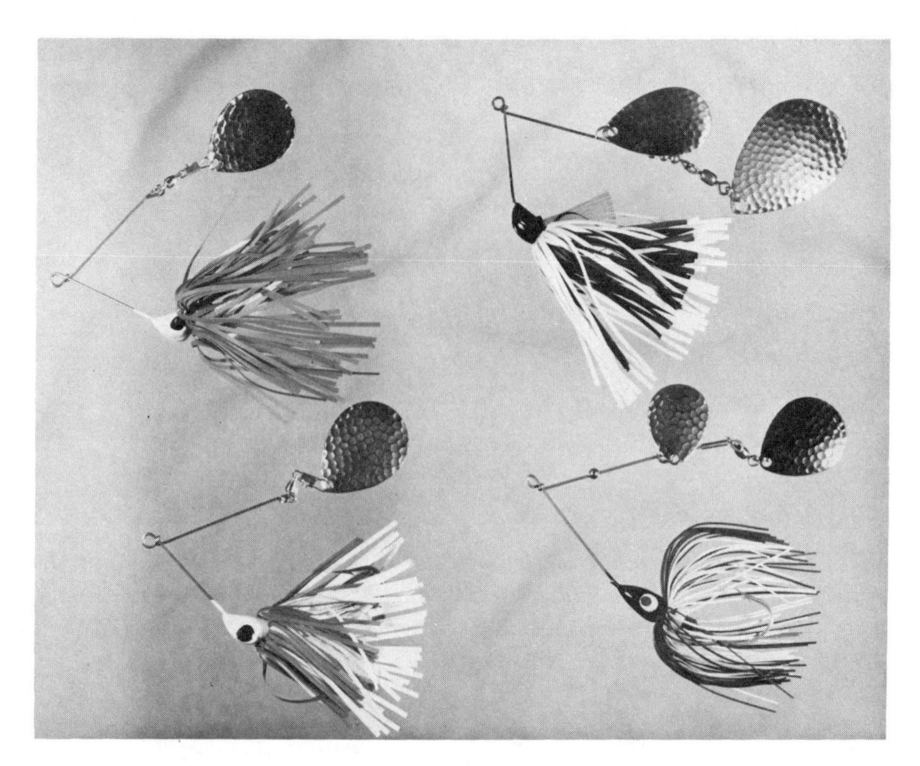

These spinnerbaits are all exactly the same size and therefore look very much the same, but there are noticeable differences. First, they are outfitted with either nickle or brass blades alone or in tandem. The upper right bait has a fiber weedguard for heavy-cover fishing. Three of the baits have vinyl skirts, while the one in the lower right-hand corner has a rubber skirt. In every case, note how the skirts have been reversed to give the lures a fuller-bodied appearance.

paled and pushed down snugly on the eye of the stinger to hold it securely in place.

Never underestimate the value of stinger hooks on spinnerbaits. I've had some days when I've caught as many as 30 bass on spinnerbaits, every one of those fish hooked on a trailing stinger!

From time to time, other embellishments may be used to dress spinnerbait hooks. The most common is a twin-tail pork frog or pork eel, but on occasion a two-inch plastic grub with a twister-type tail can spell the difference between missed strikes and solid hook-ups. Why these add-ons work is open to debate, but I believe that the soft, "meaty" texture of the pork or plastic causes bass to hold on just a tad longer, rather than immediatley trying to eject the offering, and this extra time enables anglers to more successfully drive their hooks home.

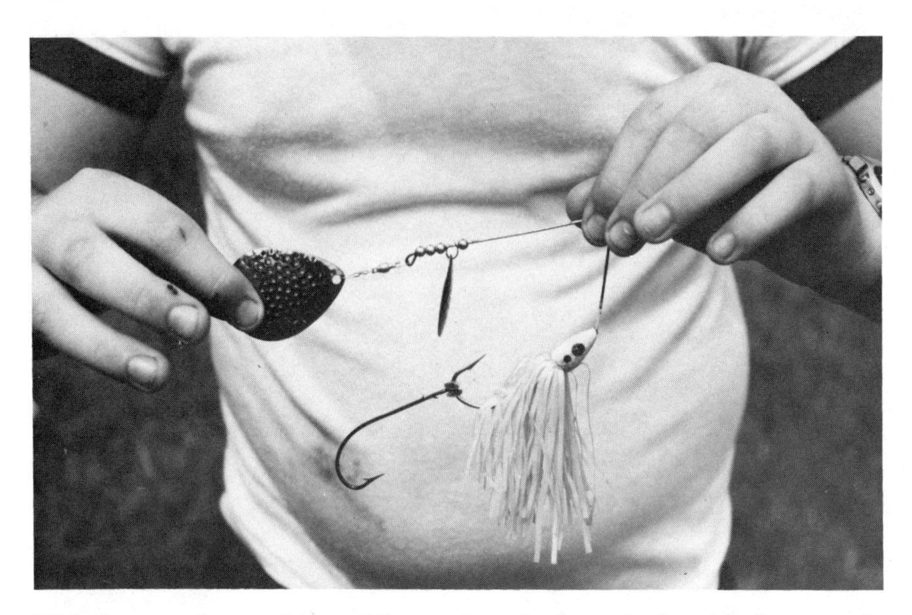

When bass are short-striking, adding a stinger hook can be the trick that saves the day. Plastic disks, ¼ inch in diameter, hold the trailer hook securely in position.

Although spinnerbaits intended for bass fishing are available in sizes ranging from ⅛ ounce to a full one ounce, the ¼- and ⅝-ounce sizes are far and away the most popular. Generally, I've had the best results using larger lures in off-colored water, and small lures in clear water. Strangely, however, oversize spinnerbaits are superior to small ones in cold water. As we've seen in previous chapters, cold water retards the feeding of bass, but when it comes to spinnerbaits they paradoxically like a mouthful. Just remember to fish them s-l-o-w.

Although spinnerbaits can be used to kick up a ruckus across the surface, tournament champ Ricky Green is one of many who claim far better results by not allowing the spinner's blades to break through the top film of water.

"Retrieve your spinnerbaits so they travel just slightly beneath the surface," Green maintains. "You should be able to see a distinct 'bulge' produced by the lure as it moves along just an inch or so under the surface."

One of the most common errors among bass anglers is to confine their arsenal of spinnerbaits to shallow-water fishing around weeds, brush and timber. This is unfortunate because these versatile lures also have many deep-water applications.

I particularly like to use spinnerbaits along steep, rocky shorelines that rapidly drop off into deep water. I cast as close to the bank as possible, work the first several feet of shallow water, and then "feel" my bait down the underwater ledges. To do this, hold your rod tip at the 10 o'clock position as you allow the spinnerbait to free-fall on a tight line. When it thumps on the bottom, lower the rod tip, take in a bit of slack line with your reel, raise the rod, and allow the bait to sink on a tight line to the next deeper ledge. Nearly all of your strikes will come as the lure is "helicoptering" or free-falling downward. Virtually the same technique can be used when fishing the irregular contours of midlake stream channel bends, underwater humps, breakline drop-offs, the rubble riprap of dam-facings, and sharply sloping timbered points.

Now let's shift gears and look at buzz-baits, one of the newest creations for bass anglers that many experts feel are destined to be among the hottest lures of the 1980s. Buzz-baits are nothing more than second-generation spinnerbaits. In other words, take a conventional spinnerbait, lengthen the lower wire arm so the leadhead and hook ride much farther back, then substitute for the teardrop-shaped Colorado blade an oversize propeller-shaped blade—you've got a buzz-bait.

Although spinnerbaits can be fished as-is, many anglers like to dress their hooks with plastic grubs, twister-tails or pork rind.

The unusual effectiveness of buzz-baits, enabling them to "call" bass out of hiding places, can be attributed to their large propeller-shaped blades.

Buzz-baits make twice the noise of spinnerbaits and this racket not only seems to attract bass out of deep water and heavy cover but is extremely effective in provoking violent strikes. Unlike a spinnerbait which, immediately after the cast, requires furiously cranking the reel handle to keep the lure topside, a buzz-bait instantly rises to the surface and stays there, even at the slowest speeds. Conversely, if a streaking-fast retrieve speed is called for, a buzz-bait can easily take it in stride and all the while continue to kick up a ruckus and track a straight course. Spinnerbaits won't. Retrieve them too fast and they'll begin rolling over or lying down on their sides and veering far off to the right or left.

As with spinnerbaits, most anglers find their best success with buzz-baits when the water is off-colored. But unlike spinnerbaits, which can be used year-round and are dynamite especially in cold water, buzz-baits are basically warm-water lures.

In addition to presenting these lethal offerings around man-made objects like docks, piers, and such, try scampering them across matted weedbeds and wherever felled timber and logs litter the bottom in jack-strawed disarray—they'll pay handsome dividends.

Noted tournament angler Rick Clunn was the first to teach me buzz-bait tricks that pay off. As we settled in our boat on Lake Texoma, I grabbed a handrail, ready for a fast boat ride to some distant part of the lake, but Clunn merely dropped his electric motor over the bow and began working docks and mooring piers only yards from the launching site.

"Most anglers overlook marinas and docking areas. They're terrific places to catch bass," Rick remarked, casting a buzz-bait underhanded.

The bait traveled fast like a low shot parallel to the surface of the water and then splatted down far back in a long dark alley between pier pilings and the bobbing hull of a moored houseboat. Then I heard the lure going to work. *Splutter, splutter, gurgle, churn, pop, splutter, splutter.* Then, suddenly KERPOW! A six-pounder streaked out of nowhere and blasted the bait; seconds later Clunn's first fish of the day was safely on board.

According to Clunn, when bass hang around docking areas they're generally close to the bottom and far back under the planks or tied-up boats, places not easily accessible to lures. Matter of fact, these places are

Because buzz-baits ride high in the water and can be retrieved at a snail's pace, they are ideal tools for working very shallow water. This is Dan Upton, wading and casting the lethal lures on the cover-filled flats of South Carolina's Lake Marion.

Tournament pro Rick Clunn gives high ratings to buzz-baits and especially likes to fish them around launching ramps, marinas and boat docks.

not very accessible to buzz-baits either, but buzzers have the uncanny ability, because of the nerve-jarring noises they produce, to entice bass from far away. Once, Rick saw the dark shadow of a bass streaking out of deep water—he guesses it was 15 feet deep—to maul his surface buzzer. This behavior contrasts with the usual precautionary, unwillingness-to-chase approach of bass, which is one of many reasons why these lures are the latest rage among bass anglers.

Buzz-baits create such a commotion on the retrieve because of the shape of their blades. Instead of the traditional Colorado or willowleaf design, like those on spinnerbaits, buzz-baits have flat, wing-shaped blades whose tips turn downward at right angles, a feature that allows them to "cup" large quantities of air and force it underwater.

Beyond this, manufacturers incorporate many different features into their particular line of buzz-baits. Some have longer or shorter arm shafts than others. Some feature only one wing blade; others sport multiple blades that spin in counter-rotating directions for perfect stability on the retrieve. They also come in as many different color and size variations as spinnerbaits.

"Unlike most other lures," Rick Clunn explains, "buzz-baits have the special ability of actually exciting bass. Even when the fish are not hungry or aggressive, they'll move out of their normal strike zone to hit a buzzer. It gives the illusion of something big on the surface, like a crippled shad, and when it's moving slowly it represents an easy target most predators simply cannot refuse."

Not surprisingly, many of the most popular buzz-baits are made by the very same companies that produce quality spinnerbaits. Just a few include Harkins (makers of the Lunker-Lure), Mister Twister (makers of Lunker-Buzz), Bass Pro Shops (makers of Uncle Buck's Buzzer), and Strike-King (makers of the Moss-Boss).

Jigs and Jigging Spoons

"The very hottest big-bass lure of the 1980s may well prove to be the jig 'n pig," Bo Dowden exclaimed as he horsed a four-pounder to the boat and dropped it into the live well. We were on the St. Lawrence River in upstate New York, and the big bass clinched a $41,000 first place award for Bo in a recent BASS Classic. Later, he gave me that very lure as a souvenir.

Although jig 'n pig lures are probably mistaken by bass for crayfish scurrying along the bottom, no one is certain why they are so appealing to very big bass. They just are.

Ideally, the jig should weigh somewhere between ¼ and ½ ounce and it should be of the banana-head design. Further, the jig should be outfitted with some type of fiber weedguard to reduce the possibility of snagging. And instead of bucktail or feathers, a majority of pros prefer a rubber skirt that breathes and pulsates as the lure is being manipulated. Undeniably, all-black is the favored color, with all-brown running a close second.

The "pig" is a size #1 black pork frog slipped onto the hook, although some pro anglers also use black pork chunks or even pork lizards. Whatever, the combination results in a heavy lure that casts like a bullet and sinks like a rock—just the ticket for summer, fall and winter bassing when most bass are away from the shorelines and hugging the bottom in deep water.

The very best place to fish a jig 'n pig is some type of edge, where moderately deep water meets very deep water. In flatland reservoirs this will primarily mean channel edges. In highland reservoirs it will mean secondary breaklines, channel-points, stream channel contours in the headwater region, and midlake humps. In canyonland waters it will mean underwater ledges and outcroppings, and "tailings" where rocks have slid into the water from high bluffs. In mesotrophic natural lakes, it will mean

One of the hottest lures of the 1980s is the jig 'n pig, particularly well-suited for deep, cold water.

steep rocky points, secondary breaklines, submerged rock-capped islands, and in some cases primary shoreline drops and shelves.

Whatever the specific nature of the bottom structure, you can fish the jig 'n pig in either of two ways. One is to work the lure vertically right beneath the boat; simply pump it up and down and hop it along as you use your depth-sounder to bird-dog the edge of the bottom contour. Or, you can simply cast this super bass-bait as you would any other. Be sure to let it sink all the way to the bottom on a tight line as many bass will grab it on the fall. Once you've felt the distinct thunk of the bait hitting bottom, then begin your retrieve by raising your rod tip, lowering it quickly while reeling in slack line, then raising the rod tip again.

The main difference between fishing a jig 'n pig and other types of jigs is that the jig 'n pig can be worked much faster. Bo Dowden and other pros even perform a bit of surgery on their "pigs" by slicing off part of the thick head of the pork rind to make it wafer in. This gives the bait more of a wavering, swimming appearance in the water and allows relatively fast retrieve speeds to simulate a crayfish routed from its hideout.

Curiously, bass don't blast the dickens out of a jig 'n pig. They usually inhale the lure and swim away with it. Be alert for a "weighty" sensation on the end of your line, as if your lure had picked up a big gob of weeds. Or you may merely see your line begin slowly moving off to the right or left. In any event, don't delay! Strike quickly before the bass discovers he's been duped by a counterfeit.

As effective as jig 'n pigs are, every serious angler's tacklebox should be well stocked with other jigs as well. I especially like Powrr-head jigs, which are shaped like anvils and have their hooks pointing up toward the surface at an acute angle. When dressed with a Reaper-Worm or curly-tail grub, these offerings actually stand up on the bottom, making themselves far more visible than other types of jigs that may lie down on their sides. With the hook point so starkly exposed, they also grab bass flesh more readily than other types of jigs.

Although many bass anglers have been devoutly fishing jigs for generations, most never seem to accept the fact that these lures must be fished close to the bottom on a tight line to be fully effective. Furthermore,

Most anglers like to doctor their pork rind pigs by slicing off half the thickness of the head. This gives the jig 'n pig a planing effect, making it look like a crayfish scrabbling across the bottom.

developing a feel for strikes is critically important, as most occur when the jig is sinking. If slack line is allowed during this crucial period, a majority of anglers are incapable of detecting the very slight ticks indicating strikes.

Jigging spoons are basically similar to jigs. I'm not referring here to conventional teardrop-shaped spoons made of thin, concave metal, such as the venerable Daredevle or Johnson Silver Minnow. Jigging spoons are a breed apart. Some call them "heavy metal" because that's exactly what they are: elongated, pencil-shaped or oval-shaped chunks of steel or lead, some with painted surfaces and others with hammered finishes, some with bare hooks and others with feathered dressing on the trebles. The most popular are the Hopkins Spoon (Hopkins Lure Company), Mann-O-Lure (Mann's Bait Company), and the Strata-Spoon (Bass Pro Shops).

Furthermore, as their name implies, jigging spoons are not meant to be

Here the author admires bass fooled by jig 'n pigs. The fish run from three to over ten pounds, proof enough these new lures are especially appealing to large bass.

cast in the usual way. They *can* be cast if necessary, for example, when you find schooling bass tearing into surface-swimming schools of baitfish; but in this situation the lure has to be retrieved very fast or it will quickly sink beyond the reach of the rampaging fish.

Typically, however, jigging spoons come into their own when fished vertically beneath your boat, just off the bottom, at depths ranging from ten to 60 feet. This makes them among the most popular lures for summer, fall and winter use on highland and canyonland reservoirs and natural mesotrophic lakes.

My own jigging spoon expertise has been gleaned from two artists of the trade, Ricky Green and Stanley Mitchell, both of whom have copped many thousands of bucks over the years in national bass tournaments. In addition to being among the few lures with which anglers can exercise precise depth and speed control in deep water, jigging spoons are incredibly easy to master.

Ricky Green particularly likes to fish jigging spoons on deltas. As discussed in Chapter 6, these are deep sand bars or ridges found along the edges of riverbeds on the floors of some flatland reservoirs. Once, I stopped fishing and just sat in total dismay watching Green at work as he boated an unbelievable 35 bass from one delta in only 20 minutes!

Jigging spoons come in a wide variety of sizes and shapes. They are ideal lures for checking deep bottom contours immediately beneath the boat.

Jigging-spoon expert Ricky Green alternately raises and lowers his rod tip as he works a spoon 30 feet deep in a river channel. The author sat in dismay as Green caught 35 bass in only 20 minutes!

Green's technique is simple. First, he presses the free-spool button on his casting reel so line can play out as the lure sinks to the bottom. Then, engaging the gears and taking up the slack, he begins slowly raising his rod tip in short jerks until the rod tip is pointed high overhead. This maneuver serves to lift the spoon about six feet off the bottom. Then he slowly lowers the rod tip back down until it almost touches the surface of the water, causing the spoon to rock and flutter in a tantalizing manner, like an injured baitfish struggling, as it descends into the depths. Most bites come as a distinct "bump" when the spoon is sinking, and Ricky quickly sets the hook and derricks the fish aboard.

Stan Mitchell, on the other hand, fishes his jigging spoons in a slightly different way. He likes to ply his efforts in only moderately deep water, especially in highland reservoirs, where some type of drowned timber is present. It may consist of stumps on the bottom, toppled shoreline trees, standing timber, or even log jams. In these situations, jigging spoons can be vertically lowered right down through the limbs, branches and trunks to bass hiding deep within the maze of cover and inaccessible to most other lures.

Mitchell begins at the bottom, working the spoon in place by pumping it up and down. Then he raises the lure several feet and repeats the effort, until he's covered all depth levels. Then, without moving his boat, he drops the spoon right back into some other hole in the cover only scant feet away and tries again. It is mind-boggling how many bass can sometimes be hiding in the thick crown of a single treetop.

Occasionally, a jigging spoon's hooks will hang up deep within the latticework of cover, but this is easily remedied. Just give a bit of slack line and jiggle your rod tip. This will cause the spoon to begin flip-flopping back and forth, and its heavy weight will eventually dislodge the hooks.

Plastic Worms

My friend Doug Hannon maintains such an intimate relationship with bass I sometimes think he's more comfortable around them than with most people. Since plastic worms have probably accounted for more tournament wins than any other lure, I recently asked Doug why he thought they were so productive.

"From watching bass in my own backyard tank," Doug explained, "I've come to the conclusion they're not very intelligent, but they can learn very fast. The way they learn not to hit a certain lure such as a crankbait or spinnerbait is by actually getting hooked by such a bait and getting away, or being released, or sensing 'schreckstoff' [an alarm substance] in the water when a school member is hooked, and associating this with the *sound* the lure was making in the water when the experience occurred.

"Plastic worms are so effective," Hannon continued, "because they are almost entirely silent baits. Therefore, it's quite difficult for a bass to learn a negative response to the lure."

I've learned that Doug is entirely right by tagging and releasing on my own experimental bass lake. Each time a tagged bass is subsequently caught, I gain more information. One thing that has become quite apparent is that a big bass caught on a particular type of lure is very difficult to catch again on the same lure. I'm not saying they *can't* be caught again, merely that each additional time it becomes increasingly harder and harder. This is not true, however, with plastic worms, at least not to such

According to bass scientist Doug Hannon, there are two reasons why plastic worms are so effective: It's difficult for bass to learn negative responses to them, and anglers can be more bold in their choice of places to work the lures.

a degree. If I catch a big bass on a blue worm today, I might not be able to catch it tomorrow on a blue worm, but likely as not that fish will be a sucker for a black worm, or a red worm, and then perhaps a week later I can catch it on a blue worm still again.

There is another thing that helps to explain the continued effectiveness of plastic worms and that, like so many other things in life, is *money.* The low cost of plastic worms has prompted a lot of anglers to begin fishing, for a change, where the largest bass call home. In contrast, when an average angler ties a four-dollar crankbait onto his line, you can bet he'll try to avoid losing that lure. So he stays away from submerged trees, log jams, drowned brush piles and other heavy cover that make his exposed treble hooks so vulnerable. After all, who can afford to lose a dozen artificial lures on every outing?

I'll tell you who can afford the loss—the plastic worm fisherman! All he's casting is a penny hook, a nickle sinker, and a few cents worth of wiggly polyvinyl chloride. With such a minimum investment tied to his line, he can afford to be bold. He can pitch that thing into the most awful looking cover imaginable. He can also work that lure across the very bottom structures in deep water that are inaccessible to many other types of lures. And he catches bass, simply because he's fishing where the fish are most likely to be and, simultaneously, where few other angler's lures ever swim.

Since plastic worms have been around since 1949, when Nick Creme of Tyler, Texas, first melted bars of plastic on his kitchen stove and molded them into lively looking nightcrawlers, it's not necessary to rehash the basics of worm fishing, which have already been chronicled in dozens of other books and thousands of magazine articles. Instead, I'll merely review a few of the more important aspects of rigging and fishing worms and then quickly move on to some of the finer points that guides and tournament anglers use to dramatically increase their catch-ratios.

Plastic worms come in numerous sizes ranging from four to 12 inches. Water clarity is the most important factor governing which size is most appropriate. Whenever the water is extremely clear, and the fish likely to be spooky, go with a very small worm. Conversely, when the water is murky or muddy, you want to produce a large visual stimulus (particularly since these lures make almost no noise) and should choose a much larger offering. In all other instances, which will be a majority of the time, six- to eight-inch worms seem the most popular among bass and bass anglers alike.

With regards to worm colors, black seems to be a universal favorite that works consistently for most anglers, in most lakes and reservoirs, under most conditions. Blue and purple tie for second place, with motor oil, red and pale green tying for third. A good rule of thumb is to use a dark-colored worm in dark water, and a light, unobtrusive one when the water is brightly illuminated and clear. The latest hit on the tournament trail are so-called *firetail* worms the tips of which are a bright fluorescent color such as hot pink or blaze orange. The colored tips cause otherwise ordinary worms to be real attention-getters when the water is off-colored or the fish are in a neutral or inactive state.

As to worm designs, Plain Jane nightcrawler lookalikes are quickly fading into history. Advanced anglers now distinctly prefer worms with wafer-thin tails that undulate when the worm is being retrieved, or wide flapper-type tails that give a worm a porpoising appearance as it swims along. Examples of these include the numerous models made by Mr. Twister, Mann's Jelly Waggler, Mann's Auger Tail, Creme's Spoiler, Ditto's Gator Tail, and Ditto's Whip Worm.

There are almost as many worm hooks on the market as worm designs themselves, and the choice is largely personal. There are two critical things to keep in mind: (1) Always match the hook size to the worm size (in other words, small hooks for small worms, large hooks for large

Although straight worms still have their calling, flapper-tail and twister-type worms dominate the market now, due to the undulating, lifelike movements they make in the water.

worms); and (2) stick with needle-sharp, thin wire hooks which are the easiest to set. Aside from this, hook sizes run the gamut from size 1 to 6/0, the most popular being 2/0, 3/0, and 4/0 in long-shanked Sproat design.

Traditionally, sliding sinkers are used in worm fishing. These have holes longitudinally through their centers through which the line is threaded, which allows the sinker to slide back and forth several feet or more at the terminal end of the line. The advantage here is that the sinker gives the light worm casting weight; yet when a bass inhales the worm, it seldom feels the weighty resistance of the sinker. Sinkers that are streamlined and bullet-shaped seem to come through thick cover much more easily than others having wider profiles.

Although the size of the sinker should be closely matched to the size of the worm, water depth and wind velocity are even more significant in determining the proper sinker size. The rule of thumb here is to use the lightest sinker possible that will allow you to cast the worm accurately, take it to the bottom, and maintain close contact (feel) with it. As water depth or wind velocity increases, progressively larger sinkers should be used. Although worm sinkers are available in sizes ranging from 1/16 ounce to a full one ounce, the 1/4-ounce size is far and away the most popular for a majority of applications.

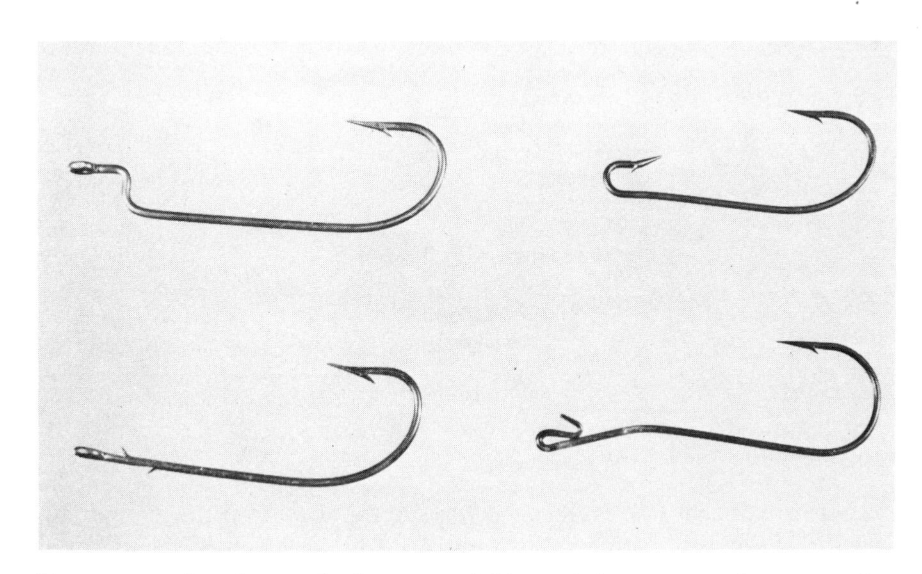

Numerous styles of worm hooks are available, and the one you select is mostly a matter of personal preference. Here are the most popular. All are 4/0 Sproats, but notice the differences in their shank designs with different features intended to hold the worm securely in place.

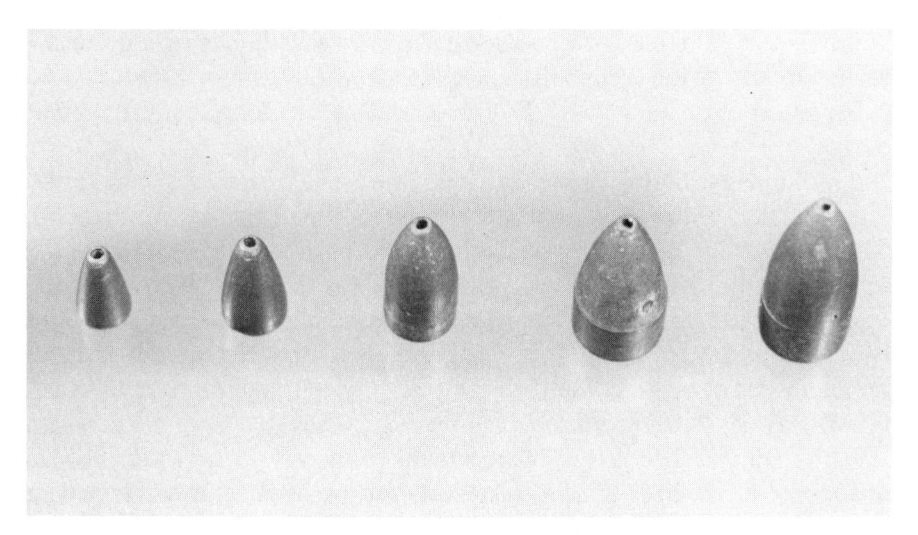

Sliding worm sinkers range in size from 1/16 ounce to one ounce; the most popular is the 1/4-ounce size, shown here in the middle.

TABLE 14–1. Combinations of Worm Length, Hook Size and Sinker Weight Suitable for Rigging Plastic Worms

Worm Length (inches)	*Hook Size*	*Sinker Weight (ounces)*
4	1	1/16, 1/8
6	1/0, 2/0	1/8, 1/4
7	2/0, 3/0, 4/0	1/8, 1/4
8	3/0, 4/0	1/4, 3/8
10	4/0, 5/0	1/4, 3/8
12	5/0, 6/0	3/8, 1/2

There are dozens upon dozens of ways to rig plastic worms in conjunction with hooks and sinkers, but most are simply novelties. Guides and tournament anglers use only two methods, the *Texas rig* and the *Carolina rig.* With any rigging method, however, it's critically important to match worm length, hook size, and sinker weight. The best combinations for average conditions are listed in Table 14–1.

The Texas rig, which is the most popular, is made by simply threading the line through a slip sinker of the appropriate size and then tying a hook to the terminal end. The hook is then pierced through the very nose of the lure, brought out the side of the worm ¼ inch lower, reversed, and the tip then impaled back into the plastic to make it weedless. Generally, a slow-sinking or semibuoyant worm is used.

In the Carolina rig, the line is threaded through a slip sinker in the usual manner, with the terminal end of the line next tied to a small barrel swivel. A two-foot length of line is then tied to the other end of the barrel swivel, the terminal end of that line to the hook, and the worm then again impaled in the usual manner. With the Carolina rig, a high-floating worm is used.

Anglers use the Texas rig when it is desirable to fish a worm right on the bottom across rocks, sand, brush, logs and similar bottom conditions. The Carolina rig comes into use when the bottom is muddy or mucky or there is sparse weed growth. In these situations, a Texas-rigged worm would be constantly buried in mire or otherwise out of a bass's visual range. With a Carolina rig and a high-floating worm, however, the sinker drags bottom but the worm floats upward about a foot or two above the bottom, remaining in clear view of nearby bass.

The big mistake most anglers make in fishing plastic worms is casting them out and reeling them in as they would a spinnerbait or crankbait. This technique, however, not only works the worm too fast, but also greatly reduces the sensitivity an angler needs to detect characteristic light bites.

So remember, a worm should always be *pulled,* never reeled. This is accomplished by casting the worm and allowing it to sink to the bottom on a tight line (many strikes will come on the fall). When the worm hits bottom, slowly begin lifting the rod tip in order to begin pulling the worm toward you several feet. When the rod tip is pointing almost vertically upward, drop it quickly, reel in the two or three feet of slack line this generates, stop reeling, then begin lifting the rod tip to move the worm forward several more feet, continuing the procedure all the way back to the boat or until you've worked what you believe to be the productive fish zone where a bass may be holding.

As previously mentioned, don't expect arm-jarring strikes when fishing plastic worms. More often than not you'll feel a very light staccato of tapping sensations, or perhaps merely a single bump. By using a sensitive worm rod made of graphite or boron, these bites often register lightly yet quite distinctly. However, other times you'll feel nothing at all but merely see your line twitch or jump sideways, or begin slowly moving off to the right or left. Still other times, a bass may pick up a worm and begin swimming toward you with it, giving a weird sensation of nothing on the

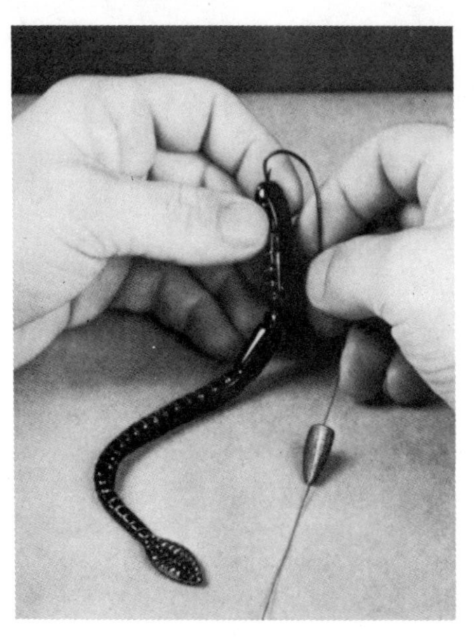

1. *To fashion a Texas-rig, thread a sinker onto the line and tie on a hook; then run hook through head of worm.*

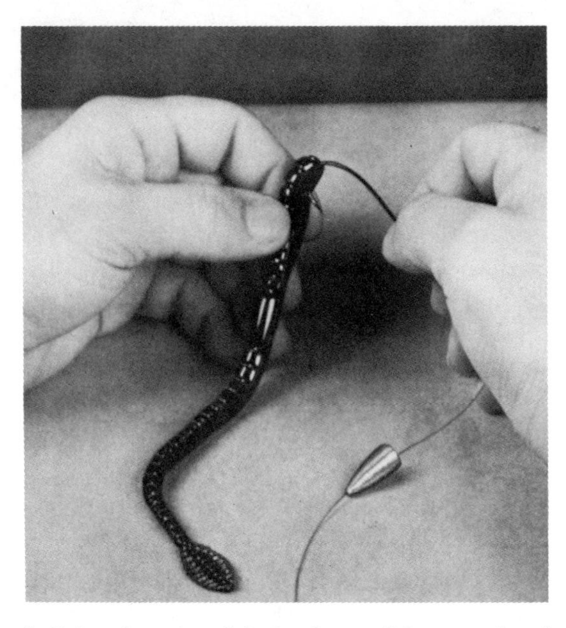

2. *Bring the point of the hook out of the worm head about ½ inch lower.*

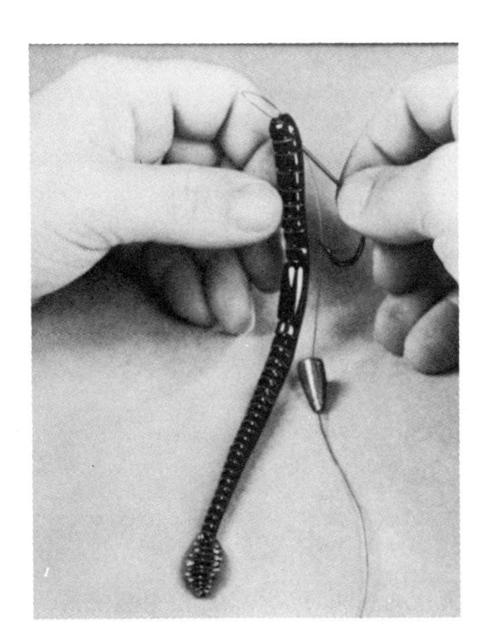

3. *Turn the hook around and bury the point in the body of the worm.*

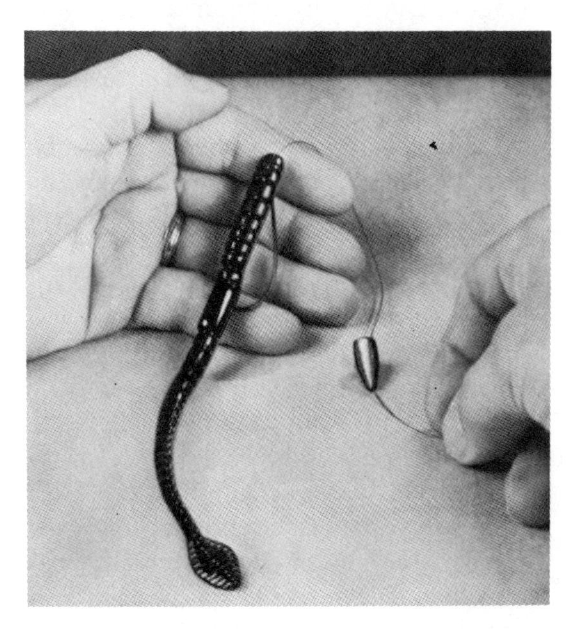

4. *In a completed Texas-rig, the worm should hang straight.*

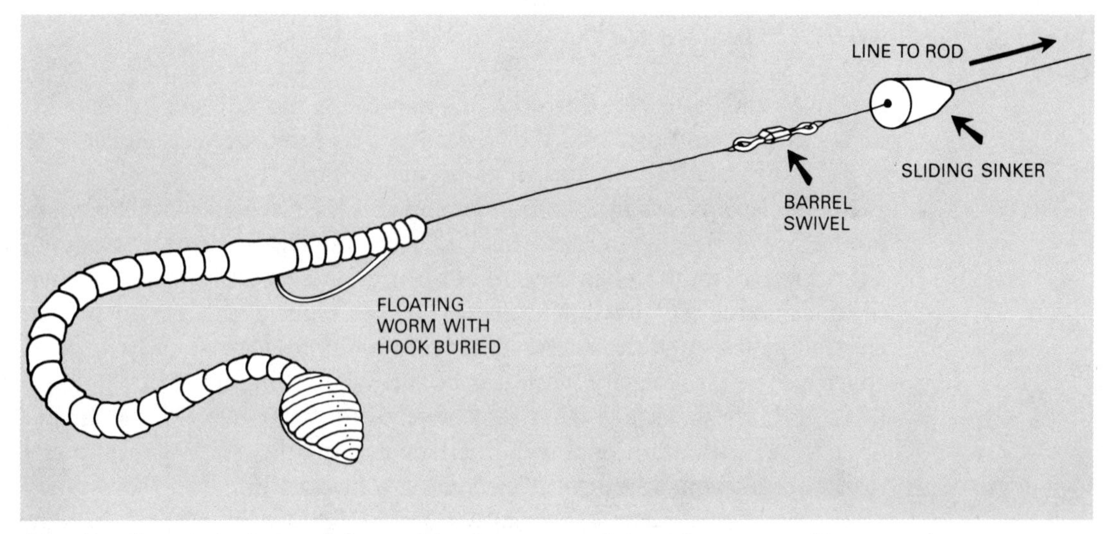

The Carolina-rig is designed for working bottom conditions that are muddy or weedy.

end of your line, as though your lure had been cut off. As bass pro Bill Dance once told me, an angler who is not an intense line watcher when worm fishing probably misses at least half of all the bites he receives.

Over the years a lot of ill advice has been written about setting the hook when worm fishing, most of it having to do with "counting to ten and allowing a bass to run with the worm." My advice is *never* get into a feeling contest with bass, for they'll win every time.

When a bass inhales a worm, it takes the bait right at the head where the hook is located. Consequently, the hook is in the proper position to be set and the longer you delay, the greater the opportunity for the fish to detect something amiss and eject the offering. The best advice is to strike as quickly as possible, the very instant you feel a "tap . . . tap . . . tap" or see the line twitch or jump. Extend your rod toward the fish, reel in any slack, and snap the rod back sharply. Right now!

When rigging hooks in plastic worms, Roland Martin, the all-time biggest money winner in tournament history, suggests pushing the point of the worm hook all the way through the worm and then backing it up just a bit. "This creates a little channel through the plastic, just ahead of the hook point," Roland explains. "When setting the hook, you have to keep in mind that you first have to drive that hook through the plastic in which it is imbedded before it can even begin to penetrate a bass's mouth. With that little channel you've created, the job is a lot easier."

When the water is murky, Tom Mann suggests using two smaller sliding sinkers on your line instead of a single larger one. "If water depth and wind conditions call for a ¼-ounce sinker," Tom advises, "thread a pair of ⅛-ounce sinkers onto the line instead. A bass's vision is retarded under these conditions, and the two sinkers repeatedly click against each other, giving the fish an added sound cue to home in upon."

Mann also advises against *pegging* slip sinkers, a technique designed to hold a sinker tight against the head of a worm. This is done by wedging a tiny piece of toothpick in the sinker's center hole where it presses against the line and thereby prevents the sinker from sliding. The slight advantage gained by this is that the worm-sinker combination snakes its way through cover a little more easily, with less chance of hanging up. But there are three great disadvantages that far outweigh this. For one, a bass picking up a worm with additional weight permanently attached is likely to feel resistance and quickly drop it. Secondly, a hooked bass can more easily throw the hook when it has substantial weight to it; with the sinker allowed to travel freely, it slides up the line several feet during the fight, and therefore cannot be used as leverage to throw the hook. Finally, pegging a sinker with a toothpick frequently bruises the soft monofilament, causing a weak spot that may cause the line to part on the strike or during the ensuing fight.

Pro angler Hank Parker stresses the need to remain flexible when fishing worms. "Never allow yourself to get so locked in to a particular color or worm size that you never try anything else," he admonishes. "The moods of bass change, and this means today's tournament champ may become tomorrow's tournament chump if he's not willing to give the bass what they want. If they refuse a four-inch worm, try an eight-incher and then a 12-incher. If they won't take red, give 'em black."

South Carolina bass guide Inky Davis offers this trick: "A lively worm will almost always out-fish one that is sloppily presented. When feeling my worms through brush and treetops, I always shake my wrist, to simulate the appearance of something crawling and gyrating as it tries to pick its way through the cover."

Pattern Fishing

Regardless of which particular lure you elect to use, one interesting phenomenon of lakes and reservoirs is that straggler bass and schools can often be found in identical situations at different locations in the same body of water.

Let's say you're on a flatland reservoir in midsummer. You know which general areas of the reservoir possess ideal water color, oxygen levels and pH. And now you are examining a contour map to ascertain the locations of structure that may be holding bass.

The fishing trip is to last several days while you're on vacation and you decide a good place to begin your search is the edge of the main riverbed. What you'll be fishing, of course, will be the breaks or substructure along the edge of the channel, and they will probably be in the form of deltas, or perhaps brush and stumps lining the channel's banks.

During the first morning on the water you fish ten different riverbed locations. None of the three locations where brush is present produces fish, nor do any of the four locations where there are stumps on a sandy bottom. However, in three places where there are stumps on a clay bottom bass eagerly hit blue plastic worms. At this point, you should note carefully other features of those locations where the fish were taken. Let's say your fish came from precisely 18 feet deep, the pH at that depth is 7.2, and the water is murky colored. If you can find this same pattern, or combination, of conditions elsewhere along the main riverbed, chances are excellent that most such areas will contain fish and they will likewise hit blue worms.

As another example, let's say that after thoroughly working several more delta locations, you discover bass clinging to those deltas where the water is 22 feet deep and whose crests are littered with rocks, and you take two very big bass in rapid succession on jig 'n pigs. The thing to do now would be to examine your contour map and mark every location you can find in which identical conditions prevail. Very likely a high percentage of those locations will contain bass, while other deltas not adhering to the pattern may be entirely barren. *Pattern fishing* is an ideal way to find straggler bass, or small groups, during early spring, late spring, and again during the fall when the fish are not schooling but are randomly scattered.

You can also pattern schooling fish at other times of year. Let's say that in a large highland reservoir you make contact with a school of bass migrating along a steep rocky point that juts out from the shoreline. The water color is murky green, the surface is windswept, and you're catching bass at exactly 12 feet deep on shad-gray crankbaits. Suddenly, while you're fighting a fish, the school spooks and vanishes into the depths. No use spending any more time there. You quickly check your contour map and note that there are a dozen additional shoreline points within a mile of your present location. Eight of those points are rocky, steep, and possess murky green water (the others are sandy, shallow, and the water is calm and gin-clear). It's a good bet that at least half of those eight points, where identical conditions exist, will also be presently witnessing a bass migration with the fish coming to the 12-foot level. The other points, which don't adhere to the pattern, probably wouldn't be worth the effort of a single cast.

On many bodies of water, you often see anglers buzzing around in their bassboats in seemingly chaotic fashion and in random directions. A certain percentage, to be sure, aren't dedicated fishermen but people ego-tripping as they display to all who care to look the roostertails their rigs can produce. But the experts on the water are undoubtedly checking patterns in a systematic way. A pair of anglers in one boat may find straggler bass clinging to submerged islands where the bottom is sandy and 30 feet deep, and the fish are slamming jigging spoons with gusto. Two other anglers may discover bass deep in potholes in moss beds, with the fish obliging them by hitting buzz-baits. Still other anglers may be working schooling fish on steep shale slides.

On any large body of water, bass are likely to congregate in certain locations characterized by a particular pattern of conditions (structure, temperature, pH, and so forth). The essence of pattern fishing is to identify those conditions on any given day (they may change from day to day or week to week) and then fish those patterns wherever they occur in a body of water. So, be an observant angler and whenever you catch a bass, never leave that location until you've doped out all you can about its specific conditions. Then locate other places with the identical pattern of conditions and head for them. Such an approach can pay off handsomely as the day wears on.

CHAPTER

15

Special Techniques For Catching Bass

The lures and techniques we've looked at in the last two chapters can be used in many situations and are popular with many anglers—amateurs and pros alike. In contrast, the special techniques I'll describe in this chapter are not everyday methods you can count on to produce bass consistently. Rather, they represent solutions to unusual situations anglers periodically run into.

More frequently than you might expect, every serious bass expert draws upon his working knowledge of these tricks of the trade to help him find and catch more fish.

Gapen's Bait-Walkers

The Bait-Walker is not a lure but an "aid" that can be used with any style or brand of lure to make it far more productive. It can even be used with live bait.

"I have invented a lot of lures over the years," Dan Gapen, the Bait-Walker's inventor recently said to me. "My Muddler Minnow fly has probably been the most popular. But there has been a fishing problem I've always wrestled with and it's shared by other anglers, no matter whether they fish lakes, reservoirs or rivers, or whether they live in the North or South or anywhere else.

"The difficulty is this," Gapen continued. "Most fish species, including bass, spend most of their lives in deep water, yet the vast majority of lures on the market are relatively shallow-runners. With the exception of heavy jigs, jigging spoons and heavily weighted plastic worms, it's quite difficult to work depths beyond the 15- or 20-foot level with most lures. That's the initial problem. The next is this. Realizing that at such depths, bass will usually be close to the bottom, often in or around cover, how do you present a lure to the fish without continually snagging on brush, logs, treetops or rocks?"

Dan's solution was dubbed the Bait-Walker, and it solves all of these problems. There is only one bad thing I can say about it. It should have been invented long, long ago!

A Gapen Bait-Walker looks somewhat like a conventional spinnerbait except that a shoe-shaped piece of lead is molded on the bottom. The line is tied to the eyelet of the device just the same as it is on a spinnerbait. From the swivel attached to the upper arm, a second length of monofilament, called a *drop-back line*, is tied. The lure or hook to be rigged with live bait is attached to the terminal end of the drop-back line.

Bait-Walkers are intended to be used either for trolling or drift-fishing. The shoe-shaped lead weight on the bottom arm takes the lure to the bottom, where the fish are, and keeps it there, while allowing the angler to continually maintain feel with the lake floor at whatever speed the water temperature may dictate.

Due to the unique design of the Bait-Walker, it very rarely will snag. It seems to just slide right through the cover, over the tops of rocks and boulders, and up and over logs only to drop back down on the other side. If the Bait-Walker does indeed happen to cling momentarily to an obstruction, all that is required is to release tension on the line and the L-shaped spring wire will push the rig backwards to free it, whereupon the troll or

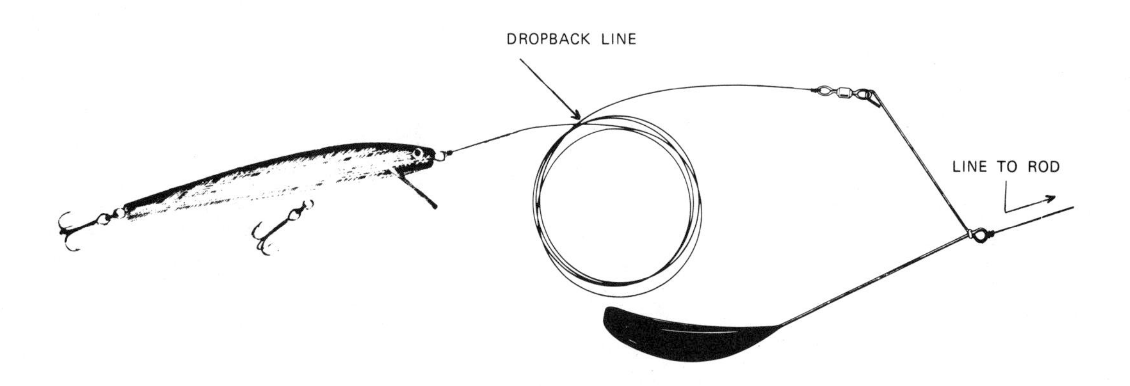

Gapen's Bait-Walkers allow anglers to present lures to bass in very deep water, without snagging on bottom debris.

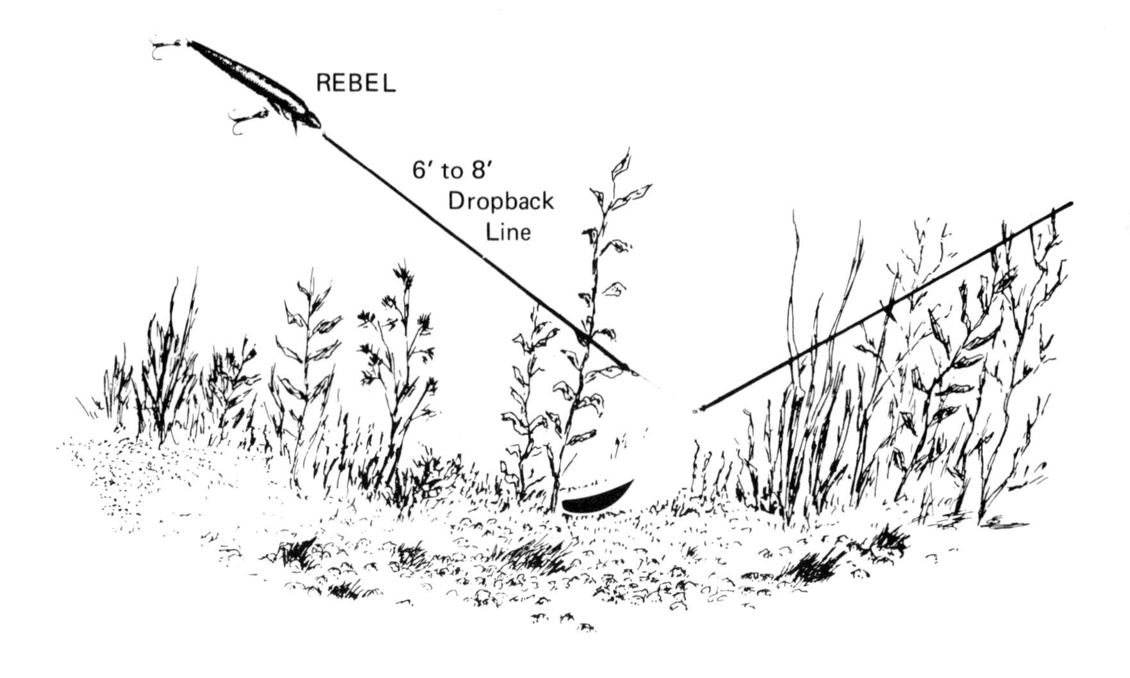

The size of Bait-Walker to use depends upon the water depth you wish to fish. Although virtually any type of lure can be used with a Bait-Walker, the author recommends floating balsa minnows.

drift can be resumed. In nearly two years of field research, Dan Gapen claims to have lost only three Bait-Walkers. That is incredible when you consider many anglers often lose twice that many lures in a single day on the water.

If the lure itself snags, and not the Bait-Walker, simply reversing the line of pull often frees it. But usually, the best lures for use in conjunction with Bait-Walkers are not likely to snag in the first place. From my experience, balsa plugs of the slim-minnow variety are tops, because they are extremely buoyant. The Bait-Walker takes the lure into deep water; while the shoe-sinker is riding the bottom, the lure, constantly trying to float back to the surface, rides slightly higher in the water, passing over the tops of obstructions. You also can use traditional crankbaits, spinnerbaits or spoons; about the only lures not particularly well suited for use with Bait-Walkers are buzz-baits and surface chuggers.

Bait-Walkers come in various sizes ranging from ¼ ounce to 6 ounces. Yet due to their "swimming" designs they offer far less resistance in the water than lead sinkers of comparable weights. Which size to use depends upon the depth of the water you are fishing. Dan Gapen recommends ¼ ounce for water 3 to 8 feet deep, ⅜ ounce for water 5 to 10 feet deep, 1 ounce for water 10 to 20 feet deep, and 2 ounces for water 16 to 34 feet deep. The largest, 6-ounce Bait-Walker will easily take a plug or spoon down 60 feet. Imagine, then, the whole new world of deep-water fishing this opens for bass anglers.

By using a snelled hook on a leader attached to the Bait-Walker's swivel on the upper arm, you can fish a wide variety of live baits in difficult situations. The method is virtually the same as backtrolling, discussed in Chapter 12. Get out your Bait-Walker when fishing very deep water or when the bottom is littered with tangled cover that would quickly cause Lindy-rigs to snag.

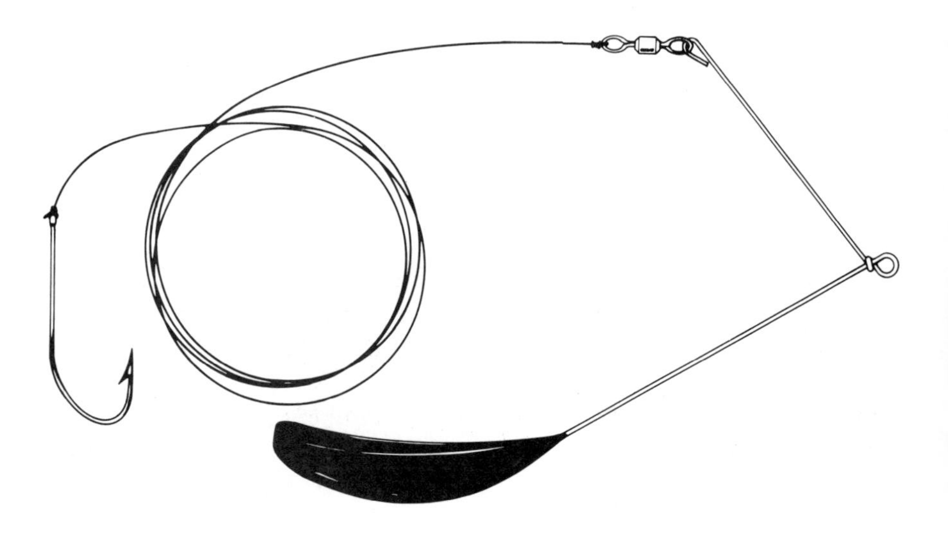

Live baits are particularly well-suited to Bait-Walkers. Simply attach an appropriate size hook instead of a lure to the Bait-Walker's drop-back line.

Every pro on the bass tournament circuit now uses the technique of Flippin' at least occasionally. Here, Rick Clunn works a submerged tree on Lake Texoma. From this one spot, Clunn and the author boated seven largemouths.

For a free booklet further detailing the use of Bait-Walkers, write to Gapen's World of Fishin', Highway 10, Big Lake, MN 55309.

Flippin' into Tight Places

The bassing technique known as Flippin' was invented by California anglers Dee Thomas and David Gliebe, both professionals who follow the tournament circuit. After winning several major contests, using nothing other than their brainstorm, other competing pros started getting wise. Currently, every one of the recognized pros uses Flippin' at least part of the time.

In Flippin' you use a rod, reel, line and lure. But you don't cast. Instead, you make a gentle flick of the wrist to execute short underhand flips that send the lure short distances from the boat. In many instances the lure travels no more than six or ten feet, although the average flip is closer to 18 feet.

Gliebe and Thomas began by using standard spinning and baitcasting rods with their technique, but these posed a number of limitations. For one, they simply were too short. What was needed was a rod that had a handle like a spinning rod, a shaft that was stiff like a baitcasting rod, and an overall length similar to a flyrod. Yet the action of the rod had to be something altogether different than either of the three.

You see, spinning, casting and fly rods are designed to cast lures. And to do so efficiently, they must have rather limber tips, slightly heavier midsections, and still heavier butts. This combination allows an angler to "load" his rod during the backcast arc, and then during the forward completion of the cast to transmit that accumulated energy to the lure (or line, as in the case of flyrods) to send it way out.

As I said, however, in Flippin' you don't actually cast. And since you are working very close to the boat, with only a short length of line out at any given time, it is important to have a good deal of strength built into the entire rod but especially in the tip section.

Anyway, about the time Gliebe and Thomas began consistently walking away with numerous tournament wins, the Fenwick Tackle Company in Westminster, California, decided to pioneer a brand new type of rod that would be specifically designed for Flippin'. In fact, they called it the Flippin' Stik.

A fiberglass Flippin' Stik is 7½ feet in length and looks somewhat like a spinning rod, but you mount a baitcasting reel on it. Another feature that distinguishes the Flippin' Stik from most other rods is that the first guide is quite far (33 inches) from the reel seat to enable an angler to strip line from his reel as he ordinarily would in flycasting. As might be expected, when Fenwick's Flippin' Stik became an instant hit, no less than six other companies quickly introduced their own versions.

Although any level-wind baitcasting reel can be used in Flippin', the experts overwhelmingly rely upon the Garcia 5500-D because with this reel you do not have to push a free-spool button to strip line. To my knowledge, this is the only direct-drive reel on the market, which means you can strip line freely, as in flycasting, yet the gears remain constantly engaged in case you have to strike quickly to set the hook.

Almost any premium-grade nylon line of 17- to 20-pound test is suitable for Flippin'. However, I suggest you use an optically brightened line that appears to glow above the surface, the reason being that you'll be fishing plastic worms or jigs and with these lures it is necessary to watch the line very closely for slight ticks or bumps that signal a gentle strike.

In the worm category, a variety of colors are in order, in six- and seven-inch lengths. And rather than use a straight worm, use one of the new kinds that has a twister-type tail, flapper tail, or long ridge of wafer-thin plastic running along its back like a fin. You'll be slithering these baits in and out of heavy cover and they are far more lifelike than regular worms. Some anglers even use slip-sinkers outfitted with rubber skirts to give their offerings a "breathing" appearance. The best way to rig worms for Flippin' is Texas-style, as described in the last chapter.

In the case of jigs, ¼-ounce models are best in a variety of colors. Either bucktail or marabou feathers are fine, with twister-tail grubs or pork frogs dressing the hooks. But make sure the jig has some type of stiff nylon or fiber weedguard to lessen the chance of the lure snagging.

Since the "flips" in Flippin' are executed while you are standing, the stable bow platform of a bassboat is the safest and most convenient place for performing this technique. If you don't own a bassboat, the next best bet is a wide-beamed johnboat. Don't use this technique from a tippy aluminum V-bottom or a canoe, or you may end up in the drink.

Once you're equipped with a Flippin' Stik or reasonable facsimile and are situated in a suitable boat, you can begin to master this effective, if somewhat unorthodox, technique. Start by holding the rod in your right hand and stripping off about eight feet of line so that when the rod tip is held high the lure hangs down and barely touches the surface of the water. Next, strip off another eight feet of line and hold it at arm's length with your left hand (there will be four feet of line going from the rod to your hand, and another four feet going back to the rod). Then simply swing the rod in a soft *underhand* manner so the lure rocks like a pendulum and gently flip the bait toward a stump or some other target. Just as you make the flip, release the line held in your left hand and the lure will travel 16 to 20 feet to the target. Of course, if the target you wish to present a bait to is closer than 16 to 20 feet, strip off less line to make the required presentation. In time, you'll be able to strip off just the right amount of line without consciously thinking about it, just like you can cast overhand to targets at different ranges without engaging in a lot of mental gymnastics.

With only a little practice, you'll soon agree that Flippin' is an extremely accurate way of presenting a bait. Not even a world champion casting artist is as accurate as an average guy who has learned Flippin'. In little time you should be able to set a coffee cup in your backyard,

In Flippin', a long rod is used to make an underhand toss of the lure a short distance, generally no more than 20 feet, from a standing position. This series of drawings show how to execute this technique, which is particularly deadly for spooky fish in shallow-water cover.

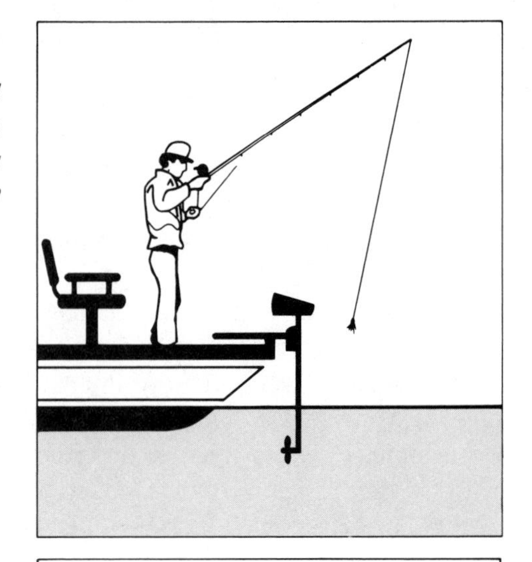

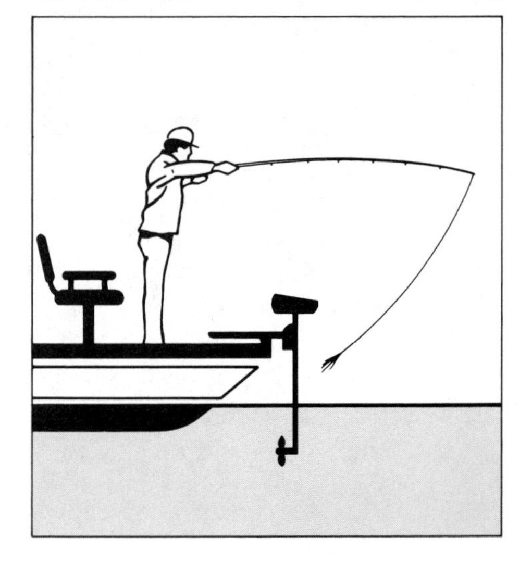

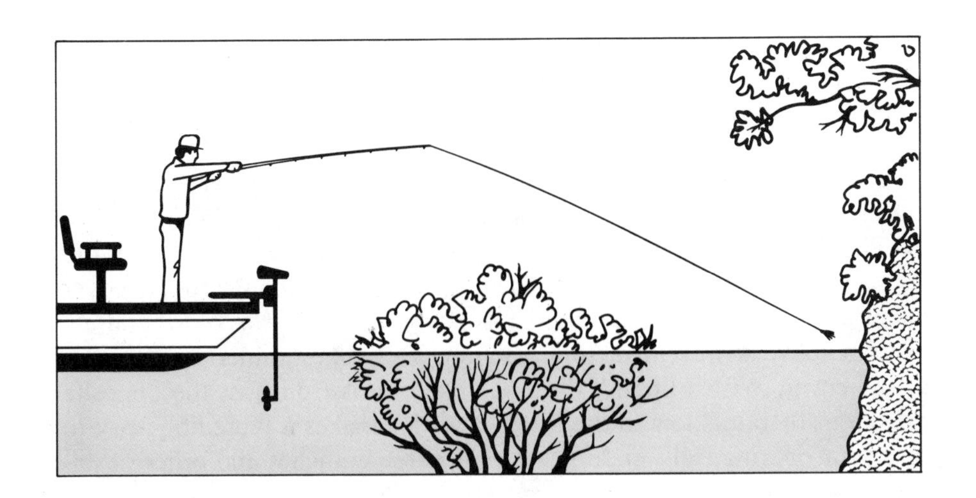

pace off 18 or 20 feet, and nine times in ten flip your worm or jig right into the cup.

Another advantage to Flippin' is that it allows you to get your lure into places not accessible with other casting techniques. In the usual style of overhand casting, the lure leaves your position from high overhead and then travels in a downward arc to the target. Yet since many types of cover have tentacles of branches and limbs extending outward, a lure coming in from above is prevented from reaching the thickest, innermost portion of the cover. With Flippin', the line approach is from just the opposite direction. It travels low to the water, and this makes it incredibly easy to toss your offering right underneath pesky tree branches and other obstacles.

The reason this is so important to successful shallow-water bass fishing has to do with the behavior of the fish themselves. When bass are in water less than ten feet deep, they typically hold extremely tight to the cover. They seldom are around the outside perimeter of the cover but usually right in the middle or thickest portions. Consequently, if you cast only around the far outside edges where the branchtips are drooping down to the water, you'll probably not get a thing because bass are very reluctant in such situations to travel far to take a lure. You almost have to hit them right on the head with it, and Flippin' is one of the most effective ways to get your lure to them.

To return to the mechanics of the technique, when your lure touches down, immediately put your left hand on the rod slightly above the reel, with the line gently pinched between your thumb and forefinger to detect light bites. From this point on, fish a worm or jig in pretty much the same way as you would if casting. Flippin', then, really doesn't involve any special way of working a lure; rather it insures an extremely accurate presentation.

Flippin' also is a very fast way of checking a large number of stumps, bushes or treetops that may be in the vicinity of your boat. Thus you do not have to go through the wasted motions of casting a lure, reeling in, then casting again, with the lure out of the water a large part of the time. Instead, you merely swing your lure to a target, fish that cover, raise your rod tip while simultaneously pulling slack line with your left hand, and then flip the lure to the next likely location. When you use Flippin', you can fish ten stumps, for example, in the same time it would take another angler, using conventional casting, to fish only two. Understandably, in a day's time, this is guaranteed to reward you with far more fish in the boat.

Aside from the accuracy and speed of lure presentation afforded by

Flippin', I'm continually amazed by how very close to a boat big fish customarily are caught, particularly if the water is a bit choppy or off-colored. You do have to be careful, however, to keep noises to a minimum. Be especially careful not to allow your electric motor's shaft or prop to bang into cover.

Don't worry too much about your lure splashing down right on top of bass and spooking them. As your Flippin' skill increases, the commotion associated with lure entry will eventually become almost nonexistent. In fact, many pros pride themselves in being able to flip jigs and worms so gently that no more than a tiny ripple is created when the lure touches down. Then they proceed to enticingly crawl and squirm their jig or worm through the cover just like a snake or eel might appear to be struggling through the water.

As in conventional worm or jig fishing, strike the very instant you feel a bump or see the line twitch. Once a fish is securely hooked, muscle it to the boat and with a gentle sweeping motion swing it right over the side. A strong nylon monofilament and stiff rod tip will handle this chore with ease, provided the fish does not weigh over five pounds; anything larger should probably be netted or grabbed by the lower lip.

That's all there is to Flippin'. I didn't say it was a complicated method, and maybe that's one reason why so many advanced anglers nationwide rely upon it as one of their foremost shallow-water strategies.

Speed-Trolling

In backtrolling, an angler runs his boat in reverse to present lures and baits on structures at slow speeds, directly beneath the boat. Speed-trolling is exactly the opposite. In this method, the craft is run forward at a much faster speed, with artificial lures dragged behind. Further, while backtrolling can be used any month of the year and is particularly well suited to cooler waters, speed-trolling is geared to much warmer waters when bass are far more active.

Speed-trolling is especially effective for quickly checking intermediate-depth structures in midlake areas, where straggler bass or school fish may be holding on the bottom at depths of six to 25 feet. More specifically, it is perhaps the most expedient method one can use to determine what type of structure the fish are predominantly using, how deep they are, and what lure speed is best for that particular day. Even though many anglers may not really enjoy trolling, I nevertheless recommend this technique as the fastest way to locate bass; once fish have been found, go ahead and anchor and cast to them if you prefer.

It was Buck Perry who refined speed-trolling to an art. He found that the most suitable tackle included a rather short, stiff trolling rod, level-wind trolling reel, and a line with minimal stretch characteristics. Compared with a soft-action, limber rod, a stiffer rod is more capable of transmitting to the angler everything the lure is doing. It is much easier to tell when the lure begins free-swimming (loses contact with bottom structure) or perhaps when it begins violently digging into the bottom (this indicates the wrong size lure is being used, the trolling speed is too fast, or too much line has been let out). With substantial amounts of line paid out behind the boat, a stiffer rod also gives the angler more leverage in setting the hook.

Most nylon monofilament lines are not suitable for trolling because they are too elastic. They're intentionally designed this way to absorb the jarring shock anglers inflict upon them when casting lures short distances and setting the hook. But when three or four times as much line is paid

Buck Perry pioneered the art of speed-trolling. Unlike backtrolling, in which the craft is run in reverse, in speed-trolling you go forward. Note the comfortable way of bracing the butt section of the rod against the leg, leaving one hand free to control the tiller.

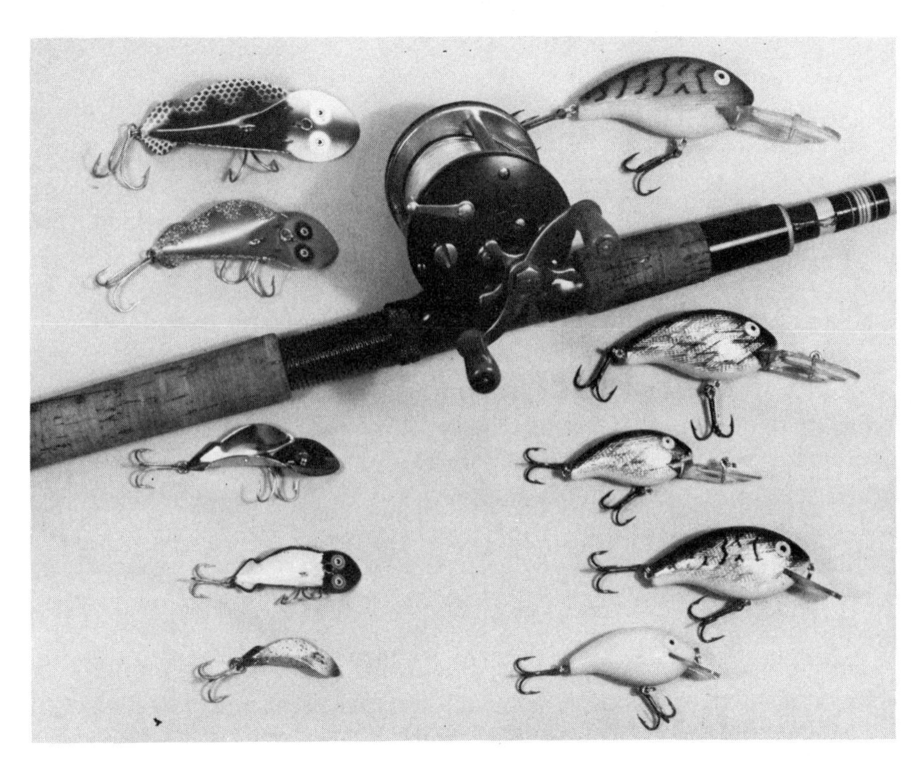

Appropriate lures for speed-trolling must run true at a variety of depths and speeds. Buck Perry invented his Spoonplugs, shown at the left, to meet this criterion, although many brands of crankbaits, such as Rebels, also work well.

out, as in trolling, this stretch factor magnifies itself to such an extent that setting the hook becomes virtually impossible. Just as important, as more and more stretchy line is let out behind the boat, it begins to bow as water resistance exerts its influence, which causes an angler to lose his depth control. A crankbait that runs 15 feet deep when trolling 30 feet behind the boat, for example, may run only 5 feet deep if 90 feet of line is paid out.

For trolling, then, I recommend using braided Dacron line, which has virtually no stretch, to which is blood-knotted a ten-foot terminal length of monofilament.

Lures used in speed-trolling must run true at a variety of trolling speeds (many lures are designed to run at only one speed and when trolling a bit faster flip over on their sides and slide to the surface). In addition, an angler must be aware of the range of depths his lures are capable of. Sometimes these depth ranges are printed on the boxes in which lures are sold; if they are not, a good way to determine the running level of lures is by casting them in a swimming pool and noting at which depths they begin bumping bottom.

Since Buck Perry wasn't satisfied with the lures available when he pioneered speed-trolling years ago, he invented his own lures, which were dubbed Spoonplugs (they're still available today). Spoonplugs are made in a variety of sizes, each intended to run at a specific depth regardless of trolling speed. An additional feature of Spoonplugs is that when they become fouled with debris such as weeds, they immediately come to the surface. This signal allows an angler to clean the lure quickly so he can return to checking his structure. Many other lures do not do this and will continue to run at their prescribed depths with weeds trailing from their hooks, which makes them very unproductive.

In addition to Spoonplugs for speed-trolling, I've had success with Hellbenders, Bombers and Rebels. These all track a truer course at various speeds and allow me to check a wider range of depths than do many other lures.

Since precise boat control is essential in speed-trolling, the best craft is something in the neighborhood of 14 feet in length and powered by a ten-horse outboard. It is also important to have some type of onboard depth sounder, mounted in such a way that the boat operator can watch it continuously.

Speed-trolling can be very tiring if you're in an uncomfortable position. I recommend holding your trolling rod in your right hand. Rest your reel and the hand holding the rod in your lap, and with the length of your rod lying on a horizontal plane, brace the butt section of the rod against your knee, allowing the opposite hand to be free for operating the outboard. A twist-grip throttle with an instant off-button on the end of the tiller handle is ideal for making quick speed changes.

One of the most difficult aspects of trolling to master is knowing how much line to let out behind the boat, and being able to let out roughly that same amount of line each time trolling passes are made. To do otherwise nearly always results in a significant loss of control over your lures. As a general rule, if you are trolling in water from 6 to 12 feet deep, let out 25 yards of line. In water from 12 to 20 feet deep, let out 40 yards of line. And in water from 20 to 30 feet deep, let out 60 yards of line.

The easiest way to accomplish this consistently is by tying your line to some immovable object in your backyard, pacing off given distances as the line peels from your reel, then using a Magic Marker containing indelible ink to indicate yardage. In other words, every ten yards, make a two-inch long readily visible colored band on the line. This way, when you later let line out behind your boat, all that's necessary is to count the bands as they

Since precise boat control is a requisite of effective speed-trolling, most anglers opt for something like a 14-foot aluminum or fiberglass boat powered by a 10-horse-power outboard. Note special mounting bracket here for depth sounder, enabling boat operator to stay precisely on course.

slowly pay from your reel and you'll instantly know exactly how much line you're letting out.

Where should you speed-troll? Well, this is where doing your home-work the evening before a fishing outing pays off. Dig out your bottom contour map and begin surveying areas you think bass will be using, based upon the type of lake, time of year, and other considerations discussed in previous chapters. Then, when you're on the water first thing in the morning, evaluate water conditions (oxygen, pH, temperature) if you're not already pretty familiar with them from recent outings. All of this should allow you to make an educated guess as to where you're most likely to run into concentrations of bass.

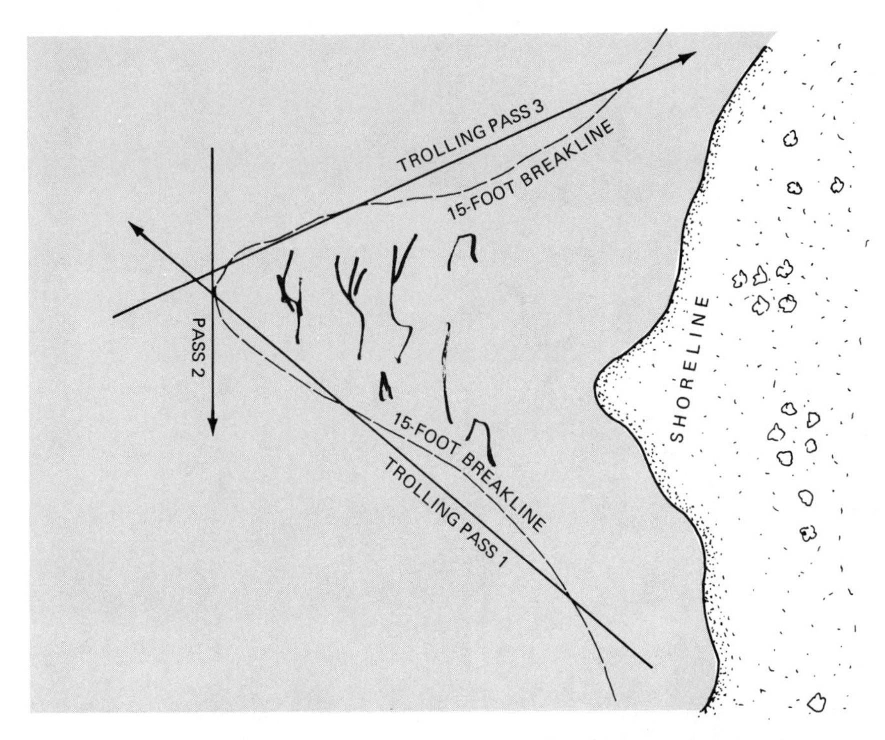

This diagram illustrates how you might speed-troll a long, wooded shoreline point. Since trolling across the point would cause lures to snag repeatedly, it's better to work the breakline drop-offs by speed-trolling, then use Flippin' or some other technique to fish the cover itself.

To be more specific, after you've chosen a particular lake area for the day's work, speed-trolling seems best suited to rather lengthy bottom features such as primary and secondary breaklines (drop-offs), underwater roadbeds, ridges, and stream and river channels. However, I would offer two pieces of advice. First, begin speed-trolling on "clean" bottom contours, as they are much more forgiving than structures littered with stumps, logs and weeds. Second, begin trolling rather straight-away bottom features until you refine the required eye-hand coordination involved in simultaneously looking at a bottom contour map and depth-sounder dial while constantly making slight course corrections by turning the outboard's tiller handle. After you've mastered this, then graduate to irregular bottom contours such as steep underwater points, stream channel bends and crooked breaklines. In these latter cases, where pods of bass may be clinging to only one of several breaks on breaklines, it will be necessary to make numerous trolling passes from perhaps several different directions to check them thoroughly.

There are two final points to keep in mind. As emphasized already,

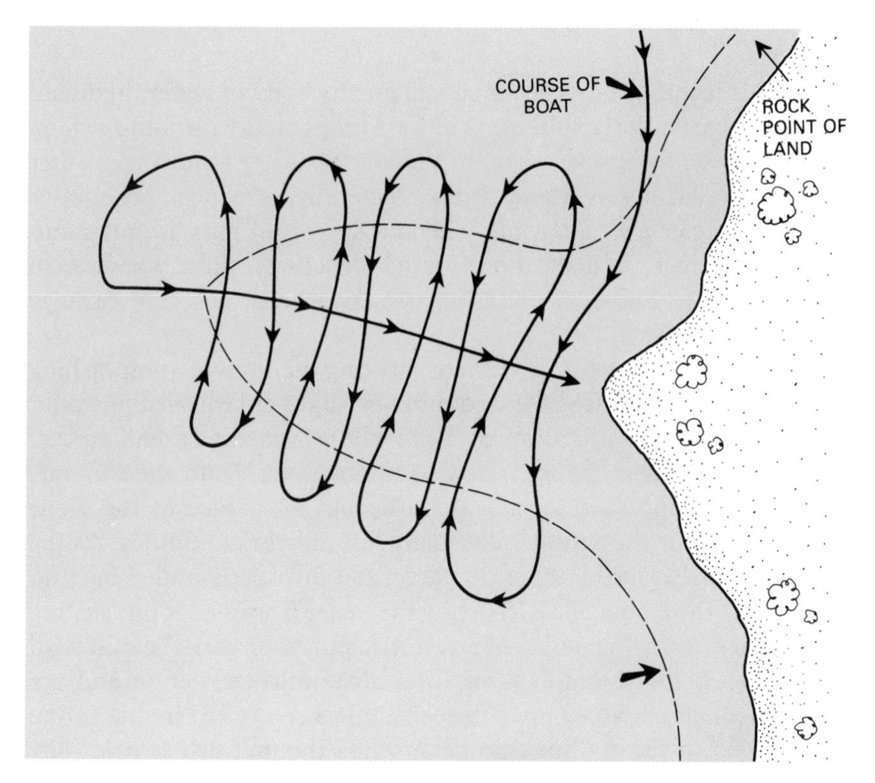

On rocky, cover-free structures such as points, methodical speed-trolling passes can be used to check the entire location in a few minutes.

when bass are in water deeper than eight feet or so, they are generally on or very near the bottom. Consequently, on or near the bottom is where you want your lures to be presented when speed-trolling. If your lures are in proper position, you'll frequently feel them ticking the bottom. If you never feel this, it means your lures are running too shallow and out of the productive fish zone; you need to switch to something that runs deeper. Conversely, if your lure is continually and violently digging into the bottom, switch to something that is intended to run not quite so deep.

Last, remember that water temperature strongly influences the body metabolisms of bass and, hence, their activity level. Lure speeds must be appropriate to the water temperature.

Jump-Fishing

The angling technique called *jump-fishing* or *fishing the jumps* can provide the most exciting bass action any angler could hope to experience.

Although this technique can be employed on any body of water, highland reservoirs are particularly suitable. The best times of day for jump-fishing are early in the morning, very late in the afternoon, or almost any other time when the surface is glassy calm. Generally, it's most productive during late summer and early fall, when all species of bass are predominantly using deeper, midlake areas or off-structures. And whenever a surface-swimming school of baitfish passes overhead, absolute carnage predictably takes place.

Anglers slowly motoring about, or drifting in known jump-fishing areas, are likely to first see only a dimple or slight splash on the water, and then another, and still another. Suddenly, as much as a half-acre of midlake water erupts in frothy frenzy as the bass slash into their forage.

Anglers witnessing such surface disturbances must race to the scene under full power for the action will usually last only brief minutes. As the boat approaches to within about 50 yards, the throttle is pulled back to avoid alarming the feeding bass. Skirting the melee from a cautious casting distance, either under the power of an electric motor or with the outboard idling, they then throw baitfish-imitating plugs into the action and are usually immediately hooked up. I've seen anglers so excited by the action that they failed to set the hook properly when the first fish struck, only to take a few turns of the reel handle and have another bass grab their offering. A lucky angler will manage to get in about six casts and boat six fish. This kind of totally chaotic fishing requires having two or three pre-rigged rods nearby; if a line breaks or tangles, or a reel malfunctions, throw the rod in the bottom of the boat and grab another!

It has long been a puzzle to anglers why a school of feeding bass, with thousands of free-swimming baitfish about, could or would single out an angler's lure. Seemingly, this state of affairs greatly stacks the odds against the fisherman, but in reality he's sitting in the catbird seat if he realizes what's going on.

For protection, baitfish school *very* tightly and as they move about they present themselves to the predators as only a shadowy, shifting mass or underwater cloudlike formation. In order to score, the bass must first charge the school to break it up and then isolate and run down individual baitfish. Usually, they are unsuccessful in their attempts to scatter the forage. Liken it, if you will, to thrusting your hand into a pail of water filled with peas in an attempt to grab one particular pea. It's almost a sure bet you'll miss the one you're after. Furthermore, the instant you extract your hand, the hole or void will fill itself in a microsecond. Essentially the same thing happens when bass charge into a highly concentrated mass of small fish.

An angler's lure retrieved through and then out of a baitfish school,

The best times of day for jump-fishing are early morning and evening hours. Here, anglers bob patiently in their boats, using binoculars to scan distant waters in the hopes of spotting surface disturbances made be feeding bass.

Popular lures for jump-fishing are plugs, spoons and similar offerings that represent shad and other baitfish.

however, gives the illusion of a baitfish that has somehow become separated from its school, and any marauding bass nearby will seize the opportunity to nail it. In fact, it is very common to catch two bass on the same plug.

To maximize your jump-fishing success, have on hand an arsenal of lures that closely represent the predominant forage in the lake you're fishing. In most cases, you'll want lures that resemble threadfin shad, gizzard shad, emerald shiners or, perhaps, small herring.

Also, try to spend as much time as possible in those lake areas where jump-fishing is most likely to occur. The number-one place seems to be over the main riverbed where there are certain bottom structures bass are likely to be holding on, such as sharp bends in the channel, deltas along the edges, or standing timber. Since these lake areas can be quite large, savvy anglers spend a good deal of time drifting at rest while simultaneously scanning the distance with high-power binoculars, searching for the beginning signs of surface-feeding activity.

Another strategy that pays off handsomely is keeping an eye pealed for birds. Watch in particular for gulls flying high and when they begin flocking to a given region, get over there quick. They are keeping tabs on a surface-swimming school of baitfish, knowing that when bass begin

It's always wise to keep your boat a considerable distance from surface-feeding bass, or they may spook and dive for the depths. Here, gulls have shown anglers where the fish are feeding and numerous boats have raced to the area to get in on the action, which is likely to last only a few minutes.

ravenously feeding they'll be able to swoop down and pick up bits and pieces of the mauled forage.

One other tactic that frequently rewards a knowing angler with larger than average bass is to allow every other cast or so to sink below the surface-swimming baitfish. As you work the lure in, from eight to 12 feet deep, make it dart and struggle. A number of much larger bass may be lurking directly beneath the smaller ones charging the baitfish. These larger fish seem reluctant to come right to the surface and engage in chase-and-catch feeding behavior, preferring instead to remain deep and leisurely pick off injured baitfish sinking down through the water from the on-going commotion above.

Graphing Suspended Bass

When bass of all species are using midlake areas, they often travel in large schools at some arbitrary depth between the surface and the lake floor. The exact depth depends upon several factors discussed in Chapters 7–9, for example, pH, oxygen levels, light intensity, or a combination of any of these.

Bass travel suspended in two situations: when they are on the prowl, searching for schools of baitfish; and when they have found a school of baitfish and are following it, waiting for some signal telling them to rise to the surface and begin foraging.

Using a graph recorder, anglers can quite easily find schools of baitfish, with bass suspended below them, and join the parade, so to speak, catching an occasional bass along the way while waiting for more surface-feeding action to take place. Although conventional depth sounders can be used for this work, with the baitfish registering as a band of thin spikes

Graphing suspended bass is generally done in midlake regions over deeper water, and it's generally a summertime activity.

near the surface and the bass as wide bands 12 to 20 feet deeper, graph recorders are far easier to use. With a print-out strip before you, you can get a much better idea of the size of the bass you're tracking, the size of the baitfish school, and the direction in which the predators and prey are moving.

Of course, it is the forage that leads the way, with the bass in pursuit, but baitfish seldom travel in random, nomadic fashion. When the water is relatively calm, look for them to follow river channels, drop-offs and similar bottom features that clearly run long distances; after a while, they will reverse their line of travel and begin heading back in the opposite direction. What the baitfish are doing is searching for clouds of plankton or algae bloom to feed upon, using the lengthy bottom contours to lead them from one part of the lake to another.

If you find a baitfish school, but then after following it for a while lose track of it, note whether or not the wind has picked up. If it hasn't, the baitfish school has probably reversed its line of travel and is now heading back in the opposite direction; turn around and you should quickly relocate the school. If the wind is gusting, however, it is now blowing the plankton or algae off course, downwind from the bottom contour, and the baitfish have subsequently made a sharp turn to follow; turn sharply downwind yourself and you'll undoubtedly find the bait again.

This print-out strip from a graph recorder, representing part of a flatland reservoir where several stream channels converge with the main riverbed, reveals the presence of suspended bass. The dark crescent near the surface is a large school of shad; the smaller crescents are bass suspended directly beneath. From above the surface, looking over a wide expanse of water, most anglers would never even suspect such fish activity in midlake.

In many cases baitfish travel too fast to be followed under the power of an electric motor and it's necessary to idle along with the outboard. If you're fishing alone, this means there is little opportunity to fish for bass beneath the forage; you have to remain behind the steering console until you see surface action beginning to erupt, whereupon you can then move to the bow and begin casting to fish in the jumps. If a partner is on board, however, or if the baitfish are traveling slow enough to be followed with an electric motor, one or both of you can fish as you travel.

Simply check your recorder and note the particular level at which the schooling bass are swimming beneath the baitfish and then work that level. Jigs, jigging spoons and leadhead tailspinners pumped up and down are the most productive lures for this kind of work because they sink quickly and can be vertically fished right beneath the boat.

Don't expect to catch a bass on every cast, as you would in periodically fishing the jumps, because most of the bass are not in an active feeding state. Most likely, you'll catch an incidental bass that has been triggered into involuntarily striking as a lure sweeps quickly by its nose, but what better way to bide your time until you can take part in another jump-fishing episode?

As noted several times in previous chapters, bass are always closely tied

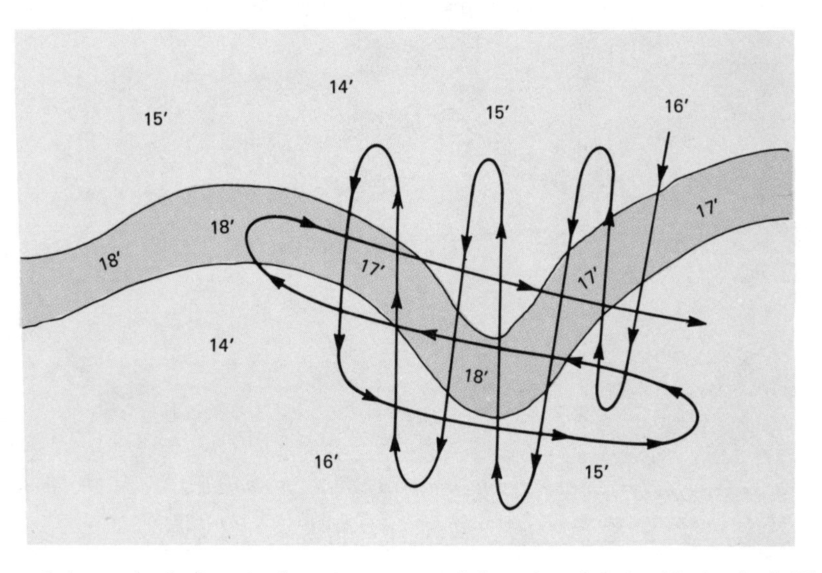

One of the author's favorite locations to graph bass is a lake's old riverbed. This diagram shows how he does it.

to their forage. This is why, in graphing suspended bass, I like to find the forage first, knowing that likely as not a school of bass will be close by. But in many instances the forage that bass are tied to are not midlake schools of minnows but crayfish or something else that does not characteristically travel far and wide during a given day. In this case, the bass will likewise remain in a given place where there is an abundance of their favorite food. These bass can be graphed as well, and you can even examine your chart paper and tell whether or not the fish are engaged in actively feeding.

One of my favorite locations to graph is a sunken, rock-capped island or long underwater ridge. Inactive bass will suspend off the edge of such structures in compacted schools. Feeding bass, however, will be scattered somewhat and, more important, closely associating with the structure. You can graph river channel areas as well. Bass that are using the depths of the channel as a resting sanctuary will be quite deep, yet if you find them moving up and out of the channel and onto deltas, bars or timbered edges, it's almost a sure bet they're now actively searching for food.

Graphing suspended fish is bass fishing's newest frontier and as this is being written, in early 1984, there still remain many aspects of suspended fish behavior we do not have definitive explanations for. Now's the time for any serious bass angler to get in on the ground level by engaging in a lot of personal trial-and-error experimentation. Maybe you'll learn something significant that eventually will prove to be a breakthrough bass-fishing technique used by thousands of other anglers nationwide.

CHAPTER

16

River And Stream Bass

River fishing is a paradox. On the one hand, the opportunities, particularly for bass, are far more diverse than those found in most lakes and reservoirs. Often all three species—largemouths, smallmouths and spotted bass—can be caught in a single day. Yet, comparatively few anglers ever bother to fish rivers. That is just fine as far as my friend and veteran river rat Tommy Wilkins is concerned.

"Fast action and few other anglers is a combination that makes me feel like I died and went to heaven," my pal remarked one day as we were pitching plugs to Ohio River bass. Incredibly, we boated nearly 30 fish in a single afternoon and saw only two other boats, both of which were towing water-skiers.

There are two reasons why America's large rivers are now the "in" places to enjoy premier fishing adventures. Foremost, we're now finally beginning to see the results of numerous anti-pollution laws and environmental campaigns launched by state and federal agencies during the late 1960s. Indeed, you name the river, be it the Mississippi, Missouri, Ohio, Tennessee, Susquehanna, or almost any other, and I'll bet the grocery money that it's cleaner now than any time in the last 40 years. Since bass and other species obviously thrive in clean water, gamefish populations have exploded almost everywhere.

Moreover, river-fishing pressure has been decreasing, which has further enhanced the comeback of the bass species. The reason for this steadily declining fishing pressure has its roots in the bass-fishing revolution spawned in the last four decades. First came a proliferation of construction projects resulting in the creation of countless manmade lakes, hydroelectric reservoirs and flood-control impoundments. Then came the bass-

Many anglers overlook the superb bass action waiting in rivers. Here, the author shows part of one afternoon's catch of spotted bass from the Ohio River. These ten were kept for the table, while 20 others were released.

boat boom, the emergence of high-performance outboards and a wide array of electronic fish-finding gadgetry, and the birth of state and national fishing clubs. A new style of fishing began to evolve that no one could have ever envisioned. A major consequence of this sudden, startling devotion to "big water" reservoir bassing was that river fishing slowly and quietly slid into obscurity.

But now, as bass fishing continues to grow in popularity and manmade reservoirs become more and more crowded, many enterprising anglers looking for more and larger fish, and for more solitude, are shifting their sights back to river fishing. In fact, the last five BASS Master Classic tournaments have *all* been staged on major rivers; Arkansas River, Arkansas (1984); Ohio River, Ohio (1983); Alabama River, Alabama (1982); Alabama River, Alabama (1981); St. Lawrence River, New York (1980). During all of these tournaments except the one on the Ohio River, the field of contenders awed spectators with large bass few local residents even knew existed in their waters.

Smaller rivers and streams that lace the countryside often provide unparalleled bass-fishing action as well. True, such habitats rarely are home to the big bass that often inhabit large bodies of water, but all this means is that an angler must scale down his tackle accordingly. Believe me, a two-pound smallmouth battled on a light spinning rod with four-pound-test line feels like you're hooked to a runaway locomotive!

Bass in rivers and streams, like those in lakes and reservoirs, use structure for resting and moving. But there is one additional condition found in such waterways that is seldom found in lakes and reservoirs: *current.*

The flow of water that constitutes a current has certain characteristics, regardless of where in the country the river or stream is located. For one, a current is always stronger just below a dam or rapids and for a few miles downstream, until it gradually begins to diminish in velocity. Also, any flow of moving water tends to take the easiest route, usually a straight line, until some land feature diverts it, creating a bend. In time, the current washes out and undercuts the outside bend, thereby making the water much deeper. Conversely, the inside of the bend has a quieter flow of water, which allows sand, gravel and sediment carried downstream by the current to settle to the bottom in such places and create a somewhat shallow bar or shoal. In flatland areas, a river or stream may be straight as an arrow for mile after mile. But in hilly or mountainous regions, or places where there are mixtures of very soft and hard ground, perhaps with occasional rocky terrain, look for a river to take on a serpentine form.

As a general rule, the current of any flowing waterway will usually be much stronger toward the surface and toward the middle of the flow.

Lesser current velocities are usually found along the floor of the river or stream and close to the banks. In smaller rivers and streams, bass commonly take advantage of this situation by resting in depressions scooped out of the bottom, letting the fast water rush above them. Or they may rest behind the protection of midstream boulders or along the shoreline where cover formations create quiet pockets of less turbulent water. In larger rivers, as we'll see in greater detail in a moment, bass living in midriver locations may seek shelter on the down-current sides of islands, in association with wing-dams, and along shoreline configurations.

The important thing to keep in mind about current is that bass will seldom be found in the swifter flows. They prefer instead to rest in quieter currents directly adjacent to the main flow. And they will always face into the current, as this allows them to maintain their positions with the least expenditure of energy. It also allows them to keep on the watch for food which the rushing current may bring their way. They may have to dart out momentarily into the fast water to capture prey, but very shortly they will return to their holding stations in the quieter edge waters.

Because of the nature of their environment, river and stream bass often look different from lake and reservoir bass, which generally enjoy a sedentary life that leads to their becoming chunky and pot-bellied. But river and stream bass, even those living in the most sluggish waterways, must continually burn energy just to maintain their positions in the constantly moving water. As a result, they develop long, lean, torpedo-shaped bodies and a well-toned musculature that can make even a smaller than average fish feel like a race horse when snagged.

Finally, I should mention that bass populations inhabiting rivers and streams are extremely sensitive to changing water levels. During the early months of the year, spring rains and associated runoff water from higher ground and feeder tributaries may cause smaller rivers and streams to swell. When this happens, and the water is rising slowly, the fishing can be fantastic around shoreline bushes, brush and standing timber. Two explanations account for this. First, the bass move to shallower water in order to get out of the main flow, which may be extremely turbulent in places. Second, rivers and streams are generally rather infertile, spartan habitats and rising water flooding the shallow banks exposes or washes into the water a sudden profusion of food. The bass may move into the shallows to feed upon insects, earthworms and other small prey; more commonly they are attracted to the baitfish and panfish seeking both refuge and food in such places.

Later, as the water level slowly begins to recede, the bass vacate the shallows and move back into their former holding stations. But if the

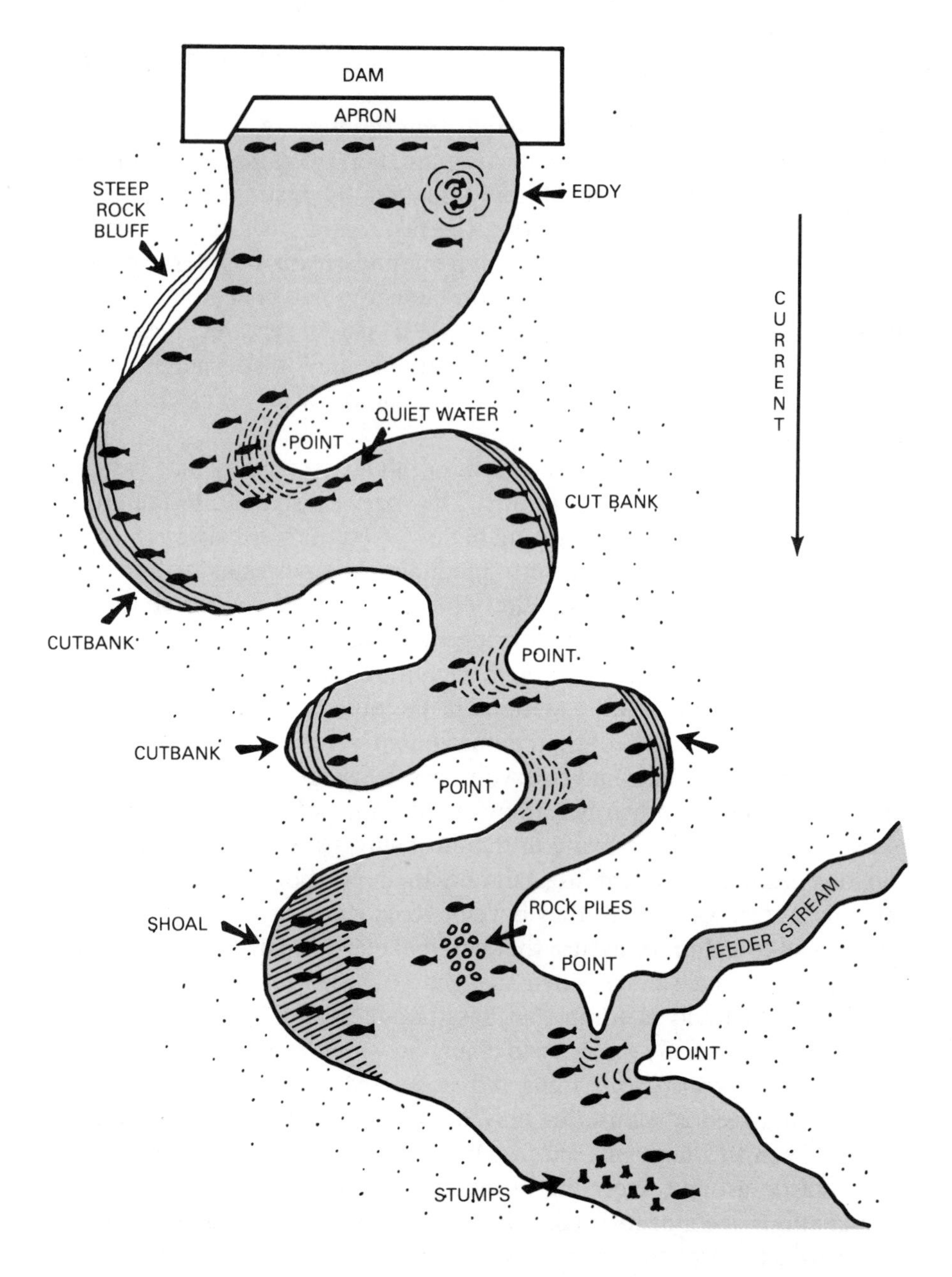

One condition seldom found in lakes and reservoirs that influences the location of river bass is current. It travels in a straight line until some land feature diverts it, which gives birth to many types of structures bass are fond of using.

water level begins to fall slowly below the norm, look for most angling action to terminate. Drops in water levels predictably send bass scurrying into the depths until conditions stabilize.

Fishing Large Rivers

Large rivers can sometimes be fished using somewhat the same strategies you might put into play when searching for bass in flatland and highland reservoirs. There will be current to contend with, to be sure, but there will also be similar depths and bank features, and bass will frequently be using them. However, bends—which may be fish magnets of the first order in smaller rivers and streams—generally aren't prime bass habitat in larger rivers. In a river such as the Ohio, Missouri or Mississippi, a bend may well be a half-mile long and several hundred yards wide.

As a result, in a majority of cases, big-river bass customarily orient themselves either to the river's shorelines or feeder tributaries. The main river channel itself is usually too deep and too swift to attract bass. Besides, the bottom is likely to have been scoured clean by dredges to facilitate barge and tugboat traffic.

I frequently like to concentrate my efforts along shoreline shelves. These features, quite common on rivers used for interstate commerce, appear as narrow benches extending out from the bank perhaps 20 yards before dropping off sharply into the main river channel. They're quite attractive to bass of all species because of a combination of desirable features: suitable water depth ranging from three to 15 feet; close access to much deeper water if necessary; the presence of a long, abrupt breakline, which facilitates seasonal and other short-range migrations; an abundance of log jams, driftwood, stumps, boulders and similar cover, which attracts baitfish, panfish and crayfish.

Whenever the water is less than six feet deep on such shelves, bass can be duped with spinnerbaits, crankbaits and plastic worms. However, if the water is more than six feet deep, the current will often carry these lures far out of position before they've had a chance to get down near bottom where the fish are holding. Now is when an angler should switch to lures such as jigs and jigging spoons.

Sandbars, which occasionally can be found in large rivers, are rather elongated structures quite similar to the deltas that exist along the edges of inundated river channels in flatland reservoirs. But a swift current caused by a torrential rainstorm can erase a sandbar overnight. Then, after

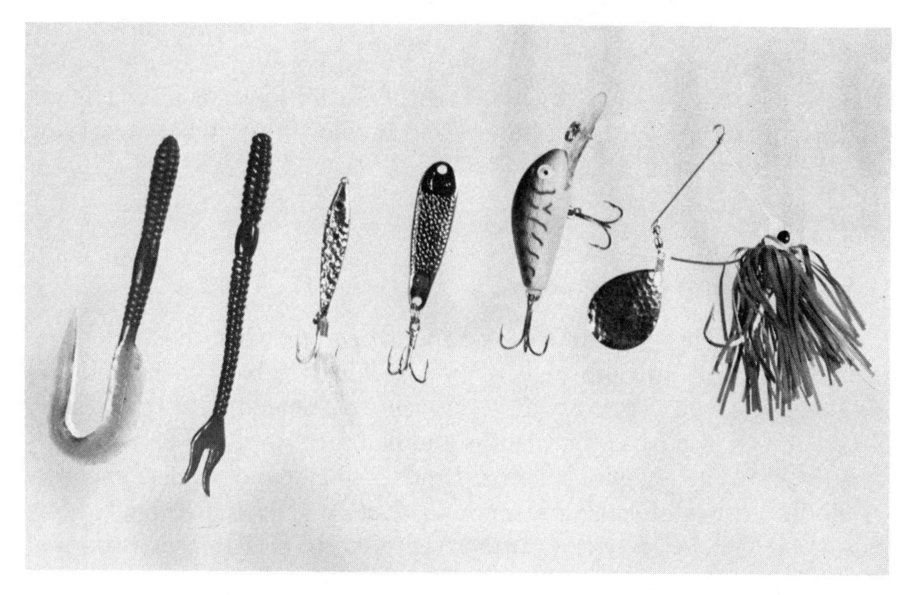

A selection of the author's favorite river lures. Since current is always present, you need offerings that sink quickly before they are out of position.

the rains have abated and the current has moderated, a new bar may begin forming somewhere else. Jigging spoons are undeniably the best lures for checking bars at a wide range of depths.

Still other features occur only in certain rivers. A prime example is an *oxbow.* This is a place where a former loop or S-turn in the river channel has been straightened out by dredges to facilitate barge traffic. The result is the formation of a crescent-shaped backwater almost like a small lake. Often, brush and logs choke these oxbows and provide optimal bass habitat.

I have fished Mississippi River oxbows not far from Memphis many times using conventional flatland reservoir tactics such as dragging spinnerbaits across fields of lily pads and throwing plastic worms to stumps and stick-ups. Unlike other river locations, oxbows often produce real lunkers. Since there is little or no current running through an oxbow, yet a profusion of cover and plenty of forage, bass quickly begin to take on the same pot-bellied characteristics as their lake-bred brethren. The one disadvantage of oxbows is their accessibility. Most times, there will be a narrow cut leading into an oxbow from the main river channel, and another cut exiting. But during low-water periods, these can be reduced to bare trickles.

Of all big-river features, however, the most attractive to bass are the numerous tributaries feeding into the main river channel. Typically, the

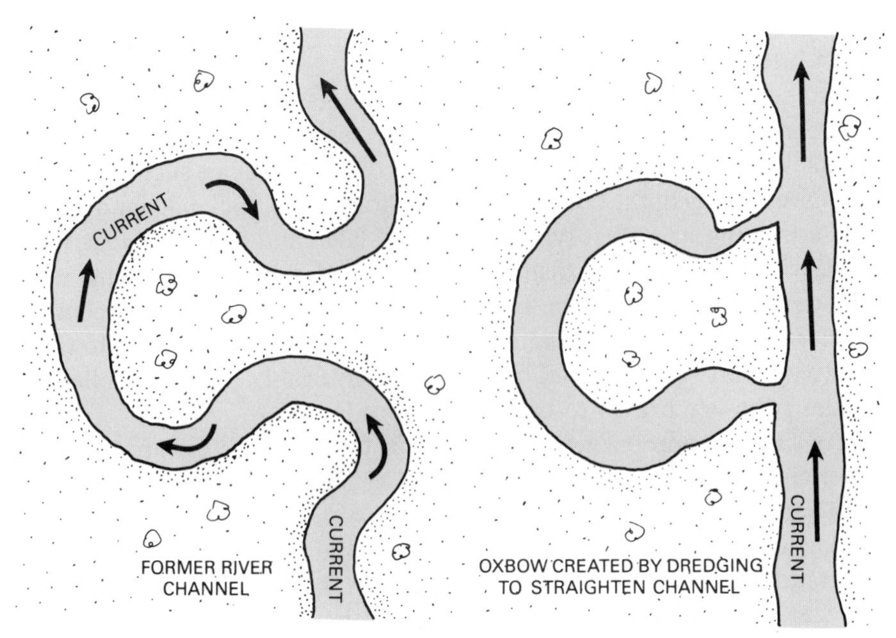

One type of hot spot common to many larger rivers is an oxbow. An oxbow is a crescent-shaped, quiet pocket of backwater that is formed when a loop in the river channel is straightened to facilitate water flow and boat traffic.

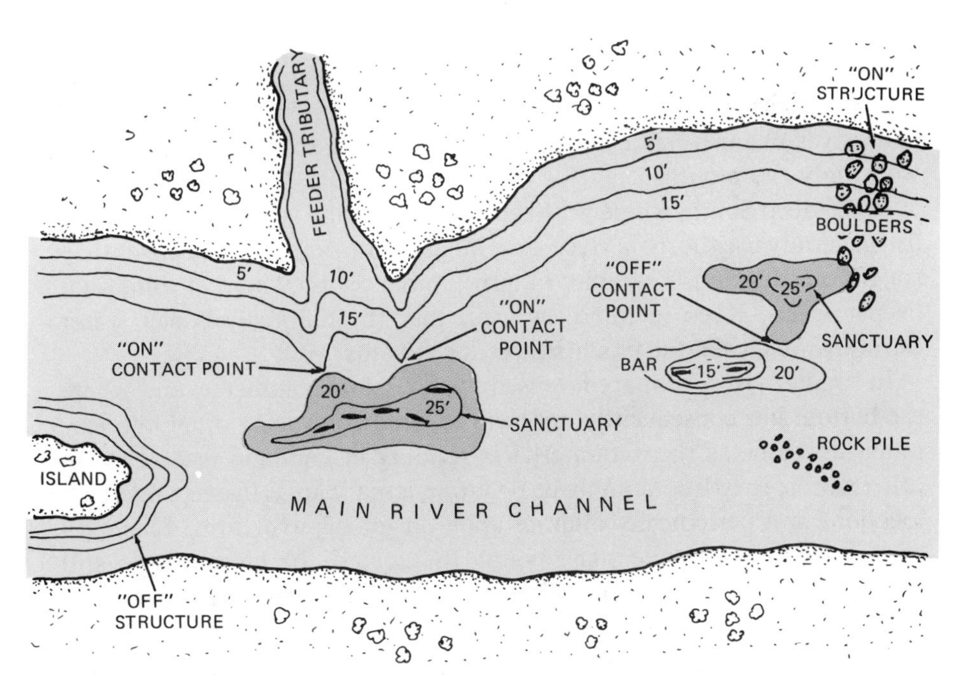

Of all big-river features, feeder tributaries probably play the most important roles in the lives of bass. Generally, the first mile of a tributary, near the mouth, is where most of the fish are found. On midsize rivers not used for interstate commerce, also be sure to look for midriver features such as islands, bars and shoals.

shorelines of such creeks and small rivers are lined with trees, stumps, rocks, weedbeds and other favored bass cover. And since such tributaries are never dredged, the bottom may have holes, bars, rock piles and similar fish-attracting structures typical of natural lakes and manmade reservoirs.

A prime time of year to fish feeder tributaries is during the spring, when all species of bass leave the main river channel where they've spent the winter months. With spawning on their minds, they are inclined to travel upstream into quieter, shallower water. Invariably, the first mile of a feeder tributary proves to be the most productive.

As summer approaches, the fish begin to drift back toward the main river channel and disperse along shoreline shelves and bars wherever they find suitable haunts.

About the time of the first hard frost in fall, bass make still another migration back toward the feeder tributaries, but they don't travel as far upstream as they did in spring. Instead, in the first 100 yards or so, near the tributary mouth, they go on feeding rampages in preparation for winter. North of the Mason–Dixon line, this is a time of year when there are large shad die-offs in rivers, so devote a majority of your time to casting baitfish-lookalike lures, making them appear to be crippled or struggling.

The seasonal keys to unlocking successful big-river bass fishing can therefore be summarized as follows: During the spring, concentrate upon the feeder tributaries; during the summer, work shorelines adjacent to the main river channel; and, during the fall, go back to the tributaries, but work only the mouths.

In the deep South, where year-round river bassing is enjoyed, wintering fish generally use the main river area, hugging the same types of cover they sought out during the summer months, only now they hold at somewhat deeper levels. Keep in mind, as well, that the markedly cooler water during winter calls for much slower lure speeds.

In smaller rivers that are not used for interstate commerce, and where the bottom has consequently not been scoured clean, bass often live very much the same as their counterparts residing in highland reservoirs. In other words, they'll commonly be tied to sanctuary areas in deep, midriver locations and periodically migrate upon on- or off-structures. Examples of on-structures are the steep points that guard the entrances to still smaller feeder tributaries and also backwater bays and coves. Examples of off-structures are midriver bars, shoals, and the tapered ends of islands.

Straggler fish in these smaller rivers will also be found around shoreline features such as docks, rubble riprap protecting banks close to roads, and the concrete pilings supporting highway bridges and railway trestles.

One thing to keep in mind, still again, is the presence of current and its velocity at any given time. When the current is gliding along at a moderate to rather swift speed, look for most bass to be holding on the protected downstream side of cover and obstructions. As the speed of the current slows, however, look for them on both the upstream and downstream sides, and a bit farther away from the banks toward the main channel. An excellent illustration of this situation is the behavior of bass around wing-dams.

Just below concrete dams, look for bass to be holding around wing-dams. These structures, made of boulders, logs and cribbing, extend into the river and shunt the current toward the middle, thus preventing shoreline erosion.

Wing-dams are manmade structures of cribbing and natural materials, usually logs and railroad ties interspersed with boulders. They may be placed almost anywhere but most commonly appear intermittently for the first mile or so just below dams. Here, the current always seems to be running at moderate to fast velocity, and wing-dams extending out into the river help to shunt the main flow of the current toward the middle of the river, thus preventing the banks from seriously eroding. When the current is strong, bass will predictably hold in the deep, quiet water close to the shoreline on the downstream side of a wing-dam. When the current moderates a bit, they'll move away from the shoreline a bit, and also begin climbing somewhat up the backside of the wing-dam toward its crest. And when the current is light, they may be at the very tip of the wing-dam, adjacent to the main river channel, on top of the wing-dam, or even on the front, upstream facing of the structure.

On both large and intermediate size rivers, the one- or two-mile stretches just below dams and locks offer other bass-fishing opportunities

Sometimes, shoreline water just below dams is shallow enough that wing-dams can be fished by wading. Other times, particularly if the current is swift, you'll want to use a boat. In addition to wing-dams, in the spring look for bass to move right up to the concrete apron of the dam structure itself.

as well. In the spring, bass like to travel upstream as far as possible, right to the very base of the dam where they hug the edge of the deep underwater concrete apron. The current is nearly always quite swift here, at least as it rushes over the top of the fish, but they find a measure of protection behind the apron, just as if they were behind a large midstream boulder. About the only way to make contact with these fish is by working jigs and jigging spoons, fishing them almost vertically right beneath the boat. But the action can be fantastic.

Most major rivers have deep water in their main channel regions and an absence of bottom structures due to dredging, both of which make for unsuitable bass habitat immediately upstream of locks and dams. But just the opposite often exists below locks and dams. Here, for several miles, the water is likely to be quite shallow due to the constant piling up of sediment.

An outstanding example of this situation is Alabama's Tennessee River immediately below the Pickwick Lake dam, where a three-mile stretch of

South of the Mason–Dixon line, many midsize rivers not used for interstate commerce have shallow water immediately below their dams, with an abundance of bars and shoals. Anglers motor up to the base of the dam, then drift downstream casting lures or paying out live baits. Anglers here are drifting for smallmouths on Alabama's Tennessee River just below the Pickwick Lake dam.

water is renowned for its superb smallmouth fishing. Smallmouths of six to nine pounds are common here, with most of the monster bass taken from the very middle of the river wherever there are sandbars, gravel shoals, clamshell beds or holes. Since these structures appear and disappear with exasperating unpredictability (due to fluctuating current velocities), finding them is largely reduced to guesswork.

The strategy most anglers use is to motor upstream relatively close to the base of the dam, let out live minnows on weighted lines or set adrift slim-minnow plugs, drift downstream with the current for several miles, then motor back to the dam and commence a new drift from a slightly different position to cover new water.

When a fish strikes, a marker buoy is thrown overboard. This is essential because by the time the fish is netted, the boat may well have traveled far from the spot; a marker guides the angler back to the exact location to see if more fish are around.

Now, once a gravel shoal or clambed has been located, anglers put into play a second strategy known as *river-slipping.* Instead of free-drifting a long distance, they use their outboards to hold them in position to fish the structure thoroughly with slim-minnow lures, crankbaits or jigs. In this technique, the throttle speed is set just a tad slower than the current velocity so the boat is not maintained in the same location, but has a tendency to "slip" back just a few feet at a time. Although any boat can be used for river-slipping, the most-favored craft seems to be a 14-foot johnboat with a ten-horsepower outboard.

Creek Savvy

Very small rivers, streams and creeks offer both the easiest and yet the most challenging bass fishing imaginable. On the one hand, an angler with even the most rudimentary knowledge of bass behavior can look at a stream or creek and immediately know where bass are likely to be holding. But trying to catch them may be altogether another matter. The water always seems to be moving too fast, or it's so shallow the fish are spooky, or the most attractive holding stations are jailed by impregnable cover.

In most shallow waters, bass do not form schools. There may be exceptions in which widely separated deep pools hold loose groupings of fish during the midsummer and winter months. But in the great majority of cases, the fish are loners.

All streams and creeks—whether they meander through rural farmlands, black-bottomed swamps, woodland tracts or deep rocky gorges—share some traits. For one, they always take the path of least resistance, carving their way through soft-soil regions, diverting right or left to skirt hardpan, which gives each the appearance of a serpent twisting across the landscape. Streams and creeks also vary widely in their bottom contours, for as the water flows to lower elevations it sluices over soft soil and hard, creating an undulating effect in a series of deep pools, bars, shallow riffles and long glides.

North of the Mason–Dixon line, smallmouths are the dominant residents of streams and creeks, but in the South they may hold a combination of smallmouths and spotted bass, depending upon the elevation. Since smallies require cooler temperatures and a stream gradient of at least 3 percent, they are most likely to inhabit mountain creeks or spring-fed lowland streams. Spotted bass tolerate water a tad warmer and are residents of nearly all streams and creeks ranging from 1,000 feet in elevation to below sea level. Largemouths generally are bonus fish in these waters since they need still warmer temperatures and a gradient less than 2 percent.

Though not common, finding all three species of bass in the same water is possible in many small rivers, streams and creeks. My friend Sam Piatt and I did so one afternoon as we floated Kentucky's Kinnikonick Creek.

"Look how the current shunts in and out along the rocky bank over there," Sam pointed out. "Along the outside edge where the current is really zipping along, we'll probably hang a smallmouth. Between the rocks, where there is a bit of protection, we may catch a spotted bass. And if there's a largemouth around, he'll be far back in that little niche of still water near those lily pads."

What happened next was almost unbelievable. Sam pitched a small spinner between the rocks, and a spotted bass grabbed it, did a pirouette on the surface, then threw the hook. Sam was reeling in for the next cast when the spinner—now in much faster water—was nailed by a smallmouth that dove for the bottom. Then I fired a floating minnow plug toward the pads, and the instant it splatted down a largemouth inhaled it.

No angler should expect to encounter very large fish in streams and creeks. Such waters simply don't produce enough food, so competition among the predators for the available prey is fierce. Another factor that limits bass size in streams and creeks is that the bulk of any food intake is quickly converted into current-fighting energy rather than allowed to accumulate in fat stores. As a result, a largemouth that weighs three pounds can be looked upon as a real trophy, and a majority of smallmouths and spotted bass will come in at less than two pounds.

However, don't allow their comparatively small sizes to fool you. Creek and stream bass that spend their entire lives in or close to fast water

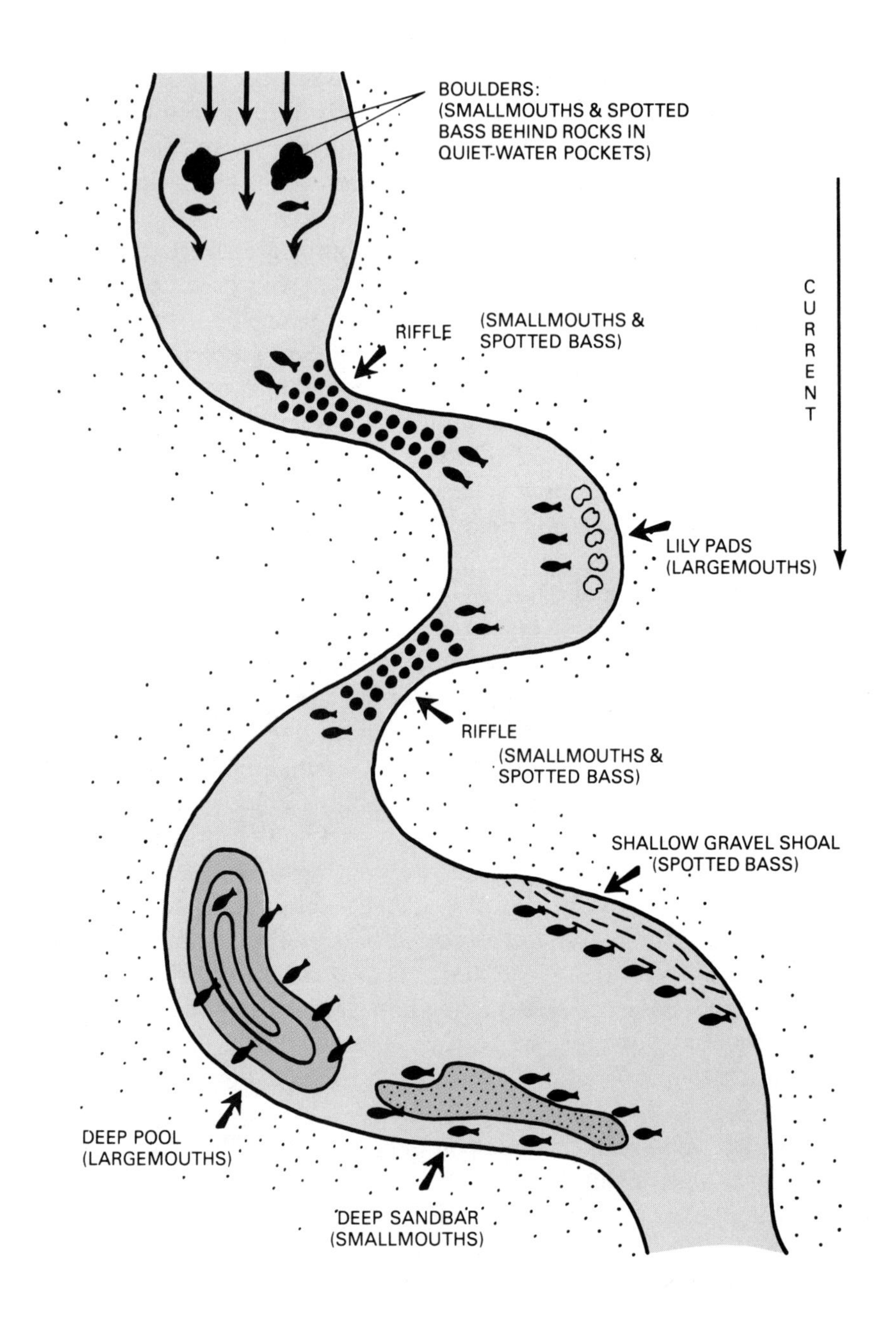

As with large rivers, the rushing current in small rivers and streams gouges out landforms and underwater structures. Depending upon the current velocity in various regions, it's often possible to make a cast and predict in advance which species of bass you're likely to catch.

become lean, missile-shaped and exceedingly strong, and they learn to use the current to their full advantage whenever they feel the sting of steel. Nevertheless, down-size tackle always is the wisest choice.

The best possible outfit is a five-foot, 3½-ounce spinning rod married to a small open-face reel. On occasion, spincasting and ultralight baitcasting tackle may be justified, but open-face spinning reels are by far the most versatile. With this gear you can quickly snap into place interchangeable spools of line to meet given conditions. I usually rely upon six-pound test most of the day, but whenever I come to a crystal-clear pool of quiet water, I like to switch to four-pound. If there's a sluggish stretch full of logjams, weeds or other cover, ten-pound test is called for.

Also, much of any stream or riverbank is lined with trees and overhanging branches, which gives the waterway a tunnel appearance. To work this cover effectively, you often must cast from rather unorthodox positions, making use of underhand or sidearm throws. In these situations, spinning gear is the easiest to handle.

Stream and creek bass feed heavily on small crayfish, hellgrammites, crickets, grasshoppers and locusts. To simulate these, nothing is better than ⅜-ounce jigs in brown, black or olive colors. Or you can use live counterparts of these crustaceans and insects. The best way to fish them is to hook them only once very lightly, add a single buckshot to the line to keep the bait near the bottom, and allow the gentle current to nudge the bait along as it tumbles slowly downstream around structural conformations on a tight line.

The fish also dote on small shiners and chubs, which are best imitated with slim-minnow plugs and straight-shaft spinners. Since you'll now and then encounter weeds and other thick cover, add a few small spinnerbaits as well.

Like their brethren in larger rivers, stream and creek bass always face into the current, and will almost always be in somewhat quieter sections adjacent to the main flow. Anglers disagree about whether such waterways should be fished upstream or down. There are advantages and disadvantages to method, and the debate as to which ploy is the most effective often causes butting of heads among the most serious anglers.

Too much ruckus upstream on your part, when fishing in a downstream direction, is likely to have one of two effects. If you dislodge gravel, silt and other debris in wading or carelessly maneuvering your craft through shallow riffles, and this tumbles downstream through locations you intend to fish next, the bass may spook. Other times, though, I've seen just the opposite occur. You may inadvertently kick up crustaceans, nymphs and other tasty tidbits; drifting downstream, these may cause bass to start

Here, author Weiss wade-fishes Kentucky's Kinnikonick Creek. In shallow waters like this, don't expect to encounter overly large bass, although fish up to three pounds may occasionally be found in scattered deep pools.

taking an interest in any potential food items—including your lures—that suddenly come their way.

Whenever the option presents itself, however, I like to fish upstream, occasionally making use of a small outboard or an electric motor if the current is just a bit too fast for comfortable paddling. The main reason for this preference is that bass, as noted earlier, face into the current, so the most natural-appearing offerings are those flowing or being retrieved with the water in the direction expected by bass.

If fishing downstream is the only practical way to work the river or stream of your choice, I'd like to make several suggestions. First, stay in your craft as much as possible. And rather than casting directly downstream, hug one bank or the other and try to cast quartering upstream. To eliminate the sounds incurred in navigating any kind of shallow-draft boat through occasional riffles or over sand and gravel bars, you may need to disembark and wade quietly. In quieter sections of water, you can sling the craft's bow rope over your shoulder and the boat will follow behind you, enabling you to sneak unobtrusively to within casting range of suspected bass lairs. If the water has any current, however, this tactic can cause endless frustration, as the boat will continually prod your backside, or try to get ahead of you. In such cases, I often beach my canoe or johnboat temporarily and hike along some gravel bar in a crouched position, casting into shoreline pockets and around various midstream obstructions. After the water has been thoroughly fished, I retrieve my craft and venture on downstream to the next likely location.

For all species of bass inhabiting small rivers, streams and creeks, it is essential to learn how to "read the water." Each pool, glide and riffle in such flowing waterways presents an entirely different picture puzzle which must be carefully evaluated. The current may slide from one side to the other, submerged rocks or logs with water rushing over the tops are sure to be present, and occasionally "sweepers" or toppled shoreline trees with their crowns lying in the water stick out into a stream.

As in larger rivers, the current in streams and creeks is always stronger near the surface and in midstream, and slower along the bottom, close to the banks, and directly behind obstructions. Bass in midstream regions are the greatest challenge. Most choose semiprotected pockets close to the main current flow (which carries most of the food), but *how* close depends at least partly upon the particular species.

For example, let's consider the situation near a large rock in the middle of a creek. On the upstream side, the current is forced to split around the rock. Right where the current splits, particulate matter in suspension will have settled out and piled up, but directly behind the rock there is almost invariably a depression. Either a largemouth or a spotted bass may select this place as a feeding station, if the current is not too swift, and a lure should be cast quartering upstream several yards ahead of where the current splits. As the slow retrieve is begun, the natural flow of the water will carry the lure around the boulder and into view of the fish behind. Approximately five or ten yards downstream of the rock, the two tendrils of diverted current join once again and the water appears bubbly or mildly turbulent. If there is any unique bottom feature present at this junction, such as rubble, expect smallmouth action.

Another hot spot for smallmouths is where two streams join, or where a still smaller creek enters the main flow of a stream. Fresh water gushing into the main channel, especially after summer showers, acts like a tonic, and if you're there with anything resembling eats you're in business. These locations, at any time of year, often present a divided appearance where the cloudy or murky water rushing in from the creek tributary yields to the clearer water of the main channel. This edge is a type of structure, and bass will adhere to it as religiously as they might to a drop-off.

It's very common for small rivers, streams and creeks to be murky, off-colored or even slightly muddy, which prevents an angler from seeing below-surface rocks, logs and other obstructions that may be serving as holding stations for bass. Here again is where learning how to read the water can pay off in handsome catches.

The trick is to take a few minutes to watch the surface of the water and any drifting bits of flotsam, twigs, leaves or even foam. A sudden change in the direction of the moving debris can indicate what lies below. If a twig or leaf suddenly deviates to the left or right from its straight downstream drift, then something below, probably a rock or log, is diverting the current. If the debris seems to hesitate, or briefly sweeps back upstream, it is being influenced by swirling eddy water, which indicates a quiet pocket directly below and some obstruction on the bottom just a few yards upstream. Similarly, a large boil on the surface indicates a large underwater obstacle, such as slab rock.

Although, as mentioned earlier, I like to fish upstream whenever possible, working sweepers—shoreline trees toppled into the water—is an exception to the rule. I first learned how to fish them effectively from tournament pro Bruce Cunagin on the Alabama River near Montgomery.

Bruce positioned our boat at an upstream vantage point and then slowly paid out line so the current carried his straight-shaft spinner downstream right into the maze of tangled branches. By keeping slight tension on the line, he kept the lure nosing into the current so it looked like a minnow trying to maintain its position. After two minutes, Cunagin paid out several more feet of line, allowing the bait to "drop back" farther into a slightly different holding pattern.

"There!" he said suddenly, striking back with a deep bend in his rod and quickly cranking the fish away from the cover before it had a chance to crochet the line through the latticework of limbs. The bass weighed only one and a half pounds, but then he proceeded to take three more of exactly the same size from the very same tree, proving the effectiveness of the drop-back technique. It's rather strange that bass anglers have only recently begun using this super tactic, because Michigan steelhead fishermen have been using it for generations to dupe big fish.

Without question, the largest stream and creek bass come from sweepers located in the longest and deepest pools. Generally, the fish will be holding right in the middle of the sweepers when the current is mild, dropping back to the far downstream side as the velocity increases.

In a deep pool on Ohio's Stillwater River I once hooked a gutsy 2½-pound smallmouth in a sweeper, on two-pound-test line. Luckily, I quickly pulled the fish away from the cover, but that was only the beginning of the battle. First the fish zipped to the right, then back to the left, apparently trying to find some trace of current that would lend it an advantage. Finding none, it leaped clear of the surface three times in rapid succession. Then it made the mistake of streaking to the head of the pool and found itself floundering on a shallow gravel riffle. I released that gallant bass. Except for one error in judgment, he'd have whipped me.

CHAPTER

17

Bass In Farmponds And Stripmine Pits

Farmponds, ranch tanks, and reclaimed stripmine and quarry ponds—ranging in size from ¼ to 50 acres—are extremely popular with bass anglers for several reasons. First, they are quite numerous and accessible. At last count there were over 6 million of them dotting the countryside, and more are built every year. Presently, the state you reside in, based upon national averages, probably has somewhere between seventy and seventy-five thousand ponds of this type. Many are created for the purposes of watering livestock, others to supply drinking or irrigation water, and still others strictly for recreation.

The great majority of such ponds are located on private or utility-owned property. But a courteous request for permission to fish, or the acquisition of some type of use-permit, will usually get you in.

Farmponds and stripmine ponds annually satisfy the angling appetites of millions of fishermen who just don't have enough time available to travel back and forth to work the larger impoundments, much less fish these behemoths. With knowledge of four or five ponds in his area, any angler can fish virtually every day of the week. All that's needed is a bit of time in the morning before heading for work, an afternoon now and then when you can sneak away from the world's cares, or a few hours of free time after dinner in the evening. If water or other conditions are not favorable at one pond (you might find the landowner's kids swimming, for example), it's usually just a few minutes' drive down the road to another.

In addition to their accessibility and abundance, farmponds and stripmine pits offer another benefit—fat and sassy bass. In my home state of Ohio, our last three state-record bass have come from such mini-bass factories. We're talking here about bass ranging in size from 9 to 13 pounds! So don't allow small waters to give the mistaken impression you're not playing with the big boys.

One study conducted by the author revealed that 80 percent of all state-record bass in the last 20 years have come from bodies of water less than 50 acres in size. This Ohio record largemouth of 13 pounds came from a small farmpond. A year later, it was surpassed by a 13 ¼-pound largemouth from a ten-acre stripmine pond.

Virtually the same story exists in most other states. Not long ago, for example, the editors of *Outdoor Life* magazine asked me to do an article titled "Forgotten Bass Waters." The gist of the piece had to do with the stampede of anglers nowadays to big reservoirs with their bassboats in tow, and the sometimes fantastic fishing action they were leaving behind. In researching the piece, I contacted every state fish and game department, requesting a rundown of previous state-record catches. I wasn't surprised to learn that in the case of largemouths, a whopping 80 percent of all state records in the last 20 years have come from bodies of water *less* than 50 acres in size.

Farmponds—Home for Big Bass

Farmponds provide excellent laboratories for learning and practicing the art of deep-water structure fishing, as well as refining numerous shallow-water techniques. Because such ponds are far smaller than lakes and reservoirs, there will not be so many productive structures, nor a profusion of cover. Consequently, bass will often be relatively easy to locate. Migration routes in particular will usually be compacted (not as long or complicated), allowing an angler to get a real feel for how bass live and move on structure. An angler can even play make-believe, envisioning the pond he is fishing as only a small segment of some larger lake or reservoir. A number of successful fish-locating-and-catching sessions under such conditions should make him more than able to venture upon expansive waters, isolate certain regions, and fish them effectively.

It may be difficult to obtain maps that accurately show the bottom contours of small manmade ponds. If maps are available, they will probably be topographic maps from the U.S. Geological Survey (addresses given in Chapter 4). But there's a great probability that bulldozers will have obliterated former land contours and in the process formed new structures during construction of such ponds, except perhaps in the case of the very largest ones.

One good source of information about the bottom contours of any pond is the landowner himself. With a pencil stub and small notebook tucked away in your fishing vest, you can ask questions and as you receive answers begin drawing a rough chart of the pond. Where is the deepest water in the pond? Is there a feeder stream channel or perhaps several of them running along the floor of the pond, or is the pond fed by springs or natural runoff surface water? Is the bottom of the pond muddy, sandy or hard-packed clay? When the pond was built, was cover such as stumps, boulders and tree crowns removed or left intact? Answers to these ques-

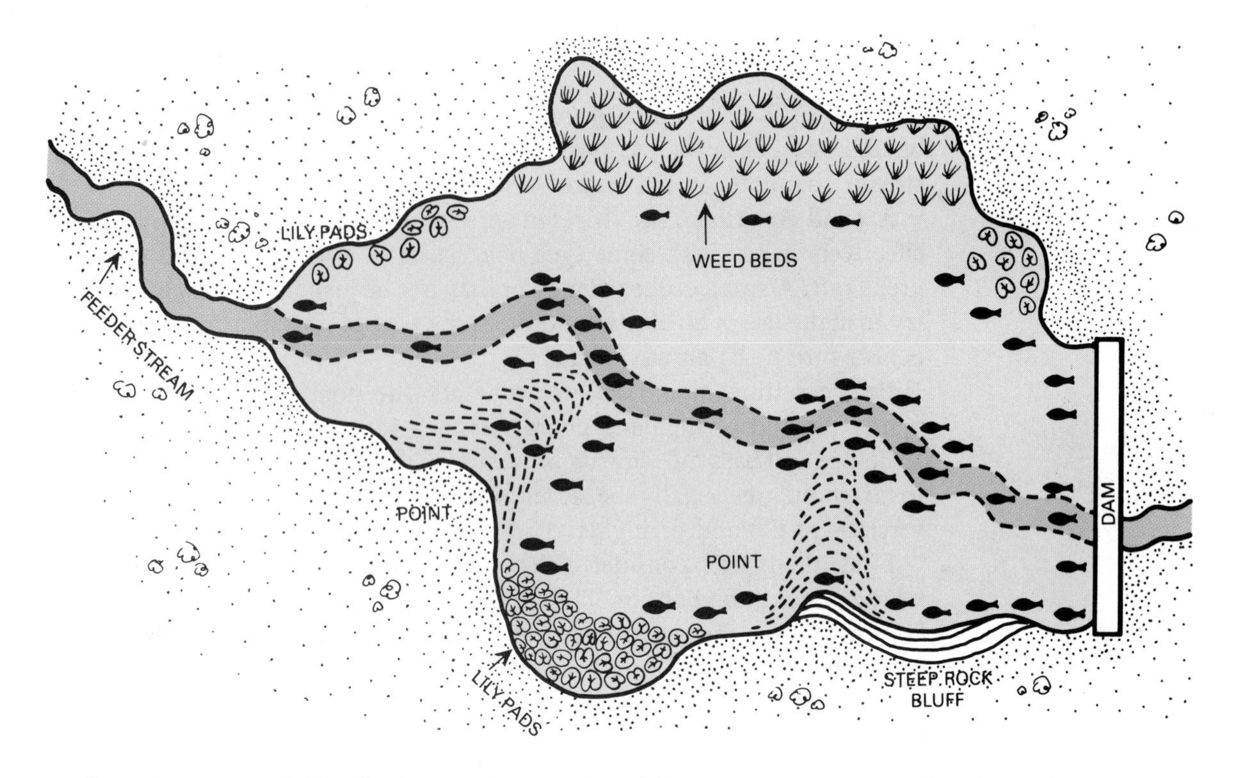

If a map is not available of a farmpond you wish to fish, you can construct one based on information gleaned from the landowner. Or, examine the surrounding landscape to get a good idea of what bottom contours may exist. If the pond was created by damming a small stream, the still-existing channel on the bottom will play a major role in bass location.

tions and others, along with the map you have been drawing all the while, will save plenty of hours of random exploration.

But if the landowner is not able to provide answers to the questions you ask (the pond may have already been there when he bought the property), you'll have to begin mapping and interpreting on your own. The first task should be a careful examination of the terrain surrounding the pond, because such land contours often hint what the bottom of the pond looks like. Is the surrounding terrain hilly, or is it flat? The answer to that question may influence whether the resident bass behave somewhat as they might in a highland reservoir or a flatland reservoir. Do you see any dominant land features such as high rock bluffs? What about the shallowest end of the pond? If a small creek is present, it's sure to continue winding along the bottom. If possible, climb a nearby hill to get a bird's-eye view of the pond and, if the water is relatively clear, you'll probably be able to spot certain bottom features, such as deep holes or winding stream channels, by the darker-colored shadows they cast.

A pond covering more than ten acres and 15 feet or more deep is most effectively fished with some type boat, such as a small johnboat or neoprene raft. A small outboard may or may not be justified, but by all means try to make use of an electric motor. Some type of portable depth sounder is also sure to be an advantage.

Before setting out, determine whether the pond possesses predominantly flatland or highland characteristics. Much of the information on structure and bass movements presented in Chapters 4 and 6 is applicable to farmponds, especially the larger ones which are really only scaled-down versions of flatland or highland reservoirs.

First, then, let's consider a flatland pond that has a stream channel winding along the bottom. This structure will be the home of the pond's largest bass for the greatest part of the year. During the spring, bass will sometimes travel the length of the channel upstream into the shallow headwater region, searching for spawning sites wherever there is suitable bottom composition. But the very largest fish seem to like to stay downstream, near the dam, leaving the stream channel wherever it loops in close to the shoreline or wherever there are signposts of some type to show them the way into nearby shallows. Then they'll select bedding sites at the bases of stumps and standing timber, and sometimes beneath overhanging bushes and willow tree branches. I think the reason the largest fish are reluctant to travel all the way upstream is that the headwater end of the pond is not only very shallow but usually very narrow as well. Add to this the fact that there is no deep water nearby and the big fish feel "boxed in." The spawning areas farther downstream, while seemingly identical with regards to bottom composition and other requisites, offer the advantage of nearby deep water if anything spooks the big fish.

During the postspawn period, the bass begin drifting back toward the stream channel, and through the warmest and brightest midsummer periods, and again during the winter, the fish will probably spend most of their time in or near the channel. Further, they will be where the channel is deepest, which is usually near the dam. As in typical flatland reservoirs, they can be counted upon to migrate from the channel toward the shallows several times a day (less often during the cold-water months). Now is when you should begin surveying the channel with your depth sounder, using marker buoys if necessary, to determine the locations (on-contact points) where the fish can be expected to leave the channel and the likely routes they will travel.

Since most farmponds have abundant weed growth during the spring, summer and fall, and since the weeds frequently extend all the way to the edge of the channel, the migration may consist of no more than the bass rising out of the channel to scatter along the edge of the weedline. This constitutes a very short migration with some location along the edge of the weedline serving as the contact point, breakline and scatterpoint all in one.

Keep in mind, however, we're talking here about large ponds of at least ten acres or more, in which the weedline may extend several hundred yards. This means you'll have to determine where, exactly, the fish will make contact with the shallows when they do migrate from the depths. Since the weedline/stream channel edge is the breakline, you'll have to look for a break on that breakline.

A break, as you will recall, is any noticeable change in the bottom contour or a place where some structural feature such as a stump interrupts the normal continuity of the breakline. If the break is rather large —say, a cluster of stumps over a five-square-yard area—I'd begin working the location by fan-casting crankbaits, beginning with shallow-running plugs and then switching to deep-divers to check areas closest to the stream channel. Remember, bass will nearly always be right on the bottom, except when the water is less than eight feet deep. If there are pockets back in the weeds at this location, you may want to check them with spinnerbaits or plastic worms for stragglers or the advance-fish of a small school already in migration.

If you fail to find fish along the edge cover (breakline), it could be that the fish have not migrated or that the water is simply too shallow for them to come all the way into the weeds during the bright, midday hours. The best bet, in this case, would be to locate deeper structures associated with the stream channel. Any sharp bends in the channel should probably be checked first. The bass could be in the outside bend where the water is deepest, or they could occasionally move to the inside bend where a slightly shallower shoal or bar has been created. You may also want to check the other side of the channel (the side opposite the weedbed). The other channel edge is still another breakline where there may be stumps, rocks, felled trees or deep weeds that may be holding straggler bass or a small school beginning to migrate toward the shallows.

When there are weedlines that run straightaway for rather long distances, and there are no features you can identify as possible breaks or contact points, try speed-trolling the entire weedline; or if the water is relatively cool, try backtrolling with live baits.

As in most lakes and reservoirs, water clarity has a crucial effect upon

When fishing a pond from the banks, wear light clothing and crouch low to avoid spooking fish that may be close to shoreline cover. Wading is often effective.

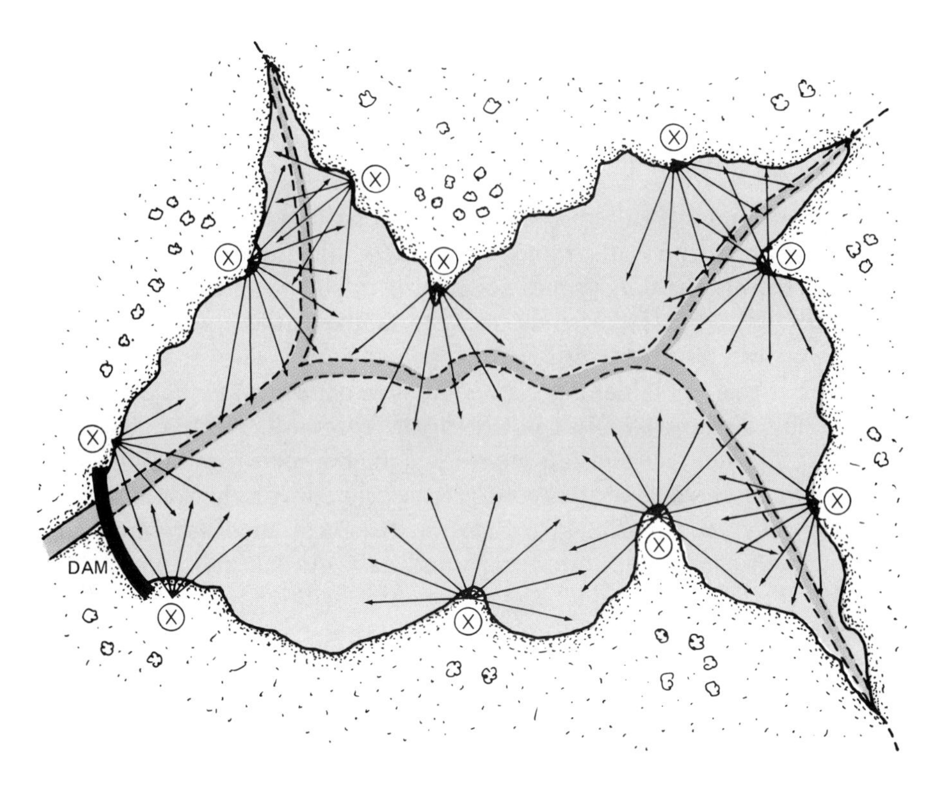

The most effective way to fish small ponds from the banks is by fan-casting your lures, then moving to a slightly different location and repeating the pattern.

sunlight penetration in ponds and consequently upon the migration behavior of bass. When they migrate in a very clear pond, you may not be able to catch them any shallower than 12 feet. But the fish in a nearby pond —almost identical in structural conformation but with cloudy or muddy water—may be randomly scattered along the banks in pockets in weeds and brush where the water is only two feet deep.

I should mention one final characteristic of flatland farmponds over ten acres in size. If there is good deep-water structure, shallow-water fishing is usually no good for anything but small fish. Large bass always prefer the depths to the shallows, even though there may be plenty of cover in the form of weeds, bushes or felled trees. But if the pond is dishpan-shaped, with little or no deep-water structure, the bass have no choice but to find hiding in and around the shallow cover.

Now let's shift our attention to highland ponds of more than ten acres. These are created just like highland reservoirs, with a dam placed between steep ridges and ravines, but seldom are they as deep. If there is a stream channel running along the floor of such a pond, it may very well be the home of the pond's largest bass. As in all highland waters, though, there are certain to be other fish-attracting structures, too, such as long steep points, bars, humps, drowned cover on the bottom, and steep wooded shorelines where the water rapidly plummets into the depths.

In the spring, highland-pond bass intent upon spawning may behave quite the same as bass in flatland ponds, but unlike flatland-pond bass they may also travel far upstream toward the headwaters. The reason for this difference is that in highland ponds, some type of deep-water escape route is invariably nearby, which is not often the case in flatland ponds.

During the summer and fall months, highland-pond bass may use the edges of weedlines and various contours associated with the stream channel. But they are also likely to use on-structures such as points and off-structures such as bottom humps and bars. As late fall approaches, look for the fish to move to deeper locations within the bowels of the stream channel and, periodically, to migrate almost vertically along steep bluffs and rocky shorelines. In all of these situations, I've found weighted plastic worms, jigs and jigging spoons to be top producers.

Small ponds (less than ten acres) are a slightly different matter and some of the gargantuan bass yanked out of these potholes are mind-boggling. These waters, in most cases, are extremely fertile, which is conducive to a very prolific food chain that allows bass to put on weight quickly. For the most part, they're also shunned by anglers.

I know of one such pond in Illinois, on the property of a rancher who raises chickens. This pond is so small that you can stand on one bank and pitch a long cast almost to the opposite side. For a number of years, however, not a single angler bothered with this piece of water, electing instead to fish its much larger 22-acre sister pond located several hundred yards away.

One morning my friend Bill Murphy decided to work the larger body of water, but upon arriving discovered two other anglers there ahead of him. Rather than intrude, he hiked to the small pond, more with the intention of passing time than anything else. Within 15 minutes he had strung a pair of seven-pounders! And since that memorable day, the pond has yielded an additional seven-pounder and half a dozen in the four- to five-pound class. As you might expect, the word has long since gotten out, and now anglers make a beeline for the tiny pond, almost forgetting about the other.

In a majority of cases, small ponds are best fished from the banks. Also in most cases, the small sizes of such ponds do not allow for much schooling activity on the part of the bass. Small pods of four or five fish may be encountered upon occasion, but most are loners associated with small swatches of cover here and there or structural deviations on the bottom. Since these bass hangouts are frequently found very close to the banks, an angler should make his approach in a very cautious, unobtrusive manner.

I wear light-colored clothing and often sneak to within several feet of the water's edge on my hands and knees, casting from behind bushes and tree trunks. An angler who boldly tramps right down to the water's edge will send sound vibrations into the water that are sure to alarm nearby fish. Furthermore, an angler who stands straight and tall with his silhouette looming against the skyline will send nearby bass into a frenzy, and in their attempt to escape from the area they may well spook still other fish farther down the shoreline.

Pulling on hip boots or chest waders and getting into the water is often a good bet in fishing small ponds. For one, the silhouette of a wading angler is much closer to the water, reducing the angle of refraction. Also, wading may help an angler to reach certain structures with his casts that might be out of range if he worked from the banks.

Small ponds commonly have stream channels running along their floors, but they are just as often dishpan-shaped and fed by surface runoff water. In such miniature habitats, the very slightest deviation in the bottom contour, for example, a one-foot drop-off, may be the best structure a pond has to offer and consequently have every large bass clinging to it. A single felled tree along the bank, in a pond which is otherwise cover-free, may be the home of the fish.

The most efficient technique for working small ponds is fan-casting. I cover various sectors of water in a clockwise direction, first casting along the shoreline edge to my left and then radiating each succeeding cast around the clock. I particularly like straight-shaft spinners on the waters because they can be used to check a wide variety of gradually increasing depths by simply counting the lure down before beginning the retrieve. After making one series of fan-casts, I then move down the shoreline a brief distance and repeat the procedure. If none of this pays off, I switch to weighted plastic worms, pitching them as far out as possible, to work the edges and other contours of the stream channel.

Both large and small farmponds have another advantage in addition to those already mentioned: Their resident bass become quite regimented in their feeding schedules. In some waters, the bass may be active mostly during the early morning hours; in others, at noon; and in others, during the early evening hours. The beauty of this, as far as the angler is concerned, is that you can test-fish any given pond for an hour or so, and if nothing's doing, you can pile everything in your car and quickly zip down the road to some other pond where the fish may be willing to chew the

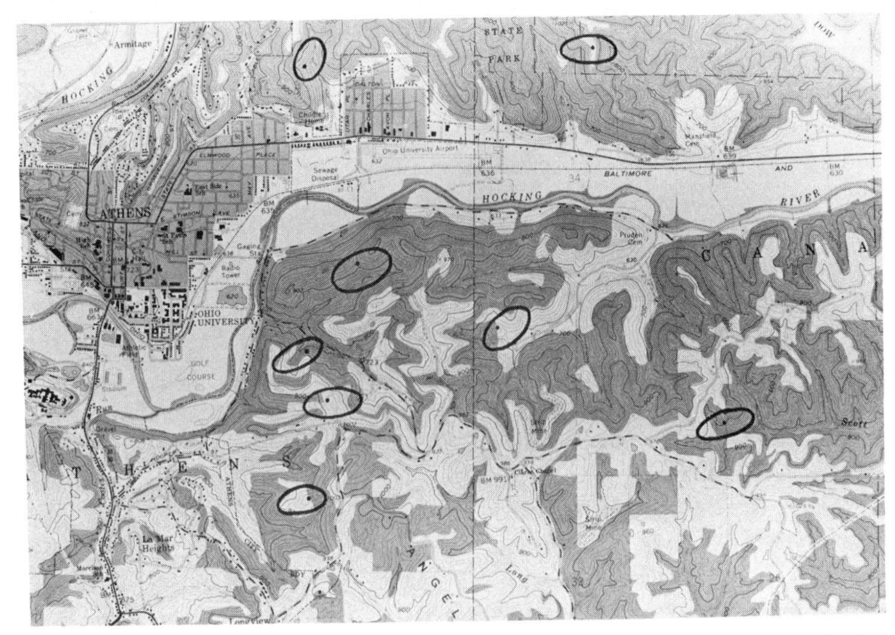

Bass living in various bodies of water often regiment themselves to certain feeding schedules. The beauty of working a farmpond circuit is that you can mark the locations of numerous ponds on a map and then begin making your rounds. If fish are not biting in one pond, you know it's only a short drive down the road to the next pond where the bass may be bent upon committing suicide!

paint off every plug in your tacklebox. And, of course, once you've deduced the dinner hour in a particular pond, you can schedule future outings to coincide.

Black Gold in Stripmine Pits

Every year increasing numbers of anglers are discovering black bass where previously there was only "black gold," the unanticipated result of state reclamation laws that obligate coal operators to restore the landscape after surface coal deposits have been removed. Reclamation involves grading the terrain with bulldozers, replacing layers of topsoil, grass seeding and some form of reforestation. It's all terribly expensive and labor-intensive, and that's why, in the mid-1950s, someone came up with an ingenious idea: Instead of grading and replanting all of the terrain, just let the gouged-out craters fill with water so lakes are created—thus cutting reclamation expenses substantially.

Nationwide, anglers have been benefitting ever since. In fact, across the

Midwest—stretching almost to the Continental Divide, east through the Alleghenies, and sporadically southward following the Appalachians, a sprawling area encompassing more than a dozen states—some of the largest bass logged each year have stripmine-pit water dripping from their gills.

To cash in on this action yourself, the first order of business is understanding how these ponds are created.

In most cases, but not always, strip mining is done in rugged, unglaciated country. Upheavals in the earth's crust bring already shallow coal seams even closer to the surface, where they are excavated by techniques that sometimes leave entire quarter-sections of mountains carved away as though some giant were merely slicing bread. The terrain, afterward, is typically a long, vaguely rectangular-shaped trench bordered on at least one side by a "high wall." There are exceptions, to be sure, with some excavation sites being teardrop-shaped, square or triangular, but the vast majority of stripmine ponds appear as long, narrow fingers encompassing less than ten acres.

When mining activities eventually are abandoned, the excavation sites slowly fill by means of natural rainwater runoff, although tiny trickle-streams, and sometimes springs, aid the effort.

Several things contribute to the very clear water typical of most stripmine ponds. First, these very small bodies of water are protected from strong winds by surrounding high walls and other steep terrain and are not fed by rushing feeder tributaries as in the case of lakes and reservoirs; thus, there is very little particulate matter in suspension to give the water color.

In addition, since the strata in which coal seams are found generally are infertile—consisting mainly of sand, shale, slate, marl or rock—stripmine ponds often are infertile, at least compared with manmade flatland reservoirs, created by inundating marshlands, river bottoms, bogs or swamps. This infertility, which often results in high levels of acidity, precludes much growth in the way of algae, plankton, phytoplankton, and other forms of zoological or vegetative life. Indeed, a high percentage of stripmine ponds are so acidic they are incapable of supporting any form of aquatic life.

I know one fisherman, a first-class dummy, who once spent day after day fishing a particular pond without even a nibble. The longer he fished without success the more exasperated he became, and that made him fish even longer and harder. Finally one morning, a game warden who stopped to check his license asked him why he was fishing in a pond where there were *no fish.* It was then, with sunken-jawed dismay, the angler learned he had wasted the last four days fishing a "hot" pond resulting from acid mine seepage.

After that disheartening experience, I now make a point of carefully checking before spending time fishing such ponds. Coal companies that have numerous ponds open to public fishing usually publish maps that indicate which waters have been found suitable for fish-stocking, as well as noting access roads and the like.

If such maps are not available, take a close look at the water itself. If it appears as though you could see a dime on the bottom, ten feet deep, and there is no sign of minnows or small bluegills around the shoreline, good advice is to try elsewhere. Look for waters that have at least a tinge of color to them. They'll still be quite clear but seem to have somewhat of a greenish, grayish, or ginger-colored tint to them, indicating decaying organic matter and, therefore, likely as not, sufficient fertility to support fish life. Also, as you hike a short distance along the bank, you should see occasional tiny panfish scurrying for cover. Another, more effective way to hedge your bet is to test the water with a pH meter, as described in Chapter 8, then concentrate your efforts in those ponds with a water pH of approximately 6.5 to 7.9.

Underwater fish-holding features in stripmine ponds are myriad, but there are some generalities and common structures found in many. The high wall bordering many, for example, is not unlike the sheer rocky bluffs, steep gravel slides, shale outcroppings and ledge-rock formations typical of highland and canyonland reservoirs. The opposite facing bank may consist of another high wall, but more commonly it will be a gradually tapering flat. Therefore, fish movements by the seasons are similar to those in other waters, with bass predominantly using the shallow, gradually sloping banks in spring and summer, then shifting to the steep banks during fall and winter.

Either end of a long, narrow stripmine pond is likely to be quite shallow, somewhat like the headwater region of a flatland reservoir but without feeder tributaries. Many ponds have a dam. In some instances, a dam is specifically created to impound the water, but more often, it is a rubble span connecting two adjacent areas of high ground and used originally as a haul road for coal trucks. Once mining activities have ceased and the gouged-out terrain allowed to fill with water, the riprap supporting the old haul road becomes transformed into fish-holding cover, the same as highway causeways spanning larger lakes and reservoirs. Spring is a prime time to find "bass on the rocks" in stripmine ponds, although these structures are worth checking virtually any time of year.

Another key bottom feature, which typically bisects the floor of a stripmine pond lengthwise, is an old *tote road.* During mining operations, such roads are used by gargantuan dump trucks to back down into the bowels of the excavation site to haul out loads of coal. Old tote roads therefore appear somewhat like long underwater ridges running the entire length of the pond bottom. Bass use these structures religiously, especially during the summer months or any other time bright sunlight or an absence of shoreline cover forces them into deeper water.

The remainder of the pond floor may consist of a wide assortment of potential fish-holding stations for small pods of fish or individual bass. Common examples include isolated large boulders, rubble piles, logs, even entire trees knocked down and pushed off to one side or the other by bulldozers. Standing timber is likely to be present as well—not only trees poking well above the surface but also those in very deep water (by peering into the depths you'll be able to see their crowns).

Along the shorelines, expect to find stumps, slab rock, sand bars, and drowned bushes and brush. When vegetation exists in stripmine ponds, it's invariably a type that favors acidic water, such as large floating masses of moss. Often, these mossbeds ring the shorelines. But even more frequently, they appear as large hovering blankets over deep midlake areas, ever shifting in both their dimensions and locations as the wind direction changes.

Bass love to suspend at arbitrary mid-depths beneath these mossbeds because baitfish and panfish are attracted to the scuds, freshwater shrimp and insects inhabiting such weeds. The trick is fishing the side of the mossbed opposite the slanting angle of the sun, which offers the greatest shade.

In most cases, a 12-foot johnboat outfitted with an electric motor for both propulsion and maneuverability around cover is an ideal choice. But in many cases, smaller strip ponds can be fished from the banks. Since there may be hidden holes, drop-offs or deep water close to shorelines, I don't recommend wade-fishing.

Since the water in strip ponds is nearly transparent, keep in mind bass tactics you'd use on any exceptionally clear lake. In a nutshell, this means concentrating your efforts during the hours of dawn and dusk when light levels are low, or even investing fishing time after full dark. Overcast skies and rainy weather are also more likely to result in nice catches, compared to bright, bluebird weather. Use smaller lures than usual, and make long casts, and when fishing from the banks keep a low silhouette.

Aside from these common, clear-water strategies, some others also fare well in stripmine ponds. When bass are using the high walls they may suspend at almost any depth and it's necessary to "stack" your lures to strain the water and determine at what level they're holding on any particular day. To do this, cast parallel to the high wall, beginning with

The high wall almost always bordering one side of a stripmine pond can be a magnet for bass during the summer. Also, determine if there is an old tote road along the bottom, as bass will use it religiously anytime conditions force them into deeper water.

a shallow-running plug, then switching to a medium-depth runner, then finally a deep-diver. The very same approach can also be used when fishing the steep rubble dam.

When working the deep, submerged tote roads that run lengthwise through strip ponds, I like to position my boat perpendicular to the structure and fish it with plastic worms. Depending upon the degree of sunlight intensity and prevailing weather conditions, bass using the drowned road may be on top of it, close to the edge or deep on the sides of the underwater ridge. With weighted worms, you can check all three locations by casting entirely across the road, bringing the fake wiggler up one side, across the top, then down the other.

Anytime you encounter shallow shoreline cover such as stumps, brush or boulders, slim-minnow plugs and tiny spinnerbaits seem to be the best bets. Around floating mossbeds, however, buzz-baits are far and away the best. Cast around the shaded edges, then skitter the bait right across the top, trying to maneuver the offering through any potholes. The surface-churning effect of a buzz-bait's prop will sometimes "call" bass up that are suspended quite deep beneath the matted vegetation, but if not, do not hesitate to switch to a deep-diving crankbait or perhaps even a jigging spoon.

Drowned treetops are another place bass like to suspend at various depths. The most effective way to fish them is with jigs or jigging spoons, as described in Chapter 14.

CHAPTER

18

Strategy For Smallmouths

Powerful runs, consecutive leaps clear of the water, head-shaking, gill-rattling, tail-walking—they're all part of the game when an angler does battle with smallmouths.

But while the smallmouth, of all the bass species, is without question a most worthy gladiator on hook and line, its physiological shortcomings make it a weakling in many other respects. Because of this, fishery biologists have had difficulty extending the natural range of smallmouths, as they have admirably accomplished with largemouths.

One trait of smallmouths in their favor is their ability to survive in water having low oxygen-saturation levels. Largemouths and spotted bass require at least 5 parts per million of dissolved oxygen, but prefer 9 to 12 ppm, whereas smallmouths can make do with only 3 ppm.

But the smallmouth is not nearly as tolerant as the other species to excessive water turbidity or to variations in water temperature. Any minor degradation of smallmouth habitat, such as an insignificant rise in pollutant levels or acid rain contamination, which the other bass species may be able to tolerate, usually leads to drastic reductions of smallmouth populations.

Smallmouths are very selective in their dining habits, too, at least when compared with their cousins who display "eat anything that moves" habits. Studies conducted on both northern and southern lakes and rivers have shown that crayfish account for close to 60 percent of a smallmouth's diet. In southern bodies of water, the remaining 40 percent of the fish's diet generally consists of various species of open-water baitfish such as threadfin or gizzard shad. In northern bodies of water, however, the presence of northern pike, walleyes and to some extent muskies, prevents smallmouths from patrolling midlake regions, forcing them to remain in relatively shallow water where any slack in their crayfish foraging is taken up by dining upon small perch, leeches, rainbow shiners, emerald shiners and other incidental minnow species they may chance upon.

Finally, a good majority of soft bottom conditions, which may be tolerated by other bass species from time to time, just won't do in the case of smallmouths. The "brownies" are usually quite averse, for example, to mud, muck, mire, loose soil, silt and abundant vegetation, such as heavily matted weeds and lily pads.

So the common angler-held belief that the smallmouth is a hardy and

The smallmouth's reputation as a hardy, tenacious species is quite misleading. It's a pugnacious, worthy gladiator on hook and line, to be sure, but its specific habitat requirements are very narrow and well defined.

tenacious species is really very far from the truth, at least if we use the largemouth's ready adaptability to myriad habitat conditions as a benchmark.

Originally, the species was confined to the Great Lakes, the St. Lawrence, the upper Mississippi, and the river systems of the Ohio and Tennessee. But in recent decades its range has been expanded considerably, though many attempts at this have failed. Smallmouth populations run especially high in natural lakes throughout New England, the southern regions of certain Canadian provinces (notably Quebec, Ontario and Manitoba), and most of the northern border states east of the Rocky Mountains. Yet the very largest fish brought to net each year come from none of these waters but rather from the large highland reservoirs and associated rivers of the east-central states, as far south as northern Alabama.

An ideal smallmouth lake or reservoir, no matter where it is located, is usually rather expansive, possessing depths of at least 25 feet and preferably more. Moreover, such waters possess only modest fertility levels (i.e., the bottom composition is low in nitrogen compounds and other nutrients), causing plant life and other vegetation to be relatively sparse. The floor of the body of water and its many associated structures generally is composed of sand, gravel, fractured sedimentary rock, hard-packed clay, marl (a mixture of clay and limestone), shale, or any combination of these materials. The water temperature must reach a minimum of 60° during the spring months for spawning to occur, and preferably should not exceed 72° at any other time during the year (though smallmouths are active and can be caught in water ranging from 48° to about 78°). If there is a bit of current, in the form of either feeder tributaries or *density flows* (a result of particularly active springs, or wind and wave action), all the better.

Since the most productive smallmouth lakes and reservoirs are those with low fertility, the water tends to be exceptionally clear. Of course, exceptions to the rule occur—often during temporary upsets in weather conditions—but the water usually ranges from crystal clear to only very slightly green, blue or brown.

Overall, the spawning behavior of smallmouths is about the same as that of largemouths, but there are several differences. First, smallmouths move onto their beds slightly earlier, usually when the water temperature is 58° to 63°, whereas the most purposeful largemouth spawning takes place when the temperature is 65° to 70°.

Secondly, largemouths typically fan out their nests in water averaging from two to six feet deep in protected backwater areas, but smallmouths often bed considerably deeper. Their nests, while frequently in water ranging from four to eight feet deep, may be as deep as 15 feet or more.

Milton Trautman, a highly respected fish scientist, has found smallmouth eggs hatching 22 feet deep in Lake Whitmore, Michigan. Furthermore, smallmouths seem to like to drop their eggs in rather exposed regions where mild current or wind and wave action can keep the water aerated. Thus, it's quite difficult to spot smallmouth beds: Not only are they often too deep to see, but the constantly moving water prevents them from assuming a nice symmetrical appearance as in the case of largemouths. Sometimes, in fact, smallmouths seem almost nonchalant about nest building and maintenance, merely dropping their eggs in some handy depression surrounded by shards of rock.

A third difference in the spawning behavior of the two species is that male smallmouths usually abandon the nests immediately after they have fertilized the eggs. Unlike largemouths, which are very protective of their eggs and newly hatched fry, male smallmouths leave the nests to whatever destruction may be wrought by the elements, panfish, crayfish, salamanders or turtles. As a result, smallmouth mortality rates in the egg and fry states are always exceedingly high.

Smallmouth Strategy

Catching bedding smallmouths is in many ways similar to catching spring largemouths, but in other ways vastly different. Generally, smallmouths are not nearly as vulnerable to plastic-worm offerings as largemouths, distinctly preferring instead some type of "hardware." Additionally, top-water lures, such as spinnerbaits and buzz-baits, and many types of shallow-running crankbaits, which largemouths clobber with abandon, are seldom effective for spring smallmouths. Although an angler may well be able to vary the speed of these lures, to determine which is best for any given day, he is restricted in his ability to probe deeper waters. And smallmouths that are bedding in water much deeper than five or six feet, simply will not come up to take a look at some offering presented high over their heads. Remember, spawning bass do not actively feed and therefore must be provoked into striking, which can only be accomplished by presenting lures right in front of their noses. The best approach, then, when smallmouths are bedding quite deep, is to use deep-diving crankbaits.

Throughout the remainder of the year, when both feeding and strike responses can be elicited, smallmouths seem to be much more spooky than largemouths; perhaps the predominantly clear water they inhabit is partly responsible for this. But whatever the reason for their habitual shyness, anglers should approach them cautiously, keeping a low profile and making long casts.

Very light tackle can and should be used, even when there is some brush, jagged rock formations or sparse weed growth present. In contrast to largemouths, which characteristically make a beeline for cover when hooked, smallmouths nearly always make a frantic rush *away* from the shallow shoreline cover and into the depths. Many times at Dale Hollow Reservoir in Tennessee, I've found smallmouths, particularly when they are in prespawn and postspawn modes, in the vicinity of brush and moss, and have had no trouble using lines as light as six- and even four-pound test. Nine out of ten fish hooked in the tangles charted nonstop courses away from the cover and into the depths of nearby creek channels, allowing me to slug it out with them in open water with little fear of losing the fish to cover.

Like largemouths, smallmouths begin drifting into deeper water to resume schooling when spawning is ended. How deep they will go is nearly always determined by the extent of light penetration, but also, in the case of northern lakes, by what larger predators, if any, may be using open-water structures. In the absence of predators, however, and all other things being equal, in those lakes containing both largemouths and smallmouths, such as Dale Hollow, smallmouths are much more depth-oriented than their bigmouth cousins. Not only will they seek sanctuary deeper, but during the course of their periodic migrations they will seldom travel as shallow.

In clear-water lakes in particular, smallmouths over three pounds may seldom venture shallower than 12 feet deep. And I know many anglers who have taken them as deep as 45 feet. Only after dark, during the winter months when the water takes on a slate-gray color, or during stormy or overcast conditions do smallmouths sometimes move in very close to the banks.

Movements of smallmouths on structure are very similar to those of largemouths described in Chapters 3 and 4. Smallmouths will make contact with the shallows at some break on a breakline and they will follow other breaks or signposts to a scatterpoint, just as largemouths do. They will also typically use on-structures during the earlier part of the year, gradually shifting to deeper off-structures as the sun shifts higher in the sky. Later in the year, during the fall and winter months, they may continue to use off-structures or they may move back to favorite on-structures. Much of the very finest smallmouth angling south of the Mason–Dixon line is during the dead of winter, when the fish move onto steep gravel points and shale slides. This probably is true because, across the smallmouth's more southerly range, water temperatures are moderate enough during the winter that bass continue to engage in regular migrations.

From about July through the remaining months of the year—in fact, until the following spring spawning season—various types of jigs undeniably account for most smallmouth action. The primary reason has to do with their versatility. They can be worked fast or slow, or any speed in between, and at virtually any depth. Add to these capabilities the infinite colors, sizes and designs in which jigs are available, plus the multitude of dressings that can be used to adorn their hooks, and they warrant a deserved place in any smallmouth angler's tacklebox. Some smallmouth experts I've fished with, in fact, use nothing but jigs.

When fishing on-structures such as steep gravel points, or ledge rocks that stair-step their way into the depths, I like to cast as close to the shoreline as possible and "walk" the jig slowly down the structure. This is accomplished by slowly raising the rod tip, lowering it quickly while reeling in the slack, and allowing the jig to "fall" on a tight line to the next depth level. The jig can be worked down to depths of 50 feet if need be. Speed control is facilitated by using jigs of different sizes and designs, and even by altering the jig head itself.

Large jigs sink faster than small jigs; likewise, roundhead jigs fall faster than flathead jigs such as Charlie Brewer's Slider or Tony Portincaso's Powwr-head. The speed with which a jig sinks can also be varied by trimming the soft leaden jig head with a penknife. To make a jig sink faster, trim the sides of the lure, so there will be less water resistance against the jig; to make it sink more slowly, trim the bottom round to flat to increase water resistance.

The type of dressing attached to a jig, and the way it's attached, can influence lure speed. I prefer marabou feathers over bucktail, as the marabou pulsates in the water like a breathing creature. Yet jigs with marabou sink faster than those with bucktail, because the deer hair is hollow, which has a buoyant effect. Other popular dressings that may be used alone or in conjunction with marabou or bucktail include plastic grubs and pork rind. When a grub is impaled on a jig's hook with the thin tail riding in a vertical position, the lure sinks fast; with the tail in a horizontal position, however, there is more water resistance and the jig falls more slowly. I'm referring here to conventional, straight-tail grubs, but I also like twister-tail and curly-tail grubs because, instead of merely sinking, they give the appearance of a small creature swimming down into the depths. Jig 'n pig combinations are sometimes positively lethal, but other anglers prefer pork rind eels (either the straight or split-tail variety). In any of these cases, an important thing to keep in mind is that smallmouths consistently seem to prefer lures that are smaller than those typically used for largemouths.

Smallmouths in Flowing Waters

Both North and South, smallmouths residing in rivers and streams also afford anglers with fast action. For any flowing waterway to sustain a healthy smallmouth population, it must have a gradient of no less than 4 feet per mile and no more than 20 feet per mile. Intermittent, shallow riffles with bottoms composed of sand, gravel and small rocks should separate long glides containing occasional deep pools. The bass will use the quiet eddy waters adjacent to the riffles for spawning during the spring if there are no nearby feeder tributaries for upstream migrations. And when the spawn is completed, the fish will move back to their holding stations in gently moving waters adjacent to the flow of more turbulent currents.

When fishing rivers such as the Tennessee, which can be wide and quite fast in places, the most effective strategy is *slipping,* pioneered by Dan Gapen and Al and Ron Lindner. As you'll recall from Chapter 16, this technique is used to hold a boat nearly stationary in fast water, without anchoring, but allows precise maneuverability whenever conditions call for it.

Say, for example, you've found a place in midriver where the water is ten feet deep and the mostly sandy bottom is scattered with boulders you believe may hold smallmouths. The current is swift enough that if you tried to drift and simultaneously cast, your boat would quickly be swept past the structure before you even completed the first retrieve. Instead, swing your boat around so the bow faces upstream into the current and keep the outboard in forward gear. Now, adjust the throttle so the boat drifts downstream but at a much slower speed than the current. You should now be able to fish the entire structure by casting upstream and allowing your lure to come back with the current, in the direction the fish expect to see food traveling. When you begin making contact with fish, you can increase the throttle speed just a tad to prevent any further slipping and hold the boat in position.

As an overview, keep these things in mind. Smallmouths live and move in very much the same way as largemouths. Therefore, much of your knowledge about fishing for largemouths in lakes, reservoirs, rivers and streams can be applied to smallmouth fishing. The major variations to remember are that smallmouth waters are usually infertile and consequently very clear, necessitating the use of light tackle. Smallmouths nearly always utilize deeper levels than largemouths. Smaller lures are usually more effective than larger ones, with jigs given top priority. And, the fish will be considerably more active than largemouths when the water is cool.

CHAPTER

19

Spotted Bass — Double Challenge

There is no question, in my friend Bill Henderson's mind, that the spotted bass is a challenging adversary, for it combines the power of the largemouth with the fighting stamina of the smallmouth. Although most anglers don't stand much chance of breaking the spotted bass world record, which Bill once did indeed accomplish, it is possible to stack the odds in your favor by learning about some of the species' unique behavioral traits.

The spotted bass, *Micropterus punctulatus,* exhibits some traits characteristic of both largemouths and smallmouths, plus some which neither are known for. Variously known as the spot, spotted bass, Kentucky or Kentucky spotted bass, the species was first identified in Kentucky in 1927. For many years, it was believed that the bass was native only to Kentucky, but it's now known that the species lives in a number of other states as well. Ichthyologists of the American Fisheries Society refer to the species as spotted bass, in accordance with its Latin name.

Unlike its largemouth and smallmouth cousins, the spotted bass is not widely distributed. As a general rule, the farther south ones goes the more plentiful the species. Although spotted bass are quite active in cold water, they do not like lakes or reservoirs or rivers that freeze over for prolonged periods during the winter. Draw a line from the southwest corner of Pennsylvania to central Kansas, then vertically drop each end of the line directly south to the Gulf of Mexico, and you'll outline the spotted bass's range.

Alabama leads all other states in the number of large spotted bass taken each year, and there the species is found in virtually every major river, stream or large impoundment. Although bodies of water that contain spotted bass very commonly also contain largemouths and smallmouths, one notable exception to the rule is Allatoona Lake in northwestern Georgia, where over 90 percent of all bass caught are spots.

Bill Henderson, showing his former world-record spotted bass, weighing a bit more than eight pounds. Although the species is known by some as Kentucky bass, Alabama leads all other states in the number of big spotted bass taken each year.

Fishery biologists have made numerous attempts to transplant spotted bass beyond the species' native range, and most such experiments have failed. However, in 1974, spotted bass from Alabama's Lewis–Smith Reservoir were stocked in California's Lake Perris; since then the species' adaptation and growth rates have been nothing short of phenomenal. At the present time, numerous seven-pound-plus fish are taken every year from Lake Perris—a fantastic record when one considers that the world trophy is only 8 pounds, 15 ounces.

Within its native range, the largest spotted bass consistently come from highland reservoirs. They seldom grow to appreciable size in flatland bodies of water, and almost never exceed two pounds in the flowing waters of rivers and streams.

Although spotted bass favor highland reservoirs, in general, an ideal body of water for this species can be described quite specifically. It is a rather expansive highland reservoir, south of the Tennessee Valley, that is at least 25 feet deep. Further, the shoreline includes high rock bluffs, ledges, shale slides and outcroppings, which frequently drop off very steeply at the water's edge. The bottom is rather hard and consists of rocks, gravel, sand, clay, crumbled shale, hard-packed soil, or any combination of these materials. In a great majority of cases, there also is standing or felled timber and brush on the bottom, with underwater structure consisting of points, bars, ridges, humps, winding riverbeds and stream channels, and similar conformations characteristic of all highland reservoirs. In addition, there are sure to be feeder tributaries gushing into the reservoir at numerous locations. Sometimes these may be only short, narrow and rather steep cuts along the shoreline, but more often they are in the form of rather long creek arms.

In such bodies of water, spotted bass are tied very closely to crayfish when they are using bank features in less than 40 feet of water. When they pack up in schools to roam midlake areas at suspended levels, small gizzard or threadfin shad are their mainstay.

Spring spawning habits of the fish are similar to those of smallmouths in that spotted bass seldom move into protected coves and embayments like largemouths. Instead, they tend to move into feeder tributaries, or remain right on the weather-exposed banks of midlake regions, wherever the bottom is gravely, sandy or scattered with rocks. If there are stick-ups

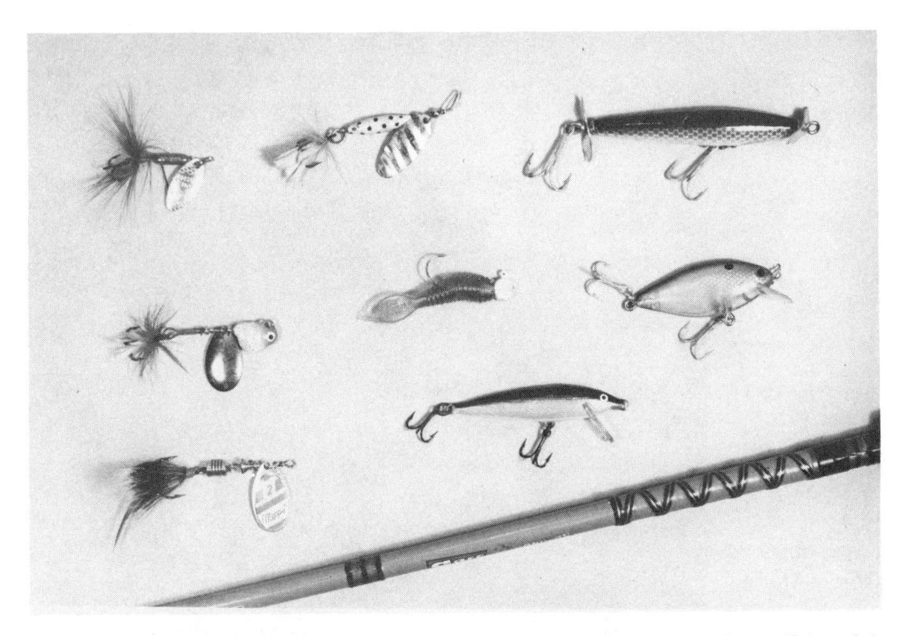

Ninety-five percent of a spotted bass's diet consists of crayfish and small baitfish such as minnows and shad. Spinners, jigs and slim-minnow lures therefore account for most of the fish taken by spotted bass anglers.

or light brush present, all the better. Also similar to smallmouths, spotted bass are not meticulous in their nest-building and maintenance activities, and their beds are therefore quite difficult to see.

The spawning instincts of spotted bass are triggered when the water temperature reaches 62° to 65°. In impoundments containing all three species of bass, then, the spotted bass begin moving onto their beds just after the smallmouths and just before the largemouths. There have been exceptions, but most of the spotted bass spawning activities I've observed have been in water averaging six to 12 feet deep; in other words, they tend to family matters slightly deeper, on the average, than largemouths but often shallower than smallmouths.

After the spring spawn, spotted bass gather in large schools during the

Unlike largemouths and smallmouths, spotted bass sometimes go as deep as 100 feet. Johnny Morris, owner of Bass Pro Shops, caught this dandy five-pounder while fishing with the author on Missouri's Table Rock Lake.

rest of the year. But their behavior varies in some respects from the schooling tendencies of largemouths and smallmouths. First, they often go to extreme depths—sometimes to 100 feet or more. Also, when clinging to structures such as deep-water rock ledges or shelves, they frequently suspend off the edge of the structure in open water, instead of staying right on the bottom. Schooling spotted bass also seem to exhibit more nomadic behavior than the other basses; they often can be found methodically working back and forth along long stretches of steep shoreline. I therefore recommend that after the spring spawn is ended, anglers concentrate the bulk of their efforts in the downstream regions of highland reservoirs, from about the midway point to the dam. Since this region offers the deepest water and the steepest rocky shorelines, it's where you can expect to encounter the largest schools of spotted bass.

Another oddity of the species is that midday produces much better catches than found with the other basses. Like largemouths and smallmouths, however, the spotted bass also is very active after full dark.

With regards to the average depths at which spotted bass are commonly found through the various seasons of the year, absolutely nothing is certain. But if pinned down, my general guidelines would be as follows: Before and after the spring spawn, look for the fish to be associated with on-structures from six to 20 feet deep; through the summer months look for them to be associated with either on- or off-structures from ten to 40 feet deep; and during the fall and winter, look for them to be associated with either on- or off-structures, again at six- to 20-foot levels. As already noted, during any time of year spotted bass periodically may descend much, much deeper than this. But that is really of little concern because the prospecting spotted bass angler will have great difficulty working deeper than 45 or 50 feet anyway, and therefore probably shouldn't even try.

Tackle and Tactics

Since spotted bass often head for quite deep water, topwater lures such as buzz-baits, and shallow-runners such as spinnerbaits and some crankbaits, are only rarely effective in attracting them. About the only time these lures might warrant consideration is when an angler finds the fish spawning in the shallower regions of creek arms.

During the late spring, throughout the summer, and into the fall months, when the fish are suspected to be at depths ranging from six to 20 feet, speed-trolling is one of the two tactics veteran spotted bass anglers rely upon most. I described this method in Chapter 15, but there are a few variations to consider when speed-trolling for spotted bass.

To begin with, even though many top-notch spotted bass reservoirs possess plenty of bottom cover or woody cover, the water often is very clear. Clear water screams for light tackle and light lines, but heavy cover demands stout tackle if the angler has any hopes of boating large fish. The only thing to do is take the middle ground, and that will probably mean a trolling rod with a level-wind reel filled to capacity with line testing from 10 to 14 pounds.

In speed-trolling for largemouths or smallmouths, which nearly always are on or near the bottom, lures must continually be kept in proper position on structure; that is, they should not be permitted to leave the structure and swim free but should continually bump or tick the bottom. Much of the time the same holds true in speed-trolling for spotted bass, particularly along a point, bar or submerged island. But keep in mind that spotted bass reservoirs often have sheer rock bluffs and steep walls adjacent to the shoreline. At Lewis–Smith Reservoir, for example, which is typical of ideal spotted bass lakes, the depth may drop from five feet to 300 feet within only scant yards of the shoreline. And as already mentioned, spotted bass often like to suspend at some arbitrary depth along these sheer walls. In this situation, then, speed-trolled lures should *not* bump along the bottom, because the fish aren't there. The fish are still adhering to structure, of course, but the structure (the steep wall) is now on a *vertical* rather than a horizontal plane, and the particular breaks the fish will be clinging to may be in the form of knobs, protrusions, indentations, outcroppings and the like. In other words, envision a bottom contour or structure that smallmouths or largemouths might favor, and tilt that structure up on its edge, and you'll have a good idea as to what spotted bass like.

In order to speed-troll such vertical structures effectively, an angler must keep his boat as close to the wall as possible without banging into it (and creating noise) and he must *stack* his lures. This means that he will make one pass down the lengthy shoreline with a lure that runs at a depth of, say, 10 feet. Then he makes a second pass, with another lure that runs at 15 feet deep, then still another at perhaps 20 feet, and so on until he has determined the depth the fish are holding at. A variety of lure speeds should also be used with each successive trolling pass.

The second strategy most often relied upon by expert spotted bass anglers is jigging. And the place it pays off handsomely is again a steep wall or bluff, but in this case where the underwater structure does not plummet straight into the depths but stair-steps its way with intermittent ledges and shelves.

For this kind of work I recommend a medium-light action spinning rod, open-face reel, six-pound test monofilament, and the same types of tiny ($1/16$- and $1/8$-ounce) jigs you might select for crappie fishing. I particularly like my jigs to have marabou feathers, with the added embellishment of a small twister-tail or curly-tail dressing. Make sure this plastic grub with its swimming tail does not exceed two inches in length; otherwise, the color of the tail or the jig itself is not overly important (I like all-white when attempting to simulate baitfish, or a combination of brown and orange when I want a representative crayfish offering).

Fishing these jigs along steep bluffs and walls can be an absolutely dynamite strategy that's been known to produce upwards of 40 spotted bass per day. It can also be a futile endeavor in which anglers go for hours without a nibble. The difference between success or defeat can in most cases be reduced to a single sentence: *The jig must remain in close contact with the vertical structure at all times.*

To accomplish this, and successfully work depths down to 40 feet or so, position your boat within relatively close casting distance (no more than 30 feet away) of the steep shoreline. Cast your jig to within a foot of the bank, but do not turn the spinning reel's handle to engage the bail. As soon as the lure hits the water, catch the line with your index finger and lower the rod tip. This allows the jig to fall downward on a tight line, which is critical because spotted bass generally take the jig on the fall and each strike is likely to be no more than a bare tick.

When the line goes slack, indicating that the jig is on the bottom (actually, on one of the stair-step ledges), release your finger holding the line and raise the rod tip, which will pull about six more feet of line off the reel's spool. Then, still again, pick up the line with your finger, raise the rod tip just a bit higher to pull the jig off the ledge, then slowly lower the rod tip so the jig begins sinking to the next lower level. Continue doing this until you've fished about 40 to 45 feet deep. If you don't make contact with fish at any level, cast eight or ten feet to the right (or left, depending upon the direction you're working) and continue slowly working your way down the shoreline. There's not much need to fish every bit of water. You can space your casts somewhat apart because fish adhering to these structures are not likely to be stragglers; they'll be in sometimes huge schools.

As mentioned earlier, spotted bass are at times quite nomadic. But at the other extreme, there are certain locations in most spotted bass reservoirs that are likely to hold good numbers of fish on almost a year-round basis. One is a shoreline bar or point that enters the water and continues on for some distance before dropping off steeply at its tip end. If the bar or point is saturated with standing timber or brush, if its tip end lies in at least 15 feet of water, and if it drops off into at least 50 feet of water, you should be able to catch spotted bass there any month of the year. The fish may be schooling by size in this situation, but the sizes of individuals may differ depending upon the depth. What I mean is, somewhat shallower on the point you'll run into a school of smaller fish, and deeper on the point a school of much larger bass. If the timber does not allow for speed-trolling, use the same types of jigs described earlier, or even jigging spoons, fishing them vertically right beneath your boat.

Another year-round holding station that seems always to contain at least a few spotted bass is a *hogback* or underwater ridge connecting two midlake structures such as islands, saddles between stream channels where they loop and wind upon themselves, or the humps created where stream channels converge or join the main riverbed. In these cases, in addition to catching spotted bass on or near the bottom, there's a bonus opportunity of frequently finding the fish slashing into baitfish on the surface. Here you can try jump-fishing, which is described in Chapter 15.

Finally, in highland reservoirs, one of the most lethal strategies an angler can consider is live bait. And *the* premier live bait spotted bass dote upon is soft-shell crayfish. Fish the baits in any of the locations discussed previously, using open-face spinning tackle. Hook the baits once through the tail and add a split-shot to the line for weight.

River and Stream Spotteds

In rivers and streams, spotted bass can tolerate cooler and swifter water than largemouths, but they do not usually prefer the low water temperatures and current favored by smallmouths. So if you chance upon a location that doesn't seem just right for either largemouths or smallmouths, it may be perfect for spots.

Although spotted bass differ in these preferences from largemouths and smallmouths, they like the structure and bottom composition sought out by both their cousins. Look for them over clean, hard bottom materials wherever there is brush, logs, or sweepers. They are not often caught in weeds, unless other, preferred types of cover are not available.

Spotted bass in the larger rivers, curiously, do not grow to much beyond two pounds. In smaller rivers and streams, even under ideal circumstances, they are certain to be smaller still, sometimes averaging only ½ pound in weight. All bass in these types of waters are products of their spartan habitat, feeding almost continually in order to replenish lost body energy, yet never getting quite enough to eat.

Light spinning tackle is the best bet for spotted bass in rivers and streams, however large or small those waterways may be. And the artificial lures or live baits that customarily are effective for either largemouths or smallmouths will do nicely as far as spots are concerned. If you want to try exclusively for the water's largest spotted bass (you'll probably never get one more than 15 inches in length, and it should be considered a well-earned trophy), ply your efforts in the scattered deep pools.

CHAPTER

20

The Amazing Florida Bass

The Florida bass is a recognized subspecies of the largemouth. Physiologically, Florida bass differ from their bigmouth relatives only in scale count and a genetic predisposition toward attaining larger proportions, though in many instances they also take on a darker color due to the nature of their abundantly fertile habitat.

The thing that makes Florida bass so exciting to anglers is their impressive size. While a nine-pound largemouth caught in a northern reservoir might well stand as a new state record to be envied by all, a nine-pound Florida bass yanked from a bed of hyacinth weeds is seldom likely to raise eyebrows among locals. There, you'll have to bring in a lunker that pulls the scales down to the 12- or 13-pound mark in order to find yourself the proud recipient of accolades and admiration. And if you're strictly a trophy hunter bent on establishing a new Florida state record, don't even begin to get your hopes up until you've landed something close to 20 pounds.

Bass attain such large sizes in Flroida (and in other places containing the Florida subspecies) not only because of their unique genetic potential for oversize growth, but also because they live in a year-round climate that allows them to realize that potential. To understand this better, let's briefly examine the growth characteristics of both the largemouth and its Florida subspecies.

In Ohio, in which largemouths exhibit typical northern growth patterns, bass enjoy a growing season of only about seven months each year. Body length steadily increases to a point, and at a rate, that is slightly less than that of Florida bass, but increases in real body weight occur very slowly. This is because a large percentage of the fat stores accumulated during the warm-water months are slowly consumed during the cold-water months of winter, when the fish fall into a type of semidormancy. The very low water temperatures severely retard body metabolism, and feeding or other activity almost ceases. But any living organism, however inactive, must maintain some minimal metabolism to stay alive. During the cold winter months, bass derive the energy to power their internal systems from the assimilation of fat stores rather than from the intake of large quantities of food as during the warm-water months.

It is true that female spring bass in Ohio and other northern states *appear* to be the largest (heaviest) of the season. But this is deceptive and constitutes only "false weight" in the form of roe sacks, which give females a pot-bellied look. After a female has dropped the majority of her eggs, one could not find a more haggard, shallow-looking fish specimen. Regular feeding activities occur during the coming summer and fall, with enormous quantities of food being consumed. But most of the weight accumulated during this growth period is stored in still more fat layers to see the fish through still another upcoming period of semidormancy. The entire affair might be likened to a person who gorges himself at every meal four days a week and then fasts the remaining three days. He will probably gain weight, but it will be slowly and only in marginal increments.

As one moves progressively farther South, of course, the period of semidormancy becomes shorter and shorter. Consequently, there is a progressive increase in accumulated fat stores, which are gradually transformed into "real" body weight. In fact, in the southernmost states there may be almost no dormancy period at all, and largemouths can realize their full genetic growth potential. But still, due to their genetic growth limitations, the fish are not likely ever to reach the sizes attained by typical Florida bass.

California Transplants

A noteworthy example of oversize bass has recently been seen in southern California. But the fish attaining impressive sizes there are not true largemouths. They are Florida bass, which have been transplanted by joint effort between California and Florida fishery officials. In southern California, year-round air and water temperatures approximate those of Florida, and for other reasons that will be discussed shortly, the aliens have been putting on weight like Fat Albert at a pie-eating contest.

For decades fishery biologists, anglers and fishing writers stalwartly maintained that George Perry's world-record twenty-two-pound-plus largemouth bass, caught in 1932, would never be bested. But when large numbers of California transplants in the 15- to 18-pound range began showing up on anglers' stringers in the early 1970s, anxious stirrings

This is the second largest bass ever recorded, a 21-pound 3-ounce giant taken in southern California by Ray Easley. If the fish had weighed only 17 ounces more, it would have broken the existing 48-year-old world record. (Photo courtesy of B.A.S.S. and DuPont Stren).

among fishermen suggested the record might soon tumble. The fishery biologists, however, were not so sure; after all, 15- to 18-pound bass had been showing up in Florida for years.

Then during the summer of 1973, Dave Zimmerlee boated a monster at Lake Miramar that weighed almost 21 pounds. Then in 1980, Ray Easley wrestled a whopper bass out of Lake Casitas that was several ounces *over* 21 pounds. This was the same year that Glen Lau, who has done extensive underwater photography of bass and who made the movie *Bigmouth,* reported seeing, close-up, a bass swimming the depths of San Vicente Lake that he estimated to be 26 pounds! It should go without saying that fishery biologists are whistling a different tune, now. As this is being written in 1984, my own prediction is that the world record will not be broken once before the decade is ended but at least twice, and that both of those bass will come from southern California.

A necklace of 13 San Diego City Lakes are currently in the limelight for regularly producing these whopper bass, though the Florida subspecies has been introduced into a total of 27 California waters. Many fishery scientists believe the oversize growth being exhibited by the fish can be attributed to a new system of fish management being practiced in California, a system that is unheard of in other states.

The San Diego City Lake managers impose a number of restrictions upon anglers. For one, most of the lakes are open to fishing for only six months, and then they are closed for six months, which allows more big bass to survive to the next season. Secondly, night fishing is not permitted on the waters. This can have an important influence because record books in other states show that many of their largest bass of the season are taken while stars are winking overhead. As noted in earlier chapters, the largest bass in any body of water are very reluctant to leave the depths except during those times when light levels are lowest. Angling pressure on the San Diego City Lakes is still further reduced by allowing fishing only on certain days of the week, such as Tuesday, Thursday and Saturday. What the California people are doing, then, is carefully regulating the annual bass harvest, so larger numbers of lunker bass are permitted to continue growing.

Catching the transplanted Florida subspecies in California does not differ markedly from catching largemouths anywhere. Many California anglers claim that the largemouths there are much easier to catch than the supposedly shy and wary Florida transplants; yet others claim just the opposite is true. Whatever the case, and I personally believe there is little difference, an angler should have success with both basses if he approaches his fishing methodically and with a working knowledge of bass behavior. This means evaluating water and weather conditions, locating bottom

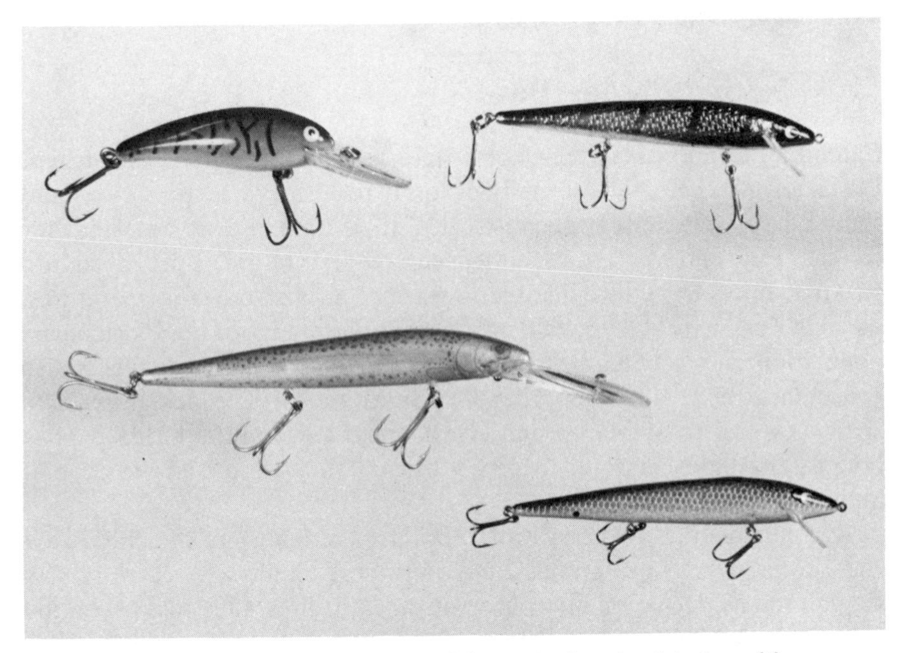

One unusual trait of Florida bass in California is that the fish there like to gorge themselves on rainbow trout. Hence, plugs that resemble trout are best.

structure the fish might be using during various seasons of the year in accordance with the lake type, and then using whatever techniques are required under existing conditions to control the speed and depth of his lures.

However, bass in many California waters have a couple of unusual habits. First, during much of the year, the bass are gorging upon crayfish. Since crayfish are nocturnal creatures, and since bass seem to adapt their feeding schedules to the circadian rhythm of this favored prey, jigs are top producers when fished during the low-light levels of dawn and dusk.

Perhaps even more unusual is that southern California bass dine heavily upon rainbow trout. Consequently, knowing a bit about trout behavior can prove helpful, for if you find trout, likely as not bass will be close by. Rainbows prefer and will seek out water that is 56° to 60°, and they commonly like to suspend themselves within this temperature band over much deeper water. So, take along a water temperature gauge and graph recorder to help in locating rainbows. Since trout may frequently be as deep as 40 to 60 feet, conventional bass-fishing techniques are inappropriate. Most California bass anglers troll slim-minnow balsa lures painted to resemble rainbows, using wire lines or Dan Gapen's Bait-Walkers.

Native Florida Bass

Catching Florida bass in their home state calls for still different strategies. Like bass anywhere, the fish are tied closely to bottom structure, cover and some type of forage; they spend most of their time in deep water, if they can find any; and they can be either tempted into biting or provoked into striking. But due to the consistently warmer air and water temperatures, an angler can expect to encounter a certain percentage of the Florida bass population on spawning beds during any month of the year (this is also true of largemouths in a few other deep South states). The most purposeful spawning occurs in March and April, but I've caught Florida bass in August that had bellies distended with eggs they were ready to drop at any moment.

Another distinctive feature of Florida bass fishing is the waterways themselves, which are practically always very shallow. As a result, although the fish occasionally consort in small groups, they seldom exhibit the diligent schooling activity involving larger fish that is common in deep, expansive reservoirs.

When we looked at the other bass species, we divided their habitats into numerous lake, reservoir, river and pond categories. But there is really little need to do this in the case of the Florida bass subspecies, because it lives predominantly in just one continuous habitat. In fact, many of the existing lakes in Florida are really nothing more than a place where some sluggish river expansively widens. An example is the Kissimmee River which, going north, widens in places to form Lakes Hatchineha, Cypress, West Tohopekaliga and East Toho.

Some may argue that since many such waters are fed by their own tributaries or springs, they are separate lakes in their own rights. But actually, much of Florida is nothing more than an endless maze of winding rivers, sometimes widening, interconnecting canals and underground rivers, and seemingly impenetrable swamp areas and flowages. There are exceptions, of course, including Lake Jackson, Lake Talquin and others. But in most cases an angler may have to check a map in order to determine accurately whether he is fishing a swamp, lake, river or other type of water, since all seem to sprawl and wander perpetually and in one way or another connect with some other body of water.

It should be noted that few manmade reservoirs exist in Florida. One of the few such impoundments, and perhaps the most productive, is the Rodman Pool, which was created in 1971 when the Oklawaha River was dammed as part of the Cross Florida Barge Canal Project. Although now 13 years old, this reservoir continues to yield large numbers of bass in the 10-to-12-pound range.

The heavy cover on many Florida waterways may overwhelm anglers fishing for Florida bass in that state. Sometimes you think you're in a jungle, as Rick Clunn demonstrates here while Flippin' with the author on a Lake Kissimmee sawgrass flat. Although bass may like the cover, it's usually an abrupt change in the bottom that attracts them to certain places.

The thing that often makes for tough fishing in Florida is the preponderance of visible cover. Most waterways contain expansive fields of reeds, lily pads, hyacinth and other vegetation, along with standing cypress and willow trees. Plenty of bass are taken from this cover, but there is one particular weed species that is far and away most attractive to bass. It's called eelgrass (*vallisneria*) and appears as long, stringy, half-inch-wide ribbons. Eelgrass is such a prolific producer of oxygen you can actually see bubbles clinging to the vegetation. Particularly during the warmest summer months, when there is little wind and wave action to aerate certain areas, and far back in swamps where the water may actually become a bit stagnant, this eelgrass is like a magnet to all forms of aquatic life. The resulting rich, diverse food chain can support the growth of many large bass.

With other species of vegetation, however, it's not so much the weeds themselves that attract the bass but the presence of some associated bottom contour. For example, look at two hypothetical weedbeds: One situated on a rather barren flat; the other situated on an underwater ridge that juts up from the bottom, extends for some distance, and then drops off again into deeper water. You fish both areas and no bass are taken from the edge of the first, but two monsters are derricked aboard from the edges of the second. In the case of the second weedbed, what really attracted bass to the area and held them there? Was it the weeds? No! If that were the case, there probably would also have been bass along the edges of the first weedbed. It was the erratic bottom contour, in the second situation, that was holding the bass; the presence of weeds was only an incidental bonus the fish could use for hiding, or as ambush stations, while relating to the bottom contour. All of this makes a good case for trying, difficult as it may be at times, to disregard the bassy-looking cover that apparently is everywhere in Florida lakes and to keep in mind the various structure-fishing concepts emphasized in the beginning chapters of this book.

Canals are one type of structural feature found among Florida waters that are not too common in other areas of the country. These channels are constructed either to connect two or more larger bodies of water, or to facilitate the flow of water by straightening a section of a winding river. In the latter case, the water in the canal generally is deeper and moves faster than the water in the old river channel, yet both waterways may afford good structure-fishing opportunities.

As noted in the discussion of flowing waterways in Chapter 16, the outside bends of smaller rivers are washed out and undercut and therefore deeper, whereas the inside bends have shallow shoals formed by settling sand and gravel. The largest bass usually are in or near the deepest water, that is in the vicinity of the outside bends or perhaps where there is an occasional deep hole. Most canals are no more than a long, uniform trench, but structure may have been created at those locations where the canal cuts across or through the old river channel. The most noticeable structures in canals are land points and underwater shelves or drop-offs where the edge of a canal meets the edge of the old riverbed. What is important is that not only are these good bass structures in themselves, but they are directly adjacent to the deepest water in the area. The best way to fish the deep outer bends in the river channel, and also the points, is with jigs or weighted plastic worms. To work the shelves, I recommend speed-trolling, just like you'd fish any breakline.

In large Florida lakes, and also in swamp areas, where the water is predominantly shallow and choked with cover, bass also head for whatever deep water exists. I'm talking now not about "popcorn" bass (fish only a foot or so in length), which may be randomly scattered, but about much larger fish that sense their vulnerability when too much time is spent in the shallows. One type of deep water they distinctly favor is a sinkhole that gushes forth spring water. I once found a sinkhole 20 feet long by ten

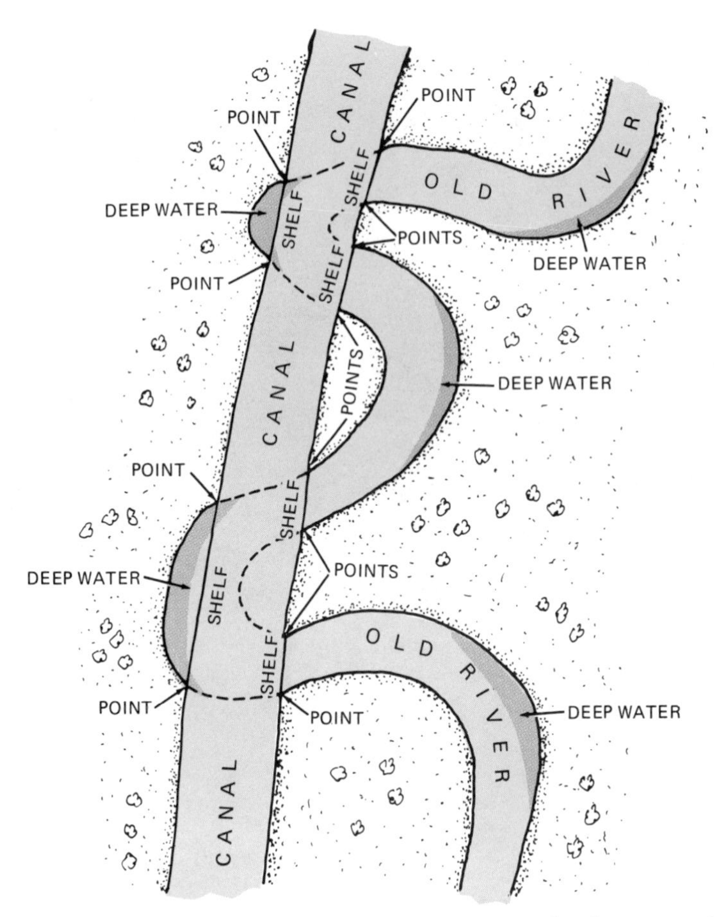

One type of structure not too common in states other than Florida is a canal where an old river has been straightened to facilitate the flow of water. This produces many favorable edges and drop-offs that bass favor.

feet wide, but they are usually much smaller. While the surrounding water may average four to seven feet deep, a sinkhole may plummet to a depth of 15 or 20 feet. Guess where the largest bass in that immediate vicinity will be found? Next to a cypress tree in the shallows? In the weeds along the shoreline where the water is two feet deep? Under a bush out on the flats where the water is four feet deep? Not on your life! The very largest fish will be in or very near the sinkhole. And you can find such holes by carefully checking bottom contour maps or through random exploration with your eyes glued to the dial of a depth sounder.

Other types of cuts, depressions or drop-offs, not necessarily associated

The most productive way to fish canals is by working the created points with jigs and plastic worms. Then speed-troll the edges. Don't overlook bridges crossing the canal which offer deep, shaded water and pilings for the fish to hide among.

with springs, may also produce fantastic catches offshore while your buddies are back in the swamp pitching plugs at the shallow weedbeds. And again, it is the change in the bottom contour and the slightly deeper water that attract the bass. Keep in mind, however, that these bass-attracting changes do not always have to be large to be productive. In a Florida swamp lake where the bottom consists of endless flats in six feet of water, a mere two-foot drop-off to the eight-foot level may have numerous lunkers clinging to that edge if it is the only noticeable variation in bottom contour anywhere in the area.

In the great majority of lakes, heavy cover along the shoreline is an indication of very shallow water with little in the way of interesting bottom structure. But sometimes midlake cover that is surrounded on all sides by open water is associated with bottom structure: A small patch of reeds or lily pads may signal the presence of a hump; a long, narrow weedbed may indicate the location of a bar; a row of trees may herald an underwater ridge. If there is no depth change, but brush, bushes or stick-ups are present in some midlake area, the cover may be indicating a place where a very soft mucky bottom yields to hardpan or sand. This location

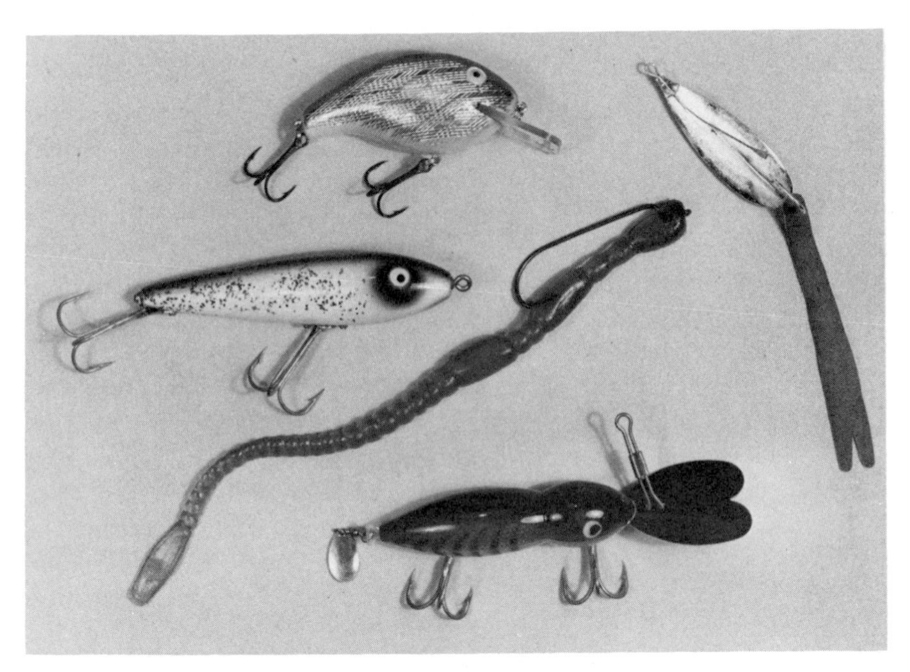

Favorite lures for Florida bass include weighted worms for deep fishing in sinkholes, weedless spoons that can be slithered over grassbeds, and assorted plugs that can be worked around the edges of cover.

could hold a bonanza of big fish during the primary spring spawn, and at other times as well. Conversely, in an area where there is acre after acre of thickly matted weeds, small openings here and there may indicate the presence of sinkholes. Any or all of these places can often be fished with the very same tackle and techniques you might use in the shallower headwater region of a flatland reservoir, with spinnerbaits, buzz-baits, plastic worms, weedless spoons and crankbaits heading the list.

In Florida, live-bait fishing also is extremely popular and at certain times of year probably accounts for more trophy bass than any other strategy. The premier bait is a large shiner six to eight inches in length, and the most productive period is the cold-water months of November through March; during the late spring, summer and early fall, artificial lures do better.

Although anglers fish with shiners throughout Florida, they are extremely popular on Lake Jackson, near Tallahassee, and similar lakes. Jackson's depths average only seven or eight feet, and almost the entire bottom is saturated with moss or weeds growing up to within a few feet of the surface. The floor of the lake is dishpan shaped, and the few holes or other variations in bottom contour are almost impossible to locate because the signals from a depth sounder's transducer will not penetrate the thick weed layer to reveal what lies below.

When fishing Florida lakes like this, an angler should hook a shiner once through the lips with a 4/0 or 5/0 hook, and add just enough weight to the line to prevent the minnow from swimming to the surface. Then the bait is suspended from two to four feet below a large float and drifted across open expanses of water just above the tops of the weeds.

When a bass takes the bait, it is permitted to run a short distance before the angler sets the hook with as much gusto as his tackle will stand. Stout rods are the rule, and lines should test from 25 to 30 pounds. When the angler has completed his drift across the lake and reached the other side, all drifting baits are brought in, the craft is quickly motored to the other side of the lake, and another drift over new water from a slightly different angle is commenced. The bass lay deep in the weeds on or near some type of bottom variation, occasionally rising to pick off baitfish cruising the tops of the weeds. When a good fish is brought aboard, it often means that the boat has just passed over some bottom contour or other structural configuration beneath the weeds. The smart angler anchors quietly and fishes the area more thoroughly to see if still more bass are around.

Shiners are also used to work the edges of heavily matted beds of hyacinth and other weeds blanketing the surface. In this situation, the largest bass are likely to be far back under the cover, hiding in dark catacombs where it is impossible to get a lure to them. A liver shiner, however, can swim right back underneath all that cover and that is exactly what it does, knowing instinctively that to remain out in open water is placing its life in jeopardy. In this case, the shiner is hooked as usual but no weight is placed on the line, and no bobber. Then the minnow is turned loose over the side of the boat, and line paid out from the reel so the shiner can swim freely.

Sometimes a shiner will swim as far as 25 yards back under the weeds, and learning to detect "bites" is one of the most exciting, explosive types of bass angling imaginable. On occasion, the line will begin vibrating because the shiner, upon seeing a huge predatory bass approach, actually begins trembling. Other times, you'll feel a steady resistance on the end of your line—a much more weighty sensation than just the shiner alone is capable of producing. Still other times, far back in the weeds, you'll see the surface water bulge up, or "boil," which indicates that a big bass has taken the bait. It's episodes like this that cause young men to grow old quickly.

CHAPTER

21

Tackle For Bass

In the long run, buying the finest and most expensive tackle you can lay your hands on is the best bargain going. It will last longer and all the while provide trouble-free, enjoyable service. More important, high-quality tackle can be looked upon as an investment in your development as a better and better fisherman, which is what this book is all about.

The selection of spinning and baitcasting reels is relatively easy because the vast majority of reels on the market today are of exceptionally high quality; your personal preference for certain features can play the major role as to which models you purchase. Simply stick with the acclaimed brand names and few problems should be encountered. In my opinion, it's quite difficult to go wrong with reels made by Daiwa, Garcia, Lew Childre or Shimano.

Rods and lines are more weighty considerations. Even a junky rod can be dressed up with pretty varnish and guide windings to look nice, which is exactly what many cut-rate outfits do. And there is a proliferation of inferior-grade lines on the market that *look* no different from premium-grade lines but will fail when subjected to the responsibilities expected of them by an expert angler.

The Super Rods

In the last few years, space-age technology has infiltrated the manufacture of fishing rods; and no clearer example is available than rods made of boron. The aircraft industry pioneered the industrial use of boron, using it in the production of certain parts for jet fighter plane wings, helicopter rotor blades and structural components for the Space Shuttle. Since boron initially cost upwards of $1,000 per pound, it's use was naturally quite

Although it's impossible to buy bass-fishing success, high-quality equipment is a good investment in your development as an expert angler.

restricted. Then, modern technology found a way to reduce the price to about $200 per pound, and the sporting goods industry subsequently began using the material in golf club shafts, skis and tennis rackets. The Browning Company of Morgan, Utah, was the very first to use boron in the manufacture of fishing rods.

Most so-called boron rods contain only about 40 percent boron because a pure boron rod would be so stiff and brittle it would snap like a piece of dry spaghetti. Browning's solution was to join metallic boron filaments with graphite fibers. The graphite component helps a rod achieve the desired action and allows it to handle light loads as well as the initial shock or strain that must be absorbed when an angler sets the hook. The boron ingredient, on the other hand, transmits vibrations much faster than other materials, so an angler "feels" far more light-biting fish than ever before. Boron also handles the very heavy or strenuous loads that may be encountered when an angler hooks a very big fish close to the boat.

To substantiate its claims about boron rods, Browning hired an independent testing laboratory to put the new rods through their paces. In one of the tests, the engineers attached transducers (similar to those used with electronic depth sounders) to the rods, "shot" the rod tips with impulses, and then measured their characteristics. They learned that when an impulse was introduced to the tip of a boron rod, it traveled to the rod handle 19 percent faster and with greater amplitude than it did with a graphite rod of identical design. The impulse traveled 120 percent faster in a boron rod than in a conventional fiberglass rod of identical design. More than

Here, Bill Weiss compares features of three boron rods. Scientific tests have revealed that impulses introduced to the tips of boron rods travel to the handle 120 percent faster than in conventional fiberglass rods, making them by far the most sensitive.

that, boron rods were found to be 23 percent stronger than comparable graphite rods and 22 percent stronger than fiberglass rods. This is amazing because the rods are so lightweight and thin: The thickest part of a boron rod, at the butt near the handle, is no larger in diameter than an ordinary pencil.

If you like to backtroll with live baits, if you like to fish with jigs, or if your specialty is crawling plastic worms across the bottom and through cover—all of which require acute sensitivity in the detection of light bites—boron rods, made by any of several manufacturers, are the best that money can buy.

While boron rods are generally looked upon as special-purpose tools, the workhorses among rods are those made of graphite, and my prediction is they will continue to be the most popular with anglers for at least the next decade. As with boron rods, it's impossible to make a pure graphite rod, so be skeptical of any advertising claims that may say otherwise. About the greatest proportion of graphite that can be put into such a rod is 92 percent because it's necessary to add to the graphite other ingredients such as resins and bonding agents.

Graphite (more properly, high modulus graphite, or simply HMG) is produced by taking a synthetic fiber called polyacrylontrile and heating it to 2,500° in order to char it. Then the material is imbedded in a special resin, wrapped around a mandrel (a stainless steel dummy rod) and baked. Finally, the mandrel is removed and what's left is the graphite rod blank, which then is sanded and outfitted with guides and a suitable handle.

These rod-making steps vary somewhat from company to company but there are three things any angler will readily notice when he picks up a graphite rod: It will be very lightweight, it will have a very stiff action, and it will be of very small diameter. The stiff action that graphite rods are known for is a particular advantage because it means a fast recovery on the cast. In other words, when the rod is flexed during the cast, it snaps back very quickly to its original shape. This means you can make long casts with a flat trajectory, instead of having a big arc in the line. As a result, casting accuracy is much better with graphite rods than with others, even when a strong wind is blowing. This feature makes them ideal tools for pitching crankbaits and spinnerbaits in and around thick cover. Probably, though, it's the extreme sensitivity of both boron and graphite rods that are their prime hallmark.

When buying either boron or graphite rods, select only those outfitted with aluminum oxide guides. This ceramic material is extremely hard and smooth, which virtually eliminates the line wear common with nickle-plated steel guides.

Graphite rods, noted for their stiff actions, have a fast recovery on the cast. This allows you to cast farther, with a flatter trajectory, than is possible with fiberglass.

Dozens of companies make boron and graphite rods, but head and shoulders above the rest are those rods made or distributed by Bass Pro Shops, Browning, Daiwa, Fenwick, and Lew Childre & Sons.

Lines and Knots

Nylon used in the manufacture of monofilament fishing lines is a synthetic fiber derived from oil-refining by-products. It is not a solid but technically a semihardened liquid, almost like window glass. The DuPont Company of Wilmington, Delaware, was the first to discover nylon in 1938 and begin making it into fishing lines; since then more than 10,000 different types of nylon have come into modern use. So when you read the label on a spool of line and it merely says "nylon monofilament," the manufacturer isn't telling you a thing, other than describing a very broad class of materials from which most fishing lines are made.

There are many attributes that spell the difference between a cheap line and a premium-grade line. Since most of these are not visible to the naked eye, evaluating the quality of fishing line is somewhat perplexing. Price alone is not a good guide because numerous lines on the market are made in Germany, Finland, Sweden, Great Britain and Japan; due to the peculiarities of the international monetary situation imported lines that are of only mediocre quality may actually cost more than premium domestic lines.

Whatever the particular brand, whether foreign or domestic, premium-grade lines are made of the highest-quality materials in an exacting, multistepped process. First the lines are extruded, that is, the raw nylon material is melted, squeezed through a tiny hole to transform it into a molten filament, and then rapidly cooled. Next, there are numerous finishing treatments in which the line is drawn, heat treated, dyed, stretched, drawn again, and so on. The purpose of these many steps is to orient the line's molecular structure to the highest possible degree of uniformity for

Buy a cheap line and you'll find it's actually very expensive because of lost fish and time-consuming problems like this.

maximum strength and performance. Otherwise, microscopic thick and thin spots would result which could cause the line to fail; in such cases, the thick spots are the weakest because these are composed of lumps of jackstrawed molecules that have not undergone proper alignment.

Cheaper lines are merely extruded, drawn and spooled. There is little in the way of quality control other than random spot checks of the finished product to ensure it is "presentable" for marketing. Otherwise, any semblance of uniformity is highly variable and imprecise. My friend Paul Johnson, at the Berkley Company, calls such products "economy lines" but explains they are actually very "highly priced" because they often cost an angler the fish of a lifetime.

Aside from uniformity, there are a number of desirable features that characterize a premium-grade line. These include high straight tensile breaking strength, high knot strength, abrasion resistance, shock resistance and manageability. Furthermore, these features must be harmoniously married. It is critically important that an advanced angler understand this because in today's world of media hype and advertising gimmickry, it's common for cutrate line companies to augment a particular characteristic, such as tensile strength or knot strength, in their products, and subsequently play it up big in sales campaigns. But such a radical alteration in the chemical composition of a line and its related physical attributes invariably destroys the balance among all the different properties, resulting in an inferior line.

For example, if nearly all of a line's stretch property were eliminated, the line would be ideal for hook setting. But its shock resistance would be adversely affected, causing an angler to lose many in-close battles with bass that unexpectedly exploded next to the boat. Or, if a line's limpness feature were greatly exaggerated, to obtain the smoothest casting imaginable, an angler would pay a dear price in another department because this line would be so soft and stretchy he could never set the hook; it would be like pulling on a rubber band. By the same token, a certain amount of abrasion resistance is desirable, particularly for anglers fishing in and around thick, brittle cover such as brush. Yet if this property is increased to extremes, as two cutrate line companies now are actually doing, the resulting line is so stiff, wiry and unmanageable that it comes off a reel in big coils, snarls easily, and is frustratingly impossible to work with.

Consequently, companies that produce exceptionally high-quality lines strive for just the right balance among a combination of attributes that most anglers will periodically have to rely upon.

Another intriguing feature of nylon monofilament lines is their visibility. Both the diameter and color of lines influence how visible they are to fish and fishermen alike. In theory, the "perfect" fishing line would be completely invisible to fish, *very* visible to fishermen (who need to watch their lines, especially when fishing worms or jigs, to detect faint ticks or bumps indicating light-biting fish), and awesomely strong. This perfect line is still hypothetical—a dream in anglers' eyes—and cannot be produced by current techniques. But the Berkley Company of Spirit Lake, Iowa, is getting close with its Trilene lines.

Berkley's Trilene lines are made from a nylon alloy that can be drawn to a much smaller diameter than all-nylon lines. A 12-pound-test Berkley line, for example, may actually have a smaller diameter than a 10-pound-test line made by another company. This may not seem terribly significant until one looks at numerous lines under water and sees how much their diameters influence their visibility. Countless times I've seen one angler in a boat go fishless while his partner, using the same type of lure but on a lighter pound test or smaller diameter line, yanked in one bass after another.

The problem with coloring dyes, and fluorescing chemicals that make

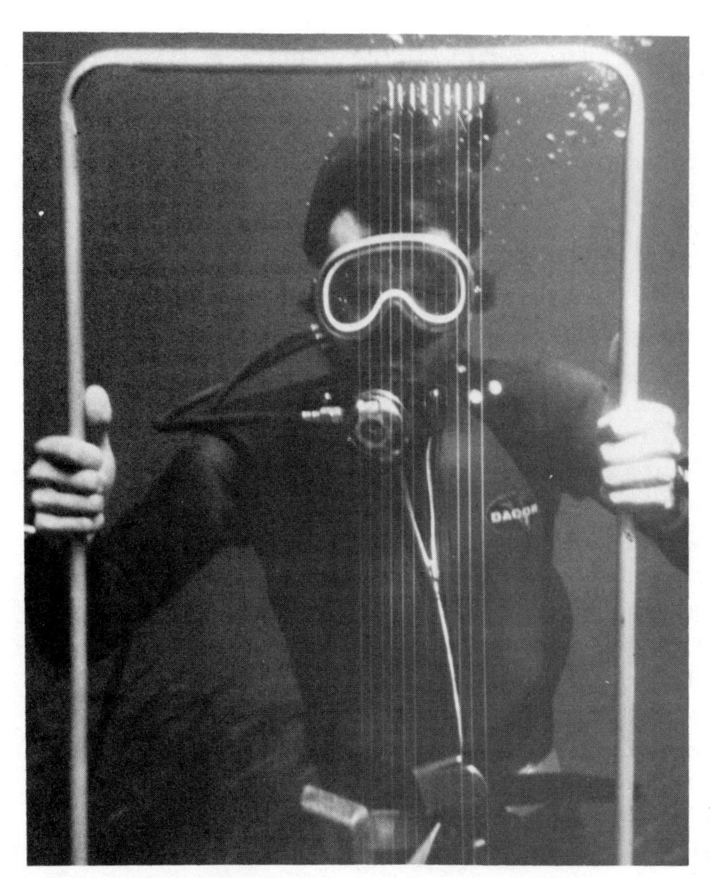

These 12 nylon lines are all the same pound test but different diameters and coloring dyes make some far more visible than others.

lines appear to "glow," is that they often are perceived in a wide variety of ways, depending upon the light intensity and the type of background the line is seen against. Although colored lines are likely to produce variable results under different conditions, I can offer a few general rules. Use translucent or clear line when casting crankbaits, spinnerbaits, buzzbaits and jigging spoons in clear water, or when backtrolling with live baits in clear water, but switch to optically brightened line when fishing plastic worms or jigs. As to which line colors are best, there is much heated debate among anglers. Some scientists, however, have very firm opinions.

Dr. Fred T. Janzow, a fishery biologist at Missouri State University, spent two years studying hundreds of bass in laboratory test tanks and natural lake situations and noted their reactions to various colors of lines. He discovered that lines of subtle hues (light blue, light green and clear) produced widely variable responses from bass, depending upon the weather and water conditions under which lines and lures were presented; that bass were definitely and favorably attracted to lures tied to lines that were bright blue and bright green; and that bass exhibited alarm responses and were repelled by bright yellow lines.

Underwater line studies by biologists have revealed that bass are alarmed by bright yellow lines, attracted by bright blue or green lines.

Exactly why bright blue and green lines drew positive responses from bass is not definitely known. Perhaps, as Janzow believes, such lines simply are accepted by bass because they "fit into" the underwater realm in which blue and green hues predominate; in contrast, yellow may be perceived as alien, triggering an alarm or avoidance response, as would any other atypical feature in the environment. The light, subtle hues, according to this explanation, are "neutral" colors which may elicit positive responses, negative responses, or no response at all, depending upon water clarity, light intensity, line diameter, or other conditions existing at any given time.

The pound-test rating of a line, which generally is printed on the spool, would seem to be a straightforward attribute that anglers could use to compare and evaluate different lines. Unfortunately, the situation is not so simple. At a Berkley Sportfishing Workshop I recently participated in, we tested ten-pound-test lines marketed by 12 different companies and were shocked to discover actual breaking strengths ranging from a low of seven pounds to a high of 15½ pounds! There are two explanations offered for such variations: differences in how line strength is measured, and willful misrepresentation.

The first thing to realize is that a nylon line will test stronger when it is dry than when it is wet. So, line companies have a choice: They can measure the breaking strengths of their lines when they are dry or when they are wet. This leads to a certain ambiguity concerning test ratings. For one, you may not be able to tell from the manufacturer's information whether a particular line was rated wet or dry. Further, if the line you are using was rated dry, then its stated pound test will decrease by some unknown amount during your fishing activities. For example, suppose you decide you need ten-pound-test line for a certain type of fishing; you spool onto your reel what you think is ten-pound test, based on what the label says, but when the line becomes wet, its breaking strength may actually be only six-pound test. To get around this problem, some companies, including Berkley, state a wet breaking strength on their line labels. If you peel dry ten-pound-test Trilene line off a spool and test it with a handscale, it may actually break at 13 pounds, yet after a half-hour of fishing the line will be reduced to its stated breaking strength of ten pounds.

The breaking strength of a line also is affected by whether or not it contains knots. Thus, some companies, when rating their lines, take into consideration not only the tensile breaking strength but the reduction in strength that occurs when various types of knots are tied in a line.

Companies guilty of misrepresenting pound-test ratings generally do so in order to be able to make some claim of superiority over their competitors. In the case of lines that are overrated, the gimmick usually has to do with an advertising campaign that touts, for example, a particular company's line as the least visible ten-pound-test line on the market—of course it is, it's really only seven- or eight-pound test. Conversely, with lines that have been greatly underrated, the ploy may involve a company's claim that its ten-pound-test line is much stronger than any other ten-pound line on the market—of course it is stronger, it's really 15-pound test.

"We are hoping in the near future we'll see some standardization in line-labeling practices," Berkley's Paul Johnson recently said to me, "and that we'll begin seeing some truth in advertising laws applied to the tackle industry. Meanwhile, the only thing an angler can do is acquire a good deal of mono line savvy and personally test prospective lines himself."

A small, inexpensive handscale is ideal for testing the breaking strength of lines. It's a modest investment compared with the value of knowing exactly what line test you're using.

In addition to measuring the breaking strengths of lines at home and on the water, you can evaluate several other features of lines right in a store. Peel off several feet of line and look at it closely. A line that appears

A small handscale is ideal not only for setting the drag on reels, but also for determining wet and dry breaking strengths of lines. In one study, ten-pound-test lines marketed by 12 different companies were discovered to have breaking strengths ranging from seven to 15½ pounds.

very shiny or glassy generally is of inferior quality. The best, premium-grade lines generally have a smooth semiluster or almost matte finish for minimum underwater light reflection. Now hold up the spool and let several feet of line dangle freely. Is the line limp and manageable and hanging almost straight down, or does it seem to hang in spirals and coils? A line that seems exceptionally soft is probably too stretchy for effective hook setting, but one that exhibits a high degree of "memory" may be difficult to cast because the line will snarl as it comes off the reel and not be able to pass easily through the rod guides. Tests such as these should make it patently clear which companies have tried to exaggerate some line property or another, and therefore which lines are inferior.

Since this book is devoted to advanced bass-fishing techniques, I told myself right in the beginning I wouldn't dwell on the subject of knots; every experienced bassman has long since become proficient in tying knots. Yet at least a few words of advice are warranted, even for expert anglers.

Take the debate over whether or not spitting on knots is beneficial. Berkley representatives have long contended that spitting on knots before snugging them up tightly does indeed help because this practice "lubricates" the monofilament line, significantly reducing heat and abrasive friction where one loop of line touches another. As a result, they claim, the hard nylon material is less likely to cut into itself and be weakened. Other companies, however, maintain that spitting makes no difference whatsoever and essentially is a waste of time.

The question puzzled DuPont scientists, so they decided to conduct knot-strength tests with a variety of pound-test lines that were either dry or wetted with saliva before knots were tied in them. The results, as measured by a sophisticated Instron Tensile Strength Testing Machine, revealed that the strength of the knots tied with wet lines was the *same* as that of identical types of knots that were tied with dry lines. However, the scientists also concluded that, spitting on knots does indeed help— a seeming contradiction worth explaining here.

As DuPont spokesman Charles Booz explained, "There are several different styles of knots any angler may elect to tie that are very good choices, such as the improved-clinch, Palomar, and Uni-Knot, as all offer from 95 to 98 percent of the line's rated pound test. Yet of these knots, the specific one an angler decides to tie is not nearly as important as the *care* he uses in the actual tying process."

This important point has been borne out time and again when professional anglers gather at some fishing clinic and are asked to tie a specific knot dozens of times and then submit them all for mechanical testing. Predictably, although the same brand and pound test of line is used and the same style of knot tied, they all seem to break under differing loads.

At an American Fishing Tackle Manufacturers Association (AFTMA) show, I once watched tournament pro Ricky Green tie two dozen Palomar knots in 14-pound-test line, which later separated under break loads ranging from ten to 18 pounds.

An explanation for these wide variations in knot strength is simple: Anglers—even professionals—are fallible human beings who are just plain incapable of precise consistency in their knot-tying efforts. In short, sometimes we tie very good knots, sometimes mediocre ones, and sometimes very poor ones. And more than frequently, it's a poorly tied knot rather than the type of knot or type of line that is responsible for a break-off.

Compounding the problem, various types of knots rely upon different principles for their holding abilities. For example, the Palomar and Uni-Knots depend upon a type of mechanical leverage. Yet others such as the clinch knots (standard-clinch, improved-clinch, double-eye clinch, and Trilene knot) depend solely upon their tightness or the cushioning effect of the many turns jammed against one another.

The bottom line in all of this is that the presence of spit on a knot probably does not add to its strength, at least if you accept the findings of the Dupont scientists. But the fact that an angler has invested the extra time and concern to go ahead and spit anyway is a clear sign he is tying his knots purposefully and carefully, and this does indeed add to any knot's strength. Keep in mind these following knot-tying tips as well:

- Where turns are required around a standing line, keep them separated as they are made and then slowly pull them together in a neat spiral when tightening the knot. If these turns are pulled up too quickly so that one or more settle on top of each other, the ones on top will cut into the ones beneath when pressure is applied.
- Jamming-type knots, such as the clinch and Uni-Knot varieties, hold best in low pound-test lines because the larger line diameters of stronger lines make it difficult to pull coils tight. Don't expect full-rated strength from these types of knots in lines over 20-pound test, unless you use pliers to grab the tag end of the line to bring the knot up more snuggly than you can with your bare hands.
- When double lines are used, as in tying the Palomar knot, keep them as parallel as possible; avoid twisting them as the knot is being tied and slowly cinched up.
- Always pull any knot up as tightly as possible with an even and steady pressure. Otherwise, if there occurs any bit of slippage when force is exerted upon the knot, tremendous friction will be generated which can cause the line to part.

The matter of which types of knots are best for different uses is greatly a matter of personal preference. When I tie a lure onto a split-ring, snap, snap-swivel, or free-floating line-tie, I invariably use the improved-clinch knot, as the nature of the additional hardware still allows the lure to exhibit all of its built-in action. But when it's necessary to tie directly to the lure, and the line-tie is nothing more than a small loop of wire, the improved-clinch is too tight and has the effect of restricting the lure's action. Now is when I switch to a Uni-Knot of the wiggle-loop variety. The same goes for jigs and jigging spoons.

When using plastic worms, however, I avoid the improved-clinch, which because of its long, slender shape, has a way of protruding from the head of the worm and then jamming itself up into the bottom hole of the worm sinker. So for all worm-fishing efforts, I use the more compact Palomar knot. The Palomar, by the way, is most easily tied with the smallest of lures, worm hooks, jigs, and the like, as it is necessary to pass the entire lure or hook through a standing, double loop of line before snugging up the knot.

Naturalized Lures

You've seen them in magazine ads and on the shelves in your favorite tackleshop. They are lures with lifelike designs imprinted on them that appear so real it seems like you'd have to keep the lid on your tacklebox locked tight to prevent them from swimming away. They are called *naturalized lures* and in many cases they are almost perfect representations of various panfish species, baitfish, and even gamefish fingerlings. These lures have revolutionized the science and art of lure design, which stagnated for more than 60 years, delivering plain plugs bearing little resemblance to the food bass commonly prey on.

After an initial period of great enthusiasm, however, many expert anglers, guides and tournament pros are beginning to report great dissatisfaction with some brands of naturalized plugs, saying that in many cases they caught far more bass on their old standard patterns. The paradox of this situation is that the tackle companies seem to have done their jobs too well! Many naturalized lures actually look *too* lifelike.

You see, nature has given all fish species markings and coloration that help them survive. In scientific terms, this is called *countershading.* What it means is that fish possess light-colored bellies that gradually blend into soft grays and greens along the sides of the fish and become progressively darker along the dorsal or back regions. Let's assume you are a bass and you are looking down upon a minnow. Against the dark-colored bottom of the lake, the minnow will be almost invisible because all you can see

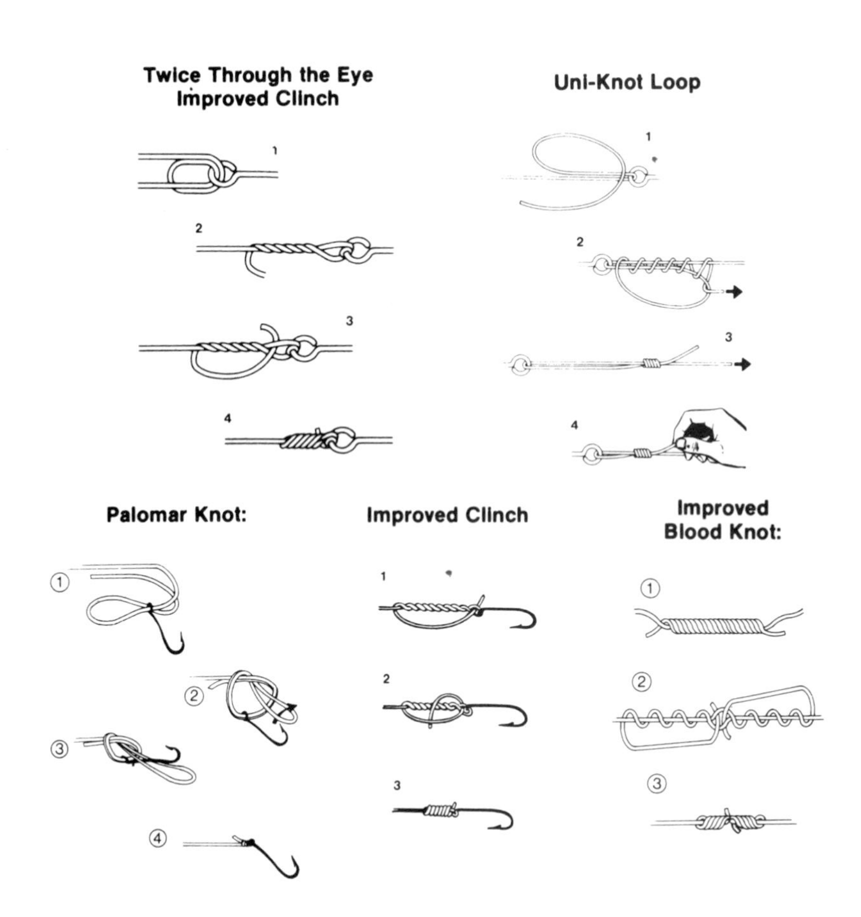

Some knots are better suited for some uses than others, but usually the most important things influencing the performance of a knot is the skill and care with which it's tied.

is its dark back. If you are at the same depth as the minnow, and looking at its side, you'll see mottled gray-green patterns that blend into the background of weeds, brush or felled trees. And if you are below the minnow, looking up, you'll again have a difficult time seeing the baitfish against the sky because of its light-colored underneath surfaces.

The major problem with many of the new naturalized lures, then, is that they blend so well with the environment—just like the small fish they mimic—that bass have great difficulty seeing them. And if bass can't see a lure, they certainly can't take it.

Scientists have recently begun studying this unusual state of affairs, and some of the most significant work has been conducted by Dr. Bill Phillips, a fishery biologist at Auburn University in Alabama. Phillips also is the president of Angling Research Associates, an independent testing company that conducts scientific investigations on fish behavior for many tackle manufacturers.

Summarizing his most recent findings, Phillips has stated, "Under most conditions, most natural lures have failed to compete favorably with other standard patterns we have been using for years that have good contrasting color schemes."

Now, I'm not concluding that the new naturalized lures are no good, and I'm not saying they won't catch bass. They will indeed. But there are some color designs and patterns that are far more effective than others, and the insightful angler will want to take many things into consideration before outfitting himself with an arsenal of these unique lures.

But let's backtrack just a minute to introduce still another angler who has engaged in extensive research on lure design. His name is Tom Seward of Carbondale, Illinois. He was the inventor of the very first naturalized lures ever to appear on the market. Seward began his career as a freelance lure designer, creating new types of lures in his home workshop and then selling the ideas to tackle companies. The first naturalized plug he invented was sold to the Lazy Ike Corporation and appropriately dubbed the Natural Ike. After designing still other lures for other companies, Seward finally created his own company called the Crankbait Corporation.

Seward's expertise in lure design is well justified because he holds a master's degree in art, and for more than 20 years he has been an avid bass

Anglers of a generation ago would be shocked to see today's naturalized lures, which look so lifelike you expect them to swim away on their own.

angler. Consequently, his knowledge of fish coloration, color theory, strike response principles, and other things that go into lure design is encyclopedic. Obviously, when Seward came out with the very first lifelike imprints on lures, competitive companies were quick to follow suit with their own versions. None, however, have really managed to duplicate Seward's efforts. So I contacted him for an interview; my questions and his answers, which are certain to benefit and intrigue advanced bass anglers, are presented in the remainder of this chapter:

Weiss: Tom, for starters, how do the naturalized lures you design differ from those of other companies?

Seward: In order to gain as much detail as possible on their lures, the companies trying to copy my ideas began producing more half-tones or grays by photographing fish images through a fine dot screen, as in producing a black and white newspaper image, and then with this as a pattern making the imprints on their lures. Conversely, my designs are straight line and dot images that stand out by producing a strong light-dark contrast. A couple of the major companies reasoned that the more photographic images on their lures would more accurately represent live creatures, but this shows a rudimentary knowledge of motion and visual acuity and has rendered many of their lifelike patterns almost useless in catching bass.

Weiss: Do you mean to say that in most underwater conditions a bass cannot see the detailed imprint on naturalized lures other than those of your own design?

Seward: Precisely! There is no way gray half-tones as photographed through a fine dot screen can ever be perceived as a baitfish or panfish species in motion in typical underwater lighting intensities. In other words, a detailed pattern held in hand, and not in motion, cannot possibly be interpreted as such at average lure speeds unless it was specifically intended to, as with my original color schemes.

Weiss: What you're saying, then, is that a lifelike imprint on a lure held in hand looks entirely different when retrieved at various speeds underwater.

Seward: Yes. Virtually all of the copies of the lifelike imprints on my original naturalized lures represent an average human's interpretation of what a prey species "should" look like underwater. But a fish will not react to or even see these patterns in human terms of perception in actual fishing situations. Worse yet, many naturalized patterns don't even fit the body shapes of the lures they adorn. The most ridiculous example of this is the crayfish patterns now flooding the market.

I knew these companies would make these mistakes because they did zero research before jumping on the bandwagon. It is an insult to the intelligence of an advanced bass angler to print and paint a backward-swimming crayfish on a front-running lure. There is no physical way a fish could perceive or react to this printed pattern in any manner that would improve strike-response behavior on the part of bass. That is why I use an abstract color scheme or pattern on many of my lures.

Weiss: Maybe a sketch would help illustrate this point. (See the accompanying drawing of two typical naturalized crayfish lures now on the market, which Seward sketched quickly.)

Seward: If you examine these two sketches, a little thought will reveal that the *high-contrast, abstract pattern* as depicted in drawing #2 will provide more visual stimulus while the lure is in motion than the ludicrous segmented pattern on lure #1, which will merely blur out to an indistinct nothingness. In behavioral psychology this phenomenon is known as *stimulus generalization.*

Since both lures only vaguely resemble crayfish, the one with the more visible stimulus features will provide the most responsive triggers. Lure #1 will still catch a few fish *despite* its printed pattern because it is of representative prey size and it moves at a lifelike speed, and that is all a bass really needs in order to react favorably.

Yet lure #2 has the great advantage because of its exaggerated contrast of light and dark hues in motion and high-contrast paint scheme. In another manner of speaking, regardless of how the two lures are presented to bass, the naturalized pattern on lure #1 by itself could never influence a strike because in motion it is indistinguishable.

Weiss: What about other imprinted features on those lures intended to imitate baitfish, panfish and fingerling gamefish?

Seward: A very common error on the part of lure companies trying to cash in on the naturalized lure fad by attempting to copy my designs has been the intricate drawing of scales on panfish and baitfish lookalike lures.

These scales only serve to mute, or kill, the chrome or pearl-colored

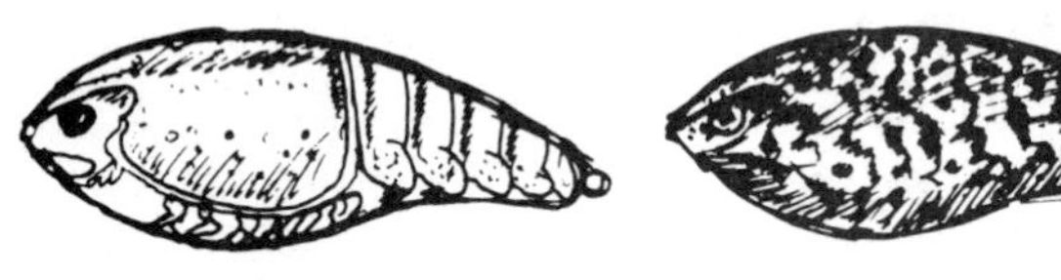

Tom Seward imprints high-contrast, abstract patterns (Lure 2) on his naturalized lures; many of his imitators use indistinct patterns (Lure 1) that blur and offer little visual stimulus to bass when the lure is retrieved.

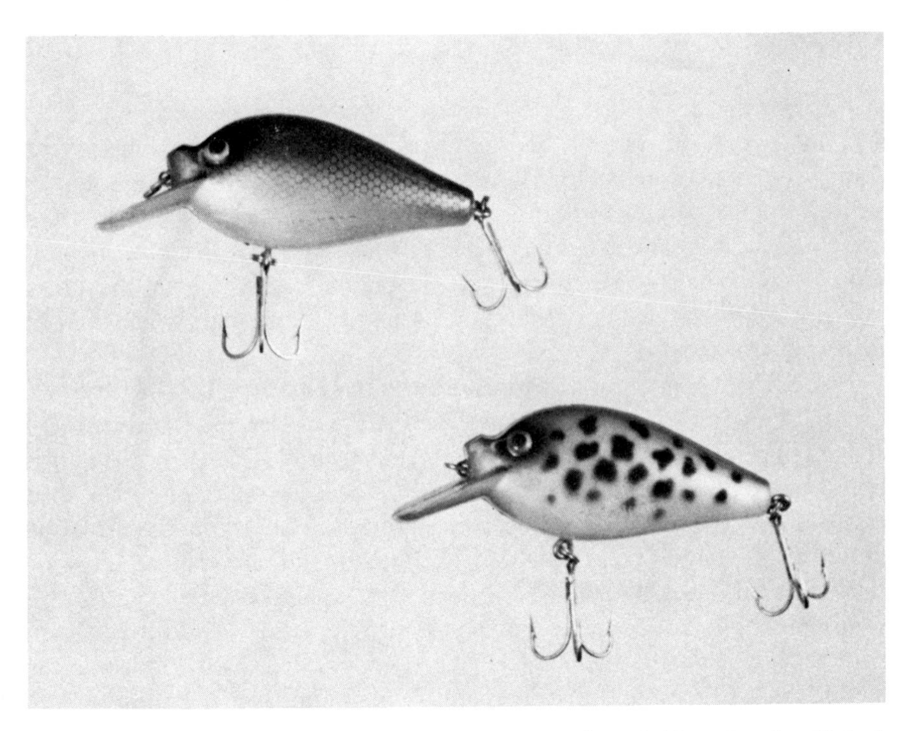

When buying naturalized lures, remember that a lure held in hand will look entirely different when retrieved at a fast speed underwater. Here are two identical lures sporting different patterns. The scales on the upper lure will blur out and be indistinguishable on the retrieve. Yet the bold, contrasting markings on the lower lure will stand out and make the plug highly visible to bass.

"flash" of the paint scheme, and biologists say it is this very flash that is the primary trigger that elicits strike responses from bass feeding upon shad or other prey. Of course, it stands to reason I never allow scales to appear on lures I have production control over.

Weiss: What about other lure features?

Seward: Other things like mouth and gill features, pectoral fins and raised dorsal fins are nothing more than attractive sculptural additions to lures, and when a lure is being retrieved through the water they are indistinguishable and therefore meaningless to bass you hope to catch.

In the tackle manufacturing trade, these additional lure features are laughingly called sales aids or *inducements.* They add to the intriguing, lifelike appearance of the lures and therefore perform the single function of tricking unknowledgeable, amateur fishermen into buying them!

Weiss: What about the eyes painted on lures? Biologists say eye size, placement and coloration all play important roles in the association between predator and prey species.

Seward: Agreed. When the eyes of two greatly dissimilar size fish meet, instantaneous recognition takes place. One of the species automatically and instinctively displays a dominant personality, the other a passive or submissive type of behavior. In fact, this reaction occurs throughout the entire animal kingdom and explains why most wild creatures tend to avoid eye contact with each other during nonaggressive or nonfeeding encounters. If and when eye contact *is* intentionally made, one or the other interprets the behavior as either a territorial threat or a sign that he's about to be made a meal of.

Aside from the eyes of creatures often serving to establish hierarchical rankings, they also, in the world of fish, serve as response features and strike triggers when predators begin engaging prey. What I mean is, the eyes of potential forage fish first identify them as such. Then the eyes additionally identify the head section of the prey as well as the direction in which it logically will try to escape, which makes ambushing, chasing, capturing and swallowing the fish head-first much easier.

Interestingly, baitfish and panfish also have certain advantages to ensure they will not be too heavily preyed upon. These advantages often enable them either to hide from predators by melting into the predominant colors of their environment or to at least display somewhat reduced response features and strike triggers through the use of unusual markings or other anatomical designs. Often the eye and head region is quite small in proportion to the overall body size, as with bluegills. In other cases, fish with somewhat larger heads and eyes have camouflage markings such as bands, stripes or bars that diminish their apparent sizes, as with rock bass and redbreast sunfish. Another feature that various baitfish species commonly display is a salt and pepper design in which the real eye is quite small and many "false eyes" in the form of numerous dots are sprinkled over the body. Certain dace and minnow species exhibit this trait and attacking bass often become so disoriented or confused by the many false eyes that the prey is given just a tad longer to escape. Also, many preyfish have so-called deflection marks in the form of a large, dark-colored splotch near the tail, as with the spottail shiner. A bass readily sees the deflection mark at the tail, misinterprets it as the eye of the fish, and upon launching its attack completely misses its target.

Since the eye and head region of prey species are such instrumental strike triggers, I always make this the largest part of my lures and even try to further exaggerate their sizes through the use of special contrasting color tones and shading techniques. Other companies designing naturalized lures go to great pains to make the eyes on their lures intricately detailed in the hopes of impressing potential buyers, not realizing those very details will blur out when the lure is being retrieved underwater and thus render it far less effective.

Weiss: In what other ways do your naturalized lures differ from those

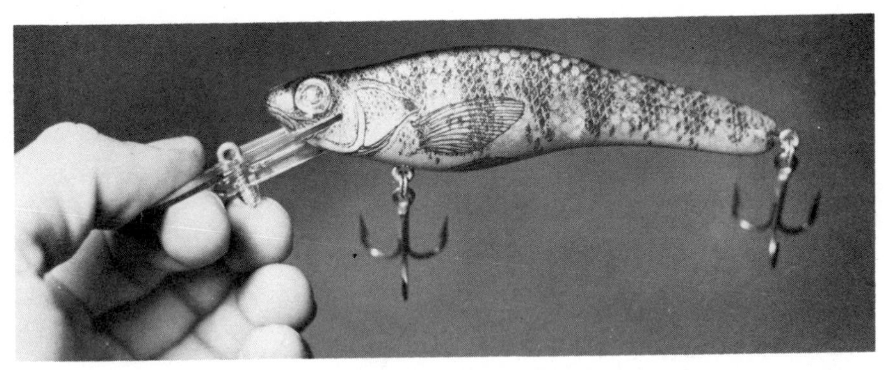

According to scientists, the eye and head region of preyfish serve as strike triggers. Consequently, lures that have exaggerated forward sections generally are best.

of other companies that might explain their acclaimed superiority?

Seward: Well, we know how all fish have countershading coloration which effectively neutralizes their overall visibility from all viewing angles and which helps prey species to avoid detection by predators. Unknowingly, other companies striving to imitate preyfish species give their naturalized lures the same countershading coloration.

But I do exactly the opposite, using what I call *reverse countershading*. Instead of my lures having light-colored bellies that gradually darken toward the dorsal region, I give them dark-colored bellies that lighten toward the dorsal region, which assures the angler that his lure will present maximum contrast from all viewing angles. A reverse-countershaded lure simply cannot hide underwater because it violates nature's laws.

Weiss: As a summary, what advice can you give to advanced bass anglers regarding the purchase of naturalized lures either designed by yourself or other companies.

Seward: First, don't be fooled by intricate, detailed print patterns on lures. Select lures that have a lot of bold, contrasting colors and patterns within the naturalized scheme being presented. These characteristics won't blur out when the lure is being retrieved but will actually enhance the print pattern. Second, try to stick with lures that have some type of pearlescent color somewhere on the lure, without the presence of scales to mute that primary strike trigger. Third, lean heavily upon naturalized lures that have large or exaggerated head and eye regions. Fourth, if you find a naturalized lure you are having some success with, and want to make it even more effective, keep in mind my reverse-countershading discovery; then, doctor that lure a bit with Magic Markers, giving the lure a dark shading near the belly and a light shading near the back. Finally, never lose sight of the fact that proper depth and speed controls over lures are always far more important than specific colors or designs.

CHAPTER

22

Battling Bass

Up to this chapter, everything has been prelude. We've looked at the behavior of bass and how it is affected by water and weather conditions. We've seen how to locate the shallow and deep homes they frequent in different bodies of water during various seasons of the year. And we've examined specific types of lure and live baits that are likely to be the most effective.

Much satisfaction can be gleaned from all of this foreplay, but it's the climax—the brief encounter with your quarry when all your preliminary work suddenly pays off and you feel solid resistance at the end of your line—that every serious angler anticipates with the greatest pleasure. These are the precious moments that anglers' dreams are made of, but whether you succeed in actually getting your prize into the boat involves more factors than you might think.

It Takes More Than a Big Jerk to Set the Hook

In time, most bass anglers develop their own way of setting the hook, and these personal styles are predictably wide and varied. Take my friend Billy Westmoreland, the smallmouth expert from Celina, Tennessee. Anyone not acquainted with this bear of a man might look at his rock-solid, oversize proportions and instantly assume that he continually breaks fishing rods and lines when setting the hook. But actually, that is very far from the truth.

On his home lake—Dale Hollow Reservoir—where the water is ultra-clear, Westmoreland uses featherweight spinning tackle, cobweb lines as low as four-pound test, and tiny jigs with needlepoint hooks. Billy has landed smallmouths up to ten pounds with this gear—proof that it takes

This is the moment every angler eagerly awaits!

Some anglers literally go overboard in their attempt to set the hook.

more than brute muscle to hook, play and successfully boat trophy bass. It takes savvy. Indeed, when this artist sets the hook it is hardly noticeable. There is a slight, authoritative snap of the wrist, like a mare's tail flicking flies, and that is that. Yet seldom does he lose a fish due to the hook not securely imbedding itself. Oh yes, he also fishes, and sets the hook, from a sitting position.

The complete opposite of Westmoreland is my friend Inky Davis who religiously plies the Santee-Cooper lakes in South Carolina. First, he's only half the size of Westmoreland. Moreover, he fishes junglelike cover with stout baitcasting tackle and lines often as heavy as 30-pound test. And as a prelude to setting the hook, Inky quickly stands, plants his feet, and then whoops and hollers. All of which serve as advance warning to his fishing partner to hang onto his seat because the boat is about to violently list to one side or the other. Davis does indeed break rods and pop lines upon occasion. But he also has a deserved reputation for being able to yank positively huge bass from the heaviest cover imaginable.

Somewhere in between these two extremes, there is a hook-setting method that is just right for you.

Two popular techniques of hook setting are referred to as the *regular set* and the *speed set.* In the first, which is commonly used when fishing plastic worms or backtrolling live baits, an angler leans forward, extends his rod tip toward the fish, quickly reels in the slack, and then strikes back. The second method, which is frequently used when casting artificial lures such as crankbaits and spinnerbaits, entails a faster, more spontaneous reaction, starting with a tight line. Since the lure already is in motion and the bass hits the lure with a jolt and often hooks itself, the speed set often amounts to little more than insurance.

These two methods, and other aspects of hook-setting, have been investigated by Homer Circle, Fishing Editor for *Sports Afield,* working with scientists at Dupont. They found that the speed set delivered 36 percent more energy at the rod tip than the regular set. In addition, the results

The most popular hook-setting methods are the regular set and the speed set.

for the regular set were about the same whether the angler was standing or sitting. With the speed set, however, 18 percent more energy was delivered to the rod tip and terminal end of the line when the angler was sitting than when he was standing.

These studies also showed that a two-handed hook set is more than twice as effective as a one-handed set, regardless of whether you're using spinning or baitcasting tackle. The two-handed method may seem awkward and uncomfortable the first time you try it, but with practice you will become proficient, and convinced that no other way is better.

Here's how you do it. Take your hand from the reel handle the very instant you feel a strike and place it higher up on the fore-grip of the rod, above the reel. Then, with a sharp snap, simultaneously pull back with the high hand and push forward with the low hand, thus gaining a distinct mechanical advantage not possible if one hand remains on the reel handle. When the fish is securely hooked, transfer the high hand back to the reel handle and play the bass. All of this hand shuffling, of course, takes place in a split second.

It may come as a surprise, but in most cases long rods do not transmit energy more efficiently than do short rods. To understand why, we have to look at several principles that come into play when rods of different lengths are flexed or "loaded." Since a long rod is capable of sweeping back in a long, wide arc and thus carries with it a substantial length of line, one might think that the stretch factor in the line would not significantly reduce the energy delivered through the rod's length to the hook. This is both true and false.

What I mean is, yes, an angler can control a greater length of line with a long rod, but this is somewhat offset by the characteristically limber nature of most long rods. This trait dampens or absorbs much of the energy the angler generates before it reaches the hook. By comparison, a shorter rod is incapable of such a wide arc and an angler cannot control as much line. Yet this is offset by the typical stiff action of most short rods, which transmits a high proportion of energy the angler imparts to the terminal end of the line during the strike.

The Berkley Company also has been involved in hook-setting research. When I recently attended one of the firm's Sportfishing Workshops, I discovered first-hand that fishermen aren't really as strong as they think, at least in terms of how much energy they can deliver when trying to set the hook. At the workshop, numerous anglers were asked to guess how many pounds of force they could register on a tension scale when striking back with any rod of their choice. Some anglers estimated they were capable of at least 18 pounds of force. Next, each angler gave slack as a scuba diver swam away underwater with the end of the line tied to the tension scale. At various distances, the diver would stop and tug on the line to simulate a bass hitting a lure. The angler would then try to "set the hook," so to speak, and the number of pounds of force actually generated was recorded on the scale for all to see.

Many egos were deflated. The average "strike" succeeded in pulling the dial on the scale down to only the three-pound mark. And although a few gorilla-types mustered as much as six to eight pounds of energy, a full 50 percent of those present did not even generate two pounds of force.

The purpose of this experiment was to show that most bass anglers greatly overestimate the amount of hook-setting force they think they are achieving when they feel the strike of a fish. Yet, curiously, as we would later learn, you don't actually require more than a few pounds of force to imbed the hook in a bass's mouth.

A variation of the above hook-setting experiment was performed during another Sportfishing Workshop, this time in Ocala, Florida. In this case, however, only one angler participated to ensure that the hook-setting data acquired remained consistent from one test to another. As the data in Table 22–1 show, anglers transmit more energy to their hooks on short casts than on long ones, regardless of whether they are using light or heavy

In workshops sponsored by Berkley Company, a scuba diver used a tension scale to determine anglers' abilities to set the hook.

lines. This can be crucial with certain fishing methods that require a high level of hook-setting energy. For example, when using the regular set with a worm in which the hook is buried in the soft plastic to make it weedless, you should stick with relatively short casts to assure consistent hook set.

The test figures in Table 22–1 also indicate that more pounds of hook-setting force is generated with 8-pound-test line than with 20-pound test. How could this be? As Berkley's Paul Johnson explained, the key thing involved here is a line's diameter, not its actual pound-test rating.

"When a fisherman strikes back to set the hook," Johnson related, "he does not have a straight pull on the hook. There is a big belly in the line. Consequently, a low-pound-test line has considerably less water resistance exerted upon it than does a thick diameter, higher-pound-test line, and so the angler succeeds in transmitting more energy to the hook."

Another test conducted by the Berkley Company involved the use of a bass to determine the pounds of force required to embed different hooks in various areas of the fish's mouth. The bass, a 2½-pounder, was held carefully while an assistant used a tension scale to determine the penetration abilities of new hooks, new hooks that had been sharpened, and dull hooks. Other than their degree of sharpness, all of the hooks were identical 2/0 Sproats with long shanks, similar to the kind anglers use in plastic worm fishing. The four areas of the mouth evaluated were (1) the left inside toward the front where there is very thin skin, (2) the right inside farther back in the oral cavity where there is thick gristle covering a hard boney plate, (3) the inside floor of the mouth in the region of the tongue, and (4) the inside roof of the mouth.

TABLE 22–1. Effect of Distance and Line Pound-Test on Hook-Setting Force Generated with Trilene XL

8-Pound Test		*20-Pound Test*	
DISTANCE OF HOOK SET	FORCE GENERATED	DISTANCE OF HOOK SET	FORCE GENERATED
100 ft	4 lbs	100 ft	3 lbs
80	5½	80	4
60	6	60	5
50	7	50	6
40	7¼	40	6¼
30	7½	30	7½
20	8	20	8½

Here, Paul Johnson measures the force required to embed hooks in different parts of a bass's mouth.

The results of this experiment, shown in Table 22–2, confirm something all anglers have long been advised of: New hooks penetrate much more easily than hooks that have been allowed to become dull through repeated contact with fish or cover; and, as sharp as new hooks are when they come right out of the box, they can be even more keenly honed for still better penetration, if an angler is willing to spend a minute working with a file or whetstone.

One thing the scientists have no explanation for is why a sharpened hook required more pounds of force to penetrate the floor of a bass's mouth than a new hook that had not been sharpened. Paul Johnson

TABLE 22–2. Force Required to Embed Hook in Various Areas of a Bass's Mouth

	Mouth Area			
	#1	*#2*	*#3*	*#4*
New Hooks	1 lb	¼ lb	5 lb	8 lb*
New Hooks, sharpened	¾	⅛	8*	4¾
Dull Hooks	5½	½	8*	9*

*No penetration

attributed this to one of those quirks of nature that sometimes occur.

"The inside of a bass's mouth is not uniform," Johnson explained. "There are areas of hard platelike material, thin skin and thick fleshy gristle. Sometimes a hook will immediately dig in upon contact, other times it will slide just a bit before grabbing, and other times it will slide and not grab and the fish will get away."

This explains the growing popularity of some new types of hooks, such as the Tru-Turn, that have offset shanks. When force is exerted upon the hook, the bend in the shank causes the throat and point of the hook to make a 90-degree turn, increasing the likelihood that somewhere during that movement the hook point will find and grab soft fleshy material.

"The placement of hooks on lures such as crankbaits has been fairly well standardized," Johnson continued, "with no thought whatever as to where those hooks will contact the inside of a bass's mouth. In the future we may learn that on some types of lures we have the hooks in the wrong places and that by rearranging them slightly we can greatly increase the number of fish that are solidly hooked on the strike.

"But as much as we may learn, we have to keep things in their proper perspective. As anglers, we'll always be dealing with a live creature in a nebulous world riddled with an infinite number of uncontrollable variables."

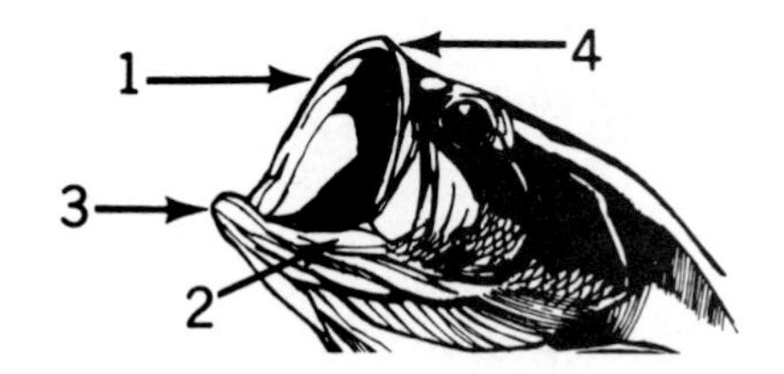

Hook penetration forces were determined in these four areas of a bass's mouth in Berkley Company tests. The test results are shown in Table 22–2.

In summary, then, the following factors have the greatest influence on hook setting:

- The degree of sharpness of the hook
- The method used—two-handed or one-handed; regular set or speed set
- The angler's position—sitting or standing
- The diameter of the line
- The length of the cast, and consequently the amount of line stretch
- The location of the hook in the fish's mouth

Factors that have little or no influence on an angler's ability to set the hook are his physical strength and the overall length of the rod.

Finally, in this section I should say a few words about drag mechanisms on reels, which are designed to slip and release line at a lower force than that required to break the line. Some anglers tighten their drags down as snug as possible, so they are completely inoperative. The philosophy here is that if a big fish is allowed to run, peeling line from the reel, it stands a better chance of reaching cover and crocheting the line around various obstacles and eventually breaking off. This reasoning has some merit, if an angler is using the heaviest of rods, reels and lines and is able to use brute strength to muscle his quarry away from cover. But in most fishing situations involving the use of medium to lightweight tackle, anglers will do better if they use and rely upon these safety features.

However, many fishermen make the mistake of leaving their drags always the same, preset as they came from the factory. Or, they merely tug on the line before the day's fishing, and if it comes off under moderate resistance, they feel they're ready for action. It's important, though, to adjust the drags on both spinning and baitcasting reels in accordance with the pound-test of line being used. The generally accepted figure is no more than 25 percent of the line's rated breaking strength.

In other words, if you're using 20-pound-test line, the drag should be set to yield when five pounds of pressure is exerted upon it. A handy way to make this adjustment is by using a handscale and turning the drag wheel or knob until it just begins to release line when the required number of pounds registers on the scale.

Also, periodically tie the terminal end of the line to an immovable object, back off the length of a cast, and then put a good bend in your rod until the drag begins slipping. Does the rod tip bounce erratically as line is being released? If so, the same "stuttering" will occur when a good fish is on, and this may allow a bass to break the line. The problem is that dirt and grit have accumulated inside the drag and the reel needs to be disassembled and cleaned.

Another critical thing is to always fill your reel to capacity because the mechanical advantages exerted upon the drag mechanism drops as the effective spool diameter decreases.

Last, be extra careful when fishing with very light lines and ultra-light spinning tackle. Carelessly setting the drag when using 20-pound line may result in an error of one or two pounds, which may not be crucial when using such heavy tackle. Yet with only four- or six-pound-test line and light tackle, that same error can be more than enough to cost you a good fish.

Get the Net!

There is no single, right way to fight a bass once it has felt the sting of the hook and charted a nonstop course for anywhere else. There are simply too many variables involved.

The aforementioned Billy Westmoreland takes his time and plays his bass with a tender touch. He has to, because of the featherweight tackle he uses. And he gets away with it, because he typically fishes cover-free water.

At the opposite extreme is my friend Inky Davis. I have seen him virtually overpower a 12-pound bass so quickly the fish was in the boat in 10 seconds flat. He can get away with this because of his fetish for broomstick rods and lines ranging from 25- to 40-pound test.

In fact, the type of swamp cover Davis fishes demands this brute strength or a big bass would surely weave his line through a logjam in an instant and shortly thereafter pop it like so much sewing thread.

"I firmly believe that if your tackle allows for it, hitting a bass hard and fast always is the best bet," Inky explained. "Many times you can actually get him coming your way before he really even knows what's happening, and once he's away from the heavy cover you've got him whipped. This is particularly important when you hook a big bass in heavy weed growth. You simply have to get his head up and moving toward you. If you just hang on and let him go wherever he pleases, he's a goner."

Regardless of the tackle being used, one thing an angler should never do when battling a big bass is point the rod tip directly at the fish. This will give the fish a straight pull on the line and if it's running in frantic, short spurts, it's bound to break off.

Neither do I recommend holding the rod tip low to the water, as many anglers do, to prevent the fish from jumping and possibly throwing the hook. An angler has little control over his tackle when the rod is in this position. Also, when the rod tip is low, a bass is encouraged to dive deep, which may take the fish into dense cover or some other predicament far worse than any it may encounter thrashing topside.

The best bet is to keep the rod high throughout the duration of the battle. Make the fish work against the bend in the rod. This ensures the fish will tire more quickly, and can be boated faster, which is essential if the bass is to be released and you want to ensure its survival. With the rod tip high, the rod also is in good position to absorb any sudden shock incurred if the bass decides to make a last-ditch effort to escape.

Another critical factor is to maintain tension on the line at all times. Otherwise, a fish that is allowed occasional slack may be able to flop the weight of the lure around and eventually throw it free. Or, the swinging of the lure may cause the holes penetrated by the hooks to become enlarged, so that the lure falls out.

No doubt, battling a bass in this manner will see the fish cavorting across the surface, kicking up a ruckus; there is a good chance one of those aerial acrobatics will allow the fish its freedom. But the thrill of such topwater antics will remain etched in your memory far longer than any other aspect of the day's outing. And in my mind, that rare enjoyment is what bass fishing is really all about.

How, exactly, a bass should be brought into the boat depends upon the size of the fish and the type of tackle being used. Most guides and tournament anglers, nowadays, use the "sweep and snatch" method, that is, the fish is led alongside the boat and as its head reaches the surface, it is swept up and out of the water and into the boat. This is a fast and easy method for landing bass up to about 2½ pounds. Just make sure you don't try to yank or jerk the fish from the water or it may break your line. The sweep and snatch method involves a continuous, fluid motion of the rod that does not suddenly place an appreciable amount of strain upon it.

Grabbing a bass by the lower jaw with the thumb and forefinger is an age-old tactic for boating exceptionally large fish because it immobilizes a bass. The trouble is, you have to learn the right way to use this tactic, or the fish is not in fact completely immobilized. When that happens, any sudden flopping or thrashing of the bass may result in one of the lure's hooks going deeply into your hand. Always bend the lower jaw down as wide open as it will go, allowing the weight of the fish's body to continue forcing downward until the hook can be safely removed.

When I'm using multi-hook lures, I generally try to avoid putting my fingers inside a bass's mouth. Better to use a net. But don't make the mistake of having on board a net that is too small for the task at hand. It should have a wide mouth, deep bag and long handle.

Whether you allow your boat partner to net your bass for you is your decision. Personally, I think it's great fun if two fishing pals can both participate in the landing of each bass. But in order to avoid tempers from flaring you have to be fishing with a partner who is an experienced net handler. I've had many sour experiences in which I mistakenly thought

Anglers often like to land a large bass by grabbing its lower jaw, but this is not recommended with multi-hook lures. This is bass-ace Doug Hannon, wrestling with a ten-pounder. (Photo by Don Wirth)

a partner knew what he was doing, asked him to net a big fish for me, and eventually lost the bass because the dummy jabbed and parried and even hit the side of the fish with the hoop, causing the bass to thrash and get away.

The best technique is for the boat partner to place the net in the water on the side of the boat opposite to where the fish is being fought. Furthermore, the rim of the net should be just slightly below the surface, so the bag expands. When he's ready, the angler fighting the fish can then lead the bass around the bow or stern of the boat and gently lead it head first into the quietly waiting net. Once the fish is two-thirds of the way into the net, the partner can then begin simultaneously pulling the net the rest of the way over the fish and lifting upward.

If you're alone, this maneuver can be a bit tricky because there is no way you can fight a bass on one side of the boat while holding the net in the water on the other side. You have to coax the bass up to the side of the boat, then reach for the net, then scoop him up and out of the water. And there's a good chance the bass will see your downward movement with the net and make a final bid for freedom. For this reason, many anglers, after bringing their fish close to the boat, like to release a bit of tension on their reel's drag, so a bass that decides to explode and attempt a hasty departure will not so easily be able to break off.

Generally, the best advice is to keep your rod high when fighting a bass close to the boat. After your partner places the net in the water on the opposite side of the boat, lead the bass around the end of the boat and gently into the bag.

Netting your own bass requires a bit of manual dexterity. This is Bill Weiss, bringing aboard a six-pounder. Note that he places his hand where the rim of the net joins the handle, for maximum control.

CHAPTER

23

Catch And Release Ethics

Moments after an angler catches a bass he finds himself faced with a weighty decision.

Should he carefully slip the fish back into the water to fight again another day? Should he clip it onto a stringer, or place it in his live well, with plans of serving it on a dinner platter to his family? Or, if it is a very large fish, should he send it to a taxidermist?

Of course, 40 or 50 years ago the question was easy to answer. A fish was food for the table. During times when mass unemployment was raking the country, money was scarce yet fish were plentiful, and waiting at home were hungry mouths to feed.

Nowadays, however, much of that has changed. Most people live in cities or suburbs and no longer acquire their food directly from the land (or water). At the same time, fishing has become tremendously popular as a recreational activity, with millions more on the water than when grandfather wet a line.

Fish and game agencies have not been able to keep pace with this trend by mere stocking or management efforts alone. During the last ten years in particular, a very high level of fishing pressure has been exerted on all bass species. The bottom line is that anglers are now being strongly encouraged to help the cause by releasing the bass they catch. They are being "persuaded" to enjoy the sporting aspect of catching bass and increasingly are frowned upon for even thinking of these gamefish as merely meat for the table.

In many regions, the catch-and-release revolution has gained such momentum an angler feels guilt-ridden for bringing bass to the dock. Some have even been known to sneak in their back door late at night with their

Years ago, anglers commonly brought home strings of bass like this, but now they're releasing most of their fish.

catch, to avoid being chastised by friends and associates committed to the catch-and-release ethic.

Like many anglers, I find myself square in the middle of this dilemma. On the one hand, releasing a fish of any size is an exhilarating feeling. If it's a small one, there's the self-satisfaction of knowing that by next year it will have grown larger. If it's a trophy, there's the heady esteem that you've bested a worthy adversary, and now, the next guy coming along will have the same thrilling opportunity. At the opposite extreme, I've always considered myself, if not a legitimate gourmet, at least an ardent devotee of the art of fish and game cookery, and consequently harbor a deep love for freshly caught fish, which cannot be compared to the cardboard representatives sold in supermarkets.

Without much fanfare, individual trout fishermen have been releasing their catch since the days of Izaak Walton. But it was the Bass Anglers Sportsman Society, in 1972, that brought its "Don't Kill Your Catch" credo to national attention. Since then, other fishing organizations have followed suit with like philosophies and equally catchy slogans.

In any case, the modern trend of releasing bass has been especially beneficial in terms of tournament fishing, whether on the national, state or local level. When hundreds of knowledgeable anglers, outfitted with all manner of modern technology, descend upon a specific lake to meet bass head on, they can devastate fish populations if all the fish caught are duly killed.

But what about the weekend angler who does not participate in bass-fishing tournaments. Is he, or should he be, as committed to the catch-and-

It was the Bass Anglers Sportsman Society, a strong promotor of tournament fishing, that instituted the "Don't Kill Your Catch" credo most anglers now follow.

release philosophy as the professional angler out pounding the water at every opportunity? Isn't it enough for every weekend angler to abide by the regulations and limit his catches to the number allowed in each state? After all, don't state fishery officials know the status of fish populations in their regions and subsequently develop regulations that allow the harvest of fish while at the same time protecting the resource? *The answer is a resounding NO!*

The problem here is that no two bodies of water are exactly the same. Each is an individual in its own right, with its own unique water chemistry and resulting fertility, resident fish populations, ratio of gamefish to panfish and rough fish, amount and type of cover, and ratio of shallow water to deep water. In other words two lakes—on opposite sides of a road, both apparently the same in appearance—may be as different as black and white beneath the surface. Ideally, each and every lake, reservoir, river and pond would be governed by laws specifically tailored to its own particular features and personality. Alas, as everyone knows, this is far from the case.

Here, biologists stock bass in a lake. Contrary to popular belief, state fishery officials do not always establish regulations that adequately protect fish populations. Encumbered by financial restrictions, they have to write blanket regulations that apply equally to nearly all waters within their jurisdictions.

State fish and game agencies, eternally encumbered by financial limitations, find themselves compelled to write blanket regulations that apply equally, or nearly so, to all waters within their jurisdiction. And this, through no fault of the agencies in question, is as ludicrous as prescribing the same medicine for 100 different sick people.

Ohio, my home state, comes to mind as a ready illustration. At the present time Buckeye anglers are permitted to take eight bass per day. And the laws state that these may consist of any species (largemouths, smallmouths or spotted bass), or any combination of the three, as long as the aggregate does not exceed eight. Although well intentioned, the blanket regulation does little to insure perpetuation of bass species in Ohio.

In the Ohio River, for example, smallmouths are present but in such few numbers that anglers look upon them as rare. Logically, therefore, anglers should be restricted in the number of smallmouths they may harvest, but they are not. If a lucky fellow chances into a school of smallmouths, he may legally kill eight of them per day. On the other hand, spotted bass are so abundant in the Ohio River that what they probably need most is thinning out, so there will not be such a profusion of undersize fish competing for the available food supply.

Now let's shift to Ohio's northern border, Lake Erie. There, the dominant bass species is the smallmouth and it is faring extremely well. Largemouths are the species in relative scarcity and require bolstering of their numbers, yet an angler may kill eight per day if he so desires.

I know of several lakes in other states where the resident bass populations have become so diminished in recent years that no bass harvest should be allowed under any circumstances until such time as the waters have recuperated; but the laws governing these lakes are the same as those pertaining to other waters where bass are plentiful. In contrast, I'm familiar with another lake that is so chock-full of bass it is common even for a rank amateur to catch 50 bass per day, although he'll be fortunate to get one that will go 12 inches. The fish obviously are stunted, and a liberal 20 fish per day limit, until such time as the water is back in proper balance, would greatly revitalize the fishery.

The point to be made is that no legislation can be enacted to benefit all fish, all the time, in every body of water. Some species need at least temporary protection, in some bodies of water, while others do not. Perhaps even a certain age-class of a species needs special protection, while in a sister lake on the other side of the road, just the opposite may be the recommended tonic.

Some states, including North Carolina and Missouri, have implemented *slot limits* in recent years, meaning that bass of certain ages or lengths must be returned to the water. No one is yet willing to predict what the long-term results of such programs may be. Undoubtedly, slot limits are a step in the right direction, but again, *only* if they are geared to specific waters to remedy specific problems, and not applied as blanket laws to cover all waters, many of which might be adversely affected.

A major stumbling block in dealing with the ecosystems of popular fishing waters is that biologists themselves frequently disagree about management policies. Many scientists, for example, subscribe to the belief that bass in the 12- to 15-inch category are the most energetic breeders and should be duly protected. Opponents say no, that if you want meat for the table, take home the 12- to 15-inch bass, but release the very largest fish, which are most important for breeding. Still other scientists contend that the largest bass have outlived their useful benefit to their race, are no longer prolific, and in fact are accomplishing little more than consuming voracious quantities of food that otherwise would benefit younger, healthier bass; so go ahead and harvest the bruins!

Another fish management controversy that has reached veritable head-bashing proportions in recent years is the issue of spring fishing when the fish are spawning. Throughout the southern states, closed seasons are unheard of, and a sport is even made of locating spawning beds with especially large fish on them, then making, perhaps, as many as 100 casts until finally the monster female becomes so enraged she knocks the hell out of the bait or lure and is hooked. Yet in the northern border states,

Whether angling should be allowed during spawning seasons draws heated controversey. One thing is certain, however: Bass that are carefully released will return to their nesting sites and contribute to propagation of their kind.

the factions are split. In many states, bass and other species are protected from the onslaught of plug-pitchers until specified dates each year. Fishery biologists in these states firmly believe that catching bass when they are spawning is greatly detrimental to their numbers. In other northern states, however, biologists of comparable expertise say anglers using conventional tackle will not harm bass or other fish populations by fishing during the spring, and no closed seasons are enacted.

I find several inconsistencies in the arguments used by those who are against spring fishing, spawn fishing, bed or nest fishing, or whatever one chooses to call it. First, even though bass generally are in shallow water at this time, they are by no means as vulnerable as many anglers suspect. During spawning, fish can be exceedingly difficult to catch, they engage in little, if any, feeding at this time; most strikes, in fact, are merely reflex responses, or in defense of spawning sites.

Secondly, it seems reasonable to say that if an angler kills a fish, no matter what the season, that is one less fish around to reproduce during the next spawning cycle. In other words, whether a bass is killed during the spring, summer, fall or winter is a moot point: That kill constitutes one less fish in the lake. In response, some would point out that spawning fish are full of eggs and milt and about to give birth to thousands of offspring, and it is therefore unconscionable to kill them at this time.

True, but bass actually contain eggs during most of the year; not just in spring. It is a common occurrence to fillet a bass caught in October, for example, and discover that it is a female with quite visible roe sacks. They are tiny, immature eggs, to be sure, that are still in their earliest stages of development and will continue to grow throughout the upcoming winter months. But they are eggs, nonetheless, that will be destroyed and never result in offspring if that parent bass is killed in October.

So if spring fishing is to be prohibited for the specific purpose of saving eggs, then logically shouldn't eggs be preserved at other times as well? If you agree, then no bass harvest whatever should be allowed for about 11 months of every year.

Another peculiar aspect of all of this has to do with bass fishing in the deep South, where temperatures are consistently warm. Here, the fish are not so regimented in their reproduction schedules as they are farther north, and consequently, at least a certain percentage of fish can be found spawning virtually every month of the year. If you're against fishing for bass when they are likely to be on spawning beds, then, logically, you should never allow yourself to take a Florida fishing trip!

Whether you actually go to that extreme is your own decision, for this chapter is not intended to be critical of any particular angler's philosophy, or the regulations established by those agencies that govern our sport.

Rather, its purpose is to point out the need for clarifying muddled issues in order to put things in their proper perspective. If we go back to basics, it must be remembered that the great majority of fish species, including bass, are not a limited, finite resource that needs to be preserved. Fish are not like crude oil, a nonrenewable resource that gradually *will* be exhausted in supply. Quite the contrary, bass and most other fish are a viable and highly renewable natural resource we can make good use of, if managed properly. This is called *conservation*, and it means to use with forethought and discretion. The opposite is *preservation*, which entails extreme, sometimes total, restrictions on use of a resource.

This preservation angle, by the way, is the very tack used by most antifishing, antitrapping and antihunting organizations in their attempts to sway public opinion and generate financial support for their causes. Unfortunately, they are having a good deal of success because, in these troubled times of dwindling finite resources, the mass public mistakenly but automatically assumes preservation always is beneficial.

Preservation may indeed be necessary for certain limited, nonrenewable

Sportsmen should learn the difference between conservation, which entails the wise use of a renewable resource, and preservation, which entails extreme restrictions on the use of a resource. Bass populations, when properly managed, can easily survive periodic harvests.

resources, but the same logic does not apply to those resources in good supply and capable of replenishing themselves (with our assistance) on a short-term basis. As a result, any organization soliciting funds or other support to "preserve" fish, game, timber or like resources should be looked upon as highly suspect. What they really want, disguised in semantic terms, is to eliminate any further harvest of those resources—particularly the ones sportsmen are interested in.

This is not meant to imply that responsible anglers can totally ignore the impact of their fishing on bass populations in specific waters. Although bass, overall, are a renewable resource that can be harvested without endangering the species, in certain waters, at certain times, certain populations may indeed be threatened. And, as already noted, regulations that apply indiscriminantly to all the waters in a state, with the intent of *conserving* bass in general, may not be sufficient to preserve specific imperiled populations. Furthermore, any angler who fishes a certain lake or

Serious bass anglers probably know their own waters better than state fishery biologists, and therefore can make intelligent decisions as to which bass species can be harvested and which should be released.

river on a regular basis soon knows more about that water and its fish populations than do the bureaucrats in charge of formulating fish and game regulations.

For these reasons, every angler is periodically faced with the personal decision of whether to keep his catch or release it, despite the detailed fishing regulations that exist throughout the country. To go back to my own experience, I release each and every smallmouth I catch in the Ohio River, even though the state says I can kill eight per day. In my opinion, that would be irresponsible behavior because I know from firsthand experience the species is not abundant there. On the other hand, if it has been a while since my family has enjoyed a fresh fish dinner, I will not hesitate to kill eight spotted bass, because in the Ohio River they are as thick as fleas on a junkyard dog.

Likely, a similar philosophy can be adopted by any bass angler, no matter where he lives. When food for the table is desired, take species that are abundant. Panfish, for example, admirably fulfill this role. Not only are they far more flavorful than bass or muskies, but are so prolific that the best thing that can happen to them is an occasional thinning of their numbers.

What I'm saying, then, is that the continuation of high-quality fishing in this country does not depend entirely on fish and game departments, and the regulations they enact. Much of the burden of conserving bass and other gamefishes rests on anglers themselves. Knowing which species to keep and which species to release, and when and where, is the responsibility of all fishermen.

Index